U0598346

INTERPRETING ZHEJIANG'S DEVELOPMENT
Cultural and Social Perspectives

WSPC-ZJUP Series on China's Regional Development

Print ISSN: 2661-3883
Online ISSN: 2661-3891

Since China's reform and opening up in 1978, the world's most populous country has enjoyed rapid economic development. This book series sheds new light on China's phenomenal success by examining its regional development and disparity. The series starts from first few volumes focusing on Zhejiang province, one of the country's forerunners in economic, social and political transformation. These volumes analyse Zhejiang's local governance innovation, regional economic development, and social and cultural changes over the past few decades.

Published:

WSPC-ZJUP Series on China's Regional Development – Vol. 1

INTERPRETING ZHEJIANG'S DEVELOPMENT
Cultural and Social Perspectives

CHEN Lixu
Zhejiang Institute of Administration, China

ZHEJIANG UNIVERSITY PRESS
浙江大学出版社

World Scientific

EW JERSEY · LONDON · SINGAPORE · BEIJING · SHANGHAI · HONG KONG · TAIPEI · CHENNAI · TOKYO

图书在版编目（CIP）数据

从传统到现代：浙江现象的文化社会学阐释 ＝
Interpreting Zhejiang's Development：Cultural and
Social Perspectives：英文 / 陈立旭著；卢巧丹，刘
美君译 .— 杭州：浙江大学出版社，2019.12
　　ISBN 978-7-308-18686-5

　　Ⅰ .① 从 … Ⅱ .① 陈 … ② 卢 … ③ 刘 … Ⅲ .① 文化社
会学－研究－浙江－英文 Ⅳ .①G05

中国版本图书馆 CIP 数据核字 (2018) 第 228277 号

Not for sale outside of the Chinese mainland
此书仅限中国大陆地区销售

从传统到现代：浙江现象的文化社会学阐释

陈立旭　著
卢巧丹　刘美君　译

总 主 编　袁亚春
策　　划　张 琛　包灵灵
责任编辑　陆雅娟
责任校对　吴水燕
出版发行　浙江大学出版社
　　　　　（杭州市天目山路 148 号　邮政编码 310007）
　　　　　（网址：http://www.zjupress.com）
排　　版　杭州中大图文设计有限公司
印　　刷　虎彩印艺股份有限公司
开　　本　710mm×1000mm　1/16
印　　张　25.75
字　　数　515 千
版 印 次　2019 年 12 月第 1 版 2019 年 12 月第 1 次印刷
书　　号　ISBN 978-7-308-18686-5
定　　价　198.00 元

About the author

Chen Lixu is Professor at Zhejiang Institute of Administration. His research interests include cultural sociology, especially China's contemporary cultural development and regional cultural studies. His research features interdisciplinary studies of philosophy, cultural studies, sociology and economics.

Contents

Introduction

Since the late 1970s and the beginning of the 1980s, thanks to the practice of the reform and opening-up, social dynamics have been unleashed in a gradual manner. However, no one could expect what kind of transformation China would undergo at that time, let alone the economic miracle that Zhejiang Province would witness. Though it is difficult to present a panorama of this process, by using simple cognition models, we can regard the process of social changes in Zhejiang as a transition from tradition to modernization. It is clear that the driving force of this transition comes from the private sector. This is demonstrated by the rise of specialized markets across Zhejiang Province, the boom of private enterprises and joint-stock cooperative economy, the rise of local economy such as "One Village One Product" and "One Town One Product," the presence of "Zhejiang Village,"" Zhejiang Street," and "Wenzhou Village." These are well-constructed, self-funding towns (as represented by Longgang Town, the First National Farmer Town) that manage their own funding in the areas of reconstructing old cities, non-government funded education, and informal talks (held in places such as Taizhou) since the reform and opening-up. It is safe to conclude that the market and civilian driving forces play a role of self-organization while the government plays a role of facilitation and support. The transition towards modernization comes both from top-down and bottom-up, in that it is caused not only by the governments' easing restrictive policies but also by people's initiative based on the anticipated benefits and costs in the face of profitable opportunities generated by imbalanced institutions. The latter cause sets Zhejiang apart from the Southern Jiangsu Pattern characterized by the governments' strong interference (especially from township governments) and the Guangdong Pattern characterized by introducing foreign capital and developing an export-oriented economy. The process of institutional innovations as well as social and economic development in Zhejiang has well illustrated the so-called "inductivity" in Neoinstitutional Economics and featured "an extended order" put forward by scholar F. A. Hayek.

The transition from tradition towards modernization is never limited in economic fields. As Nathan Rosenberg and L.E. Birdzell, Jr. point out, "The notion that economic growth is a form of transformation reminds us that the transformation is never limited in economic fields but also extends to social and political fronts."[①] Of course, the transformation is sure to extend to the cultural front. It is in the historical context of significant economic system and social transformations as well as globalization that the local culture of Zhejiang has also undergone a series of profound changes. Compared with the tradition formed by the thousand-year rural society, the changes of local culture and spirits are amazing. On the other hand, the transition towards modernization is the result of multiple factors. As put by Guy Salvatore Alitto, "From my perspective, modernization is a combination of multiple factors that coincide at one point-in-time."[②] The influential factors accounting for modern social and economic changes in Zhejiang Province are multifaceted, among which local culture plays an important role. According to Parsons, the social system consists of one social structure and three other sub-systems, which are interconnected in function. The sub-system of culture, as one of the three sub-systems,

① Rosenberg, N. & Birdzell, L.E, Jr. *How the West Grew Rich: The Economic Transformation of the World* [M]. Trans. Liu, S. Hongkong: SDX Joint Publishing (Hongkong) Company Limited, 1989.

② Alitto, G.S. *Anti-Modernization Thought Trends in a World-Wide Perspective on Cultural Conservatism* [M]. Trans. Tang, C. Guizhou: Guizhou People's Press, 1991.

plays a central role in maintaining the equilibrium of the whole system, as culture guides social actors and facilitates them in achieving their goal steadily. In other words, culture provides a notation environment for social actors and facilitates their collaboration and coordination. It is for this reason that we see the organization form of one society can find its trace in culture and that the development path and mode of a certain country or region can reflect its unique culture. In this sense, Max Weber points out that "human actions are directly dominated not by ideology but by interests (both material and ideological). However, the 'world image' created by concept often determines the direction of actions driven by interests, just like a switchman does."[①] The transition from tradition towards modernization in Zhejiang Province, though it shares some uniformity with other regions in China or even the world, features local characteristics with its cultural traditions.

I am a native of Zhejiang. It can be said that I grew along with the economic and social changes in contemporary Zhejiang. I was fortunate enough to experience Zhejiang's economic and social phenomena before and after the reform and opening-up.

When I was studying in primary school and junior high school, I also heard and witnessed or even experienced batches of ideological and political campaigns in Zhejiang. At that time, there seemed to be no big difference in appearance between Zhejiang and the rest of the country. Every day people were talking about class struggle, while they were simultaneously facing difficulties in finding adequate food and clothing.

In 1979, I was admitted to a major university in the north. Then I spent eight years working and finishing undergraduate and graduate studies in Shandong, Hubei, Guangdong, and other provinces. During this period, the Southern Jiangsu Pattern had gained prominence. Areas like Guangdong have become the forerunner of China's reform and

---

① Su, G. *Rationalization and Its Limitations—Introduction to Weber's Thoughts* [M]. Shanghai: Shanghai People's Publishing House, 1988: 84.

opening-up, which has attracted worldwide attention. Zhejiang has yet to attract much attention at this time. However, as Nietzsche puts it, major events are always quietly coming as pigeons, and the real mutation is not visible to all.

In September 1979, to register in a northern university, I took a coach from Tiantai to Hangzhou for a transit for the first time in my life. At that time, there was only one service from Tiantai to Hangzhou daily, which would only become full during the Spring Festival and the passengers were mainly those going on a business trip. However, when I returned home during the winter vacation in 1980 and went back to school, the number of services had increased to 4 times a day. Of course, some of the passengers were returning migrant workers from state-owned enterprises and public institutions outside their home. However, there were already many artisans and small businessmen who went out to make a living. Since then, during each summer and winter vacation when I went to and came back from my university, I could see more and more Zhejiang craftsmen and small businessmen going out to make a living. And I also heard many things about my fellow villagers doing business whenever I went home.

Undoubtedly, after the reform and opening-up, the willingness of Zhejiang people to make a living as entrepreneurs has begun to be released. The tide of market economy in Zhejiang has gradually surged. When I graduated as a master in 1987, I returned to work in Hangzhou, capital of Zhejiang Province. Many of those craftsmen and small businessmen who have been adventuring outside, engaging in polishing shoes, fluffing cotton, tailoring, stuffing sofas, exchanging sugar for feathers and hairdressing, have already become big traders and entrepreneurs. Specialized markets, household industries, and private enterprises appeared across Zhejiang, "Zhejiang Village," "Zhejiang Street" have sprung up like mushrooms all over the country, and the phenomenon of Zhejiang is gradually becoming more and more famous all over the world.

Since the reform and opening-up, Zhejiang's economy has developed rapidly and its economic aggregate has surged at a fast speed. In 2016, the GDP of Zhejiang Province accounted for 6.2% of the national total, ranking 4th in the country for 20 consecutive years, and its total economic output was equivalent to Turkey—whose economic aggregate ranked the 18th in the world. Zhejiang Province's GDP per capita reached 12,577 US dollars. According to the income grouping standard set by the World Bank, Zhejiang has basically reached the level of high-income economies. Other major economic indicators of Zhejiang were among the highest in the country. The urban-rural landscape has undergone tremendous changes, and people's living standards have risen significantly. At the initial stage of the reform and opening-up when the industrial foundation was weak, the proportion of agriculture was large and the resources were scarce, Zhejiang people created a remarkable Zhejiang Phenomenon. In the meantime, unprecedented changes have taken place in the local society, culture, and values of Zhejiang.

We live in a rapidly transforming society that has undergone unprecedented changes. We have been given an honor by the era in which we live, for our generation sees things that many other generations cannot see. At the same time, we bear a heavy burden and responsibility to answer the questions and challenges presented to us by this era. Though we are still unable to give in-depth interpretations or answer some of these questions, we can record the phenomena of our times and particularly our personal living experiences, which will be valuable for future studies. How did Zhejiang rapidly grow from an economically less-developed province into a province that leads the country in social and economic development since the reform and opening-up? How was the Zhejiang Phenomenon formed? How did Zhejiang form its unique regional development pattern? These questions are interesting and challenging like puzzles. However, in this day and age, it is clear that it is a utopian vision for whoever wishes to invent an interpretation model or a panacea that deals with all questions once and for all. Therefore, it may be smarter if we observe the current situation of Zhejiang's social and economic development from a limited perspective. In this book, I make a tentative study of the from-tradition-to-modern transformation of Zhejiang regional society from the perspective of cultural sociology. It is indeed a hard task to interpret the Zhejiang Phenomenon and it is obviously difficult to find a satisfactory answer if the study is simply limited to one subject. Thus, though the study uses a socio-cultural perspective, it also attempts to use theories and analytical methods of other subjects such as philosophy, economics, and politics.

The contemporary Zhejiang Pattern and Zhejiang Phenomenon are created by the people, while the government also plays an important role which, as previously mentioned, is featured with facilitation, direction, and advocacy. Hence, the study in this book values the role of government and emphasizes the tradition of the reflective few in Zhejiang's regional cultural tradition, namely the Great Tradition for ideologists. However, it pays even more attention to the popular tradition of the unreflective many, namely the Little Tradition in the folk world. The tradition of the reflective few, in Husserl's philosophical language, refers to an Ideenkleid tailored for our living world (that is, in our concrete world life, practical things are continually given to our world).[1] In contrast, the tradition of the unreflective many constitutes the living world itself, a self-evident one. This world is extant, and

---

[1] Husserl, E. *Die Krisis der Europäischen Wissenschaften und die Transzendentale Phänomenologie: Eine Einleitung in die Phänomenologische Philosophie* [M]. Trans. Zhang, Q. Shanghai: Shanghai Translation Publishing House, 1998: 61.

in the process of gaining experience, a world that can be directly understood and observed. Life is treated as an absolutely meaningful and practically verified thing without the obstruction of ideological system. The living world is the foundation of any understanding since it is a starting point and something that has been preset. The Little Tradition and the Great Tradition are not incompatible like fire and water, but are instead interactional. In history, the role of the Great Tradition have been definitely important for the Little Tradition, especially in the Chinese feudal society. On the other hand, the Little Tradition has a considerable impact on the Great Tradition. According to Gramsi's theory of cultural leadership, the process in which the cultural leadership of the ruling class is shaped and consolidated is not a process of wiping out the culture of the ruled class. Rather, it is one of constantly contacting the cultural pattern of the ruled class and absorbing the culture and value of the ruled class to different degrees. In this process, the culture of the ruling class has also changed. As a result of obtaining the cultural factors of the ruled class, the culture of the ruling class no longer belongs to only the ruling class, but rather it becomes an organic combination of cultural and ideological factors from different classes. Therefore, the ruled class will never encounter pure ruling ideology with distinctive class nature, or be oppressed by it. The ideology they face always emerges in the pattern of "negotiation format," which is formed by a compromise between the ruling class and ruled class on culture and ideology. Hence, the study in this book attempts to make a comprehensive consideration of the effect that the interaction between the Great Tradition and Little Tradition have on Zhejiang's economic and social development.

Chapter 1

Regional Culture and Spiritual Engine for the Economic and Social Development of Zhejiang Province

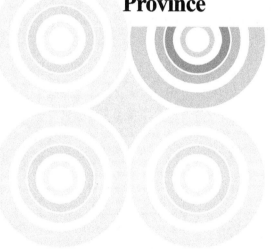

Since the implementation of the reform and opening-up, with changes in the economic system and social transformation, profound changes have also taken place in the regional culture of Zhejiang Province. Compared with the traditions, the changes in values, personality structure, cognitive disposition, life attitude, philosophy, social motivation and changes of daily life patterns of the contemporary regional culture of Zhejiang Province could be regarded as unprecedented. On the other hand, culture is not only a widely-accepted common sense or passively-accepted experience but also a series of initiative interventions that record history and moreover, changes history. The significant change in the regional culture of Zhejiang Province are bound to have an important influence on the contemporary economic and social development of the province. According to Weber's ideas on sociology, there are three interconnected and even overlapping aspects: authority, material interest, and value guidance. Among these three aspects, although value guidance does not directly decide political and economic systems since this relationship can be either direct or indirect from time to time, it is still of great impact. According to New Institutional Economics, the choice of institutions, including the informal system (namely culture), would reinforce the stimulus and momentum of existing systems. This is because it is much easier to move forward by going along the path of the existing institutional change and economic development and by following the direction already existed than to start on a new path. Cultural conventions and faith have always served as fundamental restraining factors throughout the evolution of society. Undoubtedly, since the reform and opening-up, the economic and social development of Zhejiang Province has presented distinct regional cultural characteristics.

1.1 The Origin of the Problem

Since the reform and opening-up, economic and social development has witnessed a rapid growth, with the rocketing economic aggregate and comprehensive strength. The economic and social structures have been fundamentally transformed. The social undertaking has made an all-round progress and coordinative development is gradually advancing. From 1978 to 1999, the GDP of Zhejiang Province rose from 12.4 billion yuan to 535 billion yuan, jumping from the twelfth to the fourth among all provinces in mainland China. In the late 1990s, the economy of Zhejiang Province entered a new rapid development period. In 2001, the provincial GDP rose to 674.82 billion yuan and per capita disposable income for urban residents surmounted 10 thousand yuan for the first time, reaching 10,465 yuan, with 4,582 yuan of net income for rural residents. From 1999 to 2003, the annual rise in the GDP of Zhejiang Province reached 11.7%, 3.4% higher than the average rise nationwide in the same period. From 2003 to 2016, the GDP of Zhejiang Province rose from 917 billion yuan to 4,648.5 billion yuan; per capita regional GDP rose from 4,203 yuan to 83,538 yuan; local revenue income rose from 70.7 billion yuan to 530.2 billion yuan; per capita disposable income for urban residents rose from 13,180 yuan to 47,237 yuan, ranking in first place for 16 consecutive years nationwide; and per capita disposable income for rural residents rose from 5,431 yuan to 22,866 yuan, ranking in first place for 32 consecutive years nationwide; the per capita annual income is all above 4,600 yuan, and 26 counties are no longer considered as less-developed, thus achieving the goal of phasing out poverty before the "Thirteenth Five-Year Plan." In 2016, the Zhejiang provincial GDP accounted for 6.2% of the national GDP, ranking fourth for 20 consecutive years, and equaling to the GDP of Netherland, which was ranked eighteenth worldwide; per capita GDP reached 12,577 US dollars. According to the income classification of the World Bank, Zhejiang Province has basically reached a high-income level. The economic and social development of Zhejiang Province has a promising future and continue rising.

Starting from a not so superior natural, economic and social condition, the contemporary economic society of Zhejiang Province has changed profoundly. Zhejiang is not a province with abundant resources as its composite index of per capita resources ranks third from the bottom nationwide and its per capita arable land area is far less than half of the national average. Before the reform and opening-up (1978), Zhejiang Province did not have much government investment and did not have many state-owned enterprises. From 1950 to 1978, the government investment per capita was more than 600 yuan nationwide while that in Zhejiang was only 240 yuan, less than half of the national average. In 1978, central enterprises and medium-large enterprises (MLEs) only occupied 2.6% and 16% respectively of Zhejiang's total industrial output value. Within Zhejiang Province, government investment was even lower in cities such as Wenzhou, Taizhou, Lishui, and Jinhua. For a long period after 1978, the situation of low government investment in Zhejiang did not change fundamentally. However, people of Zhejiang have created the remarkable "Zhejiang Phenomenon" since the reform and opening-up, despite having many disadvantages such as a weak industrial foundation, a large proportion of agriculture, and a shortage of resources.

Where do the "secrets" of Zhejiang's economic society lie? To answer this question, institutional variables cannot be ignored. The development of contemporary Zhejiang economic society is closely related to system changes and institutional innovation. Experiences since the reform and opening-up prove that Zhejiang is a province full of institutional innovation impulses and is eager to put it into practice. This can be reflected in the institutional innovations in economic fields such as township enterprises, private enterprises, share-holding cooperative enterprises, and specialized markets, as well as the changes in non-government funded education, self-financing for road repair, democratic deliberation and self-sufficient urbanization in the social field. Due to the realizations of such institutional innovations since the reform and opening-up, the development mode of Zhejiang's regional economic society was able to present its distinct characteristics. Unlike the "Southern Jiangsu Pattern," which focuses on developing township enterprises or the "Guangdong Pattern," which focuses on introducing foreign investment and developing an export-oriented economy, the development of contemporary Zhejiang's economic society since the Third Plenary Session of the Eleventh Central Committee of the Communist Party has reflected not only the so-called "induced" character of new institutional economics, but also the "extended order" character as proposed by Hayek. This development has also produced sound economic and social performance. Thus, in a certain sense, without the success of institutional innovations, the development of contemporary Zhejiang economic society cannot be as successful. However, there is still a question that needs further exploration—why Zhejiang active in institutional innovations?

Parsons once pointed out that any one-factor theory is naive when explaining economic and social changes. He thinks that every factor is correlated with others. Marx Weber advocates a flexible multi-factor interpretation system, that is, investigate the independent effects of institutional structures, material factors and cultural factors of society while focusing on the overall social impact of the interaction between the value system and institutional structures in a certain time and space. His discussion on the genesis of capitalism is an embodiment of such a research approach. Weber demonstrated the relationship between the Protestant ethic and the spirit of capitalism, not only from the perspective of functional consistency but also from the genealogical theory, in order to study the historical background of the rise of capitalism in the West. Despite his discontent towards the mainstream academic circles over elaborating the genesis of capitalism from a material level, Weber claimed in the meantime: "Here we have only attempted to trace the fact that Protestant Asceticism have exerted an influence on other factors. But it would also be necessary to investigate how Protestant Asceticism was in turn influenced by the totality of social conditions, especially economic. The comtemporary people are in general, even with the best will, unable to understand the cultural significance of religious thoughts nor to see the importance of religious thoughts to the formation of national characteristics. But it is, of course, not my aim to replace an one-sided materialistic with an equally one-sided spiritualistic causal interpretation of culture and of history. Each theory is equally possible, but each, if it does not serve as the preparation, but as the conclusion of an investigation, accomplishes equally little in the interest of historical truth."[1]

Marx Weber thoroughly employed the flexible multi-factor interpretation approach in his own theory. In the comparative religious studies, the analysis given by Weber and later scholars illustrates that all cultures possess the factors that can cause economic growth and decline. Examples of rapid economic growth and stagnation can be found in Protestant, Catholic, Confucian, Buddhist, Hindu, Judaist and Islamic cultures, depending on how well the economic institutional environment favors the traits of each culture. The "institutional theory" and "cultural theory" offer one-sided explanations to the conditions of East Asia's economic and social development, but fail to uncover the overall reasons that lead to such a phenomenon. Ambrose King also noted, "When explaining such complex economic phenomena as economic development, choice does not need and should not be made between 'institutional theory' and 'cultural theory'. That is to say neither should be abandoned. They are supplementary to each other rather than mutually exclusive."[2]

This has shed light on the methodology to be adopted: to understand the Zhejiang Phenomenon, one must adopt a multi-angle and

---

[1]   Weber, M. *The Protestant Ethic and the Spirit of Capitalism* [M]. Trans. Yu, X. & Chen, W. Beijing: SDX Joint Publishing Company, 1987: 143-144.

[2]   King, A. *Confucian Ethics and Economic Development: A Re-examination of Weber's Theory* [M]//Zhang, W. & Gao, Z. *Taiwan Scholars on Chinese Culture*, Harbin: Heilongjiang Education Press, 1989: 308-309.

multi-factor approach. Since China's reform and opening-up and along with Zhejiang outstripping the rest of the country in terms of economic development, many scholars within and outside the province have offered in-depth interpretations of the Zhejiang Phenomenon from the economic and political level. Yet, none have placed an emphasis on the cultural and ethical factors behind this phenomenon. This book seeks to make its own arguments instead of refuting other people's opinions, to build upon existing viewpoints and offer an alternative understanding. In other words, on the basis of existing research, this book aims to focus on following question: What is the role of regional cultural factors in the process of Zhejiang's implementation of regional institutional innovation and formation of a unique economic society?

A comprehensive understanding of the Zhejiang Phenomenon can only be achieved when we combine the interpretations from the cultural, economic and political levels. In the real world, the importance of culture cannot be underestimated. Our daily lives constantly revolve around a set of cultural environment and social context, and our daily conducts are subject to the inherent guidance and constraints of culture. In this sense, we can say that culture is an intrinsic factor of social life and an indispensable condition for any social action. Therefore, if we deviate from cultural sociology and attempt to explain the phenomenon of regional institutional innovation and economic society of contemporary Zhejiang, our research would be deemed as inadequate.

When studying the relationship between the institutional innovation and development of an economic society of contemporary Zhejiang and regional culture, many theories can be used as references, such as Weber's theory on the reasons why rational capitalism only exists in some nations and regions, the theory of later scholars on the relationship between Confucian values and the modernization of East Asia, as well as the categorization of the conditions that limit people's economic behavior like formal and informal institutional arrangements by New Institutional Economics. The latter also argues that formal arrangements can only be effective when they are compatible with things that are approved by society (informal arrangements or things that can be collectively known as culture). In addition, the theories of cultural anthropology and economic sociology can also provide important methodological and theoretical insights.

1.2　Characteristics of the Regional Development Pattern of Contemporary Zhejiang

The essential characteristics of the Zhejiang Phenomenon since the reform and opening-up can be summarized as an institutional innovation and economic development pattern that is "people-induced" and "government-improved." This pattern is a mix of top-down and bottom-up directions, which not only requires the government to loosen policies (abolish restrictive policies) but also encourages the public to make active decisions after comparing the expected benefits and cost when facing profitable opportunities caused by institutional imbalance. The core of this "people-induced" and "government-improved" pattern lies in the spontaneous and internal institutional innovation and economic and social developments, which features strong self-organizing characteristics and is motivated by the people. In other words, in Zhejiang Province, the market and folk forces play a self-organizing role, while the government is in charge of facilitation and assistance. This is precisely what distinguishes the Zhejiang Pattern from the Southern Jiangsu Pattern which features government (especially township-government) interference. The formation of such a pattern, undoubtedly, is attributed to the spirits of independent livelihoods and innovations of Zhejiang people. The strong will of self-employment and entrepreneurship is a remarkable characteristic of Zhejiang regional culture and spirit. The changes which took place after the reform and opening-up illustrate their positive effects on institutional innovation as well as economic and social developments. People in Zhejiang Province are less dependent on the government and administration officials in terms of improving their own living conditions but are more reliant on personal struggles and interpersonal cooperation. Among the large number of migrant merchants and workers who were formal residents in Zhejiang Province and then went outside to work, a majority run their own business and bear the associated risks themselves. All these phenomena reflect the will of Zhejiang people to make a living by themselves and their entrepreneurial spirit. Moreover, the will and spirit can also be demonstrated by other examples, such as the rise of specialized markets across Zhejiang, the rapid development of private enterprises and share-holding cooperative enterprises, the rise of characteristic economies named "One Town One Product" and "One Village One Product," the formation of "Zhejiang Community" "Zhejiang Street" and "Wenzhou Community" (Wenzhou is a city in Zhejiang) all over the country, the emergence of self-financing towns (Longgang Town, renowned as the "First National Farmer Town," is a typical instance), as well as the self-balance in the reconstruction funds and even the informal talks and non-government funded education in Wenling, Taizhou (a city in Zhejiang). To some extent, the spirit of self-employment is the spiritual driving force of Zhejiang's contemporary institutional innovation as well as economic and social development.

1.2.1　Government-improved Model of Regional Institution Innovation and Economic and Social Development

During the process of institutional innovation and economic development, the characteristics of "government-improved" are quite obvious. Since the reform and opening-up, governments in Zhejiang Province have offered not only a relatively loose policy environment, but also necessary coordination and protection for the institutional innovations and economic activities. For instance, in the year of 1979, the development plan of commune and brigade run enterprises in Taizhou (a city in Zhejiang) was made. However, during its implementation, the policies which were focused on the collective economy did not attach much emphasis to, nor exert limitations on other economic subjects, and thus, in the 1980s, diversified economies emerged in Taizhou. In the same year, the local government of Taizhou started to loosen the restrictions on agricultural products, and implemented the policy of "state-run, collective and individual together." As early as 1980 to 1982, the local governments of Taizhou have expanded the pilots of autonomy for state-run and collective enterprises. In the innovative process of the rural share-holding cooperation system, governments at all levels in Zhejiang provided appropriate support for this new economic form, in which they "had a look"(not interfered) at the beginning and then "made an attempt" in the development period and later "go ahead" in its promotion. Enlightened governments in regions such as Taizhou and Wenzhou of Zhejiang Province were among the first ones to bring the national joint-stock cooperation system into practice and launched a series of policies to keep pace with the development of share-holding cooperative enterprises. For example, in November 1986, the county Party committee and county government of Huangyan, Taizhou issued Some Policies on Joint-stock Enterprises, China's first systematic document on share-holding cooperative enterprises. This document explicitly affirmed that the collective economy was the main feature of share-holding cooperative enterprises, and treated these enterprises in the same way as the collective ones. In 1987, when there were still many doubts about the joint-stock cooperation system, the prefectural Party committee of Taizhou conducted a meeting with the principals of local and regional departments in order to further unify their thinking and called on people to learn from the expriences of Ningbo and Wenzhou when heading to their own ways to success. The meeting also called for further development of policies on share-holding cooperative enterprises and implemented the guidelines of encouragement, support, guidance, and administration, as well as a series of associated policies and regulations on taxation and loans. In 1987, the government of Wenzhou issued the Interim Provisions on Some Important Issues in Rural Stock Cooperation Enterprises and began to standardize the joint-stock system. Thanks to the support of all levels of government in Taizhou and Wenzhou, the share-holding cooperative enterprises in these two places have been developing rapidly.

The development of specialized markets in Zhejiang is a more persuasive example. Governments at all levels have effectively offered policy supports to the growth of a market-oriented province and the process of establishing the system of specialized markets. Although most of the earliest specialized markets were formed spontaneously by the general public, the growth of many specialized markets around Zhejiang has shown that without strong support from the local governments, it is almost impossible for these markets to develop into large-scale ones with great influence. The history of the Shaoxing Textile City of Zhejiang Province is a typical example. The Shaoxing Textile City was developed from the streets of cloth, which were spontaneously established by indigenous township enterprises. During its growth, it underwent four large-scale projects of expansion and reconstructions to which the Shaoxing governments offered huge supports both in finance, including local fiscal expenditure and bank loans, and in infrastructure constructions, including land acquisition, public transportation, and communication facilities and electricity[①]. Another reason why Zhejiang has reached a great success in specialized market system and economy is the guidance and regulation issued by the governments. For example, Zhejiang Province is one of the earliest regions to promote the separation of management and government. Many market proprietors in Yiwu are required to sell at expressly marked price, and there are also complaint handling and arbitral agencies set up in the markets. In addition, organizations such as the industry association, consumers' association, notaries, audits and law offices have all, to a certain extent, played a role in creating a levelplaying field and a regulated market order. The local governments have also made laws that are adapted to the local situations, such as The Implementation Law of Building Wenzhou by Relying on Quality that was released in 1994 by the municipal people's congress of Wenzhou. The establishment of such laws has provided an

---

① Chen, J. *The High Speed Economic Growth in Chinese Regions—A Study of Jiangsu and Zhejiang Pattern* [M]. Shanghai: SDX Joint Publishing Company, 2000: 336-337.

institutional guarantee to the prosperity of specialized markets and the normal running of the market economic system[1].

1.2.2   The People-Induced Model of Regional Institution Innovation and Economic and Social Development

On the other hand, the "government-improved" model of Zhejiang Province's institutional innovation and economic development are always based on the "people-induced" model. Compared with the "government-improved" model, the "people-induced" one is more typical. Different from the imposed institutional change which is introduced and implemented by governmental orders or laws, induced institutional change, usually advocated, organized and implemented spontaneously by person or a group of people when reacting to profitable opportunities. It refers to the change or replacement of the present institution or the innovation of a new institution. Specifically, induced institutional change has the following characteristics:

a. Profitability. Only when the institutional change's expected returns exceed its expected costs, will related groups promote this change.

b. Spontaneity. Induced institutional change is a spontaneous reaction of related groups (primary action groups) to the unbalanced institution due to the external profits.

c. Gradualness. Induced institutional change is a process from the bottom-up and from parts to the whole. Time is needed in the transformation, replacement, and diffusion of the institution. Besides, it needs to experience a lot of complex links from the discovery to the internalization of the external profits.

---

① Sheng, S. & Xu, M. *Research on Several Issues of Economic and Social Development in Zhejiang Province* [M]. Hangzhou: Zhejiang People's Publishing House, 1999: 60.

The "people-induced" Zhejiang Pattern is a market-solving, spontaneous and self-organizing model in essence. The role of government, though important, is only to facilitate, assist, advocate and host the model. Carl Menger believes that the dominant social institution is not the result of the intentional consultation of individuals but rather their unintentional behaviors. He also stated that the summation of individual behaviors would spontaneously become cooperative and coordinating behaviors, which would benefit every member in the society. What's more, a universal order would come into being throughout the society if the administrative and behavioral rules can remain stable and be followed by every member in the society.

F. A. Hayek inherited the idea of Carl Menger. He thought that, to a great extent, the social order was the result of natural evolution, namely, a "self-organizing system" or a "self-generating system." These conceptions from Cybernetics indicate that the internal interaction of the power of the systems can create a spontaneous order, which is different from a man-made order, a factitious order, a constructed order or a construction by deploying a series of elements, guiding and controlling the way they move. Among all the spontaneous orders, the most typical one is that of the organism. In Hayek's opinion, the spontaneous order is not a product designed by an individual or a group of people, but the result of the behaviors of human beings. An artificially imposed order or a guided order, named as an "organization," is an "taxis" from external forces, different from "cosmos" that is produced through internal spontaneous integration. Hayek also classified the spontaneous order into two types: one is the rule system, such as moral rules and laws; the other one is the action structure, such as the economic order in markets. These two types are different in the ways of evolution. The former takes place in an undefined environment, and its occurrence does not follow any rules of evolution, while the latter is created in a defined environment and evolves by regulations and reasons.

According to Hayek's theory, the people-induced model in Zhejiang could be regarded as a spontaneous model and a self-organizing model, which was gradually formed in the natural evolution. Many individuals have contributed to this natural order.

A key precondition for the transition of this people-induced model is that the relevant groups involved in the transition takes on a strong will of self-employment, entrepreneurship, and self-innovation, which sharply emerged in the Zhejiang civil society. For example, from 1979 to the spring of 1982, the system of household contract responsibility had taken shape initially in Zhejiang, which, however, was not established nationally until 1984. It was a spontaneous and ahead-of-the-country reaction of Zhejiang people out of their strong will to make a living against the unbalanced system. The scattered specialized markets in Zhejiang since China's reform and opening-up are not designed by someone but are a spontaneous result. They did not stem from a man-made order, a factitious order, a constructed order or a construction by someone deploying a series of elements, guiding and controlling the way they move, but rather from the non-intentional actions of a huge crowd.

The evolution of the China Yiwu Commodities Market (Yiwu Market) is such an epitome. According to Lu, Bai, and Wang, in the late 1970s, the non-official commodity markets began to diverge from the regular markets. Choucheng Town, though not the cradle of the Qiaotang Group, became a relatively ideal small commodity marketplace because of its special geographical position and its function as a political and economic center in Yiwu. Initially, only a few old men peddled in this area, later followed by a large group of people with a strong will to make a living. Within half a year, the number of street peddlers that conducted business on the Xianqian Street increased to 100. By this time, the commodity market made its way into a semi-public state and was no longer in secret. The Xianqian Street and the Beimen Street became fixed selling places. The increasing number of stalls severely affected the appearance of Yiwu. The business administration was then ordered to drive the peddlers away but failed several times because the peddlers carried only simple equipment such as buckets, which allowed them to run away easily. Moreover, confiscation would not be a big loss for them. Therefore, this kind of drive could not eliminate the peddlers' strong will to make a living. At the time, visible markets served only as places for both parties of a trade to find trading partners. The government was at its wit's end to drive peddlers away or conduct any effective administration to collect administrative fee or tax according to its regular market management approach. The two parties began to play their game of cat and mouse, but this was infeasible in the long term. Given that the order of prohibition was ineffective and the commodity market was not harmful to the society, in August 1982, after rounds of discussion, the Yiwu Government finally decided to officially open the Choucheng Town Commodity Market,[①] the precursor of the China Commodity City.

Most of the specialized markets in Zhejiang experienced a similar self-generating process. What first appeared in many towns of Zhejiang were street markets, which at that time were illegal and were known as "black markets." The government usually tried to ban, stop and drive away these markets and set up the Combating Speculation and Profiteering Office, but these methods have always ended in failure. This reality prompted the local officials to change their policies from banning, stopping and driving to persuading and guiding, first adopting the ambiguous policies of "No Public Approval and No Prohibition in Writing" and later adopting the clearer policies of "Approved in Writing and Encouraging Development." These "black markets" finally drove their way into markets that specialized in small commodities and household goods. This process is undoubtedly people-induced, spontaneous, self-generating and self-

---

① Lu, L., Bai, X. & Wang, Z. *The Yiwu Fair—From Chicken Feather for Sugar to International Business and Trade* [M]. Hangzhou: Zhejiang People's Publishing House, 2003: 37-39.

organizing and its dynamism is the strong will of people to make a living and be innovative.

The development of Zhejiang's privately-owned enterprises embodies the spontaneity of emergence and induction by the people. Even during the time of planned economy, especially during the period of the "Cut the Tail of Capitalism" movement, many household businesses had emerged spontaneously in Zhejiang. In the late 1980s, riding the wave of the reform and opening-up, individual and private economy in Wenzhou, Taizhou, Jinhua of Zhejiang emerged as a renewal of historical traditions. These spontaneously formed private-owned enterprises were kept secretly "underground" at first. For instance, at the early stage of the reform and opening-up, Wenzhou and Taizhou's private enterprises had to be attached to collective enterprises or wear a "red hat," in other words, to be covered as collective enterprises. Though the dispute over whether this economic form belongs to socialism or capitalism has never stopped, Zhejiang's individual and private enterprises continued to grow under the people's spontaneous force. The government and concerned departments have also experienced a transition from the ambiguous policies of "No Public Approval and No Prohibition in Writing" to the clear policies of "Approved in Writing and Encouraging development." Though the transformation was in line with loose national macro-policies, it was not a man-made order, a factitious order, a constructed order or a construction. The strongest impetus bringing about the transformation came from Zhejiang people and their drive to make a living and create a new path on their own.

The emergence of the shareholding cooperative system in Zhejiang has self-organizing features such as being "people-induced." The shareholding cooperative system originated from the traditions of "partnership" and "subscribe for shares in cash" in the villages of Wenzhou and Taizhou in Zhejiang. In the late 1970s, under the pressure of having a large population with a relatively little land, farmers in localities such as Wenzhou and Taizhou sought new ways to earn a living. However, a single household could not afford the costs of opening a factory. With the development of non-agricultural industries and the intensification of market competition, farmers in places like Wenzhou and Taizhou were in urgent need of a new property right system so as to adapt to their own development needs and overcome the weakness of household operation, which was difficult to adapt to the production scale expansion. The new system is able to arrange coalition and reorganization of production factors and coordinate new economic relations formed by coalition and reorganization of assets. Under such circumstances, farmers in places like Wenzhou and Taizhou demonstrated strong independent innovation consciousness. They tried to set up partnerships collectively owned by households and hire employees to expand the scale of household production. Due to loose asset coalition, unlimited joint or several liabilities of joint household enterprises, policy constraints, and inharmonious labor relations of employment, both methods hindered the further growth of the household economy, leading to its failure to become a generic form. In this case, Taizhou farmers and their families and neighbors, following the principle of "equality and free will," built a new-type of shareholding cooperative system featuring "self-funded, joint venture, benefit-sharing, and risk-sharing," which realized the privatization and sharing, of private property. And, the system became the major economic form in the further development of the household economy, especially in the non-agricultural sector. Undoubtedly, people played a major role in the process, while the government only served as an important promoter, helper, advocator and moderator. Zhejiang's shareholding cooperative system is also induced by the people, which in essence is a market solution model, a spontaneous development model, and a self-organizing model. The regional spirit of self-employment and self-entrepreneurship has, in reality, not only been reflected in the economic sector since the reform and opening-up but has widely penetrated into other social sectors in Zhejiang Province. In the 1980s, the urbanization level of Zhejiang was far lower than the national average. At that time with stretched national financial investment, a trend emerged in several places in Zhejiang where farmers worked in cities with their self-rations or built towns by self-financing. For instance, Beibaixiang Town of Yueqing City once raised 100 million yuan to renovate the town. The first folk chambers of commerce, namely Wenzhou Joint Chamber of Commerce for Foreign-invested Enterprises, Wenzhou Food Industry and Commerce Guild and Wenzhou Department Store Association were set up in 1988. Since then, Wenzhou folk chambers of commerce have gone through over 10 years of progress and made great achievements. Wenzhou folk chambers of commerce, as new rising regional governing subjects, are the inevitable results of the Wenzhou folk spirit of self-entrepreneurship and self-innovation. It was the private economy's need for self-protection and development that encouraged the emergence of these folk chambers of commerce. The need for self-protection is instinctive and spontaneous, the essence of which is to find a "spokesperson of the industry" to coordinate various social relations on behalf of the overall interests of the industry. Wenzhou folk chambers of commerce have played a unique role in Wenzhou economic and social development. First, they acted as organizers that offered services and have dealt with a number of troubles disrupting individual enterprises. Second, they acted as coordinators that solved confrontations and disputes and also coordinated internal and external relations by carrying out industry self-discipline and standardizing horizontal competition. They have taken over some tasks that are inconvenient or impossible for the government. Since China's accession to the WTO and with all kinds of anti-dumping, anti-technical barrier and anti-subsidy trade wars coming after, Wenzhou folk chambers of commerce have played a significant role in settling trade disputes, facilitating international cooperation, ushering in a new channel to acquire foreign knowledge, increasing technology and capital, exerting influence on global economic decision-making in a non-governmental way, as well as participating in unofficial global economic activities and affairs. Many new approaches of democracy at the grassroots level since the reform and opening-up originate from the incentive, assistance, initiative

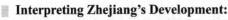

and presiding work of the local government as well as the people-induced suggestions on the one hand, and embody the folk spirit of self-entrepreneurship and self-innovation on the other hand.

1.3 The Marginal Area of the Planned Economy and People-Induced Spiritual Motivation

It was Zhejiang people's ongoing self-entrepreneurship activities that contributed to Zhejiang's astounding performance in the economic and social fields and that made Zhejiang a vibrant area of institutional innovation, demonstrating the tremendous vitality of Zhejiang's economy and society. Why does the private sector in Zhejiang Province boast such a strong sense of entrepreneurship and the urge of institutional innovation and economic development? Starting a business is a big decision for every individual. Entrepreneurship means that the entrepreneur from then on has to undertake huge financial, mental and social risks, causing a significant impact on a person's life. Entrepreneurship requires entrepreneurial motivation and enthusiasm, both of which need to be nurtured in certain economic and social atmosphere. People's motivation and willingness of entrepreneurship in an area or a nation depend on various factors, such as politics and economy, among which the cultural background plays a fundamental role. Entrepreneurial motivation and enthusiasm have to be nurtured and enhanced in a certain cultural atmosphere. For humans, the impact of culture is enormous. Schutz, a phenomenologist, argues that social culture and social knowledge consist of a variety of conventions and common practices which can be vividly described as "social recipes"— namely practices that are typical and familiar to everyone under certain conditions. Such conventions or common practices allow people to classify things, solve problems, assume social roles, disseminate and take context-appropriate actions according to certain logic comprehensible to all. Various social behaviors such as negotiation, marriage, religious ceremonies, child education and deals are carried

out according to these "social recipes."[1] Culture endows our society
with a systematic code of conduct, which provides community members
with measures, and blueprints for distinguishing right and wrong,
beauty and ugliness and reasonableness and unreasonableness. Culture
can effectively influence one's personality. In fact, people are shaping
themselves according to cultural requirements and expectations. Culture
offers people a criterion for predicting others' actions, thus enabling
people to revise their own. It is because of culture's contribution
to important social functions that different cultural backgrounds,
especially different values, determine people's attitudes toward
entrepreneurship and their different evaluations of success and the
value of entrepreneurship, thus accounting for differences in people's
motivations of entrepreneurship in different regions and countries.
Generally speaking, people tend to have stronger entrepreneurial
motivations in a social and cultural atmosphere that encourages
entrepreneurship, innovation, risk-taking, and competition, tolerates
failures and emphasizes achievement, fairness and justice. However, the
entrepreneurial motivation is bound to be weak when it is immersed in
a socio-cultural atmosphere where the entrepreneurship is not valued
and comfort to safety is preferred to risks, with no attempt to build
enterprises and little tolerance for entrepreneurship. Therefore, to study
the strong sense of entrepreneurship that is characteristic of Zhejiang
people since the reform and opening-up, we must start from the social
and cultural environment in which Zhejiang people live.

1.3.1   A Question That Needs Clarification

1.3.1.1   The Central or Marginal Areas of Confucian Culture

It is undeniable that there is a certain connection between people's
strong will to make a living and be entrepreneurs and the historical
and cultural traditions with strong local characteristics in Zhejiang.

---

[1]   Little John, S.W. *Theories of Human Communication* [M]. Trans. Shi, A.
Beijing: Tsinghua University Press, 2004: 219-220.

In what sense such connection takes place still remains a question that requires further study. While discussing the cultural factors of the Zhejiang phenomenon, some scholars argue that Confucianism is unfavorable to economic development. Since Zhejiang constitutes a marginal area of Confucian culture when compared with the central areas of Confucianism in the Central Plains, this position means fewer constraints from the traditional mainstream culture for Zhejiang people, contributing to Zhejiang people's independent innovation activities. However, this view is questionable. Indeed, according to a cultural sociology perspective, marginalization contributes to cultural innovation. The coexistence of the central culture and the marginalized culture means that the two have a trade-off relationship. E. Shils believes that "there are many forms of resistance to traditions provided and promoted by social centers. Sometimes it stems from indifference—which is only one step away from hostility—not primarily to the traditional substance, but to the authoritative expressions and their source. Indifference may be a result of incompetence and the little interest in the traditional content."[1] The existence of the marginalized culture means the fading out of the central culture, which proves the limitation of the central cultural dissemination and the declining status of the central culture's influence. Because of this, cultural marginalization is less conducive to cultural innovation. This results in the phenomenon that many culturally marginalized areas tend to enjoy faster economic and social development than the original cultural center due to the after effects, as demonstrated by numerous historical examples both at home and abroad.

However, while marginalization favors innovation, the assertion of Zhejiang as a marginal area of Confucian culture compared with the Central Confucianism center still remains an unlikely conclusion. On the contrary, at least since the Northern and Southern Song dynasties,

---

[1] Shils, E. *Tradition* [M]. Trans. Fu, K. & Lü, L. Shanghai: Shanghai People's Publishing House, 1991: 341.

the eastern part of Zhejiang has become an important area for academic and cultural development across the country. Since the Northern and Southern Song dynasties, especially the Southward Migration of the Song Royal Court, with the southward shift of the political and cultural center of the country, scholars across Zhejiang can be said to have come forth in large numbers, and the style of Confucianism has also been prominent, especially in Wuzhou, Wenzhou, and Mingzhou. These areas have witnessed regional schools of Confucianism that had an important influence on the whole country, such as the Jinhua School, the Yongkang School, the Yongjia School, and the "Four Scholars in Yongshang" who spread Lu Jiuyuan's works. In addition, the study of Zhu Xi, a preeminent Neo-Confucianist, was also widespread in eastern Zhejiang. In the Ming Dynasty, the most important Confucian school after Cheng-Zhu Neo-Confucianism was formed in eastern Zhejiang, namely the Yangming School of Idealist Philosophy. Meanwhile, the Ningbo and Shaoxing areas in eastern Zhejiang also thrived in Southeast China.

In fact, since the Song and Yuan dynasties, not only has eastern Zhejiang become the center of academic thoughts nationwide, the Confucianism in eastern Zhejiang has also been regarded as a school closely related to Confucianism in the Central Plains, rather than heresy. He Bingsong pointed out that "the so-called Eastern Zhejiang School of Confucianism is indeed an heir of the Cheng's School by direct line."[1] He Bingsong believed that there are actually two branches of the Eastern Zhejiang School in the Southern Song Dynasty, namely the Yongjia Branch and Jinhua Branch. Originating earlier than the Jinhua Branch, the Yongjia Branch enjoys a more direct affiliation than the former one. Sun Yerang pointed out: "During Yuanfeng Reign in the Song Dynasty, a new school was established, attracting a galaxy of talents to visit the Imperial College, including Jiang Yuanzhong, Shen Gongxing, Liu Anjie, Liu Anshang, Dai Shu, Zhao Xiao, Zhang

---

[1]   He, B. *Tracing to the Source of the Eastern Zhejiang School* [M]. Guilin: Guangxi Normal University Press, 2004: 148.

Wei, Zhou Xingji, and Xu Jingheng. The school was reputed for its practical statecraft. Having studied Confucianism under the School of Cheng, these talents all returned to their hometown to promote their understanding of Confucianism except for Mr. Jiang, Mr. Zhao, and Mr. Zhang, thus contributing to the so-called 'Nine Scholars' in Yongjia."[①] Among Cheng's disciples in Yongjia, Xu Jingheng and Zhou Xingji can both be regarded as precursors who introduced the Cheng School into Zhejiang. As Lou Yue in the late Song Dynasty reviewed, "Apart from Yang Gongshi in Gui Hill and You Gongzuo in Jian'an, only several persons such as Xu Jingheng and Zhou Xingji learned from Cheng Hao and Cheng Yi Neo-Confucianism in Southeast China. Therefore, schools proposing rationalism can trace their roots to the Yongjia School."[②] Quan Zuwang pointed out that "Followers of the Cheng School's Neo-Confucianism in eastern Zhejiang start with Xu Jingheng."[③] It is safe to conclude that Cheng's Neo-Confucianism has been prominent since the emergence of "Nine Scholars" in Yongjia. In the early years of the Southern Song Dynasty, the place witnessed little Cheng's Neo-Confucianism and the waning of Nine Scholars' inheritance. It was thanks to the efforts of Zheng Boxiong that the Cheng's School had been carried forward and promoted. "According to the *General Annals of Zhejiang*, Zheng Boxiong is versatile at the classics. In Shaoxing where Cheng's Neo-Confucianism waned, Boxiong came out and thrived in the School. In his book *General Meaning of Seclusion*, Liu Xie described Boxiong as a man aware of nature's principles and who fits his deeds to words. Therefore, the School of Yongjia can be said as initiated by Zhou Xingji, inherited by Boxiong and upheld by Lü Zuqian, Chen Fu Liang and Ye Shi, etc."[④]

---

① Xu, J. *A Collection of Works by Xu Jingheng* (postscript) [Z].

② Chen, F. *A Collection of Works by Chen Fuliang:* vol. 52 [Z].

③ Huang, Z. & Quan, Z. *A Record of the Origins of Schools in the Song and Yuan dynasties:* vol. 32 [Z].

④ Yong, R. & Ji, Y. *Catalogue of the Complete Collection of the Four Treasures* [Z].

Besides the Yongjia school, is it possible that the Jinhua School has a teaching-succession relationship with Confucianism in the Central Plains? There were three academic giants in Jinhua during the Song Dynasty, namely Lü Zuqian (literarily named Donglai), Tang Zhongyou (literarily named Shuozhai) and Chen Liang (literarily named Longchuan, styled Tongfu). Quan Zuwang pointed out: "The Jinhua School was the most prominent during Reign Qianchuan in the Song Dynasty. The Donglai Branch (represented by Lü Zuqian and Lü Zujian) is famous for Theory of Divination Principles, while the Shuozhai Branch for their study on classics. Given that the most prominent scholars on classics were those in Yongjia at that time, the Donglai Branch and Yongjia scholars often held discussions and shared similar interests. Therefore, the Donglai Branch was especially inclusive, while the Shuozhai Branch did not relate with other schools but rather promoted its doctrine alone."[①] He Bingsong maintained that the three giants in Jinhua and scholars in Yongjia "discussed with each other and got along well." Therefore, although the Jinhua School did not inherit Cheng's by direct line like the Yongjia School, it could still be counted as an informal disciple of the Cheng School. He Bingsong cited a large number of documents to prove this point. For example, Lü Zuqian's theory originated in Cheng's. Wang Zongbing said: "The Jinhua School prospered since He Ji, Wang Bai, Jin Luxiang and Xu Qian, while Lü Zuqian was the first to expand the source of the Donglai Branch. His ancestor Lü Gongzhu often paid visits to Cheng Hao and Cheng Yi in Henan province, and Lü Xizhe, son of Lü Gongzhu, also studied under the School of Cheng. By the time of the Southward Migration, schools in the North had faded while the Lü Family gained exclusive access to documents in the Central Plains."[②] Quan Zuwang observed, "Lü Xizhe preferred to get along with contemporary scholars. He studied and lived with Cheng Hao and Cheng Yi under Teacher Hu Anding in the imperial

---

① Huang, Z. & Quan, Z. *A Record of the Origins of Schools in the Song and Yuan dynasties:* vol. 60 [Z].

② Lü, Z. *A Reprint of Works by Lü Zuqian* (preface) [Z].

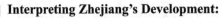

college when they were similar ages. Later impressed by the learning of the Cheng Brothers, Lü Xizhe treated them like teachers."[1]

So, would there be an inheritance relationship between Chen Liang who "focused on practical work" and Confucianism in the Central Plains? Quan Zuwang gave a negative answer, "The Yongjia Branch's classics study and practical work were consistent with the Cheng's School, while the Yongkang Branch focusing on practical work didn't inherit anything."[2] Huang Baijia also agreed that "in the Yongjia Branch, both Xue Jixuan and Chen Fuliang graduated from the Cheng's School. At the time when Chen Liang was prominent in Yongkang, he did not inherit anything from Cheng's. However, his study focused on reading and bettering the world, paying no attention to numerology. Thus Chen Liang was disregarded by people as being too utilitarian, and his school was viewed as the Zhe School."[3] However, Wang Zicai believed that Chen Liang had studied under Zheng Jingwang (namely Zheng Boxiong) in that he "called Zheng 'my sir' while offering sacrifice in Zheng's memory."[4] Quan Zuwang also counted Chen Liang as a follower of Zheng Jingwang in his book *Documents of Scholars*, in which He Bingsong believes that Chen Liang's doctrine can be traced back to Cheng's via Zheng Jingwang, and Quan's assertion that "Yongkang did not inherit" can also be contradictory.

It is more difficult to study this succession of relationships of Tang Zhongyou (founder of the Shuozhai Branch) than other scholars, for his writings were almost destroyed by Zhu Xi's disciples. However, Scholar Huang Zongxi believed that Tang's doctrine shared the same

---

① Huang, Z. & Quan, Z. *A Record of the Origins of Schools in the Song and Yuan dynasties:* vol. 23 [Z].

② Huang, Z. & Quan, Z. *A Record of the Origins of Schools in the Song and Yuan dynasties:* vol. 56 [Z].

③ Huang, Z. & Quan, Z. *A Record of the Origins of Schools in the Song and Yuan dynasties:* vol. 56 [Z].

④ Ibid.

source with representatives like Xue Jixuan and Chen Fuliang in the Yongjia Branch. "Tang established the study of classics, advocating painstaking investigations to seek ancient sages' heart and to promote such will in the world. After giving it more thought, Xue Shilong and Chen Junju decided not to identify with Tang's despite their shared origin. Therefore, Tang's doctrine continued in spite of all Zhu Xi's attempts."[①] Although Quan Zuwang disagreed with Huang's view, he also maintained that "the Shuozhai Branch agrees most with scholars in the Yongjia Branch." Judging by Tang's book *Jiujing Questions* and the postscript by Zhang Zuonan, Tang is obviously an informal disciple of Cheng's School.

The above illustrates that since the Song and Yuan dynasties, eastern Zhejiang has not only become the center of academic thoughts nationwide but also boasts a very close affiliation with Confucianism in the Central Plains. Contrary to some contemporary scholars' imagination, Eastern Zhejiang Confucianism does not constitute a kind of marginal Confucianism and differs totally from the orthodox Confucianism in the Central Plains.

Moreover, from numerous kinds of local annals, we can see the flourishing of Confucianism across Zhejiang in history, and witness the "omnipresent and all-time" infiltration of Confucianism in the private sector. For instance, according to records on *Old Stories of Wulin,* Hangzhou is "prosperous like Dongjing in terms of institutions, social etiquette, and culture." *Local Annals of Jiaxing during Hongzhi Reign* describes that Jiaxing "boasts a galaxy of literati keen on literature and learning, with rich cultural relics and brilliant clothes." Wang Shipeng observed in *Huzhou Yemiao Article* that "The prominence of education in Huzhou can hardly be matched in Southeast China, with the similar ethos like in Zhoulu (now Shandong Province) and honest people." According to Wang Yinglin's *Records of Study in Yin County*, it's a

---

① Huang, Z. *A Collection of Works by Huang Zongxi:* vol. 2 [Z].

"county of poetry and literature with good manners and a galaxy of talents." *Local Annals of Dongyang during Chenhua Reign* records that "people in Dongyang love reading. No child in respectable families does not follow a certain teacher to study, some aiming to pass the imperial examination while those intellectually and developmentally disabled seek to learn the fundamentals of literacy and manners." In the Qing Dynasty, every household in Shaoxing "observed sacrifices and took shame in not admonishing children with lectures. Most merchants and sedan carriers promoted literacy" and that "men and women there observed the proprieties strictly, with numerous documents recorded on the conduct of integrity."[1] Even citizens in Pingyang, a remote area in Wenzhou, "enjoyed prominent cultural richness and proprieties in the Song Dynasty. At that time, scholars including Chen Jingzheng, Chen Zhi, Lin Shi all studied from the Cheng Brothers and Zhu Xi. With a profound academic atmosphere, eminent scholars emerged one after another. Even today people still place a high value on Confucian classics and are keen on educating children. Private schools are widespread across the town."[2] Therefore, it would be more appropriate to say (especially after the Southern Song Dynasty) that Zhejiang is more of a central area deeply influenced by Confucianism than a marginal area of Confucian culture.

1.3.1.2 The Relationship between Confucian Culture and Contemporary Economic and Social Development

Since Zhejiang is also a central area deeply influenced by Confucianism, the question to be further explored is whether Confucianism is detrimental to the contemporary economic and social development. This question, in fact, King Yeo-Chi and scholars such as Hicks and Redding, Hofheinz and Caloler, Berger, Alatas, Aandreshi, Kahn, etc., have already done a fair amount of discussion.

---

① Zhejiang Provincial Chronicle Compilation Committee. *Annals of Zhejiang* [M].Shanghai: Zhonghua Book Company, 2001: 2298.
② Ibid. 2316.

In the interpretation of the relationship between Confucian culture and contemporary economic and social development, Max Weber has been frequently mentioned. According to Max Weber's theory, Protestant ethics are the "initiating agency" of the rational capitalism or economic rationalization. However, the attractiveness of Weber's theory lies not only in explaining why rational capitalism took place in the Western societies but also in studying why other socially reasonable forms of capitalism did not occur. Weber's comparative studies in religion, including *Confucianism and Taoism* in China, Hinduism, and Islam in the Middle East, represent precisely his attempt to account for why these societies "did not" give rise to capitalism. Weber did not intend to construct a set of historical or social "development laws." He chose these religions as objects of cultural comparison, mainly to deepen his understanding of the uniqueness of the economic development path in the West. What is interesting is Weber's analysis of China. The main idea of his book Confucianism and Taoism is to illustrate why rational capitalism did not "occur" in China. In this book, Weber basically took a two-pronged approach to address this complicated issue, from the two aspects of institution and culture. Weber first started with the institutional factors in traditional China. He chose and examined five specific factors in China's social system, namely money and city, the feudal system in China, clan system, substantive social etiquette, and social stratum. Weber's analysis shows that the institutional factors in traditional China are, in general, not conducive to generating large-scale rational capitalism.

However, his research is undoubtedly quite dialectical. Weber also pointed out that there are many institutional factors in the traditional Chinese society that are conducive to economic rationalization, including freedom of movement, non-identity inheritance, freelance employment, free education, and non-trade restrictions. Therefore, institutional factors are not sufficient in explaining the absence of rational capitalism in China. According to Weber, besides institutional factors, a "spiritual foundation" is also needed for large-scale capitalism to occur in China. Such spirit in the West refers to the spirit of capitalism originating from Protestant ethics. However, the dominant value system in traditional China—Confucian ethics, cannot provide a similar spiritual foundation. Therefore, despite certain institutional conditions conducive to economic rationalization in the traditional Chinese society, it is hard to witness economic rationality in the modern sense. For example, Confucian ethics does not appear to be "building" the world, whether in its orientation or way of behavior, but rather it is "conforming" or "adapting" to the world. Confucianism's interest is in the present world, lacking the kind of religious spiritual power that goes beyond the secular world. This naive and optimistic position of Confucianism varies totally from the huge "tension" existing between man and the world in Christian ethics. Another example is that in traditional China, all common behaviors are restricted by purely personal relations, especially kinship. Interpersonal communication is based on the associates, independent of work or career, thus lacking "businesses" based on rationality that are present in Protestant countries and "business relations" based on pure objectivity. Such traditionalism and personalism dependent on the other undoubtedly get in the way of the economic rationalization process. Therefore, the trust of all buying and selling activities in China is based mostly on kinship or kinship-like personal relations, rather than universalist relations. It is because of cultural factors mentioned above that Weber pointed out: "In this typical profit-oriented country, we can see the high esteem placed on wealth by 'profits-seeking desire,' and the 'rationalism' characteristic of utilitarianism have nothing to do with modern capitalism themselves."[①]

Weber's comparative study of world religions shows that ascetic Protestantism is a unique historical imagination consistent with the spirits and attitudes of early modern entrepreneurs in the West, promoting the early-stage development of Western modern capitalism.

---

① Weber, M. *Confucianism and Taoism* [M]. Trans. Hong, T. Nanjing: Jiangsu People's Publishing House, 1993: 273.

There is no similar religious value or form and reason in other parts of the world, which leads to the absence of native modern capitalism in those places. Weber unequivocally excluded the possible "affinity" between "China's religions" or the traditions of other non-Western countries and the modern capitalism. He believed that the "religion" or culture in the non-Western world served as a major obstacle to the development of rationalist capitalism, even after it was introduced in the West. In Weber's view, "Today, all non-Western countries have introduced economic rationalism as the most important achievement of the West, but the development of capitalism in these countries has been completely prevented by the existence of its strict tradition ... In these countries, the obstacles encountered by modern capitalism development come mainly from their religious fields ..."[①] However, although people may disagree with his viewpoint, one must admit the new perspective on research put forth by Weber is correct. What's more, his tremendous achievements are beyond doubt. Weber's analysis of traditional Chinese culture indeed conveys certain insight, of which many aspects are still valuable even today. Weber's theory is unavoidable when we reconsider the relationship between Confucian culture and economic development.

Indeed, history is unable to prove whether feudal China or non-Western societies can independently generate large-scale capitalism without the expansion of modern capitalism from the West to the world (although historical experience has shown that China did not generate large-scale capitalism before the First Opium War). What is illustrated here is that Zhejiang, nicknamed Zoulu from the Song and Yuan dynasties, can be regarded as a cultural center of Confucianism and has achieved brilliant economic and social accomplishments since the reform and opening-up. In a certain sense, this itself shows that under certain historical conditions, the Confucian culture is not necessarily an obstacle to the development of contemporary economy and society, but

---

① Xia, G. Modernity and culture: A reevaluation of Max Weber's theoretical legacy [J]. *Sociological Studies*, 2005(3).

co-exist with economic rationalism and even promote economic and social development. If, under the case where "other conditions are the same" in the sense of Samuelson and Nordhaus, Confucianism does indeed convey factors that motivate people to be achievement-oriented, as proved by the economic success of Japan and the Four Tigers in Asia. Although East Asia is more or less culturally homogeneous, namely within the "Han culture circle" or "Chinese cultural circle," or even a "Confucianized world," it has approached or exceeded the development level in the Western world when measured by indicators such as GDP per capita, industrialization, and urbanization. Even in political life, different regions of East Asia have demonstrated the compatibility and convergence with a democratic process. Thus, "there are many reasons that account for the development of modern East Asia. However, it is not hard to imagine that the traditional culture, especially post-Confucian values, constitutes the unique cultural background for East Asia development."[1]

Since the 1960s and 1970s, some scholars, such as Kahn, Alatas, Ahszynski, DeBary, Pye, and Berger, have tried to find from Confucian ethics the "alternative" of Protestant ethics conducive to economic development. Some scholars (such as Kahn) believed that the Confucian culture advocates loyalty, dedication, responsibility, and collectivism. These cultural values have created favorable conditions for coordinated development of society and economy; some scholars (such as DeBary) maintained that the family ethics of Confucianism have radiated into different social, economic and political fields and become the foundation of social cohesion;[2] some scholars (such as Alatas) maintain that strong motivation for wealth, honor, and health, as well as capability of expressing their respect for family and ancestors, are

---

① Xia, G. Modernity and culture: A reevaluation of Max Weber's theoretical legacy [J]. *Sociological Studies*, 2005(3).

② Zhang, S. Confucian culture and economic development: A review of foreign studies [J]. *Sociological Studies*, 1994(3).

undoubtedly the decisive factors in Confucian ethics that are sufficient to give rise to a vigorous economic move. Some scholars (such as Ahszynski) think that Confucianism is basically practical and rational.

What deserves particular attention is the interpretations of Berger and Pye. In his book, *Secularism—the West and East*, Berger divided Confucianism into two aspects: those of scholar-officials and those vulgar parts of Confucian officials. In his opinion, the Confucianism of the traditional literati and officials hinders modernization. As for the source of forces driving East Asia's economic development, there lies another kind of work ethics which he calls "vulgarized Confucianism," that is, the daily life of ordinary people. This is a set of beliefs and values that inspire people to work hard. Most importantly, it is a deepening sense of class consciousness, a promise to the family with almost no reservations (individuals have to work hard and save money for the family), emphasizing the norms of discipline and being thrifty. It is this "vulgarized Confucianism" that has evolved into work ethics of high production, as the Confucian norms highlighting harmony have successfully shifted from traditional institutions (such as family and stratified empires) to modern ones (companies or factories for example).[①]Pye also believed that Confucianism emphasized self-improvement and thus respected the motivation for achievement. This essential cultural value in China, as described by David McClelland, is "the need to achieve success." McClelland showed that countries with successful development, measured by the behavioral motivations taught in children's books, all got high "needs for achievement" scores. No matter what measures are taken to measure the Chinese people's need for achievement, we can all confirm that most people have the impression that the motivation of the Chinese people to strive for achievements is strong. The teaching of Chinese children emphasizes

---

① King, Y. *Confucian Ethics and Economic Development: A Review of Weber's Doctrine* [A] // Zhang, W. & Gao, Z. *Taiwan Scholars on Chinese Culture*. Harbin: Heilongjiang Education Press, 1989: 312.

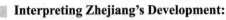
that they should accomplish something, otherwise they would fail the expectations of their parents. "In China, achievement will be rewarded within the family, and the obligations of the son to his father as well as between brothers are life-long responsibilities."①

In striking contrast to the views of the scholars mentioned above, Du Weiming disapproved of the practice of finding a substitute for Protestant ethics that was conducive to economic development of Confucian ones. He argued that "those practices intended to seek Protestant ethical equivalents in the 'modernized or vulgarized' Confucian ethics convey little meaning, in that such practices are much too superficial and mechanical." However, on the other hand, Du Weiming acknowledged that "it was not hard to see that the social and cultural capital which sustain the economic impetus of Japan and the Four Tigers in East Asia, were at least connected with Confucianism, if not derived from it. Weber once asserted that the Confucian tradition hindered the development of modern industrial capitalism in East Asia. Even if this assertion proves correct, his view that Confucian ethics is incompatible with capitalism stands untenable."② Schwartz's point of view echoes with that of Du Weiming's. According to Schwartz, "Confucianism does not offer such an equivalent at the general level." However, "in the course of modernization, certain attitudes and habits, which are related to Confucian conventions and rooted in the society, prove to be conducive to the development of modernization."③ In other words, despite the absence of an equivalent to Protestant ethics in the Confucian tradition, the Confucian tradition and modernity are not completely incompatible.

①　Pye, L.W. *Asian Values: from Dynamos to Dominos* [A] // Huntington, S. P. & Harrison, L. E. *Culture Matters: How Values Shape Human Progress*. Trans. Cheng, K. Beijing: Xinhua Publishing House, 2002.

②　Xia, G. Modernity and culture: A reevaluation of Max Weber's theoretical legacy [J]. *Sociological Studies*, 2005(3).

③　Xia, G. Modernity and culture: A reevaluation of Max Weber's theoretical legacy [J]. *Sociological Studies*, 2005(3).

Therefore, we cannot simplify the relationship between Confucianism and contemporary economic and social development and jump to the conclusion of "favorable" or "unfavorable." Within the framework of traditional Chinese systems, Confucianism could not give rise to large-scale capitalism (only sprouts of capitalism). This is above all an empirical fact in the long history of China's feudal society, rather than a mere theoretical or logical corollary. The reasons for such a fact are very complicated and scholars have made various explorations. However, a lot of detailed work is still needed if a satisfactory explanation is to be made. I do not wish to make ambitious attempts to provide a satisfactory answer to the above question. What needs to be pointed out is that Weber's Protestant ethical proposition goes back to the root cause of the spontaneous formation of capitalism, while his case regarding China is intended to prove no impetus for self-generated capitalism in China's history. If we ignore the space and time coordinates of Weber's Chinese proposition, it is not convincing to refute this proposition by using the "second modernization experience" that is later intervened and imitated by external forces. Moreover, Weber's analysis of the irrational economic orientation in traditional Confucian ethics is not all wrong, but strikingly insightful in many ways. However, the fact that Confucian states did not generate large-scale capitalism by themselves does not mean that Confucian ideas and concepts cannot be transformed into alternatives to Protestant ethics conducive to economic development under certain conditions. For example, the Confucian idea "honoring the ancestors" is very similar to "Glory to God" in Christianity and therefore its possibility of evolving into a similar "bounden duty" concept conducive to economic development cannot be ruled out. In feudal China, this possibility's failure of transformation into reality was largely due to the effects of institutional factors. Since the introduction of the imperial examination system, studying for official posts has become the most effective way to "honor the ancestors" in ancient Chinese society. It was because of this examination system that all the people in the society capable of learning devoted themselves to studying and chanting the Confucian classics.

It often took them decades to be selected as officials for their literacy and enlightenment. Therefore, in some sense, owing to the imperial examination system, studying for official positions has become the sacred "vocation" for traditional Chinese people to "honor the ancestors."

However, this notion of "honor the ancestors" is undoubtedly different from the "vocation" concept of striving for one's mundane work and creating wealth to the glory of God, which is emphasized by Protestantism. Protestant ethics, combined with other institutional factors, have introduced human behavior into a path contributing to economic development. According to Max Weber, Protestant ethics regard a human's career as a "constant practice of the virtue of containing desire," by "conscientiously" performing his profession, that is, demonstrating "thoughtful and orderly" working methods to confirm God's favor with him, which increases work discipline greatly. For Puritans, creating wealth while performing their professions is not only a morally good thing but also God's "command," which amount to pave the way for large-scale capitalism. The Puritans emphasize the virtue of containing desire by fixed occupations, thus giving "experts" an ethical encouragement. Similarly, they regard "profit-making" ideas as arranged by God and ethically honor "entrepreneurs" in modern times. In sharp contrast, traditional Confucian ethics introduces human behavior into a path unfavorable or irrelevant to economic development. In Chinese history, the system of imperial examinations, coupled with discriminatory policies on merchants, not only enabled Confucian scholars to view the act of studying to become officials as a sacred "bounden duty" for the purpose of "honoring the ancestors" but also made economically successful businessmen value studying. Carlo M. Cipolla once pointed out: "Wealthy Chinese businessmen face a deep-rooted landlord class, whose behavior is similar to any stable social class. Since their values and ideal principles are included in the noble ethical philosophy, it is not easy for the businessmen to challenge the Confucian ideal of both scholars and bureaucrats."[1] They not only failed to challenge the Confucian ideal or make the society recognize commercial success as a decent way of "honoring the ancestors" but also accepted and identified with the mainstream values that the only way to honor the ancestors was to study to become an official. Salt merchant Bao Shangzhi claimed that he had three wishes in life: "The first is to establish memorial archways for descendants, the second is to be recognized as a decent supplier, the third is that my offspring's study prospers."[2] Merchant Cheng Xiang urged his descendants: "I studied Confucianism at a young age. It is a pity that I did not continue but made my living as a merchant. You should work hard and study the classics so as to accomplish my unfulfilled cause."[3] Jiang Pei gave up Confucian studies and took up business. Though he made his business a success, he could not help feeling regretful. Jiang Pei once warned his younger brother, who also intended to be a businessman after failures in the imperial examination, "A farmer's faith in the agriculture is so solid that he shall never give up farming because of one year's crop failure. I have already regretted my choice; will you repeat my former mistake?"[4] Such views were undoubtedly widespread among ancient Chinese merchants. This shows that although traditional Confucianism contains favorable factors that could be transformed into Protestant ethics equivalents conducive to economic development, the institutional arrangements in the feudal society apparently impeded such transformation. Therefore, if institutional arrangements directed human behavior into the path where creating wealth brings glory to ancestors, things may have been completely different.

However, this assumption is of little significance to ancient Chinese

---

[1]　Cipolla, C. M. *Economic History of Europe*: vol. 1 [M]. Trans. Xu, X. Beijing: The Commercial Press, 1988: 12.

[2]　She, X. *Genealogy of the Bao Clan Preserved in the Ancestral Hall:* vol. 1 [Z].

[3]　Ming, J. & Xiu, N. *Pedigree of the Jiang Clan in Xinan* [Z].

[4]　Ibid.

society. This is not only because the traditional Confucian culture itself enjoys affinity with traditional institutional factors but also because the Chinese culture's development and institutional evolution rely on its special path. Without the introduction and impact of foreign culture and institutional factors, it is impossible for China's traditional Confucianism and institutional factors to change the deep-rooted path and generate the transformation to a large-scale market economy.

The above shows that if we confirm Confucian ethics' positive effect on East Asia's economic development during the 1970s and 1980s (that is also true in modern China's case), this does not mean that such an effect is universal regardless of history, culture, institutions, time or space. Du Weiming pointed out that businessmen without political interference could mobilize the initiative of Confucian ethics, while government-supervised and merchant-managed Confucian enterprises played a negative role in the process of modernization. Confucian ethics can stimulate creativity and initiative in a free and open environment, yet give rise to negative effect when coupled with certain political culture. The great success of East Asia's economic development resulted from the fact that these societies have achieved a unique effect in introducing the institutionalized structure and culture of the West as well as their coordination with local cultural factors. Therefore, when interpreting the East Asian phenomena, if we simply proceed from a cultural perspective, we would inevitably raise the following question: Why did this culture affect the economic development in traditional China? If we simply proceed from the perspective of institutional innovation, it is thought-provoking to ask, why have the other countries in the world not witnessed significant economic achievements after the same practice of introducing social and economic systems from the West, while in East Asia it is a completely different story. Why do the social and economic systems introduced from the West have different characteristics in East Asia (such as strongman politics, the important role of professional bureaucrats in East Asia's economy, etc.)? Obviously, we can answer these questions only by Weber's multi-factor "flexible explanation system" and taking a holistic approach to the structure and cultural factors of East Asia's social system. Undoubtedly, the modernization of East Asia is not a self-generated process in the early period, but a response motivated by foreign forces in the later period. It is a result of both voluntary and involuntary absorption of the Western systems by East Asian society after the long-term expansion of Western modernity. In this sense, the economic growth in East Asia during the 1970s and 1980s is a kind of "artificial engineering and art." The key to this project lies in handling the coordination between the institutional structure of the West and the culture in the local area, as well as recreating the national culture and national mentality. On the other hand, it is obvious that the introduction and establishment of the factors of the Western capitalist system had objectively cut off the affinity between the Confucian culture and the traditional social system, leading to not only the rejection of the unfavorable factors in Confucian ethics but also the affinity with the favorable ones. Meanwhile, this also provides an opportunity for a creative transition to Confucian ethics, which is good for economic development. Ethics make the creative transformation that can promote economic development.

However, even if we can prove that the Confucian culture is at least not necessarily an obstacle to economic and social development, but rather can coexist to some extent with economic rationalism under certain conditions, and even contributes to economic and social development when coordinated with other factors, we still cannot regard Confucianism as the only reason for the contemporary economic and social phenomena in Zhejiang. This is because Confucianism itself, as a culture upheld by Zhejiang and other provinces in China, is not enough to explain the "multiple institutional innovations" in Zhejiang compared with other parts of the country since the reform and opening-up and the prevalence of self-employment and entrepreneurship. Otherwise, it would be hard to explain why some central areas of Confucianism are imbued with entrepreneurship while others do not. Therefore, although Confucianism is compatible with contemporary economic and social

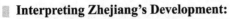
development to a certain extent, and even contains elements conducive to the development of contemporary economy and society, it needs to be coupled with other factors to achieve the desired effect, as already shown in the Four Tigers of Asia.

1.3.2 The Marginal Area of the Planned Economy and the Self-Entrepreneurial Spirit

The above shows that the idea that Zhejiang is on the verge of Confucianism is flawed. Also, Confucianism is not necessarily detrimental to the development of the contemporary economy and society and its tradition can actually be compatible with modernization. In light of this, it is not so convincing to account for the prevalence of entrepreneurship in Zhejiang since the reform and opening-up by resorting to the fact that Zhejiang constitutes the marginal area of Confucianism. In this case, it is necessary to find a new path of explanation. According to a cultural function theory, cultural ethos originates from people's efforts in adapting to the environment. Therefore, to account for the forming of entrepreneurship, besides analyzing factors of cultural traditions, it is necessary to analyze the national system and policy background since the reform and opening-up, as well as the specific social conditions facing Zhejiang people, and the initial natural and social conditions of institutional innovation and economic development in Zhejiang around the time of the reform and opening-up.

Institutional innovation is an evolving process, including the replacement, conversion and transaction process of systems. Institutional innovation is achieved through the marginal adjustment of complex rules, standards, and enforcement. It generally begins with the weakest part of its former system, rules, and regulations. As for those innovations with a higher degree of heterogeneity than the former one, they are more likely to emerge from places with the weakest power of the former systems. Correspondingly, the awareness of self-innovation and entrepreneurship are also more likely to be formed on the marginal areas of the former system. This view is not only consistent with the principles of New Institutional Economics but also in line with the theory in cultural sociology that "marginalization contributes to cultural innovation."

Before the reform and opening-up, Zhejiang, like other parts of China, implemented the planned economy. Under such a system, state-owned and controlled resources have been assigned to different levels and types of governments and departments according to the delegation of administrative power and were then redistributed to various organizational units. Different units gained access to allocated resources in accordance with the distance from the center of state power, and assumed the responsibility of using resources in line with national directives. Therefore, different units were endowed with the legal status of controlling corresponding resources according to their granted administrative authority. At that time, the differences in resource ownership or control originated from the hierarchy of the units such as their ownership's nature and administrative level, etc.[1] Differences among regions, on the other hand, resulted from resource abundance, largely due to the size and number of the state units. During the period of the planned economy, China adopted the "one-size-fits-all" approach. However, due to the different number of units and amount of resources among regions (mainly demonstrated by the size of state-owned enterprises and level of centralization), the whole country has formed central and marginal areas under the planned economic system. The central areas in the planned economy refer to those heavily-invested-by-the-state, resource-preferential areas where state-owned enterprises (SOEs) are concentrated; while the marginal areas are those with lower levels of investment or with less concentrated SOEs. Due to different property right basis, in general, the "quantity" of "traditional system accumulation" in the central areas of the planned economy was

---

① Lu, F. Unit: A special form of social organization [J]. *China Social Sciences*, 1989(1).

markedly higher than that of marginal areas. According to the above standards, Zhejiang obviously falls within the category of marginal areas or the weak part of the planned economy. Since the founding of the PRC, Zhejiang is a province with less state-owned elements or accumulative state investment. From 1950 to 1978, state investment exceeded 600 yuan per capita nationwide, while that figure in Zhejiang amounted to only 240 yuan per capita, ranking last among all provinces and less than half of the national average level. Therefore, before the reform and opening-up, Zhejiang was characterized by numerous local enterprises and small enterprises. For the total industrial output value of Zhejiang Province in 1978, the share of central enterprises and large or medium-sized enterprises was only 2.6% and 16% respectively. Since 1978, the low level of investment in Zhejiang has not fundamentally changed. From 1978 to 1992, state investment in Zhejiang Province equaled three-quarters of the national average. Comparing the seven coastal provinces (namely Liaoning, Hebei, Shandong, Jiangsu, Zhejiang, Fujian, and Guangdong), in terms of state investment from 1985 to 1997, Zhejiang ranked sixth, only higher than Fujian. Since 1949, Wenzhou, Taizhou, Lishui, and Jinhua areas in Central and Southern Zhejiang Province have witnessed even lower state investment. For example, from 1950 to 1978, the state investment in Taizhou amounted to only 460 million yuan, of which 42% was in agricultural infrastructure construction. In 1978, the GDP of Taizhou reached only 1.013 billion yuan and its industrial and agricultural output value totaled 1.343 billion yuan, of which the former was 650 million yuan. Meanwhile, the fiscal revenue of Taizhou topped 100 million yuan, and the per capita income of farmers was 120 yuan.

"Poverty gives rise to the desire for change." The marginal areas or weak part of the planned economy and the relative "poverty" status of Zhejiang have been precisely the sources of Zhejiang people's strong motivation for independent living, entrepreneurship, and innovations, which determined Zhejiang's potential for institutional innovations when the policies were eased.

Although Zhejiang Province ranked last nationwide in terms of
state investment per capita from 1950 to 1978, and despite its small
number and size of state-owned enterprises, the collective industry,
which demonstrated people's strong motivation for independent
living, innovation and entrepreneurship, has gained momentum to
some extent. By 1978, the province's collective industrial output value
accounted for 38.75% of the industrial output value, ranking first in
China. Despite the widespread repression and severe crackdown on
private industry and commerce since the early 1950s, subsistence
businesses, namely the so-called "speculation" activities, were
common in Zhejiang. For example, in the mid-1950s, against the
backdrop of the state's strict control of production means, acquisition
of iron scrap by merchants occurred in Taizhou. They even traded such
material on the Yangdian markets during the fair days. According to
the *Taizhou Local Annals*, "In 1957, the local government focused on
cracking down on foreign traders and local law-breakers who illegally
colluded with them. A total of 228 speculators were investigated and
treated in Tiantai County, 51 in Xianju County and 44 in Huangyan
County. In 1959, Tiantai County handled 492 speculative offenders,
of whom 17 were sentenced, two arrested, 17 public surveillance, 15
suspended and 62 fined. In 1961, Wenling County cracked down on
habitual speculative offenders, with six people arrested, six sentenced,
one public surveillance, imposing a penalty of 126,000 yuan. In 1963,
Yuhuan County investigated 83 cases of speculation." Despite such
crackdown, the trading of clothing coupons, food stamps, chemical
fertilizers, non-ferrous metals, and Chinese herbal medicines in
the private sector of Taizhou still remained consistent throughout
the 1960s and 1970s. "In 1973, more than 100 large-scale cases
of selling tickets and state monopoly materials were investigated.
From December 20th to December 23rd, 1975, nearly 30,000 people
in the entire district were organized to investigate speculators,
banning 59 illegal markets and over 2,200 undocumented traders and
handicraftsmen. In 1977, there were 39 learning classes held for 7,555

undocumented and illegal operators in the district. In 1979, 3,409 cases of speculation were investigated and addressed."[1]

In Wenzhou, people's motivations for making their own living and entrepreneurship have always been very strong. In the era of the planned economy, Wenzhou's commodity production proceeded on a small scale. Jinxiang Township processed quotation cards and badges of Chairman Mao in the early days of the "Cultural Revolution." [2] Despite the widespread suppression of private industry and commerce since the 1950s, farmers in the vicinity of Hongqiao in Wenzhou still adopted various ways to conduct market trade. There were still 20,000 to 30,000 people on each market day, with 400 plus listed products. Even under strict control, food sales have not been eradicated.[3] There were less than 5,000 laborers in Qiaotou Town of Yongjia, of whom 3,000 worked outside the town, accounting for 60% of the total workforce. 200 cotton fluffing workers went out in 1962 and up to 1,000 in 1968. In the 1960s, more than half of the workforces in Xianyangchen Village, Hongqiao, were malt vendors wandering about the streets. Due to the limited supply of food and clothing coupons, many people began to travel back and forth between Wenzhou, Shanghai, and Hangzhou, buying and reselling such coupons for a living. Some even dealt with gold and silver ware. Pressured by subsistence, more and more farmers voluntarily entered the field of circulation, causing Wenzhou to receive harsh criticism as a typical example of "taking the capitalist path."[4] According to a survey, unlicensed street vendors in Wenzhou

---

[1] *Taizhou Local Annals* [M]. Hangzhou: Zhejiang People's Publishing House, 1995: 150-151.

[2] Wang, X. & Zhu, C. *Private Enterprises and Family Economy in Rural China* [M]. Taiyuan: Shanxi Economic Publishing House, 1996: 18.

[3] *Annals of Hongqiao Township* [M]. Beijing: China International Radio Press, 1993: 104.

[4] Zhou, X. *Tradition and Change: The Social Psychology of Peasants in Zhejiang and Jiangsu and Its Evolution since Modern Times* [M]. Beijing: SDX Joint Publishing Company, 1998: 196-197.

City amounted to 5,200 in 1970, 6,400 in 1974 and 11,115 in 1976. "Underground contractors," "underground transport corps," private markets and "black markets" were also widespread. In the retail sales of social products in 1976, the volume of transactions in the private market actually accounted for 90%.[1]

The above phenomenon shows that the informal economy or "illegal economy" in many parts of Zhejiang was still quite active even in the period when the state was in strict control of the economy, which typically illustrates the so-called paradox of state control in economic sociology. According to socioeconomic theory, when the state seeks to eliminate informal economic activities by strengthening its regulatory control, such activities would become even wilder. As Noiz observes, rules give rise to the irregular, and the formal economy generates its own informality. To include all economic activities in the planned economy often produces an opposite effect, leading to the expansion of the informal sector. The problem is that in the planned economy period when the state was in strict control of the economic field, not all areas had a relatively active informal economy or "illegal economy." Therefore, under what conditions can the society witness a relatively active informal economy or "illegal economy" after the government strengthens its regulatory control to eliminate informal economic activities? This question reveals that the occurrence of the "state control paradox" in Zhejiang requires other explanations in addition to the one of "state control." Among many factors, the strong desire of Zhejiang people to make their own living and the cultural spirits of entrepreneurship and self-innovation is an important factor accounting for the occurrence of state control paradox.

Such desire and entrepreneurship awareness have their profound social and psychological foundations. This can be highlighted through

---

[1]   Shi, J. et al. *Institutional Change and Economic Development: A Study of Wenzhou Pattern* [M]. Revised Edition. Hangzhou: Zhejiang People's Publishing House, 2004: 65.

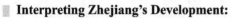
comparison with social groups in the central areas of the planned economy. The research by Li Lulu and Li Hanlin suggests that people's behavioral freedom refers mainly to their ability to simultaneously rely on a number of different actors in the process of achieving their goals and satisfying their needs. It also means that in the process of pluralistic dependence, they can maintain the independence of their own behaviors completely. By contrast, behavioral dependence in the strict sense emphasizes the process and orientation of actors subject to certain groups or individuals, which is caused by the monopoly of resource supply.[①] In the central areas of the planned economy, on the one hand, with the state's mandatory power and administrative control, the legitimacy of occupying resources other than state and collective property was denied, thus there was literally no alternative resources for individuals' independence. On the other hand, in the central parts of the planned economy, because of the relative concentration of the state-owned units and enterprises, people can enjoy more benefits of paternalism more easily. For example, they benefit from medical treatment welfare, housing, recruitment, food, and non-staple foods subsidies, etc. In general, they had a weaker desire to make their own living or for entrepreneurship, leading to a correspondingly stronger dependence. As mentioned earlier, such dependence is more "mandatory" than "dependent," more of "attachment" on administrative power than of "exchange behavior" in essence. Individual dependence or obedience to units and organizations is regarded as obedience to the state's mandatory commands under the planned economy, a "passive" choice without any other alternatives. Wald pointed out that in the period of planned economy, there existed a kind of traditional authority relations in China's state-owned factories and organizations, namely the individual's "organizational attachment" to the unit or organization with the "system of asylum relationship" at the core of authority relations. The basic economic and political structures determine the individual's

---

① Li, L. & Li, H. *Resources, Power and Exchange in the Chinese Work Unit Organization* [M]. Hangzhou: Zhejiang People's Publishing House, 2000: 55.

strong economic and political dependence on the unit or organization to obtain the legal identity and special benefits. The political characteristics of the unit or organization result in such individual attachment to the unit as manifested in the dependence on unit leaders who are in control of resource distribution and political power. Wald argues that the formation and maintenance of such authority-dependence relationship result from a particular authoritative culture, namely the network of asylum relations between leaders and activists. In this network, personal loyalty, institutional roles, and material interests are intertwined through exchange, including the exchange of material and immaterial interests.[1] Li Hanling compares the unit to "a village in the urban city"[2] and believes what unites unit members are a kind of spiritual culture characteristic of China's traditional rural society. The specific unit organization is similar to the "home" in the sense of China's traditional culture. The acquaintance society, paternalism in the unit, and the normal life style of "always being in the same unit" all reflect touches of local culture. The unit leaders have the power of distributing resources, social supervision, and judgment, or even ethics control, which are similar to the authority in traditional Chinese patriarchal culture.[3] These spiritual cultures, with strong local culture features, provide both a "social structural basis" and a "cohesive spiritual bond" for the hierarchical order in the units' society.

The central area of the planned economy is full of state-owned factories. With more state-owned factories, on the one hand, it means more national resources; on the other hand, it means that the social groups in the area attach more dependency on unit organizations.

---

① Li, L. & Li, H. *Resources, Power and Exchange in the Chinese Work Unit Organization* [M]. Hangzhou: Zhejiang People's Publishing House, 2000: 48-49.
② Li, H. *The Unit Society in China: Discussion, Thinking and Study* [M]. Shanghai: Shanghai People's Publishing House, 2004: 46.
③ Ibid. 47.

However, as for those marginal areas or weak parts like Zhejiang, which boast less state-owned enterprises, most people have no access to resources through state-owned enterprises and find it hard to share the benefits of the planned economy. In other words, most people (especially the farmers) do not have the chance of one-way dependency on enterprises that is enjoyed in the central areas of the planned economy, so everything depends on themselves. As a result, accordingly, the intentions of self-employment and of self-innovation tend to be intense. The practice of the planned economy before the reform and opening-up has shown that, as a response to the central and marginal areas of the planned economy, the corresponding central and marginal areas influenced by cultural values under the planned system would also take its own shape. In the central area of the planned economy, people have more chances to "learn while working" and to "study in work." Some practical or individual cultural values related to the planned economy are not bound to be gained through written text but more through individual and group practices, from which people are influenced unconsciously. The practice of the planned economy creates the necessary environment for individuals and groups to "practice" and to "be influenced unconsciously." For example, the planned economy covers people's birth, aging, illness, and death, which would make people gradually gain dependency without autonomy; the lack of flowing labor employment system as well as cadre and personnel system under the planned economy would make people gradually get resigned to the situation and unwilling to move ahead; the distribution model of communal pots contributes to people's mentality of egalitarianism and the social environment lacking in competition under the planned economy would finally weaken people's consciousness of innovation, risks, competition and so on.

The situations mentioned above obviously show a trend of weakening from the central areas of the planned economy to its marginal areas. Generally speaking, the closer to the central areas one is, the more likely the above situations will dominate, and vice versa.

On one hand, owing to the lack of state investments and state-owned enterprises during the time of the planned economy, there is no denying that Zhejiang has witnessed weaker consciousness of dependency and stronger self-employment and self-innovation consciousness. As Li Lulu and Li Hanlin remarked: "When people are no longer dependent on or controlled by the behavioral orientation of a certain social group or individuals during the process of meeting demands and realizing goals, behavioral dependency would gradually disappear, and people would become gradually aware of the independence and degree of freedom in the course of their own behaviors."[①]On the other hand, if people are deeply influenced by the cultural values of the planned economy in the central areas, they tend to stand at the negative ground during the transformation from a planned economy to a market economy, and their cost of "transforming ideas" would be relatively higher. However, for people in Zhejiang who were at the marginal areas of the planned economy, it is very likely for them to stand at the advantageous ground and correspondingly, endure lower cost to transforming ideas because they are less constrained by mainstream cultural values. For example, if people in the central areas have a stronger consciousness of dependency and are resigned to current situations, thus rejecting changes and lacking consciousness of self-innovation, competition and so on, then due to a lack of protection by "paternalism" under the planned economy, Zhejiang people in the marginal area could foster consciousness of risk, competition, and especially the consciousness of self-innovation at a quicker speed when coupled with other factors against the background of economic system transformation. It is because of this, when changes of power lead to policy changes, such changes quickly pass on to the "nerve endings" of the planned economy, which are waiting for them. Consequently, the consciousness and the impulse of "self-employment" and "self-innovation" of people in Taizhou who lack the protection of "paternalism" are thus released.

---

① Li, L. & Li, H. *Resources, Power and Exchange in the Chinese Work Unit Organization* [M]. Hangzhou: Zhejiang People's Publishing House, 2000: 56.

The cultural spirits of self-employment and self-innovation are especially reflected on the farmers in Zhejiang. Since the reform and opening-up, institutional innovation and economic growth of Zhejiang, as characterized by the booming of township enterprises, private enterprises, specialized markets, share-holding cooperatives and thriving non-government financial system, have all been closely linked to activities of the farmers who account for 86% of total population in Zhejiang in the early stage of the reform and opening-up. Since modern times, farmers have been regarded as a conservative social group that is incompatible with modernization from the traditional perspective, and as the main target of the intellectuals' so-called "Chinese Citizens' Character Reform." Why do farmers who have always been regarded as conservative show intense spirits of self-employment and self-innovation in Zhejiang since the reform and opening-up? To answer this question, it is necessary to analyze the social environment under the planned economic system before the reform and opening-up.

During the planned economy period, the state gained primitive accumulation for national industrialization from farmers by means of "the price scissors." From the First Five-Year Plan to the end of the first stage of national industrialization (1953–1989), the country obtained more than 700 billion yuan from the countryside, roughly taking up one-fifth of the newly created value of the countryside. Although China's farmers made a historical contribution to industrialization and urban construction, the planned economic system set restrictions on farmers. Corresponding to the planned economic system, the government issued a series of restrictive policies and regulations for the farmers. Among them, the policy with the most profound influence was the implementation of a strict household registration system that divided the urban people and rural people, which in essence restricted farmers to enter cities. The farmers not only had no access to preferential policies enjoyed by urban residents, such as medical treatment, housing, cereal, subsidy on non-staple food and so on, but were also restricted to professions with a relatively high social evaluation under the planned economic system.

For example, they could not enter state-owned enterprises or public institutions. Such restrictions and discrimination did not disappear even after the reform and opening-up. For example, the limited industries and professions for migrant workers from outside Beijing in 1998 included: the finance, insurance and postal service industries, and the professions of various managerial staff, salesmen, accountants, cashiers, dispatchers, telephone operators, price auditors, shop assistants, taxi drivers, various ticket sellers, inspectors, child-care workers, elevator operators, computer operators, civil aviation stewards, attendants and office staff of star-rated hotels (restaurants) and hostels. Other large and medium-sized cities also had similar employment restrictions.

In order to facilitate the analysis, we can roughly divide social groups under the planned economic system into two main types, namely those within the system and those outside the system. The dividing standard of in-system groups and out-system groups is whether the group is entitled to some special benefits under the planned economy, such as medical treatment, housing, employment, subsidy on non-staple food, etc. Obviously, the out-system group is restricted and discriminated by the planned economic system and it lies at the margin of the planned economic system. Due to the restrictions imposed by the household registration system, commodity grain policy, labor employment system on urban and rural population mobility, it is difficult for the out-system group members (whose main constituent are farmers) to transform into in-system group members except through narrow channels such as joining the army, entering schools, etc.

Restrictive and discriminative policies under the planned system are definitely adverse to farmers who are a part of the out-system social group. However, it is exactly these restrictions and discrimination that contribute to Chinese farmers' more intense desire for self-employment and self-entrepreneurship when compared with the urban residents. Regarding this point, the following opinions of Max Weber, Braudel and Lewis can provide an important theoretical reference.

Max Weber pointed out: "The minorities or minority religions, which yield to a hierarchy, would generally intervene in economic activities by means of an unusual power because they are excluded from politics whether they are willing or not. All the most talented members seek opportunities in this field to have their talents recognized, since they do not have the chance to work for the governments. The Polish and the people of East Prussia are certainly examples of this. Their influence develops much faster than that in Galicia, where they serve as the dominators."① Of course, Weber also believed that, since the Protestants had a special spirit or disposition, they might be an exception. Whether the Protestants are dominant or dominated, whether they are in the minority or majority, "they always show a tendency towards promoting economic rationalism."② Even so, Weber does not deny the universality of the phenomenon that the minority "intervene in economic activities by means of an unusual power" because of social restrictions.

Likewise, Braudel believed that while society needs commerce, mainstream social valued discriminate and restrict commercial activities. Restricted by such values, it is inconvenient for mainstream social groups to conduct business that is disdained by them, which provides an opportunity for those social groups who are restricted to work in professions with a relatively higher social reputation. Braudel pointed out: "In a society with special taboos, like regarding debit and credit, along with the taboo of finance industry, doesn't the society force 'non-normal human' to do things that are needed, yet despised by the whole society? Alexander Gershclone thinks that this is exactly the reason why the separatist arises from the Orthodox Eastern Church in Russia. If the separatist had not existed at that time, they would have needed to show up... In this debate, it is better to say that society

---

① Weber, M. *The Protestant Ethic and the Spirit of Capitalism* [M]. Trans. Yu, X., Chen, W. et al. Beijing: SDX Joint Publishing Company, 1987: 26.
② Ibid.

makes a difference and not the 'capitalist spirit'. Political disputes and religious fanaticism in medieval and modern European history impelled many people to leave their home. They went into exile and formed minority groups... They were impelled to leave home, which helped them make a great fortune." [1]

There is no doubt that Lewis's points are consistent with those of Weber and Braudel. He thinks that in some cases, the discrimination against one group would contribute to their prominent development in aspects that are of no interest to the ruling class. For example, if the ruling class looks down on economic activities, and at the same time restricts other groups to show themselves in activities that are taken as an honor by the ruling class (like military professions, the government or church), then the discriminated groups would make use of the chances of economic activities to show their features. It immediately reminds people of the status of Jews in Western Europe during medieval times: When making money, as a means of livelihood, was discriminated, which was almost the only opportunity open to Jewish people, they would gather in this industry. If the discrimination was banned, Jewish people can also work in any profession without restrictions, and they could be seen in areas of science, agriculture, the army, and all relatively 'respectful' lifestyles. They may not be better at making money than most other groups. Furthermore, in response, they would despise such a way of living and become incompetent in this respect. [2]

In medieval Europe, economic motivation was regarded by mainstream culture as a powerful desire in people, which scared people with absolutely no encouragement because economic activities had

---

① Braudel, F. *Civilization and Capitalism, 15th to 18th Century* [M]. Trans. Gu, L. & Shi, K. Beijing: SDX Joint Publishing Company, 1993: 160.

② Lewis, W. A. *The Theory of Economic Growth* [M], Trans. Liang, X. Shanghai: SDX Joint Publishing Company, 1994: 108.

nothing to do with morality. According to the mainstream values in medieval times, the property is the embodiment of people's interest in real life, which distracts people from focusing on their future and saving their souls. The accumulation of property leads to people's rising selfishness, resulting in people fighting with each other for wealth. In this process, greed and hatred would beat altruism. Thomas Aquinas thus said in *Summa Theologica*: "Willingly staying in poverty is the most important and fundamental condition to get perfect love." In the Medieval period, the Roman Catholic Church never acknowledged the value of mundane businesses, and it depreciated profitable commercial activities with no mercy. So, the Medieval period was pervaded with an idea that making money was immoral. Even though Florence was a financial center in the 14th and 15th centuries, at that time, seeking profits was still regarded as ethically suspicious or as an intolerable behavior. Sayings like "making the rich go to heaven is more difficult than camels threading a needle" reflect the "anti-merchant complex" that people fostered under Catholicism to some degree. However, through phenomenon, resistance against commercial interests is actually an expression of interest. Western Europe during the Medieval period was an agricultural society, and mainstream society looked down on commerce and even carried out oppressive measures because large-scale commerce would overthrow the self-sufficient economy that had developed. Nonetheless, complementary commerce is still of necessity in any self-sufficient society. The so-called "pure" natural economy without any division of labor and total independence from others, actually only exists in theoretical models rather than in the real world. The self-sufficient natural economy, in reality, is always complemented with commercial exchange to some degree, which is shouldered by complementary marginalized people. The Jewish people during the Medieval period played exactly that role. Before Babylon was kept in captivity, the Jewish people were also divided into different ranks and classes. The knight, the farmer, the handicraftsman and a few businessmen are examples of this. The prediction and results of captivity led Jewish people to drift about from their settlement, so from then on, Jewish conventions prohibited settling in a fixed place. Anyone that sticks to Judaism cannot be a farmer. Therefore, on the one hand, Jewish people had to run commercial businesses, especially currency commerce, because of their religious custom, which also caused their dealings to be limited to commerce among tribes or among conventional groups with regard to religious custom, accounting for their status as marginalized men. On the other hand, compared with Western Europe, the Jewish people are foreigners, but when compared with civilizations outside Western Europe, they are Western Europeans. Although they are biologically in Western European society, they cannot actually enjoy the same political and economic status as Western Europeans. This feature makes them marginalized men as well.

As marginal men in Western Europe, the Jewish people do not have any rights and benefits, which are "naturally" owned by the locals. So, they need money to compensate for it, namely to "purchase" such rights with money. "The Jewish people can only depend on money to live, which should be understood in a deeper sense rather than the mere definition of money in modern capitalist society, namely the right to purchase life, because the Church of Christ allows Jewish people to 'purchase' the rights as pure farmers at a certain interval. In this case, money is given the pre-sacred meaning for the Jewish people."[①] Therefore, when Islam and Christianity prohibited their believers from lending money for profits, discriminated "marginalized men" and "heretic" Jews then had a chance. As Abba Eban said, "Churches in Western countries prohibit Christians from lending money in stricter measures day by day, so there is a vacuum in the Christian Europe in this respect, which is left to be filled by the will of the Jewish people. Though many Christians and Christian churches are still lending money, those Jewish who come from developed countries and have plenty of cash are still able to lend money publicly, while the

---

① Bermant, C. *The Jewish* [M]. Trans. Feng, Y. Shanghai: SDX Joint Publishing Company, 1991: 27.

church must operate only for certain reasons."[1] Under this circumstance, it is no wonder that people directly relate usurers to Jewish people.

Among other racial or religious groups, like "the Huguenot believers under French Louis XIV's rule, non-followers of Anglican Church in the UK and the Whig believers,"[2] as well as the Armenians, Jain in India, and ethnic Chinese in Southeast Asia, similar cases can also be found. Max Weber thought that there could be various ways when a group runs a commercial business with their own products. He explained that the business often developped as the avocation of farmers and domestic industry operator, which is usually seasonal. Independent professional traders and vendors, together with tribe communities specializing in managing commerce, arise accordingly, but there were also some tribes engaged in certain specialized industries, which were needed by other tribes.[3] Weber discovered that it was also possible that some religious believers became professional businessmen because of religious restrictions, whose typical form can be seen in India. In India, commerce is mastered by a certain caste. That is to say, due to rejections of religious customs, the "commercial" caste has commerce all to themselves. With the exception of commerce based on group conventions, there are also certain commercial activities limited to certain religious sects, whose members cannot work in any other industries because of witchcraft and religion restrictions, as manifested by the case of Jains. Since Jainism prohibits killing creatures, especially those vulnerable ones, the Jains cannot be warriors nor work in other industries, like those using fire, because fire would kill insects; they cannot travel in rain because they would step on insects in water.

---

① Abba, E. *Jewish History* [M]. Trans. Yan, R. Beijing: China Social Sciences Press, 1992: 160.

② Weber, M. *The Protestant Ethic and the Spirit of Capitalism* [M]. Trans. Yu, X., Chen, W. et al. Beijing: SDX Joint Publishing Company, 1987: 26.

③ Weber, M. *Weber's Portfolio*: vol. 2 [M]. Trans. Kang, L. &Wu, N. Nanning: Guangxi People's Publishing House, 2004: 126.

Therefore, the Jains have no other choice than business which settles in one place. According to Carsten Herrmann-Pillath, nowadays, the affluence of overseas Chinese is to a great degree the result of discriminative policies adopted by many countries in the Asian-Pacific region of Chinese people's economic activities, which seems like a paradox. In the past, the economic activities of overseas Chinese were limited to economic gaps, which later became extraordinarily profitable departments. For a long time, the Philippines had stipulated that Chinese people cannot be involved in key industrial departments while their dominant role in the Philippines' banking industry rose up. At the same time, since all countries do not allow ethnic Chinese to develop socially and politically, they can only promote their social status through economic achievements.[1]

In light of the above interesting paradoxes generated by religious restrictions and social discrimination, Lewis pointed out: In some countries and regions, the minority may not be allowed to succeed politically, or they cannot enter any upper-status social professions in the military, administrative, management, scientific professions, etc. So their abilities cannot be put to effective use anywhere but the industries. Additionally, most religious taboos may stop most of its members from engaging in some activities (trading, money-lending), from touching certain things or animals (fertilizers, leather, pigs) or from making use of some advantageous chances, whereas if these minorities have different biases, they could thrive on the opportunities from which the majority exclude themselves. When the minorities come into being, their religious disciplines are not always more helpful to economic growth than those of the majority. Time itself can make a difference. As the minorities adjust themselves for existence, their religious

[1] Herrmann-Pillath, C. *Internet Culture and Chinese Social and Economic Behaviors* [M]. Trans. Zhu, Q. Taiyuan: Shanxi Economic Publishing House, 1996: 7.

disciplines would also change.[①] This phenomenon could be seen as an implicit function that arises from religious restriction and social discriminative policies, the operation of which produces imperceptible and unintentional results that are beyond people's expectation.

The opinions of Weber, Braudel, and Lewis mentioned above are definitely enlightening for understanding the more intense desire for self-employment and spirit of self-entrepreneurship shown by farmers in Zhejiang, compared with the urban residents since the reform and opening-up. Under the planned economic system, the farmers' situation is similar in many ways to that of the "Minority" according to Lewis's view. They cannot engage in professions occupied by in-system groups. However, it is exactly because of this that they can thrive on those chances from which in-system social groups exclude themselves. The questions in demand of further investigation are why do farmers in Zhejiang show more remarkable desire for self-employment and spirit of self-entrepreneurship than their counterparts in other places? Why is it that the farmers in Zhejiang are called the Chinese Jews rather than the names of their counterparts in other places?

Before the reform and opening-up, if we say that Zhejiang was on the periphery of the planned economy, then farmers in Zhejiang were at the margin of the planned economy's periphery. As has been mentioned above, owing to restrictions in the household registration policy that control mobility of urban and rural population, the commodity grain policy, labor employment system, etc., it was difficult for out-system members like farmers to change into in-system ones. It was especially difficult for Zhejiang to witness such transformation before the reform and opening-up because of its marginal status under the planned economy. Compared with the central areas of the planned economy, farmers in Zhejiang were no doubt an outside social group facing

---

① Lewis, W. A. *The Theory of Economic Growth* [M]. Trans. Liang, X. Shanghai: SDX Joint Publishing Company, 1994: 123.

greater pressure to survive. In the central areas of the planned economy, with more investment from the government and higher levels of urbanization, it meant that more people entered in-system social groups and accepted the protection of paternalism under the planned economy. Meanwhile, it also meant that with the same resources, the out-system social groups' pressure of survival was relieved efficiently. For example, in Liaoning Province, part of the central areas of the planned economy, the non-agricultural population took up 23% in 1952, which reached 36% in 1957. From 1957 to 1960, the percentage of urban residents kept rising sharply. Urban residents took up 42.3% in 1962, with 36.5% non-agricultural population. Then, like most areas nationwide in the same period, the mechanical growth of urban population in Liaoning reduced markedly. In 1970, urban residents took up 34.9% and non-agricultural population 30%, with the number of cities reduced from 12 to 10. The urban population then witnessed slow growth. Despite the slow growth rate of only 1.7% from 1970 to 1978, the percentage of urban population in Liaoning in 1978 still reached 36.6%. In sharp contrast to Liaoning, the government made small investments in Zhejiang since the founding of the PRC. Zhejiang witnessed not only slow economic development but also backward urban construction. Urban population and non-agricultural population in Zhejiang took up 11.81%, 14.79% respectively in 1949, after which the urban population rose and fell sharply. However, in 1978, the figures still remained at 14% and 12.26% respectively. From 1949 to 1978, the proportion of urban population in total population rose by only 1.2%, while non-agricultural population fell by 2.53%. Since non-agricultural population almost equaled in-system social groups during the planned economy, the low proportion of non-agricultural population in the early days of the reform and opening-up meant that very few people could enter the in-system social groups and accept the protection of paternalism under the planned economy. Meanwhile, given that resources are limited, the large population of out-system social groups faced greater pressure to survive.

However, the dialectics of history found expression precisely in the fact that when policies eased, it was exactly the out-system social groups (mainly farmers) at the margin of the planned economy's periphery that promoted institutional innovations in Zhejiang and "economic growth outside the system." This phenomenon can be explained by many aspects, among which is the spirit fostered in an adverse environment is definitely not negligible. In this respect, Toynbee provided an enlightening opinion. He believed that if a creature lost the inborn function of a certain organ and thus became disabled in some mechanism compared with other congeneric creatures, then the creature would probably witness the extraordinary advancement of another organ or function in response to this challenge. This would make up for its flaws in one respect by surpassing counterparts in another respect. "In society, if a certain group or class has social flaws—by accident, because of individual behavior or others' behavior in society—it would react in the same way. Once hindered in one respect, they concentrate on developing in the other respects and thus gain dominance in those aspects."[1] Given its special historical reasons and real situations as well as the resulting survival pressure, out-system social groups in Zhejiang, especially farmers, tend to have relatively stronger impulses for self-employment and spirit of entrepreneurship (depending on themselves rather than the state), which is in sharp contrast to those in-system social groups and out-system groups in the central areas under the planned economy. The lesser survival pressure of out-system groups in the central areas under the planned economy means a weaker desire for self-employment. Meanwhile, the greater pressure faced by those in Zhejiang means that they must come up with ways to survive and that they must possess a stronger impulse of self-employment and spirit of entrepreneurship.

On the other hand, under the planned economic system, in terms of Zhejiang Province and the whole country, values of the "in-

---

[1] Toynbee, A. J. *A Study of History:* vol.1 [M]. Trans. Cao, M. et al. Shanghai: Shanghai People's Publishing House, 1966: 155.

system" groups at the "center" obviously belonged to mainstream social values. In accordance with the planned system without market mechanism, mainstream values, to a great extent, discriminated and even restricted economic activities outside the system (namely the so-called "capitalist" economic activities). When policies eased, in-system groups influenced by mainstream values looked down on or were not in a position to engage in out-system activities conducted by "Getihu" (self-employed entrepreneurs), such as mending shoes, weaving, cutting hair, doing business, etc. At the early stage of the reform, however, numerous businesses were waiting to be dealt with and the country was desperately in need of "peace and unity" as well as production recovery to secure adequate food and clothing, etc. Meanwhile, limited by insufficient capital, it was hard for the state to invest a great deal of initial funding. Against this macro background, the actual social needs for out-system economic activities require market activities outside the system to serve as a necessary "complement." Therefore, the society objectively "asked" out-system social groups to engage in out-system economic activities, which provided a rare opportunity for them under such special circumstances. Meanwhile, at a time when the policies eased, while the planned economic system did not, it was still a difficult task for the outside groups to enter the system. This was because the planned system had set limits for them, restricting them to engage in out-system economic activities despised by in-system social groups. It is this dialectic that strengthened the impulse of self-employment and spirit of self-entrepreneurship of the outside-groups in Zhejiang (namely, farmers who take up 90% of the total population). Since the reform and opening-up, tens of thousands of Zhejiang people (especially farmers) have been doing business on small wares, fluffing cotton, contracting constructional engineering, cutting hair, mending shoes across the country and also forming production bases of plastic products, models, producing pumps, parts of cars, motors, etc., and innovating the joint-stock cooperative system, and financial system in the private sector, etc. All of these epitomize the impulse of self-employment and spirit of entrepreneurship of out-system social groups (especially farmers) in Zhejiang.

1.4 Large Population with Limited Land and the People-Induced Spiritual Motivation

To analyze the reasons accounting for the spiritual motivation induced by people in Zhejiang, it is obvious that we should follow Max Weber's interpretation principle of the so-called multi-factor "flexibility." Although the marginal status under the planned economy constitutes an important reason for economic development and spiritual motivation for institutional innovation induced by people in Zhejiang since the reform and opening-up, it is apparently not the only one. Notably, besides the marginal status under the planned economy, and greater survival pressure faced by a large population of the outside social groups and other factors, the natural environment with vast population and limited farmland and resources is also an extremely important reason for the intense spirit of self-employment and self-innovation.

1.4.1 Influence of the Natural Environment on the Spirit

As for the influence of the natural environment on human society and human spirits, many discussions have been made by thinkers. Humboldt pointed out, "I try my best to testify in any aspect where the natural environment has a continuous influence on the moral structure and human destiny."[1] Ritter thought that people were "a mirror of nature." The UK, being "located in the center surrounded by straits, it naturally becomes the dominator of the ocean."[2] Kant believed that society and nature had a causal relationship and every nation was divided by its natural boundary (mountains, rivers, etc.). Breaking the boundary means breaking the balance which follows certain laws, thus resulting in inevitable wars. Kant determined the

---

① Humboldt, A. *My View of Nature*[M]// Anuqin, B.A. *The Theoretical Problem of Geography*. Trans. Li, D & Bao, S. Beijing: The Commercial Press, 1994.

② Ritter, C. *General Geography*[M]// Anuqin, B.A. *The Theoretical Problem of Geography*. Trans. Li, D. & Bao, S. Beijing: The Commercial Press, 1994.

objects of political geography studies as the location of the country, products of labor, custom, handicraft, commerce, and local residents. He also viewed the influence of the natural environment on society as the influence of natural conditions favorable to production activities on social lives. From Hegel's perspective, the natural connection that helps foster national spirit is exactly the geographical basis, "contrasted with the universality of the moral 'Whole' and with the unity of that individuality which is its active principle, the natural connection appears an extrinsic element; but inasmuch as we must regard it as the ground on which the Spirit plays its part, it is an essential and necessary basis."[①] Hegel thought that there were three different political systems in the world. The first one is plateau areas with extensive steppes, where residents are mainly occupied in stock farming and move from place to place in search of water and grass as the seasons change. Sometimes they gather together to plunder residents in the plain areas. Due to lack of reliable means of livelihood, laws are not needed and a strict patriarchal system dominates the society where there are two extremes in people's personality, namely hospitality and robbery. The second one is plain areas in large river valleys where residents are occupied in agriculture. The production proceeds with the seasons in an orderly way. Land ownership and various legal relations come into being accordingly, which make the basis and foundation of the state possible. As a result, great empires like China, India, Babylon, Egypt, and others emerged. The third one is coastal areas connected to the ocean with a developed handicraft, commerce, and maritime industry. The ocean invites people to conquer, and engage in piratical plunders, and at the same time encourages people to seek profits and to take up commerce. Since taking risks for profits is a frequent activity, coastal residents are full of courage and reason, thus contributing to the democratic regime in coastal states.

---

① Hegel, C. *Lectures on the Philosophy of History* [M]. Trans. Wang, Z. Shanghai: Shanghai Bookstore Publishing House, 1999: 85.

Another tendency regarding the influence of the natural environment on human society and human mentality came into being after Hegel. Ratzel discussed three questions in his book, *Human Geography*, namely, these were the distribution and clusters on the earth surface; dependency of those distributions on the natural environment as a result of human migrations; and the natural environment's influences on individuals and society including the direct physiological effect, the psychological effect, the effect on human organizations and economic development, the effect on human migrations and their final distribution. Ratzel's thought was later extended to the political field, leading to his *Political Geography*. In *Geographical Environment*, Semple expounded Ratzel's thought and reached a conclusion on the basis of comparing the cultural stages of typical nations living under the same natural conditions: If these nations share similar or related social and economic development, then it is safe to conclude that such similarity or correlation is caused by the environment rather than the race. Ellsworth Huntington also developed Ratzel's points in *Civilization and Climate*. He thought that people's daily life depended on geographical conditions. When meeting their material demands, people in different places on earth usually chose those professions with the most chances of success determined by the geographical environment. Every person's health and energy are mainly influenced by the occupied profession and material living conditions, which mainly depend on the geographical environment. Even human's high-level demands, like management, education, religion, art, and others, are also influenced by geography. Though these demands are mainly decided by racial features, accidental incidents in history and genius figures, the geographical environment would influence high-level demands in five aspects, namely, population density, affluence, and closeness, regional differences in interests or resources, and energy level. Huntington believes that among the five elements of the geographical environment, namely location, type of territory, water body, soil and mineral, as well as climate, climate matters the most since temperature, humidity and weather changes are most influential on human health and energy.

Though different scholars hold different opinions, they all believe that the natural environment exerts an important influence on human society and human mentality. There is no doubt that the primordial natural environment plays an essential role in the divergence of culture. Besides influencing cultural traditions by means of securing livelihood, the environment also has a direct impact on people's personality. Just as Hegel said, "what we focus on is to understand the close connection between the natural type of the place and its people's character and type, instead of regarding the occupied land as the external land. The character is exactly the way every nation emerges in world history and its adopted status."[①] Following the directions of the above opinions, we can draw the conclusion that the important element of land condition in the natural environment undoubtedly plays a big part in people's thinking.

In Chinese and world history, many examples demonstrate that local people would initiate a desire to make their living in the non-agricultural field and thus form a cultural tradition of commerce due to limited or infertile land. The typical ones are found in Venice in medieval Europe, as well as Huizhou and Shanxi during the Ming and Qing dynasties of China.

The merchants of Venice were good at commerce and had initiated a strong desire to make their living in the non-agricultural field. They formed a unique cultural tradition of commerce, which was largely made by the special natural environment rather than their inborn talent. Venice was far away from the European continent with barren soils. Since there was no normal land or island, the soil was often immersed in salty water or marshes, causing Venice to have no arable land, quarries, iron to cast, wood for houses or even clean drinking water. Generally speaking, it is a misfortune to have such a terrible natural

---

① Hegel, C. *Lectures on the Philosophy of History* [M]. Trans. Wang, Z. Shanghai: Shanghai Bookstore Publishing House, 1999: 85.

environment. However, such misfortune actually provided Venice with a certain opportunity. On the one hand, barren soils posed restrictions to Venice. On the other hand, Venice was naturally advantageous in terms of geographical location, for it sat exactly between the Western Europe civilization and Eastern Byzantium civilization, allowing it to function as a natural communication hub between Central Europe and all Mediterranean countries. Such a favorable location contained a huge commercial opportunity. Therefore, "The most important commercial center was in Italy: the retention of urban traditions in Roman times, the constant connection between some places in the peninsula and empires east of Constantinople, as well as its location in the Eastern Mediterranean, naturally made it a place of large-scale commercial renaissance. Seated on the Adriatic Sea, Venice enjoyed advantageous geographical environment, which enabled it to make use of commercial chances."[1] Barren soil put heavy pressure on Venetians for living, leading to their strong living desires and entrepreneurial spirits. This not only constituted a powerful spiritual motivation for them to break the constraints of barren soil but also provided strong mental support for breaking the solid religious ideology and bans in the Medieval period and instead forming their unique commercial cultural tradition. Under the guidance of strong living desire and entrepreneurship, friends or enemies of Christianity do not matter as long as there was profit for the Venetians. The Venetian "spirits of entrepreneurship and desire for seeking profits were too intensive and necessary. They did not allow religious hesitation to stop them from resuming connections with Syria for a long time, though they were now in the hands of heretics." "As for the Italians, customers' religion was nothing as long as they can get profits. Seeking profits would be condemned by the church and would be viewed as greedy. However, here, it found its expression in

---

① Phillips, J. R. S. *The Medieval Expansion of Europe* [M].Oxford: Oxford University Press, 1988: 26.

the most undisguised way."[①] Motivated by strong desires for living and entrepreneurship, the sacred Crusade of Christians also became a golden opportunity for the Venetians to gain profit. The Genoese and Venetians made the passenger ship service of sending Crusaders through the Mediterranean into "an extremely profitable business. They charged exorbitant prices which the Crusaders (who were mostly poor) could not afford. At that time, these Italian 'speculators' then mercifully allowed them to 'work unpaid all the way to compensate for ship fares', the amount of which from Venice to Acre would push Crusade knights to engage in several wars for their shipowners."[②] In this way, Venice largely expanded its territory along the coast of the Adriatic Sea, Greece (Athens was colonized by Venice), Cyprus Island, Crete Island, and Rhode Island. In addition to the normal trading with the heretic world, some merchants of Venice even dared to break the bans of European Christian churches and trafficked weapon materials to the Muslims for profit.

Like the merchants of Venice, the special natural environment also serves as an important reason for the strong desire for a livelihood and entrepreneurship of the Huizhou and Shanxi merchants in the Ming and Qing dynasties. Huizhou was in charge of She County, Xiuning County, Wuyuan County, Qimen County, Yi County, and Jixi County, which were all surrounded by high mountains and lofty hills in the south of Anhui Province. During the Song Dynasty, the contradiction between people and land in Huizhou has been prominent, with rice supply dependent on Raozhou. During the reign of the Chunxi Emperor in the Song Dynasty, *The History of Xin'an* recorded the following: "Xin'an is a prefecture that sits in the mountains, it is characterized by narrow and rugged terrain, solid and infertile soil as well as surging water with

---

① Canter, N. F. & Werthman M. S. *Medieval Society 400–1450* [M].NewYork: Thomas Y. Crowell Co., 1972: 139.

② van Loon, H. W. *The Story of Mankind* [M]. Trans. Qin, Y. & Feng, S. Guilin: Guangxi Normal University Press, 2003: 177.

little deposits. Since its establishment, the city has fortified itself in the mountains, and word of this has spread to the neighboring townships, making the city known. The city sits at the foot of the mountains, at the deepest part of the valley. Layers of cultivated land are dug against the mountains, and the farmers would climb up step by step. Yet, even with 10 or so layers they still count to less than an acre. The farm cattle with high efficiency and sharp tools are not enough. Resorting to slash-and-burn cultivation, the farmers look up to the sky and sigh when it does not rain for more than ten days. However, as soon as the rain falls, the water from the mountains rush down and wash away the soil or crops, so the diligence of people can be seen." In sharp contrast, Raozhou and Xuancheng had hundreds of acres of land where the farmers cultivate once a year, and then comes the rain. The grouth of crops was dependent on each other, and thus the people there can have enough food all year round, without the need to exert all their energies. People in She County carried out farm work in March or April, then came May and June. At this time, the water in plough became warm. The father and son take off their shoes, and work knee-deep in the mud and suffer the burning heat of the day and mosquito bites become the key problem. They also have to endure insects and leech infestations as they had no other choice.[1] It is at these times that people's diligence can be seen. The intensive labor and hardship caused by adverse natural environment can be strongly felt. Shulin also said that Huizhou "has vast mountains and limited land, and most poor households depend on farming."[2] "Although Xin'an ranks among the six prefectures, it features numerous high mountains. Its waters run west to Zhejiang Province and east to Pengli. The two sides of the river are as if covered with sands, but the plain cannot be seen."[3] The poor farmers and lower-class people have to rely on millet, wheat and other arid crops for livelihood because of the scarcity of plains.

---

① Luo, Y. *The History of Xin'an*: vol. 2 Discuss Tribute[M].

② Shu, L. *Anthology of Shu Wenjing*: vol. 2 When I Was in Chencang[M].

③ Shu, L. *Anthology of Shu Wenjing*: vol. 2 Manage Cases Raised by Officers with Chen Yingzhong[M].

What the aforementioned shows is that the economy of Huizhou cannot be centered on mere agriculture. Therefore, it is natural for people in Huizhou to have a desire to make their living in the non-agriculture field. As for the relationship between the natural environment in Huizhou and the rise of the Huizhou merchant group, scholars in the Ming and the Qing dynasties had a lot of precise and excellent discussions. Wu Rifa said in *An Overview of Huizhou Merchants*, "Our Huizhou is surrounded by numerous mountains with rugged roads and hidden hills, which contribute to vast mountainous areas and limited lands. Wherever there are plain lands between mountains and roads, people would gather and settle together. Because of population increase, the crops grown there cannot meet the demands of the population there, thus giving rise to commercial activities."[①] Tang Shun said as well, "The land in Xin'an is narrow and limited with insufficient plough. People virtually count on commerce for livelihood and even people from respectable families do not mind being merchants."[②] Wei Xi pointed out that, "The economy of Huizhou surpasses others in regions south of the Yangtze River. Due to the contradiction between land and population, more than half of the population goes to other places to conduct business. Some newly-married indigenous people go out for ten years, twenty years or even thirty years without returning. When they come back, even the descendants may not recognize them."[③] Hong Yutu also thought that "She County witnesses vast mountains and limited land, with barren soil and little production. Since the soil is not suitable for crop production, the cereal has to be transported from other counties. Therefore, it is a trend that most local people engage themselves in

---

① Wu, R. *Overview of Huizhou, Starting with Predestined Relationship* [M].

② Tang, S. *Overview of Cheng Shaojun's Journey* [M] & *Anthology of Tang Jinchuan*: vol.15 [M].

③ Wei, X. *Anthology of Wei Shuzi*: vol.17 [M] & *Chaste Women in Four Generations of the Jiang Family* [M].

commerce rather than permanent jobs."[1] According to statistics, the average farmland area per capita in Huizhou during Emperor Zhu Yujun's reign in the Ming Dynasty was only 2.2 Mu (a unit of area), and 1.9 Mu during Kangxi reign in the Qing Dynasty, which was later reduced to 1.5. According to current standards, the figures of 2.2, 1.9 or 1.5 Mu are not that small. However, given the productivity level at that time, the contradiction between people and land was quite prominent. As Hong Liangji, a scholar in Huizhou during Qianlong reign said, at that time "The food a person consumes in a year requires a land of nearly four Mu, so if a family has 10 people, they would need a land of 40 Mu."[2] In other words, the average farmland area has to be four Mu to provide enough food for people. According to this standard, Huizhou in the Ming and Qing dynasties were obviously an area in desperate need of crops. Scholar Gu Yanwu thus remarked that Huizhou County "in most cases counts what is produced in one year, yet cannot afford one-tenth of the whole demand."[3] Xu Chengyao, a local of Huizhou, also said, "Our county sits in high mountains and the grain produced cannot afford a month's demand, so in most cases the grain needs supplements from other places, which can be thousands of miles away from Jiangguang, or as near as hundreds of miles away from nearby counties. Because of high transportation costs including trade cost, shipping cost, and others, the price of rice in Huizhou is especially high in the South of the Yangtze River."[4] The fact that local land could not afford to provide for its people inspired the strong desire for people in Huizhou to be entrepreneurs and to make their living in non-agriculture fields. Old sayings consider commerce as a means of livelihood, and no commerce

---

① Zhang, H & Wang, Y. *Study of Huizhou Merchants*[M]. Hefei: Anhui People's Publishing Press, 1995: 19.
② Hong, L. *Juan Shi Ge Wen*: vol.1, Meaning of Words and Life [M].
③ Gu, Y. *The History and Situation of all Counties, Regions South of the Yangtze River* [M].
④ Xu, C. *Casual Talks about She County*: vol. 6 Situation of Rice Transportation in Mingji County [M].

means no hope. How can they not be in a hurry and feel urgent? "People all need livelihood and cannot live without commerce."[①]

Just like Huizhou merchants, the strong will of making a living and the enterprising spirit displayed by Shanxi merchants in the Ming and Qing dynasties are also intrinsically linked to the natural environment, which bears "cold climate, impoverished land, and sparse vegetation." Being at high altitude, with rugged terrain, continuous ridges, and valleys, Shanxi Province, located in the Loess Plateau, may not be blessed by the warm and humid climate from the ocean due to the obstruction of Taihang Mountains. Instead, it has endured sand erosions from the northwest deserts. The arable farmland is dominated by dry lands, with few water areas. According to a survey conducted in 1935, the dry lands accounted for 97.18% among the total arable land—of which 48.51% were hillsides, with only 2.82% water area[②]. There was land alkalization in the plain basins, water shortage in the terraces, and soil erosion risk in the hilly areas. Kang Jitian, a hydraulic expert in the Qing Dynasty, once commented on Shanxi, explaining that "it is a place where there is no fertile soil, no water irrigation, and no abundance of traffic and food," "few creatures can survive with such cold weather and infertile land," "it is nearly impossible to farm on the hills and lands here"—Shanxi indeed offers poor conditions for living.[③] Barren land and poor natural environment resulted in low output of grain per Mu in Shanxi during the Ming and Qing dynasties. Ren Qingyun, a researcher in the Qing Dynasty, said: "From the north of Zhili to Shanxi, most of the lands are broad with sparse population; however, in Jiangnan (region

---

① See *Collection of She County* in Wanli Reign.
② Xu, S. The agriculture of Shanxi in modern times [M] //Office of Shanxi local Chronicles Compilation Committee. *Shanxi in Modern Times*. Taiyuan: Shanxi People's Publishing House, 1998.
③ Ge, X. *The Development of Commerce in Five Hundred Years—Jin Merchant and Traditional Culture* [M]. Wuhan: Huazhong University of Science and Technology Press, 1996: 1-2.

south of the Yangtze River), one-tenth of its 240-feet Mu land produces even more food than that of 1000-feet Mu in Shanxi."[1] It is not hard to believe that there would be a serious food shortage in Shanxi. Zhu Shi, a Qing's governor also said: "I've known that in Shanxi and its ajar province, even in harvest year the food cannot cover people's living. Only by those business ships transporting rice from the Jiangnan region to Shanxi can the Shanxi people survive."[2] Like the cases of Venice and Huizhou, the land of Shanxi was not able to feed its people, which inspired Shanxi people's strong will to make their living and their enterprising spirits. As Conchita put it, "To the south of Taiyuan, most people travel far to conduct business for livelihood without returning for years, for their poor hometown cannot support their basic life. Therefore, they have to travel far and exchange needed goods."[3] Zhang Siwei also said, "Though Wupu (now named Yongji) is located at the turning of the Yellow River; its soil is too poor to yield crops to raise so many people. With little supply from the land, people seek their means of livelihood from commerce. So many people travel away to survive that among ten houses nine were empty."[4] According to surveys, more than 60% of households in Shanxi's Qi County at the end of the Qing Dynasty and in the early days of the Republic of China had a history of engaging in trading. On such prediction, in a county of 100,000 people, 15,000 of them went out for business.[5] *History of Taigu County* also said, "Yangyi (now named Taigu) witnesses rich labor and poor fields. Even in the rich year, the food produced cannot sustain people for two months. Therefore, besides farming, people are all good at making

[1]   Ren, Q. Suggestion about mobilizing people to establish water conservancy project [M] // *Anthology of Governing Country by the Royal Court*: vol 43.
[2]   Zhu, S. *Collection of Public Documents of Zhu Wenduan*: Filling vol. 4 Counsel the Ban on Purchasing Grains with Officers of Henan [M].
[3]   Kang, J. *Jin Cheng Tu Lue* [M].
[4]   Zhang, S. *Tiao Lu Tang Ji:* vol. 20 [M].
[5]   Zhang, Z. *The Rise and Fall of Shanxi Merchants* [M]. Taiyuan: Shanxi Ancient Books Publishing House, 2001: 289.

their living and they take little of traveling 1,000 miles away. That is why despite the poor fields, the local people themselves are rich."[1] For example, Taigu County in Shanxi was originally a poor place, but people strove to make a living with their businesses, which has brought them fortune and has made Taigu County a rich place. After Daoguang Reign, this county had been famous for its richness, ranking among the top three business places in Shanxi as a place "controlling the economy of the whole Shanxi Province."[2]

Most merchants' groups in history (not just the Venetian merchants and the Huizhou merchants) have been linked to a natural environment characterized by overpopulation or poor soil. In history, the hometown of most merchants' groups is densely-populated or rarely-cultivated so that people cannot rely solely on farming for their livelihood but have to find another means. Of course, it needs to be emphasized in particular that although the special natural environment is one of the necessary conditions for the rise of commercial associations, it is not an essential one. Otherwise, we would not be able to explain why in similar places with limited lands and dense population, only some formed commercial groups while others did not, or why people in certain areas had the willingness and initiative to make a living outside of agriculture, while others chose to be resigned to circumstances. Therefore, a comprehensive examination is necessary while attaching importance to the relationship between the natural environment and people's willingness and initiative to make a living by themselves and the rise of commercial groups. Hegel attached great importance to the role of the natural environment and pointed out: "We should not overestimate or underestimate the role of nature: Ionian's bright sky certainly contributes to the beauty of Homeric poetry, but it cannot

---

[1]   See *Annals of Taigu County*.

[2]   See Preface of *Annals of Taigu County*.

produce Homer alone."[1] Hegel didn't deny the role of the geographical environment in shaping national character and national spirit. However, he believed that the direct cause of differences in character and spirit lies in the different economic lifestyles of different ethnic groups—the natural conditions only serve as indirect reasons. However, researchers both before and after him are trapped in the error of exploring the mere psychological or physiological influence of nature on people while completely neglecting nature's influence on social productivity and its influence on the entire social relationship of mankind and their superstructure through social productivity. But Hegel completely avoids such grave errors, not only in individual aspects, but also in the entire formulation of the whole question."[2] Marx pointed out that "without its own natural routine, a single being cannot be called a natural being, nor can it participate in the life of nature."[3] Meanwhile, he also pointed out that "an abstractly understood, isolated and supposedly separated nature also means nothing to humans."[4] Tang Lixing believed that in the study of the phenomenon of Huizhou merchants, we should not only pay attention to the relationship between geography and people's livelihood, but also the relationship between geography and culture. Take Huizhou for instance, even in terms of geography, while paying attention to the inherent mountainous areas in Huizhou, it is also necessary for us to form a macro grasp of Huizhou's location in the Jiangnan region of South China. It should also be noted that social interaction and the rise of Huizhou merchants are precisely the results of social changes under the specific conditions of time and space as well as the consequent

---

① Hegel, C. *Lectures on the Philosophy of History* [M]. Trans. Wang, Z. Shanghai: Shanghai Bookstore Publishing House, 1999: 82.

② Plekhanov. *The 60th Anniversary of Hegel's Death* [M] & *Anthology of Plekhanov's Philosophical Works*[M]. Beijing: SDX Joint Publishing Company, 1959: 484-485.

③ Marx, K. *Economic Philosophy Manuscript 1844* [M]. Beijing: People's Publishing House, 1985: 125.

④ Ibid. 135.

series of social interactions.[①] Harriet Zurndorfer's research on Huizhou shows that what happened at the same time as the transformation of the system along territorial boundaries was the change of tax policy in the Ming Dynasty. In 1494, the varnish and tung oil expropriated by the Department of Labor would not be taken by deducting land tax, while it would be a dependent annual tax separated from land tax, which hugely increased local tax to 3,777 taels. In 1515, the Department of Labor imposed tax on 20,000 thousand pine trees on Huizhou to a further degree; then in 1523, it increased the tax on logging. When miscellaneous additional tax sharply increased during Emperor Jiajing's reign, the cost on making money from farm land became so large that many people preferred to do business rather than occupy land. The opinions of Tang Lixing, Harriet Zurndorfer are not only significant in meaning but also in value, both theoretically and methodologically, for the study of Huizhou merchants and other commercial groups.

1.4.2   The Contradiction between People and Land and the Spirit of Self-entrepreneurship

Since the reform and opening-up, Zhejiang, like Venice, Huizhou, and Shanxi in the history of China and foreign countries, has been given a natural environment with a small land and large population. This has been an important factor for Zhejiang people to form willingness for self-employment and spirit of entrepreneurship.

With a land area of 101,800 square kilometers accounting for 1.06% of the country, Zhejiang Province is one of the smallest provinces in China. In Zhejiang Province, mountains and hills occupy 70.4%, plains and basins 23.2%, rivers and lakes 6.4% and the farmland area take up 1,613,800 hectares. Therefore, there is an old saying that "70% of the lands are mountains, 10% are water, and the remaining 20% are

---

① Brook, T. *The Confusions of Pleasure: Commerce and Culture in Ming China* [M]. Trans. Fang, J., Wang, X. & Lou, T. Beijing: SDX Joint Publishing Company, 2004: 137-138.

farmland." According to the research report of the Research Institute of Rural Development Research Center of the State Council, with the national average of 100, Zhejiang's per capita Resource Index among all provinces and municipalities in China is as follows: the water resources 89.6, energy 0.5, mineral 4.9, available land 40, cultivated land and climate 117.2; of the "Per Capita Resource Ownership Index" of all provinces and cities, Zhejiang ranks third from the last and the last five are Shanghai 10.4, Tianjin 10.6, Zhejiang 11.5, and Jiangsu and Guangdong both 26. The research report shows that Zhejiang is indeed a "province with few resources" in terms of the abundance of basic natural resources. According to the "per capita Resource Index," the contradiction between the crowded people and limited land in Zhejiang is more prominent. In 1993, the population density of Zhejiang reached 423.7 people per square kilometer, many times higher than the national average of 123 in the same period and the average of 41 in the world. In 1978, the per capita arable land area in Zhejiang Province was 453 square meters, which became 410 square meters in 1990 and 380 square meters in 1995, and now has dropped further to less than 367 square meters. The per capita arable land in Zhejiang is less than half of the national average, and only 1/6 of the world average. In some parts of Zhejiang, especially in Taizhou and Wenzhou, the representative of the Zhejiang Model and the most economically viable regions in the first 20 years of the reform and opening-up, the per capita arable land area is even lower. In 1978, per capita arable land in Wenzhou was 346.7 square meters whereas in Qiaotou Town of Yongjia, the per capita arable land area was only 186.7 square meters. At present, the per capita arable land area in Wenzhou has dropped to below 220 square meters. Before the reform and opening-up, the per capita arable land in Taizhou was less than 333.3 square meters, much lower than the national and provincial level of 1066.7 square meters and 453.3 square meters, respectively.

How would natural conditions of dense population with limited and barren land and few people with a vast and fertile land impact the spirit of people? Montesquieu pointed out that "The law should have taken into consideration the natural state of the country; the cold, hot and warm climates; the quality, situation and area of the land; the way of life of the peoples of farming, hunting and animal husbandry; and the residents of different religions, sexual addictions, wealth, population, trade, customs and habits. Finally, the purpose of the law and the legislator, as well as the order of things that underlie the establishment of the law, is also linked. The law should be examined from all these points of view."[1] Not only should the formation of the law be combined with the analysis of the natural state; the formation of human spirit should also be combined with the analysis of the natural state. Different natural states can have different effects on human spirit. According to Montesquieu's view, a barren land breeds the enterprising spirit, while a fertile land develops a person's inertia. "Meager land makes people diligent, perseverant, hard-working, and brave. People have to make what lands do not give them by themselves," whereas "a fertile land makes people lazy and cowardly because of the peace and happiness it brings."[2] "A country rich in land naturally develops dependency on the land."[3] Hegel pointed out: "The sea has given us an indefinite and boundless vision. When human beings feel themselves infinite in the infinite sea, they are inspired to surpass all that is limited. The sea not only invites humankind to conquer and plunder, but also encourages them to pursue profits and engage in commerce." However, "an ordinary land and an ordinary plain basin bound mankind to the soil and draw him into an endless dependence."[4] Marx also believed that "too abundant a nature makes 'human inseparable from the hand of nature, just as a child cannot do without a guide.' It cannot make man's own

---

① Montesquieu. *The Spirit of the Laws:* vol.1 [M]. Trans. Zhang, Y. Beijing: The Commercial Press, 1961: 7.

② Department of Philosophy, Peking University. *French Philosophy in the 18th Century* [M]. Beijing: The Commercial Press, 1979: 56.

③ Ibid. 54.

④ Hegel, C. *Lectures on the Philosophy of History* [M]. Trans. Wang, Z. Shanghai: Shanghai Bookstore Publishing House, 1999: 96.

development become a natural necessity. The country of capital is not the lush tropical, but the temperate zone. It is not the absolute fertility of the soil, but the difference and diversity of its natural products that form the natural foundation of the social division of labor. The changes in the natural environment then encourage people's needs, abilities, labor materials and way of working to become diversified."[1]

Therefore, although the geographical environment is not the only factor that determines the spirit of people, it is an important factor that affects people's spirits. According to one theory, man is an organism. Human spirit is first controlled by the human body, which is subject to the "nervous system, nutrition, and digestive system as well as energy." Obviously, this view is very different from subjectivism. In the view of subjectivism, the body is only an insignificant factor. But it is undeniable that there is a reasonable degree of rationality in exploring the origin of social history from the needs of the body and physiology.

According to Marx and Engels, people must be able to live in order to "create history." However, in order to live, clothing, food, shelter, and other things are needed first. Therefore, the first historical activity was to produce information that met these needs, namely the productive material life itself. This activity is also a historical activity that people have to conduct every day at every time (now as thousands of years ago) in order to make a living. This is the basic condition for all history. "The first premise of all human history is undoubtedly the existence of a living individual. Therefore, the first fact to be confirmed is the physical organization of these individuals and the resulting personal relationships with other aspects of nature. Of course, we are neither here to study people's own physiological characteristics in depth, nor to study in depth the various natural conditions in which people live—geological conditions, geographical conditions of mountain and hydrology,

---

① Marx, K. & Engels, F. *Complete Works of Marx and Engels:* vol.23 [M]. Beijing: People's Publishing House, 1972: 561.

climatic conditions and other conditions. Any historical record should be based on these natural conditions and their changes due to people's activities in the historical process."[①] Therefore, the needs of the body with "nervous system" and "digestive system," which need nutrition and energy, are the most essential needs of a living organism in a certain natural environment. However, different natural environments, like dense populations with a limited land and barren soil and a sparsely populated land with a vast land and fertile soil, will have different effects on the body, the physiology, the needs, and the mental state. When the land can basically meet the basic needs of the body such as eating, clothing and inhabiting, the body may tend to become lazy and "stick to the land" and form a corresponding "security of homeland." However, when the land cannot meet such basic needs, the body will break through the shackles of any strong ideology and sprout a strong desire and entrepreneurial spirit to make a living.

Since the reform and opening-up, what effect has the natural environment of dense population with limited land had on the spiritual state of the people of Zhejiang? On the one hand, in those sparsely populated but fertile land, although people can obtain certain living materials and living security, they may also be bound by the land at the same time. In other words, the guarantee of access to subsistence materials may be at the expense of free movement. It is possible that people may deal with land year after year so that just as children cannot live without guardians, people cannot live without the land and the land may exhaust the time and energy of most of the capable laborers in those areas. However, in areas such as southern Zhejiang where there are more people and less land, after the implementation of the contract system with remuneration linked to output system in rural areas, the farmers' enthusiasm for production and their production efficiency have been largely increased. As long as there is enough labor to handle

---

①   Marx, K. & Engels, F. *Selections of Marx and Engels:* vol.1 [M]. Beijing: People's Publishing House, 1995: 67.

the land, it is hard for the land to bind people. Some people claim that since the reform and opening-up, many lands in Zhejiang have been cultivated by the elderly, women and children. This statement may be exaggerating, but it is undeniable that the natural environment with a greater population and less land indeed liberated a large number of young and middle-aged men in Zhejiang from the land so that they could both leave their farmland and homeland to go out for business activities. This is especially true in Wenzhou, where the contradiction between people and land is serious. In 1978, the beginning of the reform and opening-up, the rural labor force in Wenzhou was 1.8 million, of which 1.6 million engaged in farming, whereas in 1985, of the 2.1 million labor force, only 600,000 people engaged in agriculture, accounting for 28.8% of the total while the remaining 1.5 million farmers have been freed from farmland. Therefore, the natural environment with dense people and limited land not only poses pressure of survival for Zhejiang people but also gives them free space to engage in non-agricultural activities. People in Zhejiang gained valuable things after ridding themselves of the shackles of land, that is, freedom—the freedom to move freely and act freely. Such personal freedom is exactly what is necessary for engaging in non-agricultural activities, especially commercial exchanges. This experience is also very similar to that of medieval merchant groups who once had been wanderers. In the Middle Ages in Europe, land decided the distribution of living materials of a member of society and at the same time decided the stability of one's social status. In an era when the acquisition of real things was more important than coinage, nobles, manor owners, and serfs were all closely bound up with the products of the land. Therefore, at that time, leaving or losing land meant losing the basis for making a living as well as one's due status in the community. However, it was also because of the loss of land that these wandering people were freed from the various land-based systems and rules. "Both Jews and Venetians, who are free to move, are all people who are free from agriculture and are basically have no relationship with the land in Western Europe. They are people who are on the more, familiar with many local conditions

and good at facing all sorts of dangers but getting high profits in the
end. There are too many similarities between the people in the Western
Europe who abandoned agriculture and these 'predecessors.' Both of
them were socially trapped people. Following the sustainable paths of
the 'predecessors,' they eventually took their way of life as their own
survival capital which is a very natural thing."[1]

Zhejiang people, especially Zhejiang farmers, are not inherently
more willing to make their own livelihood and independent innovation
when compared with other regions. In fact, as far as normal is concerned,
people who make a living directly from agriculture are clinging to the
land. According to Fei Xiaotong, as already quoted earlier, agriculture
is directly financed from land, unlike nomadism or industry. Nomadic
people who live based on gazing area are erratic and uncertain; people
engaged in industry can choose where to live, their migration will not be
obstructed. Alternatively, a society directly relying on agriculture makes
itself "a society living and dying on the same land due to the restriction of
locality. Their normal life lies within their hometown from the cradle to
the grave."[2] "We can say that for people who depend on agriculture for
a living, it is normal for their generations to settle down while migration
is frowned upon. Severe drought and floods or turmoil for successive
years can cause some farmers to leave their hometowns. I believe that
the flow of grassroots population during such major incidents as the War
of Resistance is still negligible."[3] Of course, this does not mean that the
rural population is fixed. Because the population is increasing, as long as
there are several generations in a certain land, the population will reach
its saturation point. The excess population has to go out and create new
lands for themselves. But the root is not moving. The excess people who

---

① Zhao, L. *The Formation of the Merchant Class and Social Transformation in
Western Europe* [M]. Beijing: China Social Sciences Press, 2004: 131.
② Fei, X. *Earthbound China* [M]. Beijing: SDX Joint Publishing Company,
1985: 4.
③ Ibid. 3.

go out are like seeds blown out of the old trees. Those who find new land survive and create a small family colony whereas those who fail to find new lands are eliminated or "make a fortune" under different kinds of circumstances.

Chayanov believed that traditional farmers not only "stick to the land" but also are "indolent" even on the land. Once the traditional farmers produced enough grain for their own consumption, they would reduce their own labor or even stop their work. In other words, for traditional farmers, the satisfaction of consumption was not an infinite process, but a process that would settle to a certain standard. In 1924, Chayanov collected and rearranged the household survey materials in four counties of Russia at the time and concluded that "the extent to which laborers in family farms develop their labor capacity is driven by the demand for household consumption. When the consumer demand increased, the extent of self-development of farmer labor also deepened. On the other hand, the consumption of labor capacity is also constrained by the intensity of labor itself. With the same income, the harder the labor, the lower the standard of living will be; however, farmer families often have to make great efforts to reach such a low standard of living, but when it lowers to a certain extent, they will give up their arduous job. In other words, we can say with certainty that the degree of self-development of farmer labor is determined by a certain relationship between demand satisfaction and labor intensity."[1]

Of course, traditional farmers "stick to the land" and even show some "indolence." This does not mean that they are irrational. On the contrary, farmers are rather rational. They seem to be "conservative" and often even behave "unscrupulously." In fact, "conservative" and "unscrupulous" are also rational choices under the given constraints. J. Migdal stated that "The farmers are pursuing a strategy of 'minimum

---

[1] Chayanov, A. *The Economic Organization of Peasants* [M]. Trans. Xiao, Z. Beijing: Central Compilation & Translation Press, 1996: 53.

for maximum,' that is, taking the least risk and striving for the maximum environmental control. Farmers are suspicious of change because they realize that the so-called advances may bring them to somewhere worse than they are now. To farmers who are struggling to survive, this is an unacceptable risk."[1] T. Schultz, an economist, argued in the 1960s theoretically and empirically that farmers, like everyone else, are rational and have "normal" sensitive reactions to price and other market stimuli. In Africa, for example, he pointed out that the farmer supply response was highly elastic when the export prices of cocoa, cotton, coffee, peanuts or oil palm fruits became profitable. Therefore, the traditional smallholder economy is not as inefficient as some people believe. It is enough to prove that the attempt to forcibly change the allocation of resources contrary to its wishes, resulting from the "irrationality" of farmers' economic psychology, has resulted in a more inefficient result than that of the farmer economy. In his view, treating a farmer as a "leisure-lover who prefers leisure rather than extra work to increase production," a "squander" who is reluctant to save to increase investment, and an outdated conservative who is an inefficient user of the available resources, is all "defamatory" to farmers.[2] Mendras quoted M. Malitot in his *The Finality of Peasants* the study of farmers in the Ganges Valley, where Malitot discovered that although farmers were aware of the benefits of a complete irrigation technique, they are not willing to use the water because "it is in their view that irrigation system a conspiracy of the government in order to

---

① Migdal, J. S. *Peasant, Politics and Revolution: Pressures toward Political and Social Change in the Third World* [M]. Trans. Li, Y. & Yuan, N. Beijing: Central Compilation & Translation Press, 1996: 42-43.

② Qin, H. The price-supply reaction of agricultural market in history and reality—An investigation on "Rationality of Farmers" from the economic history [M] //Jia, D. *Chinese Farmers in Modernization*. Nanjing: Nanjing University Press, 1993: 3.

extract more labor and money from them."[1] If uncontrollable factors such as natural disasters are excluded, then the traditional agriculture based on self-sufficiency is all determined and transparent, or the information is sufficient. Therefore, under normal circumstances, farmers tend to prefer having a relatively low-income but relatively stable life. Farmers are afraid of trying out new things, mainly because these kinds of attempts often entailed some risks and uncertainties. In other words, under certain condition of existence, the farmers' reform must bear the corresponding risks and may fail in the end, while failure means devastation in reality. A smallholder is very vulnerable, the death of a cow is enough to put him into bankruptcy. Therefore, when the output level of a producer can only meet the minimum consumption needs of the family, the risks and uncertainties in the innovation and development of production make the survival threat the most basic problem that the producer faces. At this time, the main purpose of the productive activity is not the maximization of income, but to maximize the family's likeliness of making a sufficient living. The low level of production technology has caused smallholders to face pressures of this kind from time to time, resulting in inherent necessity to minimize risks. Thus, the normalization of production has become their primary choice.

On the other hand, farmers' rationality is manifested not only by its usual trade-offs between input and spiritual gains but also by the trade-offs it often places between input and spiritual gains. The motivation of the farmers to make progress and the desire to get rich are not only restricted by the conditions of material productivity, but also by cultural meanings and values, by the "non-economic factors" such as rights, status, prestige, trust and evaluation. In other words, their entrepreneurial motivation and the desire to get rich are also a social and cultural construction. In a social and cultural atmosphere that advocates "being satisfied with small wealth," "shoot the bird which takes the

---

[1]　Mendras, H. The *Finality of Peasants* [M]. Trans. Li, P. Beijing: China Social Sciences Press, 1992: 42.

lead," "dreads fame as a pig dreads being fat," and "the rafters that jut out get rotten first," the farmers who are ambitious and prosperous will inevitably be seen as heterogeneous and later be punished. In this situation, the traditional farmers unavoidably embody what Wolf calls "arrogant," "infatuated with poverty," "ascetic" and "obeying poverty as virtue," in the cultural conception. They also have "collective jealousy" and "blind faith in witchcraft" and are "fond of spreading privacy" to deal with the trauma of materialism and the "upward crawling" from other worlds to maintain economic averages and traditional codes of conduct.[①] That is, to limit the infinite pursuit of wealth for individuals contributes to the collective survival of the community. Scott therefore believes that the farmer economy is a kind of moral economy. Scott's point of view can be demonstrated in the Chinese People's Commune System. Under the People's Commune System, the farmers' incentive to pursue profits was constantly suppressed by the "petty-bourgeois ideology." Families that had made fortunes beyond their social groups had also been continuously hit with the policies. Therefore, although the state encouraged farmers to work hard for a collective enterprise, farmers appeared to be "inertial" in their personal enrichment. In fact, the reason why farmers were "inertial" is that they were worried that they would be punished by the social "community."

However, this does not mean that "slow development," "no development," or even stagnation, etc. are inherent features of the farmer economy or agricultural production system, neither does this mean "conservation," "inertia," "reluctance to take risks" or "inefficiency" will always be an option for farmers to conform to rationality. Migdal quoted Crookes as saying: "In the past, winter wheat has always been regarded as a risky crop because it depends entirely on the weather. However, when the tax revenue became so heavy that people could not bear it and when the rent rose as much as 50% or

---

① Harding, T. et al. *Evolution and Culture* [M]. Trans. Han, J. & Shang, G. Hangzhou: Zhejiang People's Publishing House, 1987: 52.

more, a handful of richer farmers began betting on such risks."[1] Scott also believed that Safety First behavior did not rule out all innovation, but exclude those high-risk innovations. The principle of Safety First does not mean that farmers are subordinate to their own habits and cannot afford even the avoidable risks. When crops in dry seasons, new seeds, planting techniques, and new things like market production provide a clear, substantial return with no or low risk to survival and safety, one can see that farmers tend to be at the forefront. When "continuing to do routine activities always leads to failure, this once again makes risk-taking meaningful; such an adventure is in the interest of survival. Farmers whose survival programs have failed because of climate, land shortages or rising government rent do their utmost to maintain their own fledgling status—which may mean to re-use crops for sale, run into new debt and take risks to use new rice varieties or even to descend to banditry. A large number of farmer innovations have this desperate character. This has the same peculiar social and political implications as the economic background in which farmers cannot but fight for things unknown and share a common skepticism."[2]

When the scarcity of land, coupled with the inefficient production of the People's Communes, made farmers' survival difficult, "taking the risk" may also have been a reasonable choice, especially in some areas in southern Zhejiang where the per capita cultivated land was only 200 square meters. For example, before reform and opening-up, in Jinxiang Township, Cangnan County of Wenzhou City, people once went to the district office canteen to get food to eat. The number of farmers who went out to flee the famine was not easy to count. It

①　Migdal, J. S. *Peasant, Politics and Revolution: Pressures toward Political and Social Change in the Third World* [M]. Trans. Li, Y. & Yuan, N. Beijing: Central Compilation & Translation Press, 1996: 43.

②　Scott, J. C. *The Moral Economy of the Peasant: Rebellion and Subsistence in Southeast Asia* [M]. Trans. Cheng, L., Liu, J. et al. Nanjing: Yilin Press, 2001: 32-33.

is said that the percentage of Pingyang County reached 60%.[①] Under such circumstances, leaving the land is a rational choice or a worthy risk for the farmers. The dense population with limited land means that the land could hardly feed its people, continuing to rely on land could have led to starvation. In other words, the Zhejiang people, especially people from southern Zhejiang (such as people from Wenzhou, Taizhou, Yiwu, and Yongkang) who most vividly reflected the Zhejiang spirit later in the reform and opening-up, had no choice but to leave the land and make a living in the non-agricultural sector. This also meant that under the circumstance in which the most basic needs were difficult to meet, Zhejiang people, especially those in southern Zhejiang, had to have a strong will for self-employment and a spirit of self-innovation. As more and more farmers leave their land to make a living in the non-agricultural sector, the concept of group culture of farmers in southern Zhejiang gradually changes. Pursuing wealth is now regarded as "glorious" instead of "shameful." However, this new social and cultural construction will in turn change the subjective utility function of farmers, so as to further encourage and strengthen their progressive motivation and desire to get rich.

The above situation undoubtedly forms a sharp contrast with those living in the vast and sparsely populated areas of northeast China. Northeast China wa not only the center of China's planned economy before the reform and opening-up but also a fertile land with a sparse population. For example, in Heilongjiang Province and Jilin Province, called "land of black earth," the cultivated area per capita is 4,000 square meters and 1,580 square meters, respectively. With the vast and fertile black soil, people can eat well and dress warmly without much effort. Therefore, if not forced to do so, people from northeast China will not easily leave the affluent black earth land. A few acres of land, two cows and a wife and children by the warm hearth make for a very

---

① Fei, X. Small commodities, big market [M] // He, F. *Overview of Zhejiang*. Hangzhou: Zhejiang People's Publishing House, 2003.

comfortable life, not to mention the good living environment where "pheasants fly into the rice pot." The descendants who "reluctantly braved their journey to the northeast" therefore relied on nature since then. Adhering to the monotonous homeland and lacking pressure and excitement from unfamiliar environments, they gradually formed a conservative character lacking entrepreneurship and innovation and a stubborn and tenacious sense of "sticking to the land" that adheres to convention and lacks adaptation. As Bing Zheng, a Jilin scholar said, "Compared with Zhejiang Province, there is a clear gap between our province in awareness of innovation, development, and mobility. The reason behind this apparent gap is that the sense of 'sticking to the land' is at work."[①] Under the survival pressure owing to the scarcity of land with a large population, the first pot of gold for many private entrepreneurs in Zhejiang was earned by doing businesses like repairing shoes, umbrellas, glasses or selling cotton and hinges in the northeast of China. The northeast people however did not bother with this. The result was that the shoe repairers, cotton and hinge sellers and their sons became the boss, and the recipients and their sons became their employees. As Bing Zheng thinks, the formation of the sense of "sticking to the land" had a process. Historically, the majority of the Northeast people was the immigrants from inside the Shanhaiguan Pass who had been innovative, mobile and seeking development. However, the northeast is located in the interior with rich resources, fertile land, good weather, and few natural disasters. It was easy for the immigrants from Shanhaiguan Pass to obtain living materials and rely on the produces from the mountains. As time passed, immigrants have lost their original pioneering spirit. In other words, the formation of the sense of "sticking to the land" was inseparable from the relatively abundant geographical environment of the northeast. The northeast is "sparsely populated with little space pressure." Farmers could still use the traditional mode of production to survive.

---

① Bing, Z. Break through the sense of "Sticking to the Land" and promote nation-wide entrepreneurship [N]. *Jilin Daily*, 2004-06-04.

However, the marginal areas of the planned economy as well as natural endowments such as the crowded population on the limited land and lack of natural resources, make Zhejiang people (especially people from southern Zhejiang where the contradiction between people and land is more prominent) face greater pressure for their subsistence. Their most genuine desire to survive compelled them to leave the land and "think" of a solution. Therefore, they have stronger senses of self-employment and entrepreneurship, which constitute the "historical tradition" and "spiritual resources" of Zhejiang's institutional innovation and economic development. In fact, Zhejiang Province has long lost the condition for a life and work in peace and contentment due to the long-term survival pressure that arose from the crowded population and the limited land. For example, "Ningbo is a city with a mountainous area and a narrow and thick population. Its people often go out to trade and concurrently enjoy the maritime advantage. Their boats ship north to Liaoning and Shenyang, south to Fujian and Guangzhou, middle to the Yangtze River and Shanghai served as the central market for the stock."[1] Because of "the growing population and inadequate production of its land, people of Ningbo went out everywhere for business, their merchants were therefore spread all over the world."[2] Siming breasted mountain with the sea, with its narrow land and dense population, the rural people either farmed or went out to make a profit. Dinghai's "plain soil by the sea was mostly saline marsh, whose center was in the middle of the mountains with barren land and limited water which was unsuitable for plantation. The produce each year could not even sustain the people on the land."[3] It can be said that before the Movement of the Taiping Heavenly Kingdom, the contradiction between people and land

---

① Zhang, R. Archives of siming club in Shanghai [J]. *Archives and History*, 1996(6).

② Shanghai News Agency. *Sequel to Research Materials of Shanghai* [M]. Shanghai: Shanghai Bookstore Publishing House, 1986: 291.

③ Shanghai Museum Library. *Selections of Monument Materials in Shanghai* [A]. Shanghai: Shanghai People's Publishing House, 1980: 259.

in Zhejiang had already been very sharp, otherwise, there would not have been a large number of overseas Chinese who went across the seas to make a living.

It needs to be further explained that, compared with other parts of the country (such as northeast China), both southern Zhejiang and northern Zhejiang are areas where there are many people with little land. Historically, the phenomenon of "overcrowding" has also appeared in northern Zhejiang, but the two differ to some extent. Especially after the Movement of the Taiping Heavenly Kingdom and the War of Resistance against Japanese Aggression, the contradiction between people and land in the south of Zhejiang Province was even more prominent than that of northern Zhejiang and southern Zhejiang. According to Zhuo Yongliang's research, the population of Zhejiang Province decreased by two thirds during the Movement of the Taiping Heavenly Kingdom. In the ninth year of the Xianfeng period during the Qing Dynasty (1859) when the Movement of the Taiping Heavenly Kingdom was conducted, the population of Zhejiang was 30.4 million. Whereas in the 13th year of the Tongzhi period in the Qing Dynasty (1874), only 10.84 million people remained, a decrease of 64.3%.[1] Northern Zhejiang was the region where the population of Zhejiang decreased most during the Movement of the Taiping Heavenly Kingdom. For example, according to *Annals of Lin'an*: "After the havoc and turmoil caused by war in the first year of the Tongzhi period, the gathered exiles in Lin'an County were only between 8,000 and 9,000 people. Having been urged to conduct reclamation for three years, the people were gathered and multiplied. By the 20th year of the Tongzhi period, the population of Lin'an started to exceed 40,000 people. However, from the Tongzhi period to the 12th year of the Guangxu period, the records are incomplete, therefore the information cannot be verified."[2] According to *Annals of Huzhou*, the households

---

① Zhuo, Y. Sweet potato, war and entrepreneurship—The causes and predicament of the Wenzhou Pattern [J]. *Zhejiang Social Sciences*, 2004(3).

② See *Annals of Lin'an* in Xuantong Reign. [M].

of Linghu Town "long had stabled at 5,000, but decreased to 4,000 after the wars."[①] Shuanglin Town also lost more than half of its population due to warfare, and less than 4,000 households remained. Other towns, such as Shanlian, Digang, Daitou, Lianshi, Daqian, Hongxingqiao, and Jiapu have all been affected and lost much of the population after the war. Several thousand households in Shanlian Town survived the war; Digang Town "used to have about 3,000 households, but only 2,500 remained after the war"; 600 to 700 households remained after the war compared with the formal stable 2,000 in Daitou Town and 1,300 in Lianshi Town.[②] The total population of the seven counties (Jiaxing, Xiushui, Jiashan, Haiyan, Pinghu, Shimen, and Tongxiang) in Jiaxing Prefecture was only 953,053 in 1863, less than one-third of the 2,933,764 in 1838.[③] Due to the declining population in northern Zhejiang during the Movement of the Taiping Heavenly Kingdom, the per capita arable land in this area was also larger than that in southern Zhejiang. During the War of Resistance against Japanese Aggression, the population in northern Zhejiang dropped sharply again. There were 306,000 people in Haining County in 1946, 61,000 fewer than in 1936. Jiashan County was once where the seesaw battles happened. In 1942, there were only 147,000 left in this County, nearly half the value when compared with that of the early Republic of China.[④] The impact of the war on the population in other areas of Zhejiang Province was relatively small, while the population in southwest Zhejiang was scarcely affected by the war. Therefore, the density of people on land in southern Zhejiang has been far bigger than in northern Zhejiang. Now, in Zhejiang, Jiashan County in the north is the county with the largest arable land per capita. In 1979, per capita arable land of Jiaxing in northern Zhejiang was 2.15 times that of Wenzhou. At

---

① See *Annals of Huzhou* in Tongzhi Reign. [M].

② Liu, S. *Research on Regions South of the Yangtze River Towns in the Ming and Qing dynasties* [M]. Beijing: China Social Sciences Press, 1987: 79.

③ See *Annals of Jiaxing* in Guangxu Reign. [M].

④ Zhuo, Y. Sweet potato, war and entrepreneurship—The Causes and predicament of the Wenzhou Pattern [J]. *Zhejiang Social Sciences*, 2004(3).

the beginning of the reform and opening-up, the average per capita arable land in Jiaxing was 746.7 square meters while in Wenzhou of southern Zhejiang, it was only 346.7 square meters, less than half that of Jiaxing. Compared with the northern part of Zhejiang, contradiction between people and land in southern Zhejiang was more prominent, people there lived under greater pressure. Therefore, in the process of the reform and opening-up, the people from southern Zhejiang showed stronger spirits of self-employment and self-innovation than those from northern Zhejiang. At the same time, with the less prominent contradiction between people and land in northern Zhejiang, the historical tradition there was the same as that of southern Jiangsu: "Agriculture supplements industries and the men plough whereas the women weave, forming the legend of love."[①]

Due to the relatively abundant land resources, the agriculture in northern Zhejiang had much resource accumulation, and was developed into the commune- and brigade-run enterprises and the later township collective enterprises. In the beginning of the reform and opening-up, compared with individual economies like stone carving, bamboo weaving, cotton fluffing, bucket hooping, sewing, hairdressing, cooking, hardware selling, shoe repairing and sugar or sundry goods selling, entering collective enterprises, after all, could bring a more stable income and fewer uncertainties and risks. For example, according to the survey conducted by Cao Jinqing et al., there were artisans in the villages in northern Zhejiang, "but their work was harder, especially for those bamboo carpenters working from home, who have long working hours. Masons workedd outdoors and had high labor intensity. There had been many apprentices learning mud, wood, or bamboo crafts, but after the mid-1980s, they moved to country enterprises. One of the reasons for this was that becoming bamboo-making craftsmen,

---

① Fei, X. Small commodities, big market [M] //He, F. *Overview of Zhejiang.* Hangzhou: Zhejiang People's Publishing House, 2003.

masons or carpenters was too bitter and too tiring."[①] On the other hand, like the southern Suzhou people, due to the relatively abundant land resources, there is no urgency for the northern Zhejiang people to leave the land. At the beginning of the reform and opening-up, they entered the township collective enterprises and engaged in industrial activities, as a complement to agricultural activities and in large part to help out with the family expenses. This was preferred by the people in many parts of southern Zhejiang who sought to first solve the food problem. Of course, with the rapid development of rural collective enterprises later on, in some developed areas in northern Zhejiang, the focus of many household economies gradually transferred to the rural collective industry and commerce, while agriculture as the original main industry has been pushed to the veritable "sideline." To a certain extent, the materials of investigations of Chenjiachang Village and Y Town conducted by Cao Jinqing et al. can serve as an example of the above-mentioned phenomena. According to the statistics in 1988, as many as 58 people entered the collective enterprises and private enterprises of village or town level among the total of 167 people of 49 households in Chenjiachang Village. Among the 58 people, there were 51 people working in various companies within Y Town, the remaining seven were located in the neighboring town, and most of them lived in Chenjiachang Village to grow rice and engage in sericulture. In this sense, it can be said that neither did they leave their homes (the administrative village), nor did they leave their lands (the contracted field). This is also the case with Y Town. According to the statistics of the Y Town government in 1986, a total of 2,045 staff worked in township collective enterprises, 2,233 people in village collective enterprises, with 4,278 people altogether. The town had a population of 16,423 people. Among them the male and female labor force accounted for over half of the population, that is, about half of the labor force had

---

① Cao, J., Zhang, L. & Chen, Z. *Social and Cultural Changes of the Villages in Contemporary Northern Zhejiang* [M]. Shanghai: Shanghai Far East Publishers, 2001: 248.

entered into all kinds of rural collective enterprises.[①] Employment in collective enterprises does not generally mean that people in northern Zhejiang had completely abandoned agriculture. In most cases, while some members of a family work outside agriculture, the other family members still do the farming. And even the members who engaged in the industries would still help do the farming during the busy seasons. These semi-industrial and semi-agricultural families still lived in the village where their census had been registered, and are still doing farming work for a living to varying degrees.

These could clearly show that compared with farmers in southern Zhejiang, northern Zhejiang farmers have a relatively stronger notion of dependence on land and awareness of a homebody. It should be noted that this trait is very similar to the farmers in southern Suzhou, which could be verified by the investigation on Zhouzhuang in northern Suzhou and the "Zhejiang Village" in Beijing in the mid-1990s conducted by Zhou Xiaohong.

According to Zhou, "in the 1960s and 1970s in Zhouzhuang or even the whole southern Jiangsu, despite the restoration of private plots for farmers and some sideline production, farmers were still effectively controlled in terms of food production on the collective land (which to a certain extent is thanks to the relative abundance of land). Moreover, with a certain agricultural commodity rate and accumulating ability, the commune economy showed a further development (which is the starting basis for the development of township enterprise since the 1970s)."[②] According to the raw data from the investigation, Zhouzhuang farmers and "Zhejiang villagers" differed in their career choices. Up to 43.6% of

---

① Cao, J., Zhang, L. & Chen, Z. *Social and Cultural Changes of the Villages in Contemporary Northern Zhejiang* [M]. Shanghai: Shanghai Far East Publishers, 2001: 92.

② Zhou, X. *Tradition and Change: The Social Psychology of Peasants in Zhejiang and Jiangsu and Its Evolution since Modern Times* [M]. Beijing: SDX Joint Publishing Company, 1998: 197.

the "Zhejiang villagers" chosed to do business whereas only 8.5% chosed
to enter township enterprises. Although as high as 27.1% of Zhouzhuang
people chose to do businesses, as high as 19.5% chose to enter township
enterprises while 14.4% chose to continue farming. From the raw data, as
many as 16.1% and 34.8% of the "Zhejiang villagers" were very willing
or willing to develop in places with poor conditions and high risk, but
rich in opportunities and money, amounting to more than half of the total
population, whereas only 6.2% and 22.3% in Zhouzhuang made these
two choices, respectively, accounting for only about half of the percentage
of the "Zhejiang villagers." Zhou Xiaohong believed that this difference
could be explained by many factors. The main reason lied in the better
natural and geographic conditions enjoyed by Zhouzhuang people than
by the "Zhejiang villagers," which made the Zhouzhuang people's
attachment to their home and land higher than the latter. Moreover,
precisely because the "Zhejiang villagers" felt greater pressure to survive
at home and because they had to go to other places, they had a much
higher sense of flow and risk awareness than the Zhouzhuang people.[1]

The above shows that, in sharp contrast to northern Zhejiang and
southern Jiangsu, the agriculture accumulation in southern Zhejiang
was minimal and its collective economy was also very weak as
the contradiction between people and land was more intense. The
southern Zhejiang people therefore cannot rely more on commune-
and brigade-run enterprises or collective enterprises, they can only
rely on themselves through entrepreneurship. In other words, at the
beginning of the reform and opening-up, people in northern Zhejiang
generally relied on collective entrepreneurship while people in southern
Zhejiang generally relied on their own by entrepreneurship. Compared
with the former, people in the latter area were more pressured to
survive but also had far more intense spirit of entrepreneurship. This

---

[1]   Zhou, X. *Tradition and Change: The Social Psychology of Peasants in
Zhejiang and Jiangsu and Its Evolution since Modern Times* [M]. Beijing: SDX
Joint Publishing Company, 1998: 272.

could be fully confirmed by the differences in development seen with different ownership enterprises in these two places during the reform and opening-up. For example, in 1990 in Jiaxing in northern Zhejiang, among industrial enterprises above the town level, the private enterprises accounted for 9.44% of the total enterprises, the collective enterprises 89.37% (where the number of township enterprises accounted for 65.5% of the number of collective enterprises) whereas other companies (including joint ventures, self-employed) accounted for only 1.19% of the total. In the same year, the output value of the rural and urban private sectors accounted for only 4.91% of the industrial output value in Jiaxing.[①] In 1998, 1,362 of industrial enterprises in Jiaxing had an output of more than five million yuan, 130 of which were from the private sector, less than one-tenth of the total.[②] Their output only accounted for 4.43% of the overall output value of the enterprises which had over five million output in that city.[③] In sharp contrast, Wenzhou in southern Zhejiang already had 133,000 small family businesses in the mid-1980s.[④] In the late 1990s, for the total industrial output value of Wenzhou, the public-owned enterprises (state-owned & collective) contributed only about 15% (the state-owned enterprises accounting for less than 4%), whereas the non-state-owned industries (privately-owned, stock cooperative enterprises, etc.) contributed as high as 85%.[⑤] Huang Zongzhi believed that in general, the self-employed economy prevails easily in poor areas, which was mainly due to the financial constraints of the township government. The

---

① *Annals of Jiaxing City* [M]. Beijing: China Books Publishing House, 1997: 136.

② *Jiaxing Statistical Yearbook of 1999* [M]. Beijing: China Statistics Press, 1999: 136.

③ Ibid. 140.

④ Guo, Y. Comparison and assessment on the industrialization models of countries and towns in China [J]. *Zhejiang Academic Journal*, 1987(4).

⑤ Shi, J. et al. *Institutional Change and Economic Development: A Study of Wenzhou Pattern* [M]. Rev. ed. Hangzhou: Zhejiang People's Publishing House, 2004: 48.

towns with substantially developed industries have gained significant revenue from profits generated from the affiliated companies. In such towns, the governments' public service expenditures could only spend a small portion of the total income while the majority would be invested in other industries, which in turn created more income and investment. However, "poor towns with industry lagging behind had low income and could sometimes not even afford the necessary public service expenditures. Some of these towns would in turn implement harsh fiscal policies to its subsidiary enterprises, forcing some enterprises into debt to borrow money to pay for money acquired by the higher administration, resulting in a vicious cycle of poverty. It was in these backward regions that the private enterprises with less investment could thrive better than the collective enterprises."[1] It can be said that Huang's analysis was quite reasonable. However, a more thorough explanation of why the private economy would become prevalent more easily in poor areas should also consider the significant factor of the relationship between people and land and its impact on the human spirit. Although the condition of people and land and its impact on people's spirit is not the only reason for the aforementioned phenomenon, it is at least one of the important factors.

On the other hand, relying on the land itself can hardly solve even the most basic food and clothing problems for the southern Zhejiang people, so they must abandon their lands or leave their homes to survive. In fact, because the relationship between human and land has been highly stressful in southern Zhejiang, people there have long been used to going out to make a living, therefore the outflow population often accounts for a considerable proportion. For example, according to Customs, the 6th volume of *Annals of Yongkang County,* "The farmers in our county worked in four seasons without rest, lacking time for pleasure. There was no more land, and with the ridges on earth, the

---

[1]   Huang, Z. *Small Peasant Families and Rural Development in the Yangtze Delta, 1350–1988* [M]. Beijing: Zhonghua Book Company, 2000: 263.

grains gained are limited. A little sloth will end up having nothing to eat. Although the wealthy seldom save for themselves and do their best to offer food, trade their extra fields with the poor and let them cultivate the land, half of their rent is used for taxes, the poor lease the farming fields from the wealthy, and feed themselves on half of their rented land. Therefore, supposedly, both the rich and the poor have no more power." The tense relationship between human and land must have been a significant reason for Yongkang to become the "homeland for a hundred kinds of jobs." Since the beginning of the Song Dynasty, people such as coppersmiths, blacksmiths and tinsmiths from Yongkang have already traveled extensively, which has hence become a tradition and has led to a widespread saying that "Hardware craftsmen walk everywhere, and all counties in the nation could not live without the ones from Yongkang." Dongyang County, which also belongs to Jinhua like Yongkang County, also had a quite intense man-land relationship; therefore, many craftsmen sold their skills in alien lands. From 1933 to 1934, as many as 90,000 people went out to make a living, most of them were carpenters, bamboo crafts makers, tailors, and masons. Their remittances to the county amounted to as much as three million yuan.[1] According to the *Annals of Wenzhou* during the period of Emperor Wanli in the Ming Dynasty, in Wenzhou, "the thin land could not rear the people," "people survived through their extensive labor work" and "they could use the little money earned to do their businesses." The *Annals of Wenzhou* in the period of Emperor Qianlong also said that because of the "thin land," many people were pushed to the sidelines or went out to make a living. In Pingyang, "the social vogue is much worse than in western Zhejiang. Once they graduate, the scholars would stop reading and start to learn businesses." "No scholars are ambitious. Once they want to go out to play, they would put away their books and start to earn money."[2]

---

[1] Bao, W. *Studies on Zhejiang Regional History* [M]. Hangzhou: Hangzhou Publishing Group, 2003: 201.

[2] Fu, Z. *County Annals of Pingyang—The Annal of Climatography* [M]. 1926.

Northern Zhejiang's situation was in stark contrast to that of southern Jiangsu. The survey of Kaixiangong Village on the southeast coast of Taihu Lake conducted by Fei Xiaotong in 1936 could help illustrate the problem to some extent. The total area of Kaixiangong Village was 2.04 million square meters, of which the agricultural land accounted for 90%. If 1.84 million square meters of farmland is allocated to 274 households, it means that every household can only get about 6,707 square meters of farmland. In normal years, 0.009 bushels of rice can be produced per square meter. A male, a female, and a children's consumption in a year amounts to 33 bushels. In other words, in order to get enough food, each family has to own 3,666.7 square meters of land. At that time, even if all the land was used for food production, a family could only produce about 60 bushels of rice. Fei Xiaotong therefore concluded that: "Calculating with four people as a household unit, after meeting the food needed to supply the average family, the area of land that each family owned could barely pay for other necessities roughly equivalent to the value of food. Therefore, we can see that in this village where every household has four people on average, the population pressure on land is quite heavy."[①] Although Kaixiangong Village in southern Suzhou is faced with a very heavy population pressure, this pressure is much lighter when compared with villages of southern Zhejiang in the same period. This is because land in the former area could still meet the food needs of the average family and could barely pay for other necessities with a value roughly equivalent to the food supplied, the latter's land area, however, could not even meet the basic human needs for food and clothing. Therefore, a few farmers in Kaixiangong Village also left their homes to make a living, but the number was not that significant. Although cottage craft as a parergon has long been a common practice to earn a living for the farmers in Kaixiangong Village, and the sericulture industry has even become a second income source for them, their traditional cottage craft was an endogenous demand, which was generated from

---

① Fei, X. *The Life and Change of Peasant in Jiangcun Village* [M]. Lanzhou: Dunhuang Literature & Art Publishing House, 1997: 33.

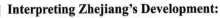
the natural condition of large population with limited land. This industry could supplement their shortage of income from agriculture and has thus become a part of the farmers' production. Therefore, unlike the traditional handicraft industry of southern Zhejiang which arose to fully meet their people's consumption needs, the cottage industry in Kaixiangong Village was for income, rather than just for self-consumption. However, such cottage industry, which was not for people's own consumption, was actually a paragon for farmers and enabled the usage and exploitation of the surplus labor time of farmers. Its meaning lies in the increase of farmers' income rather than the change of their occupation.

Besides, according to a comparative study of Hongqiao in southern Zhejiang and Zhouzhuang in southern Jiangsu, during the Republic of China, "because Zhouzhuang had relatively better farming conditions, the ratio of farmers going out to work was not big." However, due to the tension between people and land, "the ratio of farmers leaving Hongqiao was higher than that of Zhouzhuang, which had a looser relationship between people and land. This phenomenon was particularly evident during the famine."[1] For example, in 1929 when the famine struck Hongqiao, "since January, the people fleeing to other provinces or counties met each other on the road. The number was difficult to investigate at that time; we could not make sure how many millions there were. It was common for the remaining people to eat things such as leaves of sweet potatoes or crab shells; it could also be heard that people committed suicide by taking drugs or jumping into rivers."[2] Due to the lack of land, by 1949, more than half the farmers in Hongqiao had small businesses or small industries on the side. Although most of the vendors had little investment and gained less profits, they had quite a keen business sense. The Hongqiao phenomenon can be

---

① Zhou, X. *Tradition and Change: The Social Psychology of Peasants in Zhejiang and Jiangsu and Its Evolution since Modern Times* [M]. Beijing: SDX Joint Publishing Company, 1998: 120-121.

② Recent News on Famine [N]. *Yueqing Messenger*, 1929-10-29(69).

seen as a microcosm of Zhejiang, especially in Wenzhou, Taizhou, Jinhua and other places in southern Zhejiang.

After 1949, due to the rapid population expansion, coupled with the production inefficiencies of the people's communes, the contradiction between human beings and land in Zhejiang became more prominent. Douglas North said that: an efficient organization was a key factor in economic growth, and reasons for the rise of the Western world lied in the development of an effective economic organization. "Efficient organizations need to make institutional arrangements and establish ownership to create a stimulus so that personal efforts could become activities where a private rate of return could be close to the social rate of return."[1] The private rate of return getting closer to the social rate of return is also a process for property ownership rights in society that is continuously improving. Effective ownership includes all laws, regulations, practices, and rules that help each person to determine how to possess, use or transfer rights produced by the wealth. If a system of social ownership clearly defines everyone's exclusive rights and provides effective protection for such exclusive rights, the society would be full of "innovative spirit," and the economic growth could be promoted. However, the People's Commune is a social-economic system with unclarified stipulations on individual rights. Under the People's Commune System, it was easy to produce ill-defined property rights as it was difficult to "personify" the owner, or the cost "personify" the owner was too high, or the monitoring costs for the owner to the operator was too high. This would result in the "free rider" phenomenon in the use of resources, which could be shown as using resources or the products of others' for free, even transferring the expenses or costs of one's own economic activities to the groups whose property rights were ill-defined. The field surveys on Chenjiachang Village in northern Zhejiang conducted by Cao Jinqing and others shows that during the People's Commune period, the farmers' attitudes toward collective land and private plots stood in stark

---

[1]   North, D. C. & Thomas, R. *The Rise of the Western World* [M]. Trans. Li, Y. & Cai, L. Beijing: Huaxia Publishing House, 1999: 5.

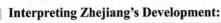

contrast. The collective land was everybody's land; everybody's land was not my own land—this was often a farmer's reasoning. Therefore, farmers' behavior could be typically expressed as dragging along at a snail's pace on the collective land, whereas those with individual plots were working like Wu Song fighting a tiger. As a rule, fertilizers and pig manures used by those with collective land, whereas private plots usd only people's manure. However, before the pig manures were brought out of the swinery, villagers would often fertilize them on their private plots first, and these fertilizers would also be stolen from their home for use on private plots. Some private plots and collective land were separated by only a ditch or a dike, but these channels would always move toward the collective land. When private plots were re-measured every time due to the re-division, you could always find that some people's private plots had spread over the stipulated area. The different attitudes of members of the people's commune toward collective land and private plots could be seen from the different outputs from the same area of different types of land. This could be roughly seen from the household income details of a member Mr. Zhu in 1972. There were seven people in Zhu's family. They had a small private plot of 233.3 square meters, planted with cabbages, grapes, pumpkins, sweet potatoes and seeds in sheds. They were sold for 226.79 yuan except for those used for household demands. The total revenue for Zhu obtained from the collective land that year was 1,027.66 yuan (including 266.70 yuan in cash and the rest in-kind). Thus, private plots, which accounted for only 5% of the per capita arable land, provided 22% of the income of the collective land, which accounted for 95% of the per capita arable land. If calculated in cash, the income from private plots was almost similar to that of the collective land.[①] Since in the 1960s and 1970s, the entire rural Zhejiang has had no exceptions to the implementation of the People's Commune System, the above phenomenon in Chenjiachang Village in northern Zhejiang could be seen as a microcosm of the whole Zhejiang. Therefore,

---

① Cao, J., Zhang, L. & Chen, Z. *Social and Cultural Changes of the Villages in Contemporary Northern Zhejiang* [M]. Shanghai: Shanghai Far East Publishers, 2001: 65-66.

the rapid population growth, together with the production inefficiencies of the People's Communes, produced a worsening effect for Zhejiang which already had a sharp contradiction between people and land. In this case, the wish of self-employment became more intense for people in Zhejiang.

Under the high pressure brought by the ultra-leftist policy as well as the contradiction between people and land, it seemed impossible to eradicate those who went out for fluffing cotton, doing woodwork, becoming goldsmith, selling sugars or handicrafts, or vendor activities conducted by those who set up their booths everywhere and sold their products along the roads. For example, before the reform and opening-up, Yiwu had over 1,100 square kilometers with a population of 630,000 and thus the per capita arable land area was 373.3 square meters. With the barren land, farmers' per capita annual income distribution has been around 60 yuan in the 1960s and 1970s. Yiwu was thus a typical "poor county." In the 1970s, the total agricultural labor force in Yiwu County was more than 200,000, while the arable land only accounted for 253.3 million square meters. Even with some of the most backward production tools, there were still hundreds of thousands of surplus laborers. For this reason, small underground wholesale markets have already emerged in the regular markets in Yiwu. During every market day, many professional vendors for small commodities appeared at the peddler's market in Niansanli Town. Later, dozens of vendors who only sell small commodities appeared in Xianqian Street in the downtown area of Choucheng Town. They used bamboo baskets, wicker baskets, travel bags or plastic sheeting as tools to set stands anywhere and peddled their wares on the streets. They set stands in the morning and shut the shops at noon.[1] At that time, specializing in trading small articles of daily use was very dangerous, therefore, the Yiwu traders had to maintain high vigilance and be equipped with a simple, easy

---

[1]   Zhang, W. & Zhu, H. *A Research on the Small Commodities Market in Yiwu—The Practice of Socialist Market Economy in Yiwu* [M]. Beijing: Qunyan Press, 1993: 34.

outfit to escape. This phenomenon was not limited to Yiwu, but had existed in many places in Zhejiang. To make a living, farmers in many parts of Zhejiang even carved unofficial seals, forged letters of introduction to go out and engage in the individual economy. A large number of decisions issued by the Yueqing County authorities in the 1960s and 1970s could still be found in the file room in Hongqiao Town of Wenzhou. Those who were dealt with were people who had resold food stamps, gold, and silver, many of them were even Party members, grassroots cadres and demobilized soldiers.[1]

As already stated earlier in this book, despite the fact that Zhejiang people had already begun to develop a strong will for an independent living and an urge to start their own businesses in as early as the planned economy period, this impulse has suffered serious repression under the socio-cultural context of the planned economy. In previous ideological and cultural movements, the kind of self-employment and entrepreneurship impulse displayed by Zhejiang people were often regarded as synonymous of expressions such as "taking the capitalist road," "individualistic," "selfish," "advancing their interests at the expense of others" and "people with selfish considerations." Slogans of "cutting the tail of capitalism," "criticizing the moment the flash of selfish considerations appears," "getting rid of bourgeois' idea of law" and the repudiation of the so-called thoughts of "playing the market," "material incentives," "money in command," and "pursuit of personal interests" rose one after another, becoming a big attraction in the previous ideological and cultural movements. Under this historical condition, the Zhejiang people's willingness to be entrepreneurs may only become a lurking undercurrent. Only under the institutional, policy and socio-cultural environments since the reform and opening-up could entrepreneurship form in the brim place of the planned economy

---

① Zhou, X. *Tradition and Change: The Social Psychology of Peasants in Zhejiang and Jiangsu and Its Evolution since Modern Times* [M]. Beijing: SDX Joint Publishing Company, 1998: 196.

and under the pressure of limited land with numerous population, obtain affirmative moral assessment and therefore be fully released and become part of the spiritual impetus for the economic and social development of Zhejiang.

It was because of the marginal position of the planned economy and the limited land with numerous people that people in Zhejiang had faced tremendous pressure to survive. Therefore, people can imagine how Zhejiang will be when the policy loosens. Since the reform and opening-up, the utilization of the "historical tradition" and "spiritual resources" of Zhejiang people—self-employment and self-innovation as well as entrepreneurship—has been the reason for the formation of "One Village, One Product" and "One Region, One Industry" in Zhejiang, the rapid development of the individual and private economy, the innovation of the system of stock cooperative enterprises, the cultivation of various specialized markets, the path of the self-financing construction of towns (Longgang Town, "the First City for farmers in China," is a typical representative of the road), the practice of agricultural scale operation, the exploration of establishing universities through the stock-holding system (such as Wenzhou University) via the self-balancing captial transformation of the old city, the "four selves" road for building transportation—"self-loan, self-construction, self-charge and self-pay," and the "five selves" policy in water conservancy construction (with extra "self-management" compared to the previous "four selves") as well as the spontaneously emerging democratic deliberation meetings in the towns and villages in Zhejiang, such as in Taizhou. Zhejiang's economy is regionally diversified. For example, Ningbo is famous for clothing, Wenzhou for leather shoes, Shaoxing for synthetic fabrics, Haining for leather clothes, Yiwu for smallware, Yongkang hardware, Yueqing low-voltage apparatus, Dongyang magnetic materials, Huangyan for fine chemicals, Qingyuan for mushrooms, Xinchang for tea and pharmaceutical, and Anji is famous for bamboo products. The list of characteristic regional economies could be longer. It is particularly worth mentioning that

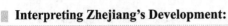

the "Zero Resource Economy" phenomenon has been shown in many parts of Zhejiang since the reform and opening-up. The so-called "Zero Resource Economy" refers to the regional economic development that does not rely on local natural resources, but follows the economic development mode in which both raw materials and the sales market are in the outer areas. For example, being located in the plains, there is neither native forest nor timber production in Jiashan County, yet Jiashan is the country's largest plywood production base. Their plywood accounted for one-third of the domestic market share. Yuyao does not produce the raw material for plastic, but it is the largest distribution center for plastic raw materials in southern China. At present, Zhejiang has more than 300 characteristic industry groups, which conduct a "Zero Resource Economy" that relies on no natural resource.[1] If this distinctive regional economy and the formation of the "Zero Economic Resources" phenomenon deviate from the willingness to be self-employed, self-innovating entrepreneurs, which sprouted from being at the edges of the planned economy and the scenario of little land with a vast population, the results would be unthinkable.

---

[1] Sheng, S. & Zheng, Y. *"Zhejiang Phenomenon"—Industrial Cluster and Regional Economic Development* [M]. Beijing: Tsinghua University Press, 2004: 59.

Chapter 2

The Cultural Tradition of "Striving for Practical Results" and the Zhejiang's Economic and Social Development

The contemporary Zhejiang cultural spirit features the "pursuit of practical results." Since the reform and opening-up, many practical economic reforms in Zhejiang have been implemented on the basis of the unchanging formal rules, "names" and "forms" of the planning system. Many people first took concrete actions that conflicted with the formal rules of planned economy, which thereby changed the actual code of conduct, created various new economic relationships and provided people with opportunities to earn profits. By all appearances, this cultural spirit of "striving for practical results" has an inner connection with the traditional Zhejiang cultural spirit. Throughout the history of Zhejiang Province, the cultural spirit of striving for practical results and stressing utility are summarized and epurated by the Eastern Zhejiang Practical Schools and have infiltrated the minds of Zhejiang civil society widely. With the passing of time, the cultural spirit of striving for practical results and stressing utility has taken root in civil society firmly and continuously. This spirit constituted the cultural psychology and "gene" of contemporary Zhejiang people and has had quite a positive effect on the institutional innovation and economic and social development of contemporary Zhejiang Province. In what aspects do Zhejiang people show the cultural spirit of "striving for practical results?" How do Zhejiang people practice their cultural spirit? These are questions worthy of discussion.

2.1　The Spirit of "Striving for Practical Results" and the Contemporary Phenomena of Zhejiang Economic Society

2.1.1　The Spirit of "Striving for Practical Results" under the Planned Economy

In *The Protestant Ethic and the Spirit of Capitalism*, Max Weber pointed out that in the process of secularization, the Protestant ethic not only created the conditions of capitalism, that was, the never-ending businessmen and diligent workers, but also gave birth to the capitalist spirit, namely the Franklin's capitalist spirit, which meaned that people made profits but didn't enjoy life as they were motivated by money-making. According to Weber, the rationality of modern economic organization derived from the rationality of the Protestant calculation formula. "If one behaves based on purpose, means and consequence, and considers reasonably between means and purpose, purpose and consequence, and the ultimately various possible ends, then, his behavior is objective rational, that is, neither emotional nor traditional."[1] Weber believed that it was the rationality of the Protestant calculation formula that forged the spirit of capitalism to a great extent. "Under any circumstances, the Puritan world outlook is conducive to the development of a rational bourgeois economic life. It is the most important and, above all, the only consistent one in the development of this life. It fostered the modern economic man."[2] The landmark meaning of "refining the designs of appropriate means to achieve some specific practical purposes systematically" is "planning."[3] The Puritans and the merchants are identical in this regard.

---

① Weber, M. *The Protestant Ethic and the Spirit of Capitalism* [M]. Trans. Yu, X., Chen, W. et al. Beijing: SDX Joint Publishing Company, 1987: 163.
② Ibid. 136.
③ Weber, M. *Confucianism and Taoism* [M]. Trans. Wang, R. Beijing: The Commercial Press, 1997: 32.

In Protestantism, untiring labor is the only means of obtaining the grace of God and the obligation to God, which also adds to the glory of God, cools the greed of the flesh and at the same time expresses the rebirth and sincere faith of the Puritans. As a vocation of labor, once it is willingly practiced by a diligent believer, it is bound to accumulate wealth. However, if it is not a desire for greed and not for the purpose of wealth itself or the consumption in Hedonism, but only a faithful fulfillment to the vocation, then such wealth is justified and necessary. This wealth is also a signal of God's blessing on him. Therefore, the initial motivation for the formation of Protestant ethics is for religious purposes. However, after the purely religious passion, pragmatic, calm and rational economic men replaced those ardent pilgrims. "At this time, the fervor to seek the Kingdom of Heaven begins to gradually change into a calm economic morality. The root of religion slowly dies and gives way to secular utilitarianism." In this way, "the peculiar consequence of Western internal asceticism is the rational materialization and socialization of social relations." In Weber's opinion, the rationalization of the capitalist organization derived from the Protestant ethic is a starting point of modernization, as well as the uniqueness of the West. Weber's so-called rational calculative rational spirit, which is regarded as the starting point of Western modernization, can be said in a sense that it is a pragmatic and cultural spirit of efficiency moving from the insubstantial Kingdom of Heaven to the down-to-earth reality. In other words, the rationality of calculating costs and benefits, means and ends is applied as a method of enhancing efficiency.

It is obviously not necessarily appropriate to make a simple analogy of Zhejiang's regional cultural spirit of "striving for practical results" with the rational spirit and pragmatism of European Protestant ethic. However, it is certain that Zhejiang people also have a pragmatic and rational group character, which has imposed a profound imprint on Zhejiang's economic and social development. In the ultra-left social and cultural atmosphere of "asking for the grass of socialism rather than the sprout of capitalism" during the planned economy period, quite a lot of Zhejiang people treated or even broke the constraints of ultra-leftist line, principles, and policies in a pragmatic, rational and flexible attitude. Activities including fixing farm output quotas for each household and engaging in trade always continued despite repeated prohibition and were seen by many local people as an effective way to solve the subsistence problem and even to get rid of poverty and become better off. Under the tight control of planned economy and the overflow of left-wing ideology, the market mechanism still played a persisting role in the gap and fought against the control of planned economy.

In May 1956, in order to improve the production efficiency of agriculture, after the approval of the Director of the Agriculture and Industry Department of CPC Wenzhou Committee, the Yongjia County Committee decided to conduct a trial of the production responsibility system, which was later renamed as the "system of fixed output to household," in Xiongxi Village, Liaoyuan Commune in a fairly pragmatic spirit according to the productivity back then. In 1957, there were 255 cooperatives in Yongjia County with more than 178,000 thousand families that carried out the system, accounting for about 15% of the farmers in the Wenzhou area which had more than 1,000 cooperatives. After that, the system of fixed output to household in Yongjia and even the Wenzhou area was quickly criticized and "corrected." However, in 1961, this system reappeared in some areas in Zhejiang Province under the context of the system being advocated by the ultra-left political forces as a conflict between socialism and capitalism. By mid-June, among 1,880 production brigades and 9,498 production teams throughout Shengxian County, there were 357 brigades and 1,468 teams that carried out this system, accounting for 19% and 15.5% of the total number respectively. By November, among 49 communes, 832 brigades and 4,881 teams in Xinchang County, 46 communes, 472 brigades, and 2,735 teams carried out this system, accounting for 93.8%, 57% and 55% of the total number respectively.[1] Soon after, the system of fixed output to household was once again prohibited and "rectified." However, such "rectification" violated the wishes of the people and lowered the efficiency of agricultural production. Therefore, it was boycotted by "pragmatic" people. In some places, in order to cope with the superiors, the system of fixed output to household was applied under the disguise of collective labor. Since then, although the system was restrained for having evolved into a matter concerning political line struggles, it continued to expand gradually in rural areas such as Xinchang and Shengxian. By May 1962, in Xinchang County alone, 67.6% of the production brigades and 70% of the production teams either carried out fixed farm output quotas for each household or parceled out land to individual households. In the province, production teams which practiced the system of fixed output to household with most of the land or all the land accounted for about 2% to 3% of the total production teams.[2] While the Tenth Plenary Session of the Eighth CPC Central Committee held in September 1962 reiterated the class struggle, it criticized the system of fixed output to household as the "single-handed working style" of capitalism and strictly forbade it. Zhejiang certainly could not escape from this. From 1975 to 1976, the ultra-left political forces preached on a larger scale that "the People's Commune System has a strong vitality. However, a small number of landlords, rich peasants, counter revolutionary, bad elements and the rights have not stopped sabotage activities. The remnants of small-scale production still exist. Some peasants still remain the habit of small-scale production to varying degrees. The spontaneous forces of capitalism have also often been on the rise in some rural areas. The

---

[1] CPC Zhejiang Provincial Party History Lab & Contemporary Zhejiang Institute. *Brief History of Contemporary Zhejiang 1949–1998* [M]. Beijing: Contemporary China Publishing House, 2000: 161,198.
[2]   Ibid. 200-201.

struggle between socialism and capitalism is still fierce."[①] However, it is interesting to notice that under such hostile political atmosphere, the cultural spirit of "striving for practical results" of Zhejiang people has emerged once again. For example, in 1975 and 1976, 77% of the production teams in Yongjia County of Wenzhou City realized the system of fixed output to household. In the second National Agricultural Science Conference held in the winter of 1976, Yongjia County was criticized violently for being the county in Zhejiang Province that "practiced single production in separate fields and did the most serious damage to the collective economy."[②]

2.1.2 The Spirit of "Striving for Practical Results" Since the Reform and Opening-up

Since the reform and opening-up, under the background of the gradual loosening of national policies, the cultural spirit of "striving for practical results" has been further embodied in Zhejiang Province, which has enabled Zhejiang people to deal with the original institutional arrangement with a more daring, pragmatic, rational and flexible attitude. In the process of gradual reformation from a planned economy to a market economy, Zhejiang's economic and social development has clearly displayed characteristics of Hayek's so-called "extended order." During the formation of the "extended order," the spirit of "striving for practical results" played a lubricating role. According to Hayek, the market order is formed during the course of competition and exchange, and the market order can only be proven in the advent of the market order. First of all, market competition is a process of groping and discovering, in which the remuneration that each individual receives does not depend on whether his purpose is good or bad, but on the value of his performance to others. In this way, one learns how to work with others in practice and how to improve his own welfare

---

① Chi, H. Study the theory of the dictatorship of the proletariat carefully [J]. *Hongqi*, 1975(2).

② *Wenzhou Chronicles* [M]. Beijing: Zhonghua Book Company, 1998: 1041.

in error. Secondly, only by participating in the market exchange and competition will people find the information they need to achieve their goals. Besides, the price system will automatically deliver that information in the most efficient way, which will dramatically reduce the amount of information everyone needs. Thirdly, market competition is not controlled entirely by "contingency" but represents the order and complexity, which can be seen as an individual learning process. Through the market exchange process, people not only pass on what they consider to be "good" ideas, but also share some common ethics, values, and laws. In this learning method, the abstract general rules of conduct are formed, inherited and evolved to form the "extended order." The process of forming the expanded natural order is a process in which the parties continue to participate and compete for interests. Through repeated competitions and bargaining, the final system will generally achieve institutional equilibrium.

Practice shows that the gradual reform process in Zhejiang is, in fact, the formation of Zhejiang's "extended order." The gradual reform process or the formation of the "extended order" is neither to devise an "economic" system in advance by reason, nor to destroy the old and establish the new in one step, but a process of natural evolution. During this process, some new institutional arrangements are derived at the edge of the old system and gradually reduce the space of the old system through continuous expansion, which promotes the change of the old system, and then achieve the innovation of the entire economic and social system. At the same time of the economic system reform, the political system remains relatively stable, so as to create a relatively stable social environment for the further adjustment of the system and maintain strong government forces to regulate the reform. Since the reform and opening-up, the reason why the gradual innovation system reform in Zhejiang has been able to succeed and the "extended order" has been gradually formed is because they have benefited largely from the application of the cultural tradition of "striving for practical results." This pragmatic cultural tradition is conducive to the growth of the new rules under the old system, without necessarily breaking the old system first to open up the way for the growth of the new system. Since the reform and opening-up, many substantive reforms of Zhejiang's society and economy have been implemented under the planned system with no changes in the formal rules, "names" and "forms." Although the formal rules of the planned system still exist, many people first take actions that conflict with formal rules, change the actual behavior constraints and create new kinds of economic relations that allow people to capture profit opportunities.

The development and institutional innovation of Zhejiang's various ownership economies fully demonstrated the role of the "striving for practical results" cultural spirit. In the initial stage of the reform and opening-up when national policies began to loosen, although the individual and private economy made some progress, "leftist" thinking still had a great impact. Engaging in the individual, private and share economy meant that people not only had to face political risks, they also had to bear the accusation of "privatization" and the social discrimination that "individual operations were crooked." For example, during the campaign of cracking down on serious economic crimes in the early 1980s, eight people were sentenced among the former "eight kings" in Wenzhou, including the "junk king", "electromechanical king" and "directory king." Although those "eight kings" were rehabilitated and the individual, private and share economy re-emerged soon after, the nationwide controversy of "pertaining to socialism or capitalism" had never stopped. The resurgence of "leftist" thinking often triggered more arguments on the "Wenzhou Model." When the individual and private economy was still subject to discrimination, individual and private enterprises in many places (such as Wenzhou, Taizhou, Yongkang, Yiwu, and other places) registered under the name of "state-owned or collectively-owned enterprises" in a flexible way. When the joint-stock system, shareholding cooperation system and institutional innovations such as specialized markets and public works that started among the people were still subject to dispute, many places flexibly adopted the approach of "naming the enterprise after establishing one." When reform attempts had not been accepted, many places took the policy of "observing the development without drawing a conclusion." When privately-owned enterprises and joint-stock enterprises failed to get policy recognition and preferential policies, they chose to register the enterprise under the name of "collective" joint-stock cooperative enterprise, which was extensively adopted by private enterprises and joint-stock enterprises in the coastal areas of Zhejiang Province.

In the late 1970s, individual enterprises and private partnerships began to emerge in Yuhuan County, Taizhou Prefecture and rapidly developed in the first half of the 1980s. At that time, the national system allowed the private economy to exist, but only to the extent that it was supplemented to public ownership. Although the discriminatory system and policies on the private economy decreased, they were still widespread. During this time, the Yuhuan County government chose to take time to observe its development and neither stopped nor supported it. In a policy document of 1988, the Yuhuan County Commission stipulated that privately funded joint-stock enterprises were allowed to register under "collective" name while maintaining the nature of the shares internally if they voluntarily applied for it. However, no department or individual may use the "collective" name to transfer property. The affirmation of the "collective nature" of the joint-stock cooperative system by the government became an "amulet" to private, joint-stock and other enterprises that lacked the policy recognition and preferential policies. At that time, the Taizhou Prefectural Committee and Administrative Offices, which were also home to the superior of the Yuhuan County, took the same workaround. In 1987, the No. 242 document of the State Administration for Industry and Commerce denied the public-owned nature of the joint-stock cooperative economy, while Taizhou clarified the "public" nature of the joint-stock cooperative system in the document and allowed it to enjoy the preferential policies of the collective economy. In 1989, the Zhejiang Administration for Industry and Commerce and Zhejiang Tax Bureau jointly issued a document stating that joint-stock enterprises should not be named under "collective joint-stock cooperative enterprises" and stipulated that "rural collectives must occupy at least 50% of the fixed assets in every collective enterprise." Through flexible arrangement with several parties, the Taizhou Administrative Office successfully cut the collective proportion to 20%, so that most joint-stock cooperative enterprises could still run under the name of "collective enterprises" and enjoy the preferential policies. Under such circumstances, a large number of private enterprises, individual industrial and commercial households, and joint-stock cooperative enterprises in Taizhou registered under the name of "collective enterprises." In 1993, when the clarification of property rights became an urgent issue for the further development of enterprises, the government issued another document to remove those "collective" names, which helped more than 4,000 individuals, privately owned, village-run, and rural shareholding cooperative enterprises to resolve the problem of property rights.

In the early period of the reform and opening-up, the pattern of "household workshops using the brand of rural enterprises to do business" was invented by Wenzhou people, which fully reflected the spirit of "striving for practical results." In 1980, Gold Star Brigade Stationery Factory, a village-run enterprise with more than 40 people, in Cangnan County, Jinxiang Town decided to decentralize production under centralized management for it was not profitable. On the premise of insisting on the name of a collective factory externally, a unified factory name, bank account number, tax payment, commission, and management fee were carried out, while an independent financial accounting was implemented internally. This method of decentralized production under centralized management became the prototype of "household workshops using the brand of rural enterprises to do business." The mature form of this in Wenzhou means that under the conditions that the private economy is still under discrimination and the state policy still imposes strict control over privately engaged commodity operations, individuals or unions that have not acquired independent legal person status for various reasons are affiliated to collective or state-owned enterprises to engage in production and business activities. The specific practice is that after the consultation of the two parties, with the approval of collective or state-owned enterprises, they provide services to affiliated units and charge a management fee. The service can be concluded as "three substitutions and three borrowings," that is, to open unified invoice for affiliated units, set up accounts and do bookkeeping for affiliated units, collect national tax revenue for affiliated units and allow affiliated units to borrow the recommendation, blank contracts, and bank accounts.[①] This pragmatic method of letting "household workshops use the brand of rural enterprises to do business" not only allowed the individual and private economy to gain legitimacy, but also enabled them to avail themselves of the preferential treatment conditions of collectives and state-owned enterprises. Thus, this method was imitated widely in Wenzhou. According to a survey of 1,750 enterprises in Rui'an County, Wenzhou City in 1985, 926 private partnerships, private-shareholding or privately-owned enterprises were registered with collective brands, accounting for 52.9% of the total number.

In the business pattern of "decentralized production under centralized management," a covert norm corresponding to the open norms was formed in Wenzhou's economic realm, which was a vivid manifestation of Wenzhou people's spirit of "striving for practical results." The so-called open norms refer to those publicly announced norms by groups, organizations, and society, such as laws and regulations, ethics, technical norms and other various provisions of the express regulations, rules, systems. Covert norms refer to those tacit norms that the open norms neither prohibited nor advocated. In general, covert norms do not violate open norms and are not expressly permitted by public norms, so they are neither supplements nor violations of the

---

① Shi, J. et al. *Institutional Change and Economic Development: A Study of Wenzhou Pattern* [M]. Hangzhou: Zhejiang University Press, 2002: 364-365.

open norms. Covert norms are elusive, which means not open to the public, and this type of norm without public announcement and clear written form is beyond law, morality, rules, and regulations, etc. One of the salient features of it is that it grazes the edge of the open norms without violation. Those behaviors guided by covert norms do not violate the law, morality, rules and regulations. In fact, the pattern of "decentralized production under centralized management" was a kind of covert norm, which did not violate the open norms of collectives and state-owned enterprises. The enterprises that provided the services of "decentralized production under centralized management" grazed the edge of the open norms of collective and state-owned enterprises. Although they were registered under a collective brand, they were actually private partnerships, share-holding or private enterprises. At the same time, they did not violate the open norms of collective and state-owned enterprises for although they were actually private partnerships, shareholding or private enterprises, they still belonged to collective and state-owned enterprises nominally.

Under certain conditions, covert norms can be transformed into open norms. If open norms approve and institutionalize actions under the guidance of covert norms, covert norms can turn into open norms. The "pragmatic" spirit and actions embodied in Wenzhou's non-governmental ownership system such as "decentralized production under centralized management" actually obtained the government's acquiescence, encouragement and support, which was an extremely important condition for the transformation of covert norms into open norms. In line with the pragmatic approach of Wenzhou's private sectors grazing the edge of collective and state-owned enterprises, all levels of Wenzhou government clearly staged a pragmatic attitude in formulating policies. For example, the Interim Provisions on Several Issues Concerning Rural Stock Cooperative Enterprises in 1987 and the Report on Certain Policy Issues Concerning Several Issues Concerning Rural Stock Cooperative Enterprises in 1990, which were promulgated by Wenzhou government, not only affirmed the collective nature of the joint-stock cooperative enterprises but also granted concessions in taxes, loans, land use and production licenses on a collective basis. Under such circumstances, a large number of privately-owned enterprises and individual industrial and commercial households registered under the name of joint-stock cooperative enterprises. Among the 435 shareholding cooperative enterprises that passed the formal acceptance tests in 1990, the total number of employees was 28,563, of which only 5,003 were shareholders, accounting for 17.5% of the total number. Even with 5,357 dependents of the shareholders who worked as employees, the proportion was only 36.3%, while 17,858 were non-shareholder employees enrolled in the society, accounting for 63.7%. According to a survey of 90 joint-stock cooperative enterprises conducted in 1993, only four enterprises held full shares, accounting for only 4.4% of the total; 86 enterprises (95.6%) held by part shareholdings (mainly two or three people).[1] These figures showed that there were still many joint-stock cooperative enterprises which were standardized by the government including privately-owned or joint-stock enterprises. Moreover, according to the investigation of local government officials, the actual figure was greater than these proportions. In Wenzhou, some investigators found that when talking about joint-stock cooperative enterprises, although "government officials emphasized its legal legitimacy and necessity, the boss of a joint-stock cooperative enterprise always admitted frankly that it was actually a private enterprise."[2] This showed that the affirmation of the "collective nature" of the joint-stock cooperative system by the government was seen as an "amulet" by private, joint-stock and other enterprises which did not receive policy recognition and preferential policies. Although not publicly announced,

---

[1]   Wang, T., Yang, H. & Qiao, C. *Cooperative Economy of Shares in China— Theory, Practice and Countermeasures* [M]. Beijing: Enterprise Management Publishing House, 1997: 166.

[2]   Investigation team of all-China federation of industry and commerce. A survey report on private economy in Wenzhou, China [M] // *China Private Economy Yearbook (1978–1993)*. Hongkong: Economic Herald Press, 1994.

the covert norms had actually been legalized. After the adjustment of national policies and the relaxation of system environment, a large number of enterprises under the name of "collective enterprises" had resumed their original forms. Since the promulgation of the "Company Law," some "affiliated enterprises" and "joint-stock cooperative enterprises" that were known as collective enterprises in Wenzhou City had been directly registered as limited liability companies. By the end of 1995, 1,100 limited liability companies, five joint-stock companies, 90 enterprise groups, 63 Sino-foreign joint ventures, and 70 enterprises under private management and leasing operations had been set up in Wenzhou.[①] Since then, covert norms have transformed into open norms.

The spirit of "striving for practical results" is reflected not only in the economic field, but also in other areas of society. Since the reform and opening-up, Zhejiang's non-governmental colleges and universities, democratic deliberation, non-governmental public welfare social and cultural facilities and other phenomena have all reflected Zhejiang people's practical and pragmatic regional cultural spirit.

Therefore, in the above-mentioned sense, the "pragmatic" cultural tradition has, to a certain extent, played a very important intermediary role in the institutional innovation and economic and social development of Zhejiang since the reform and opening-up. It has enabled Zhejiang people to take a pragmatic attitude toward the old institutional arrangements and to urge the government to make adjustments in the formal institutional arrangements to provide people with a broader space to choose new institutional arrangements independently through their own pragmatic actions. In this sense, the application of the cultural tradition of "striving for practical results" is the spiritual lubricant and catalyst for the innovation of contemporary Zhejiang system and the

---

① Wang, T., Yang, H. & Qiao, C. *Cooperative Economy of Shares in China—Theory, Practice and Countermeasures* [M]. Beijing: Enterprise Management Publishing House, 1997: 169.

economic and social development of Zhejiang, and is also of great significance to institutional innovation activities including the evolution of Zhejiang specialized markets, the development of the joint-stock system and private economy, the establishment of non-governmental public works and the construction of democracy at the local level. It is because of this regional cultural and spiritual tradition that the institutional changes in Zhejiang since the reform and opening-up can be carried out in a gradual pattern for the new rules developing under the old system, which presents the Hayek's so-called character of extended natural order.

Compared with the radical pattern and the artificially designed and constructed pattern, the advantages of the gradual and naturally evolving institutional changes pattern are undoubtedly obvious. The artificially designed system generally excludes most parties from the system design. Although it solicits the opinions of the parties through certain means, the solicitation is still very limited due to the costs and expenses. Therefore, artificially designed system is difficult to achieve Pareto Optimality. According to Hayek's induction, the advantages of a gradual or naturally evolving institutional changes pattern are at least as follows. First, the interests of socio-economic life are complex and the spontaneous order of the market is based on mutual benefits. Thus, the natural order is the best order. Second, the spontaneous order based on the abstract rules that allow individuals to freely use their own knowledge for their own purposes is more efficient than the organization or arrangement based on orders. Third, the extreme importance of spontaneous order or the rule of law is based on the fact that it expands the possibility of peaceful coexistence of people for mutual benefits. These people are not small groups with common interests nor do they follow a common superior, thus enabling a huge or open society to be generated.[1]

---

[1]   Lu, X. *The New Institutional Economics* [M]. Rev. ed. Beijing: China Development Press, 2003: 114.

In addition to the above, the gradual and natural evolution of the institutional changes pattern has other advantages. According to the hypothesis of "learning by doing" or "learning in doing," human knowledge can be divided into two categories. One is technical knowledge which can be expressed in words and languages with certain rules and procedures and people can master it through receiving education or reading books. The other is practical or personal knowledge which is unable to be preached and the only way to obtain it is through physical experience. Personal knowledge includes information about particular people and organizations formed in a specific political, economic, and cultural environment. In general, the original knowledge and information stock still have great utility in the process of economic system change and the updating of the knowledge and beliefs of the economic subjects. The rapid reform of the social structure will undermine people's long-term accumulation of such knowledge and information, thus hindering the social and economic system and the main body functions. A typical example is that the organs of a healthy person can adapt to changes in temperature of about 50 degrees in a few hours. However, if this happens within a few minutes, his body will be seriously damaged or ill for there is no time for him to react to the changes. Therefore, avoiding the sudden destruction of information and organizational resources can reduce the organization and information costs of reform. If radical reforms are adopted, it will inevitably undermine the existing organizational structure and information stock. Therefore, people cannot form stable expectations and the organization and information costs of reform will increase.

On the one hand, institutional changes can only function effectively if it is compatible with certain cultural values. In New Institutional Economics, institutional changes are always accompanied by cultural changes, and the speed of institutional changes also depends on the speed of cultural changes. The cracking of the mystery of institutional changes needs to start from the point when human beings began to study culture. It is through constant cultural studies that human beings were able to move into civilization and progress from truculence, ignorance, and backwardness. History has shown that the speed of institutional changes is a function of learning speed, and the direction of institutional changes depends on the expected rate of return on access to different knowledge. Many rules, habits and their systems are the results of learning. Learning and institutional change are interrelated and mutually reinforced. The changes of systems and rules are the result of trying and learning; in turn, the effective system encourages people to keep learning. A good foreign system, if it is far from native values, ethics, habits and lifestyles, may as well be "good-looking but not for use" or a mere formality after "publication" or a distortion in implementation. This shows that institutional changes must be synchronized with cultural changes. Institutional change requires a process. If the changes in the cultural values that are compatible with the old economic system require a process, the formation of new cultural values that are compatible with the market economy also requires a cumulative phase. This makes it virtually impossible for the changes in the economic system to completely "deviate" from the original track overnight (such "changes" may have taken place in the history of mankind but the vast majority has ended in failure). Otherwise, the reform will encounter enormous social resistance, and its cost may even be so great that the reform cannot proceed. Gradual reform continually corrects the original institutional arrangements, which will be in turn gradually replaced by cultural values with new institutional arrangements and cultural values with higher efficiency. Thus, various kinds of systems and arrangements of the market economy will be conceived in the old system through "entry" and competition.

On the other hand, in the process of gradual reform, new rules which breed under the old system impact on the existing irrational legal forms and call for the advent of new law. The demonstration effect of the new rules leads to institutional innovation demand on a wider range and larger scale. Therefore, it is exactly the application of the spiritual tradition of "striving for practical results" that, in fact,

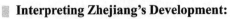
Zhejiang's original restrictive policies have gradually been relaxed and the original economic and social systems have gradually been adjusted. This in turn has expanded the collection of economic and social system choices, provided new profit opportunities, and eventually formed a new social and economic system framework through the accumulation of quantitative changes in institutional changes.

2.2 Regional Great Tradition and the Cultural Spirit of "Striving for Practical Results"

2.2.1 A Dilemma That is Hard to Justify

Why do Zhejiang people have a cultural spirit of "striving for practical results"? In recent years, scholars who study the Zhejiang phenomenon tend to explain it from the cultural tradition of eastern Zhejiang (the impact of Great Tradition). The perspective that attracts the most attention is that of the eastern Zhejiang Practical Schools which dates back to the Southern Song Dynasty, claiming that the purpose of learning lies in its humanistic pragmatism. It seems to make sense in a way. Some schools do have the distinct cultural character of "striving for practical results" such as the Yongkang School represented by Chen Liang, Jinhua School by Lü Zuqian and Yongjia School by Ye Shi. As different as they might be, all the Practical Schools share a common essence—advocating the combination of learning and its practice with patriotism and pragmatism. The purpose of learning is humanistic pragmatism.

The arguments on "Wangba Yili" (hegemonism and fame, righteousness and benefit), which lasted for several years, between Chen Liang and Zhu Xi, representative figures of the Yongkang School, demonstrate their concepts of righteousness and benefit. Chen, discontent with Zhu's exhortation of being "pure Confucian," demanded him to abandon the thought of "practice of both righteousness and benefit, hegemonism and fame." Chen thought, "if hegemonism can be practiced along with benevolence, so can the principle of nature and human desires."① Chen also proposed that "one should stay realistic and pragmatic," noting that the purpose of the study was to apply it. In *Da Chen Tongfu (Answering Chen Tongfu)*, Chen Fuliang summarized Chen Liang's thought as follows, "it was a virtue to get things done."

The Jinhua School, being a large school, explores the origin of life, values the practice of self-restraint, and advocates "being educated and practicing what you preach." It gives much emphasis on humanistic pragmatism and goes against empty talk of the truth about things and the nature of minds. It also attaches importance to stability as well as the value of ancient laws and regulations. Tang Zhongyou advocated that the value of learning was its practice and humanistic pragmatism and said that "the essence of learning lied in pragmatism and concentrating attention. Drawing bread on the ground could not allay your hunger. Covering with thousands of willow catkins could not keep you warm. Learning without putting it into practice was as useless as drawing bread and covering catkins."②

Lü Zuqian was well-known and had a great number of students when he gave lectures in eastern Zhejiang, where he taught both classics and history. He taught his students to learn in order to practice. Lü claimed "scholars should strive for pragmatism"③, "pursue truth, nurture talents and seek pragmatism," and "scholars should be engaged in scholarship that can be put into practice"④. He thought "craftsmen regard utility as important when they are making implements. If they cannot be used, all the work would be wasted. Similarly, if learning cannot be put into practice, why would scholars study in the first place?" In the second version of *Comprehensive Textual Research of*

---

① See Chen Liang, "Letter Recording Replies to Zhu Yuanhui in the Year of Bingwu."

② See *Posthumous Papers of Tang—Sequel of Book Jinhua: Collectanea of Yuezhai.*

③ See Lu Dian, *Answers to the Imperial College.*

④ See Lü Zuqian, *Legend of Zuo.*

Historical Coin Documents, he also analyzed the origin, function as well as the advantages and disadvantages of the currency system.

"Striving for practical results and stressing utility" are also the pursuits of the Yongjia School. The leading figure, Chen Fuliang, valued practical results. Ye Shi advocated the governing concept of "ruling the country by dealing with concrete matters." He opposed to the discussion of morality and justice without the background of material gain and proposed new values which advocated that "if there was no material gain, morality would be empty talk" and "material gain and morality can coexist." Xue Jixuan thought that "one should study Confucian classics and make clear the advantages and disadvantages of the current affairs" and "one should avoid empty talk and violent behavior." He put emphasis on "exploring the inner workings of things." Therefore, as Huang Zongxi said, "The Yongjia School tought a person how to comprehend things steadfastly, keep the promise and hence understand the truth and handle affairs accordingly."[①]

The ideals noted above show that it was the cultural character of the Eastern Zhejiang Practical Theory to stress reality and practice, emphasize practical results and focus on the material gain. However, it should be further pointed out that although they are indeed the distinctive features of Practical Theory, Zhejiang people's spirit of "striving for practical results" cannot be entirely attributed to the school. There is still a dilemma that is hard to justify.

First, if we attribute "striving for practical results" to the Schools, it can easily remind people of Max Weber who attributed the spirit of contemporary capitalism to the renovation of the Protestant ethic. It should be noted that Weber came to the conclusion based on sufficient evidence. He thought that it was not the individual case but a common phenomenon shared by many important churches and religious sects that

---

① Huang, Z. *Learning Case in the Song and Yuan dynasties: Genzhai Learning Case* [M]. Beijing: Zhonghua Book Company, 1986.

an extraordinary commercial awareness of capitalism and religious zeal coexist perfectly among the same group of people. In *The Protestant Ethic and the Spirit of Capitalism*, Weber states at first: A glance at the occupational statistics of any country of mixed religious composition brings to light a situation which has several times provoked discussion in the Catholic press and literature, and in Catholic congresses in Germany. This discussion centers on the fact that business leaders and owners of capital, as well as the higher grades of skilled labor, and more so the higher technically and commercially trained personnel of modern enterprises are overwhelmingly Protestant. "This is not only true in cases where the difference in religion coincides with one of nationality, and thus of cultural development, as in Eastern Germany between Germans and Poles. The same thing is shown in the figures of religious affiliation almost wherever capitalism, at the time of its great expansion, has had a free hand to alter the social distribution of the population in accordance with its needs, and to determine its occupational structure. The more freedom it has had the more clearly is the effect shown."[1] Weber also found that among the Catholic graduates the percentage of those graduating from the institutions preparing, in particular, for technical studies and industrial and commercial occupations still lags farther behind the percentage of Protestants. In addition, the factory has taken its skilled labor to a large extent from young men in the handicrafts; but this is much truer of Protestant than of Catholic journeymen. To further elaborate, among journeymen, the Catholics show a stronger propensity to remain in their crafts. This means that Catholics more often become master craftsmen, whereas the Protestants are attracted to a larger extent into the factories in order to fill the upper ranks of skilled labor and administrative positions.

This has shown that Weber analyzed the relationship between the Protestant ethic and the spirit of capitalism from the fact that business

---

[1]   Weber, M. *The Protestant Ethic and the Spirit of Capitalism* [M]. Trans. Yu, X., Chen, W. et al. Beijing: SDX Joint Publishing Company, 1987: 23.

leaders and owners of capital, as well as the higher grades of skilled labor, and even more the higher technically and commercially trained personnel of modern enterprises, are overwhelmingly Protestant. "The supposed conflict between other-worldliness, asceticism, and ecclesiastical piety on the one side, and participation in capitalistic acquisition on the other, might actually turn out to be an intimate relationship."[①] Protestants, both as the ruling class and ruled class, both as the majority and minority, show a propensity of economic rationalism. Similar to Weber's research method, if we can prove that business owners of modern Zhejiang have also been influenced by the Eastern Zhejiang Practical Schools, or have grown up in such environment, it can be inferred that their spirit of "striving for practical results" can be attributed to the Eastern Zhejiang Practical Theory. The problem, however, is that it can hardly be proved based on empirical facts.

Zhejiang's institutional innovation and the miracle of economic and social development since the reform and opening-up were initially created by social groups outside the system. Those who can best reflect the spirit of "striving for the practical results" are farmers and new Zhejiang merchants, which represent 90% of the Zhejiang population. The latter was from the lower class and made their fortune from scratch, exchanging feather for candies, mending shoes, fluffing cotton, tailoring clothes and doing woodwork. The majority of them have never heard of the significant figures of the Eastern Zhejiang Practical Schools such as Chen Liang, Ye Shi, Xue Jixuan, Chen Fuliang, and Huang Zongxi, let alone their thoughts and teachings. Because of this, giving credit directly to the Schools seems to be untenable and not convincing. This is what Samuelson and Nordhaus called post hoc fallacy. In *Economics,* they illustrated the viewpoint by a silly idea of a wizard who thought that witchcraft and arsenic are both necessary ways to kill enemies.

---

① Weber, M. *The Protestant Ethic and the Spirit of Capitalism* [M]. Trans. Yu, X., Chen, W. et al. Beijing: SDX Joint Publishing Company, 1987: 28.

Or citing remarks from a journalist saying since Florida is the state with the highest mortality rate, living there is especially bad for health. Samuelson and Nordhaus defined post hoc fallacy after giving two examples, "Event B following event A does not prove that A causes B. It is post hoc fallacy if one thinks that an event which takes place before another is the cause of it."[1]

Then can't we avoid the fallacy by collecting more materials? The answer is negative. Even if the mortality rate of a thousand years is available, we cannot jump to the conclusion that Florida has a high mortality rate. Careful research is required and "factors except for the location should be kept the same."[2] For instance, the age distribution in a state should remain the same or similar after correction. Only after adjusting death figures based on age distribution, gender, previous health-detrimental risks, and other such factors can we know whether living in Florida is detrimental to one's health. Samuelson and Nordhaus's theory noted above is methodologically significant to our study of the regional cultural spirit. Explaining its cause from the perspective of "striving for practical results" of the Eastern Zhejiang Practical Schools would be making a similar mistake to post hoc fallacy. A more detailed, in-depth and comprehensive analysis is required to explore the source of the cultural spirit in contemporary Zhejiang.

---

[1] Samuelson, P. & Nordhaus, W. *Economics*: vol.1 [M]. 12th ed. Trans. Gao, H. et al. Beijing: China Development Press, 1992: 12.

[2] According to Samuelson and Nordhaus, economics is extremely complex, with millions of people and businesses, hundreds of prices and industries. One possible way to explore economic laws in this environment is through controlled experiments. A controlled experiment is one in which everything else remains the same except for the studied subject. Therefore, a scientist studying whether saccharin can cause cancer in mice will ensure that the "other conditions are kept the same," changing only the amount of saccharin with the same air, light, type of mouse. See Samuelson, P. & Nordhaus, W. *Economics*: vol.1 [M]. 12th ed. Trans. Gao, H. et al. Beijing: China Development Press, 1992: 11-12.

Second, even though the Eastern Zhejiang Practical Theory might have an impact on social psychology, the ideas of scholars like Chen Liang, Ye Shi and Lü Zuqian can only develop from the Great Tradition into popular belief of Zhejiang people through a medium. Written and printed media, since their advent, have been technologies that decipher and use language. Hence, the cultural transmission has become the privilege of the minority who can master the technology. Under such circumstances, those who acted as the medium were the literati and officialdom who mastered linguistic and literary skills. That is to say, the Eastern Zhejiang Practical Thought should first influence the intellectuals and then be used as a medium to affect change within the general public.

It is true that the Eastern Zhejiang Practical Schools has had a profound impact on society during the Southern Song Dynasty. In his letter to Shi Tianmin, Zhu Xi made a basic assessment of the prevailing Zhejiang school, "Since I came to central Zhejiang, I have found that friends of mine hold a totally different idea. When I met Chengzhi in Danzhou yesterday, he said righteousness and material gains were an integral whole and cannot be separated, which startled me. I think this is the severest evil of our society. The other evils are unworthy to worry about."[1] Zhu Xi and Chen Liang debated repeatedly but did not reach a consensus. The long debate enabled Chen's thought to be spread widely.

Even during the middle of the Southern Song Dynasty when the theory proposed by Zhu Xi and Lu Jiuyuan dominated, the Eastern Zhejiang Practical Schools could still contend against it, therefore its social impact cannot be underestimated. The theory that has the most profound impact on Chinese intellectuals is Cheng–Zhu Neo-Confucianism rather than the Eastern Zhejiang Practical Schools of Chen Liang and Ye Shi. This is because the former was officially admitted to be handed down directly from Confucianism and gradually established its supremacy in China. Until the Yuan, Ming, and Qing

---

① Zhu, X. *Collected Work of Zhu Xi*: vol. 53 Answering Shi Tianmin [M].

dynasties, Cheng–Zhu Neo-Confucianism has become the national school. It was even a common practice among scholars that theory which was inconsistent with Confucianism can be accepted, but one that was inconsistent with Cheng–Zhu Neo-Confucianism cannot. During the Yuan, Ming and Qing dynasties, the court stipulated that the imperial examinations should be set based on the Four Books and the Five Classic, while Zhu Xi's annotation of the Four Books was taken as the criterion. As the modern philosopher Feng Youlan said, after the Four Books annotated by Zhu Xi became the official readings, especially for the imperial examinations, "Generally, intellectuals who read the Confucian classics are actually only reading the Four Books. Their understanding is limited by Zhu's annotation. Just as the constitutional monarchy in the West in which the monarchy is merely a figurehead and it is the Prime Minister who had the real power, although Confucius was still revered as the 'Greatest Sage and Teacher' in the Yuan, Ming, and Qing dynasties, he did not have real power. Zhu Xi was his 'Prime Minister' and was called respectfully as Zhu Zi."[1]

Confucian scholars thought that theories inconsistent with Confucianism can be accepted, but one inconsistency with Cheng–Zhu Neo-Confucianism cannot hold up and the court wanted the public to believe in Confucianism and Neo-Confucianism. Therefore, under such social background, the theory that could exert a profound impact on intellectuals could only be the latter rather than the Eastern Zhejiang Practical Schools. The same is the case with the hometown of the leading figures of the Practical Schools, Chen Liang and Ye Shi. But under the political background of national unity, "all the lands in the world belong to the King, and all the humans in the world are King's people." When Zhu's thought ruled China, Chen Liang's hometown would naturally be dominated by it. There are many records on books of Yongkang local customs since the Song Dynasty.

---

[1]   Feng, Y. *The New Chinese Philosophic History*: vol. 5 [M]. Beijing: People's Publishing House, 1988: 159.

2.2.2 The Confucian Cultural Tradition and the Spirit of "Striving for Practical Results"

In Chinese intellectual history, the Eastern Zhejiang Practical Schools is viewed as the opposite of Neo-Confucianism. As Zhou Yu pointed out in *Zhu Xi and the Contemporary School*, "In the early period of the Zhejiang school, figures were no match for Zhu Xi both in knowledge and debating skill, such as Chen Liang who was careless and Chen Fuliang who was cautious. But since Ye Shizhi's *Records of Learning and Practice* was published, the schools dominated together with the schools of Zhu Xi and Lu Jiuyuan. It had the potential to overthrow the ideas of Zhu."[1] In the Southern Song Dynasty, Chen Liang once started a tit-for-tat argument with Zhu Xi, who was a representative figure of Neo-Confucianism, while in the same period Ye Shi's arguments with Neo-Confucianism on the concept of righteousness and interests were also seen as another echo of war. The divergence between the Eastern Zhejiang Practical Schools and Neo-Confucianism can be clearly seen through the debate over the "righteousness and interests" and "hegemonism and fame." Zhu, from the principle of heavenly principle and human desires, gave a new interpretation of the Confucian idea which valued benevolent government and righteousness and despises hegemonism and interests.

Under the disguise of benevolence, the emperors of the Han and Tang dynasties ruled the country by hegemonism. Therefore, although they built a prosperous country, they lacked morality and were "blinded by material gains."[2] Zhu opposed judging a hero by a success or failure and telling right and wrong from the perspective of utilitarianism. Chen Liang thought that ever since the world was created, benevolence and hegemonism, righteousness and material gains, as well as reason and desire, could not be separated. Even in the three generations where

---

[1] *Zhou Yutong's Selected Works on the History of Confucian Studies—Zhu Xi* [M]. Shanghai: Shanghai People's Publishing House, 1983: 178-179.

[2] See Zhu Xi, "8th Letter to Chen Gongfu."

righteousness prevailed, righteousness and interest, hegemonism and fame were practiced simultaneously. Benevolence and righteousness are nothing more than caring about others with a kind heart through deeds that benefit the people. If benevolence is in the material gains, then hegemonism comes from the former. Benevolence is in the hearts of both the three emperors and those of the Han and Tang dynasties.

However, it is still an internal debate of Confucianism. According to different opinions towards righteousness, interests, reason and human desires, we can regard Neo-Confucianism as extreme Confucianism and the Eastern Zhejiang Practical Schools represented by Chen Liang and Ye Shi as the moderate one. Although there was a serious disagreement between the two ostensibly and they were antagonistic to each other culturally and spiritually "because of differences in saving the world with morality and practical results,"[1] in the final analysis, the spirit of seeking "utility" and "practical results" was permeated by both schools. It notes that even the traditional Chinese culture, only moderates were "explicit" and extremists seemed to be "implicit."

In a sense, the traditional Chinese mainstream culture and the intellectual elites (literati and officialdom) seem to give less importance to and even abandon interests, which can be seen by their debates on "benevolence, righteousness, and desires." "Pursuing interests and personal gains" is the proposition of non-mainstream schools (such as the Yangzhu School which emerged in the Warring States with developed businesses). In fact, placing a high regard for righteousness over material gains indeed seemed to be the dominant value in traditional Chinese culture. Taking the Chinese mainstream culture after the Han Dynasty as example, Buddhism and Taoism advocated standing aloof from this mortal life. Their opinion to give up interests can be clearly revealed. Although Confucianism advocated throwing oneself into the

---

① Shu, J. *Biography of Zhu Xi* [M]. Fuzhou: Fujian Education Press, 1992: 498.

worldly affairs, it also showed a tendency of valuing righteousness over material gains.

Throughout the history of Confucianism, whether it is the "debate of righteousness and interests" or later "the debate of reason and desire," a common theme seems to be on worshiping righteousness or reason. They advocated that righteousness and reason outweigh interests and desire. There is an ambiguity on both sides concerning whether interests can be properly taken into account under the above precondition. Extreme Confucian scholars proposed that interests and desires should be abandoned, while righteousness and reason should be preserved. For instance, Zhu Xi said, "Scholars must abandon their human desires and pursue heavenly principles. This is the true learning." While Wang Shouren claimed, "The heart must be innocent and free from desires." They also believed that there was a certain degree of opposition between heavenly principles and human desires, righteousness and profit. According to Zhu Xi's view, due to human desires, the innate and noble heavenly principles of humans are weakened, and fail to function well.

But heavenly principles are righteous and serve the public well, while human desires are wrong and serve personal interests. The two are antagonistic to each other with no room for compromise. Therefore, the attitude towards human desires is "Overcome it." Moderates such as Wang Chong, Sima Qian, Wang Anshi, Chen Liang, Ye Shi, Yan Yuan, Dai Zhen, and others advocated giving certain status to interests and desires and priority to righteousness. For example, Sima Qian said, "People were kind and just when they were affluent." On the other hand, Dai Zhen said, "It was impossible for one to have no desire and take no action" and "Sages were selfless but they do have desires." He also said, "People had desire, love, and conscience by birth." Therefore, human desires have own reason to exist and do not run counter to heavenly principles. Properly pursuing desires and interests does not collide with righteousness, but is beneficial to nurture morality. However, both extreme and moderate schools of Confucianism seemed to regard "upholding righteousness" and "upholding reason" to be of absolute value, which outweighs interests and desires.

But we should also see the other side in a dialectic analysis. In fact, while extreme schools advocated that "Scholars should get rid of human desires and recover heavenly principles," they did not deny human desires and material gains altogether. For instance, Cheng Yi thought "Ordinary people won't survive without material gains. How can it be of no benefit?"[1] and "People who do not interfere with others are fond of material gains while those who do dislike it."[2] Zhu Xi claimed, "The most important morality is righteousness."[3] Cheng Yi thought "Righteousness is rooted in the human heart and is the character bestowed by heavenly principles. Pursuing material gains comes from our heart and is manifested in the pursuit of materialistic satisfaction. This shows that human desire is selfish. Following the heavenly principles, one will not seek gains but will never encounter any misfortune. Following human desires, material gains cannot be obtained. Worse still, he will do harm to himself."[4] "One must prioritize benevolence rather than material gain."[5]

Meanwhile, Cheng Yi thought "How can it be possible that the sages do not talk of material gain?" and "People who rarely mention material gain will follow this principle when they handle affairs. The gain will naturally come to them."[6] Righteousness is more important

① Cheng, H. & Cheng, Y. *Posthumous Papers of Cheng of Henan Province*: vol. 18 [M]. Shanghai: Shanghai Classics Publishing House, 2000.

② Cheng, H. & Cheng, Y. *Posthumous Papers of Cheng of Henan Province*: vol. 19 [M]. Shanghai: Shanghai Classics Publishing House, 2000.

③ Zhu, X. *Collected Works of Zhu Xi*: vol. 24 [M].

④ Zhu, X. *The Annotation of Four Books: Mencius* [M]. Beijing: Zhonghua Book Company, 1983.

⑤ Zhu, X. *Collected Works of Zhu Xi*: vol 76 [M].

⑥ Li, J. *Quotation from Zhu Xi*: vol.36 [M]. Beijing: Zhonghua Book Company, 1986

than material gain and following heavenly principles is to have both simultaneously. Zhu thought on the other hand, "Material gain will come when one has the right opinion and clarifies the truth. Bothering about material gains and losses will not necessarily lead to gain."[①] Zhu was not opposed to material gain that is derived from righteousness but that from desire.

Moreover, even in traditional Chinese mainstream culture featured by "laying less emphasis on and abandoning material gain," it cannot hide a strong propensity of favoring "practical gain." In other words, the absolute value and priority of "righteousness" rather than "material gain" is clearly shown in Chinese mainstream culture, especially in Confucian ethics. But in real life, it is always the other way around.

On the one hand, extremist schools of Confucianism, such as the school of Sima Guang, Cheng Hao, Cheng Yi, Zhu Xi, Lu Jiuyuan and Wang Yangming, had very tough attitude which can be shown in "Scholars should get rid of human desires and recover heavenly principles" and "The existence of heavenly principles is at the expanse of human desire and vice versa." The value orientation of practical utility is revealed. In fact, the propensity of "laying less emphasis on and abandoning material gain" shows value orientation to some extent, but it is not absolute, central and fundamental. Righteousness and reason are not absolute and ultimate values although they seem to be. In real life, they are not the core value orientation or the cultural center, but they should be adapted to "benefit all people through one's own conduct."

On the other hand, "laying less emphasis on and abandoning material gain" has different pertinence. So righteousness and reason are not mutually exclusive but supplementary to each other. The tendency is usually employed by those engaged in the handicraft

---

① Li, J. *Quotation from Zhu Xi*: vol.37 [M]. Beijing: Zhonghua Book Company, 1986

industry, commerce or other profitable businesses that are despised by bureaucrats, with a purpose of gaining more profits, namely making more money as government officials. Hence, the essence of giving less emphasis to material gain is the marriage with bureaucrats and authority on the basis of natural economy with the aim of working together to exclude all other profit-making industries regarded as improper and ultimately carved up all the interests.

Take commerce as an example. Although the comparison between the poor and the rich is as follows: Farmers cannot compare with craftsmen; craftsmen are poorer than merchants; and men who do embroidery are not as good as officials. Doing business was the best way to earn money compared with farming and making craft. But bureaucrats did want to see businessmen devise strategies to contend for the emperor's interests and impair the achievements of the Kingdom of Qi, and even use their wealth to get acquaintance with the nobility and have more power than influential officials. So they adopted the strategy of giving less importance and even abandoning profits as well as merchants, which drove people back to farming. The scenario above which shows the practical spirit of excluding the profits of others and capturing the larger interests of national bureaucrats can be seen directly in the measures adopted by the traditional bureaucrats and in the Chinese mainstream culture, especially Confucianism.

In a positive light, traditional Confucian bureaucrats in China advocated that the value of knowledge depended on whether it can be implemented in the world. Utility is an innate impulse of Confucianism. As Lu Xiangshan said, although Confucianism is completely unrecognized, the belief system lays emphasis on utility. In Confucian culture, utility is the expectation, priority and ultimate value. It takes on a dominant position. "Living in seclusion" is the last resort. As Yu Yingshi said, "The tyranny of Chinese autocracy reached its peak in the Ming Dynasty. Confucian scholars cannot preach what they believed but concealed their ideas, which was the last resort. However,

Confucianism did not completely abandon its original impulse of utility. Therefore, whenever the political and social crisis deepens, the concept of managing world affairs begin to rise. Examples can be found in both the late Ming and early Qing dynasties."[①]

Such utilitarianism definitely leads to unitary value orientation. Although on the surface, Confucianism insists on using ethics as the final criterion for judging things in the world, it is, in fact, the utility that is used as the judging standard. In Confucianism, morality and even culture as a whole are instruments of the world. This is undoubtedly the reason why Confucian culture in history has shown great tolerance for other cultures. As long as they were useful to the world, Confucianism often incorporates things of diverse nature.

On the other hand, the criterion of "utility" is indeed the sharp weapon that weakens the unique values of all the other schools. The historical debate between Confucianism and Buddhism strongly illustrates this point. Buddhism has its own unique value orientations and this is especially true with its belief of being aloof towards worldly affairs. But according to Confucian cultural standards, such belief is exactly the downside of Buddhism since it cannot manage the family, run the state and govern the country peacefully. Hence it is of no use. The conflict between Confucianism and Buddhism ended when the former found its own orientation of development, stating that "Buddhism can nurture morality. Taoism can strengthen physical health. Confucianism can govern the world." This statement embodies the cohesion and tolerance of Confucianism using "utility" as the standard. One prevailing principle of Confucianism is stressing the use of literature to civilize people. The concept of "literature manifesting the Tao" which became famous in the middle of the Tang Dynasty began to take shape after the efforts of Xunzi, Yang Xiong to Liu Xie.

---

① Yu, Y. *Modern Interpretation of Chinese Thoughts* [M]. Nanjing: Jiangsu People's Publishing House, 1989: 249-250.

According to Huang Kaifa[1], it was in the middle of the Tang Dynasty that literature was further related to Tao. The rulers of the middle Tang Dynasty revived Confucianism in order to meet the needs of politics, which led to the ancient literature movement advocated by Han Yu and Liu Zongyuan. "Literature manifesting the Tao" was the slogan of the movement. Han and Liu showed a propensity of valuing Tao over literature to varying degrees. In the Song Dynasty, this phenomenon evolved into a phenomenon that emphasized Tao and despised literature. The two aspects had a relationship similar to that of master and servant. This can be reflected in Zhou Dunyi's remarks of "Writings are for conveying truth." Articles are used to nurture morality and civilize people, or otherwise it would become a vehicle of no use and could only be called "art" rather than "literature." Therefore, as Zheng Zhenduo said, "Chinese literature cannot be fully developed because it is affected by the traditional literary concepts. Most people are brainwashed by Confucianism, regarding literature as vehicles and Ci and songs as insignificant skills. Others are willing to compose beautiful articles and see literature as an instrument to divert them from boredom. The two opinions have not been fully eliminated until now."[2]

In short, according to the Confucian standard of "utility," different cultures and their value orientations are bound to move toward forming a unitary view. Moreover, the ultimate pursuit and value orientation of culture (the orientation of truth, goodness, and beauty) will dissolve. This is in sharp contrast to intellectuals of Western Europe who considered seeking truth as their ultimate value and pursuit.

In Western Europe, scholars who pursued truth, learning and art would not be despised. On the contrary, their deeds were praised far

---

[1] Huang, K. Practical literary concept of Confucianism and "Writings are for conveying truth" [J]. *Journal of Jiangsu Administration Institute*, 2005(5).

[2] Zheng, Z. Suggestions to change Chinese literature [J]. *Literature Quarterly Magazine*, 1922(10).

and wide: Pythagoras came to a sudden enlightenment and found the principle of buoyancy. Thrilled by his findings, he ran out of the bathroom naked to announce it. Wittgenstein wrote down the essence of philosophical thinking amid gunfire. The pursuit of Copernicus, Brahe, Kepler, and Galileo in scientific research is not in the utility. As Schmidt put it, "There are four names that struck people's ears like the roar of thunder: Copernicus, Brahe, Kepler, and Galileo. But it is undeniable that they are all devout Christians whose scientific work is influenced by their beliefs. This is usually neglected in most science textbooks."[1] "Inventing a law of causality is much happier than being the Persian king." Western intellectuals can rest easy through the pure pursuit of knowledge without social utility. In Comparison, because of excessive pursuit of utility, ancient Chinese intellectuals are not able to support their career and life.

However, one downside in the traditional Chinese mainstream culture, knowledge is a stepping stone for intellectuals to obtain a high position with matched salary and bring glory to their ancestors. This value orientation of the traditional literati is clearly expressed in the remarks of Confucian masters. Xuncius said in *Following the Examples of Confucian Scholars,* "I was from poor families but want to become wealthy. I was born stupid but want to be smart. Is that possible? Mencius said the only way is through learning." Therefore, Chuang Tzu accused Confucianism of "engaging in loose talk to stir up trouble and confusing the emperor in order to be conferred as marquis." The criticism strikes home. Wang Yangming once criticized those who wanted to pass the imperial examinations, saying "He does not manage the family economically, but make a merit of entertaining guests. When he wants to invite guests, everything is borrowed. When guests come, they are impressed by the wide range of items. After they are gone, everything will be given back. If the guests do not come, the housing

---

① Schmidt, A. *Under the Influence* [M]. Trans. Wang, X. & Zhao, W. Beijing: Peking University Press, 2004: 205.

items are unprepared and he will be exhausted."[1] That is to say, Confucianism is only a stepping stone for wealth and fame for some people.

Ostensibly, merchants pursue fame while Confucianism value righteousness. But Neo-Confucian scholars of Huizhou who were the spokesmen of Huizhou merchants pointed out that the two share similarities in terms of value orientation. First, "Scholars pursue fame while merchants seek wealth."[2] It seems that they have different goals, but in essence, their pursuit is the same. There seems to be an antagonism between businessmen and scholars. Righteousness and material gain are interlinked in Huizhou's Neo-Confucianism. As the saying goes "Scholars and merchants have different theories but the same aspiration."[3] The difference between the two is only in form but not in essence. "Confucian scholars are industrious only to attain fame and material gains. They inherit the will of parents and bring glory to them."[4]

Second, doing business and being officials have similarities. The former is helpful for them to become a government official and the latter is conducive to do business. As Wang Daokun said, "The number of merchants is three times that of Confucian scholars in the new capital. Merchants seek wealth whereas scholars pursue fame. When scholars fail to get things down, they will be expelled and businessmen will be assigned to an important position. When the merchants benefited from it, they will be banished for the good of the next generations and scholars will be employed. Different methods are alternatively

---

① Wang, S. *Collected Works of Wang Yangming* [M]. Shanghai: Shanghai Classics Publishing House, 2011.

② Wang, D. *Collection of Taihan*: vol.17 [M].

③ Wang, D. *Collection of Taihan*: vol.61 [M].

④ Wang, D. *Collection of Taihan*: vol.54 [M].

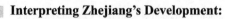

used and hence a balance is stricken."[1] Similarities can be found not only in government affairs but also in daily life. In the Ming and Qing dynasties, it was usually fathers and elder brothers who ran the business, and sons and little brothers who attended school and brought benefits to the next generations in Huizhou. Juniors who became famous for studying Confucianism and were senior officials did not care about commercial interests.

Third, merchants who strive to obtain an official rank want to make his family well-known, which is also the purpose of learning and becoming a governmental official. Doing business and studying Confucianism are both ways to honor ancestors.

Fourth, since doing business and being officials have similarities, the two kinds of fame can also be transformed into each other. As Wang Daokun said, "In the south of the Yangtze River, the new capital is famous for artifacts. Their tradition is that one will do business if he does not study Confucianism and vice versa. After all, a good businessman who has notable achievements bears comparison with a learned man."[2] Li Daqi expressed his attitude towards abandoning Confucianism to do business, "A real man is ready to realize his aspiration anywhere all over the country. What shouldn't he do? He should neither be unable to become a government official and bring glory to his parents nor be incapable of starting a business, getting married and leaving assets to children." After he became prosperous, he rushed to attend the school.

According to the view of modern economics, both "studying Confucianism for fame" or "doing business for profits" embodies the pursuit of personal interests. According to Granovetter, social behaviors such as job search is also a matter of rational choice, but here, the object

---

① Tang, L. *Social and Economic Research of Huizhou Since the Ming and Qing dynasties* [M]. Hefei: Anhui University Press, 1992: 212.

② Wang, D. *Collection of Taihan*: vol.72 [M].

and the field of activity have all begun to expand. It includes not only economic gains, but also occupation, social status and reputation, etc. The rational choice also moves from the market area to the broader social network. Becker argued that people were pursuing utility (interest) in their particular cultural structures according to their own value judgments. In addition to goods and services, "social values" such as respect, social status, reputation, and knowledge may also be the source of utility and form an integral part of personal interests. In other words, the personal utility function includes both economic and non-economic variables. Therefore, when economic men make their choices, they need to make trade-offs between different commodities and between commodities and non-economic goods. Conversion between studying and doing business is a choice made by a typical economic man after the trade-off between material and non-material goods.

The scenario above shows that although the interests of the market (doing business) and fame and fortune (studying Confucianism) are clearly different in terms of the objective of pursuit, both are still pursuing the same value orientation of utilitarianism. Undoubtedly, they arrive at the same end by different means, pursuing practical utility as their ultimate and absolute value orientation. The ancients called failing the imperial examinations as repeatedly "failing to sell the talents," which implies that doing business and studying Confucianism are both offered for sale. Then, when the social situation changes, it is easier to shift one's profession from being an official to doing business. Looking further, when doing the two jobs has the same purpose of bringing glory to ancestors and the family, their gap in utility is eliminated. New classical economics has clearly revealed the point. Although Marshall also considered the concept of economic man as the analytical basis of his economics, he thought that it is inaccurate to regard "economic man" as a person who is driven by self-interest.

Marshall pointed out that the economic men were generally working diligently for the interests of the family and trying to accumulate capital. An economic man is defined as "a person who has a desire of bringing benefits to himself and others and is willing to work hard and sacrifice himself to support his family."[①] Marshall showed an intriguing image of the "economic man," specifically, that the economic man also has an ethical character. If his remarks are translated into the language of Huizhou Neo-Confucianism, then the "economic man" also appears to have a motivation of glorifying and illuminating the ancestors. However, this kind of noble motive does not change the defining characteristics of the economic man who maximizes his interests.

In fact, although Confucianism has the most prominent value orientation of utility in traditional Chinese culture, the indigenous schools like Mohist, Taoist, and Legalist also have similar value. Taoists seem to be the most detached (advocating being aloof towards worldly affairs), but they still insist one should do nothing and then everything would be done. After the Taoist school evolved into Taoism, it has shown a stronger propensity to pursue longevity and immortality, and practical utilitarianism through their own efforts.

Therefore, both the moderate and the extreme Confucian schools clearly or implicitly incorporate the value orientation of practical utilitarianism. The two schools are only opposed to each other on the surface.

Ironically, Zhu Xi strongly advocated that "Seeking justice is not for material gain. Understanding the truth is not for merits," but his hometown Xin'an (Huizhou) revered Neo-Confucianism. "The theory of the human nature prevailed after Zhu Xi."[②]

Since the Song and Yuan dynasties, Neo-Confucianism has been

---

① Yang, C. *Economic Man and Analysis of Order* [M]. Shanghai: SDX Joint Publishing Company, Shanghai People's Publishing House, 1998: 138-139.

② See *Annals of Jixi County* in Qianlong Reign.

illustrated. It passed on from generation to generation. "The world calls Xin'an the 'birthplace of culture and education'."[1] Guild halls in Huizhou revered Zhu Xi. The existing pedigree of Huizhou's clan is a clear proof of their reverence for him. Therefore, that is to say, it has been a common ethos since the Song and Yuan dynasties. Neo-Confucianism formed a unique cultural environment, or as Tang Lixing put it, "Neo-Confucianism comes first." "This has enabled Huizhou merchants to have a different group mind compared with other merchants, which further affected and determined the formation and tendency of their psychology. This is the reason why Huizhou merchants vary from the others."[2]

Neo-Confucianism, which advocated keeping natural principles and abolishing human desires and contrasted with the Eastern Zhejiang Practical Schools represented by Chen Liang and Ye Shi, became the ideology of Huizhou, which was particularly thought-provoking.

In fact, as a connecting link between Confucian, Mencius and Zhou Dunyi, Chen Hao, and Neo-Confucianism undoubtedly also had the common core value orientation with Confucianism, namely pursuing "humanistic pragmatism" as the ultimate goal. Zhu Xi once called his theory the "theory of emperors," regarding it as one that can bring benefits to a country and purify folklore and scholars who want to cultivate themselves and manage others. He believed that an emperor with a pure mind could run the court successfully. When the court is well-managed, all officials can be governed. When the officials are governed, all citizens can be ruled. When the citizens are ruled, the whole world can be reigned over. Therefore, Zhu Xi, as a master of Neo-Confucianism, did not have a viewpoint of utilitarianism as Chen Liang and Ye Shi did. However, in the deep sense, he pursued "utility"

---

[1]   See *Records of Xinning County* in Wanli Reign.
[2]   Tang, L. *Social and Economic Research of Huizhou Since the Ming and Qing dynasties* [M]. Hefei: Anhui University Press, 1999: 115.

as his goal. As a result, Zhang Xuecheng, a real expert in the Qing Dynasty, also praised Neo-Confucianism to be "an integration of life, practical results, knowledge, and article" and claimed that learning in later dynasties "inherits real learning from Zhu Xi."[1] Because of this, it is possible for Huizhou merchants who take substantial profit as their ultimate goal to find available spiritual resources from Zhu Xi.

Studies of philosophical hermeneutics show that man will never live in a vacuum, and until he has self-awareness or reflection, he is in his own world and belongs to this world. Therefore, he does not understand things from nothingness. His cultural and social background, traditional concepts, customs, knowledge of his time, spiritual and ideological conditions, material conditions, the ethos of his nation are things that are bound to belong to him since he was born and affects him throughout his life. This is the so-called "preconceived idea," "prejudice" and "prejudgment."

A different horizon corresponds to a different prejudgment system. Although both the reader and what he wants to understand have their own horizons, understanding does not mean abandoning his horizon and placing himself in a different one. In the beginning, the reader should go into the horizon he wants to understand and enrich him as his understanding expands. Our horizon is continually formed in contact with the past horizons. This process also includes the fusion with the past horizon, which Gadamer called "the fusion of horizons." Hall, a contemporary cultural researcher, also believed that the sending of information does not mean it can be received in the same way. At each stage of communication, it takes on a special form. There are special conditions to restrict communication both with coding (the formation of information) or decoding (the reading and understanding of information).

---

[1] Zhang, X. *On Literature and History*: vol.3 Zhu and Lu [M]. Shanghai: Shanghai Classics Publishing House, 2015.

There is no consistency between coding and decoding. A given message can be decoded differently by various readers. Hall's decoding theory shows that the meaning of the text changes as the code used alters. It is not easy for the reader to completely agree or disagree with the text, but rather to lean towards a certain text and a group of readers who are in the same social context. Another contemporary cultural researcher, John Fiske, argued that meaning comes not only from the text but from the connections with readers in a particular social context. Different readers often interpret a text in a variety of ways, and the meaning of the text can be delivered in various tones.

Eggertsson said, "When people's experience does not conform to their thinking, they will change their view." However, "When people change their ideologies, the contradiction between their experience and their consciousness must be certain accumulation."[1] The reason why Neo-Confucianism became the ideology of Huizhou, the hometown of Huizhou merchants who pursued utilitarianism, is because it has the common value orientation as Confucianism with the purpose of humanistic pragmatism. It is also the result of the "fusion of vision" or "compromise reading" between Huizhou merchants and Confucian texts, through which improper contents are 'neglected' whereas positive ones or those relevant to their daily life are promoted.

This "fusion of horizons" between Huizhou merchants group and Neo-Confucian texts are not identical or homogenized, but only partially overlapping, including both differences and interactions. It is clear that the new fusion of horizon created includes both the horizons of the Huizhou merchants and that of Neo-Confucian texts, which are hard to distinguish clearly. Zhu Xi described excessive lust as human desire, which is the principal meaning, and proper ones as heavenly principles, which is the secondary meaning.

---

[1] Eggertsson, T. *New Institutional Economics* [M]. Trans. Wu, J. et al. Beijing: The Commercial Press, 1996: 68-69.

Zhu's opinion of "keeping heavenly principles and giving up human desires" is to abandon the principal meaning and preserve the secondary since it conforms to heavenly principles. Neologists of the Ming and Qing dynasties, starting from their own reading horizons, apparently attached more importance to the principal meaning of "human desire." However, Huizhou merchants valued the secondary from the perspective of their own horizon. Since "there is heavenly principle in human desires," the two are not mutually and absolutely exclusive. In the process of the merging of scholars and merchants in the Ming and Qing dynasties, Huizhou merchants introduced the concept noted above to the explanation of their relationship, putting forward the new concept of "merchants and Confucianism are interlinked." They also proved the concept from gains, righteousness, interest, filial piety and fraternal duty as well as fame and material gains.

Therefore, as Tang Lixing said, "Huizhou merchants integrate Neo-Confucianism for their own economic interest, which is clear from their method of studying." Most of them are not devoted to the systematic study of Neo-Confucianism, but rather take certain chapters, sentences and aphorisms to serve the immediate needs of the business. "Huizhou merchants reformed Neo-Confucianism and integrated it into their economic interests with the power of the community, which can reflect their values and aesthetic taste."[1]

Tang also cited many examples to illustrate that the pragmatic attitude towards Neo-Confucianism that Huizhou merchants had and the "compromise reading" of its original texts stemming from their own interests.

Therefore, the texts of Neo-Confucianism were unwillingly used by Huizhou merchants who saw the fragility and limitations of "imperial study." The texts allow different opinions while at the same time they

---

[1]   Tang, L. *Social and Economic Research of Huizhou Since the Ming and Qing dynasties* [M]. Hefei: Anhui University Press, 1999: 210.

also try to submerge those different voices. Their complex meaning cannot be explained in itself, which enables Huizhou merchants to generate new texts that meet their needs. That is to say, texts are controlled by the merchants. The production and circulation of Huizhou merchants' culture rely not only on the significance and blankness provided by Neo-Confucianism but also on the active participation and creation of Huizhou merchants. Their hermeneutic conversation with Neo-Confucian texts is like a real dialogue involving equal and positive interaction. It presets that both sides have considered the same topic and one common problem so that they can discuss it since there is always a focus of a conversation.

It is in this process that Huizhou merchants passed on the history of Neo-Confucianism to its current deliverer. That is to say, they understood Neo-Confucianism with the current background in nature. This is a kind of adaptation or translation. The understanding is an event or a movement in the history in which both the interpreter of Neo-Confucian texts and the theory itself cannot be regarded as an autonomous part. As Gadamer said, understanding itself cannot be seen as merely a subjective activity, but rather a transformative one in which the past and current mutually understand each other.

The experience of Neo-Confucianism in Huizhou during the Ming and Qing dynasties indicates that Confucian extremists, like the moderates, also valued practical results and utilitarianism, except that the former was implicit whereas the latter was more straightforward. When the society has a need, the value orientation of the extremists passes through the "fusion of horizons" or "compromise reading" of a certain social group. It will not only become prominent, but also be transformed and used by utilitarianism and further develop into an ideology that can benefit merchants like the Eastern Zhejiang Practical Schools represented by Chen Liang and Ye Shi. This also means that "striving for practical results" and "stressing utility" is not only a spiritual heritage exclusive to the school. As a result, both

Neo-Confucianism of Huizhou and the Practical Schools, through their own development path, have found fresh water coming from the value orientation of Confucianism which pursues practical results. Certainly, thanks to such spirit, they have developed distinctive cultural personalities with unique geographical features that are different from Confucianism and Neo-Confucianism.

There have been profound expositions on this point. American scholar, Hoyt Tillman distinguished moral ethics from practical ethics and "ethics of utilitarianism" from "ethics of morality and motives" in *Utilitarian Confucianism—Ch'en Liang's Challenge to Chu Hsi*. The disagreements between Zhu Xi and Chen Liang are merely the basic political inclination developed during the polarization of Confucianism. "In the process, they materialized the tension between absolute ethics and ethics of political gain, ethics of morality and ethics of utilitarianism."[1] Although Zhu Xi and Chen Liang's views seem to be completely opposite ostensibly, in Zhu Xi's absolute ethics, virtue or righteousness has supreme command. In other words, the reason why people must show mercy is that doing so is good rather than stemming from the utility. The virtues of benevolence also contradict pragmatism.

Compared with Zhu, Chen Liang built his morality on results. His utilitarianism represents the rejuvenation of traditional Confucian thought and its political orientation. "He combined benevolence and hegemonism and denied discussing them separately. Chen Liang incorporated material gains into the moral concept of benevolent government through connecting the emperor and practical politics. Hence, his unification of king and king bridged the gap between the means and the result. Through the ethical proposition, he can focus on the effects of political behavior without being bound by the moral issues. The unification of benevolence and hegemonism denies the

---

① Hoyt, T. *Utilitarian Confucianism—Ch'en Liang's Challenge to Chu Hsi* [M]. Trans. Jiang, C. Nanjing: Jiangsu People's Publishing House, 1997: 94.

negative connotation of utilitarianism and provides ethical support for the main orientation of social politics."[①] However, it should also be noted that on the other hand, as Ye Tan put it, mind and social practice are topics of Neo-Confucianism. Both Neo-Confucianism and the Practical Schools have inherited the concepts of cultivating one's moral character, regulating the family, running the state and governing the country peacefully, covering moral cultivation and humanistic pragmatism.

However, the Practical Schools pursue social utilitarianism while Neo-Confucianism seeks knowledge, moral cultivation and practice. The principal belief of the former is to transform the society and achieve practical results whereas the latter is in pursuit of knowledge and morality and despises material gains. Although they are all after pragmatism, they differ in human pragmatism and personal practice. "This difference has very far-reaching significance— in the Song Dynasty, Confucianism split into different schools that existed simultaneously. Human pragmatism then developed into two major aspects, seeking personal practice and humanistic pragmatism respectively. The latter has influenced the later societies and ideologies profoundly and played an important role in the evolution of social form."[②]

Therefore, areas that are influenced by Confucianism have spiritual resources laying emphasis on "striving for practical results" and "stressing utility." Whether they can be developed and harnessed effectively, however, depends on other social and historical conditions. It is a social existence that determines the ideology of society rather

---

① Hoyt, T. *Utilitarian Confucianism—Ch'en Liang's Challenge to Chu Hsi* [M]. Trans. Jiang, C. Nanjing: Jiangsu People's Publishing House, 1997:135.
② Ye, T. Study on economic thoughts of real learning in the Eastern Zhejiang Practical Schools in the Song Dynasty—Centred on Ye Shi [J]. *Researches in Chinese Economic History,* 2000(4).

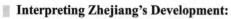
than the other way around. When social and economic development has an urgent demand for spiritual resources, they will be explored through "fusion of horizon" or "compromising reading." In this sense, it is not Neo-Confucianism of Huizhou that breeds its economic and social life but the opposite. It is not the Eastern Zhejiang Practical Schools that contribute to the cultural spirit of "striving for practical results" but certain social and historical conditions. Undoubtedly, once the social consciousness of "striving for practical results" is explored and spread, it has a reaction to society to a certain extent.

It should be noted that social awareness can be divided into two different levels, namely social mentality and social ideology. The former is directly related to daily life. It is a spontaneous, unsystematic and indefinable form of reflection that mirrors social existence. The latter is an indirect reflection of social existence and a more systematic and conscious form of abstract reflection summarized in social life. The social mentality is the ideological basis and provides the initial foundation for its formation and development.

According to the classification method noted above, both schools can be incorporated into social ideology which is an indirect reflection of social existence and a more systematic and conscious form of abstract reflection summarized in social life. Although a systematic and theoretical form of social ideology might have a negative effect on social existence and psychology, as the folklorist Sumner said, the folk custom that people unconsciously form in their activities has finally become the paradigm for them to consciously safeguard themselves. "All members are obliged to follow" because "folk custom is a social strength," which dominates social life. "All human lives in all times and all stages of culture are largely dominated by folk customs."[1] In this sense, social psychology, which has a more direct impact on the

---

[1] Gao, B. *Folk Culture and Folk Life* [M]. Beijing: China Social Sciences Press, 1994: 96.

economic and social life of the ancient people, should have a more direct impact on the development of contemporary Zhejiang.

2.3 Regional Folk Tradition and the Cultural Spirit of "Striving for Practical Results"

As previously mentioned, "striving for practical results" and "stressing utility" have indeed created a cultural spirit vital to the economic and social development and institutional innovation of Zhejiang since the reform and opening-up. At the same time, an attempt has also been made to prove from multiple angles that the source of the "striving for practical results" spirit of contemporary Zhejiang people can be traced back to the Eastern Zhejiang Practical Schools. However, this point of view seems to lack evidence. In fact, on the one hand, the viewpoints of the Eastern Zhejiang Practical Schools can find their spiritual resource from Confucianism or even the traditional mainstream culture of China as a whole. As indicated by the other sections of this book, the Eastern Zhejiang Practical Schools, despite having its distinct characteristics, can be directly linked to Confucianism of the Central Plains. More importantly, on the other hand, suppose that the theory of "social existence determines social consciousness" is acknowledged, it can then be concluded that the spirit of "striving for practical results" and "stressing utility" is not only a reflection of social existence in the Zhejiang region throughout history, but also a refining and generalization of the social mentality of the people. In other words, this spirit does not merely act as the source. It can be said that the Eastern Zhejiang Practical Schools are able to demonstrate their distinct regional characteristics due to the existence of the Zhejiang regional society and the stimulation from the people's social mentality. Therefore, it is more important to prove whether a spirit of "striving for practical results" exists in traditional Zhejiang society, rather than proving whether the cultural spirit is embodied in the Eastern Zhejiang Practical Schools. To achieve this goal, the real source of the pragmatic spirit of contemporary Zhejiang people can be determined. However, this is no doubt a very difficult task.

2.3.1 Practice of the Folk Industry and Commerce and the Spirit of "Striving for Practical Results"

Using one factor to negate another factor or regarding one factor as the only factor to explain why the spirit of "striving for practical results" of the Eastern Zhejiang Practical Schools was formed is clearly one-sided. In this context, continuing to follow Max Weber's multi-factor "flexible interpretation principle" should still be the correct approach. Firstly, many factors have had a significant impact on the formation of the "striving for practical results" cultural spirit of the Eastern Zhejiang Practical Schools, including the collapse of facing the Northern Song Dynasty; unique natural conditions of Zhejiang; political, cultural and economic positions enjoyed by Zhejiang compared to the Central Plains; as well as other social existence factors such as Zhejiang's unique methods of production and living. Apart from the nation's macro-political and social situation, amongst Zhejiang's many factors of social existence, the well-developed practice of the private industrial and commercial sectors is particularly notable.

The development of industry and commerce during the Song, Yuan, Ming, and Qing dynasties will be specifically addressed in the other chapters of this book and will not be explored in this section. It is worth noting that throughout the history of China and foreign nations, people have generally focused more on the reality and practical results, which are determined by the unique characteristics of industrial and commercial activities. According to modern economics, industrial and commercial activities are acts performed to ensure one's survival and to improve one's well-being, which is a kind of economic activity.

In classical and neoclassical economics, participants of economic activities are rational and act on their self-interest. This is typically reflected in the concept of an economic man who is the basis of traditional economic theories. It can be said that the existence of an "economic man" who handles everything in a strictly rational manner is the basic psychological hypothesis of British classical schools. The philosophical foundation of the economic man hypothesis is individual utilitarianism.

From the time of Adam Smith, the economic man hypothesis has already been clearly defined (before Smith, including mercantilism, this hypothesis had already been implied). The characteristics of the economic man hypothesis put forward by Smith can be categorized into the following: self-interest, rationality, and the pursuit of the maximization of self-interest which would lead to the promotion of social interests. In neoclassical economics, the interests of an economic man are extended and are linked with one's subjective evaluation. Thus, the economic man no longer pursues merely the maximization of self-interest, but rather the maximization of subjective utility. This has expanded the "economic man" hypothesis' scope of explanation on human behaviors. There seems to be notable evidence for the abstract reliance that economists have on the economic man. The first is the Darwinian survival mechanism. Market competition only commends entrepreneurs and businessmen who pursue profit maximization rationally, while bankruptcy or stagnation is used to punish those who act in a different way. In this manner, only entrepreneurs or businessmen who pursue maximization can survive. Therefore, it seems that the economic man hypothesis matches the concept of "survival of the fittest." Second, by applying the economic man hypothesis into the analysis and forecast of specific issues, the results have proven to be identical.[1]

Of all the characteristics of an economic man, the one that can best demonstrate the pragmatic or the "striving for practical results" spirit

---

[1]   Yang, C. The theoretical value of the economic man and its experiential basis [J]. *Economic Research Journal*, 1996(7).

is rationality, which refers to the continuous weighing, comparison and calculation conducted by an economic man between costs and benefits, so as to select the course of action that would bring him the greatest benefits. In other words, the maximization of effectiveness can only be achieved through calculation, and its principle is inseparable from the calculation principle. In this sense, Waters has pointed out that "the individual continuously calculates the return of participation relative to the cost, therefore human behavior is considered as rational."[1]

In Max Weber's system, rationality and rationalization are vitally important concepts, yet he has never clearly defined the term "rationality." According to Rogers Brubaker's analysis, there are no fewer than 16 apparent meanings of the term "rationality" as used by Weber: "Thus modern capitalism is defined by the rational (deliberate and systematic) pursuit of profit through the rational (systematic and calculable) organization of formally free labor and through rational (impersonal, purely instrumental) exchange on the market, guided by rational (exact, purely quantitative) accounting procedures and guaranteed by rational (rule-governed, predictable) legal and political systems. Ascetic Protestantism is characterized by rational (methodical) self-control and by the rational (purposeful) devotion to rational (sober, scrupulous) economic action as a rational (psychologically efficacious and logically intelligible) means of relieving the intolerable pressure imposed on individuals by the rational (consistent) doctrine of predestination."[2] These different connotations of "rationality" are in fact the different forms of the same matter that are demonstrated in different contexts. This "same matter" is a kind of reasonable state that should be confirmed through reflection, and sometimes refers to the ability to achieve this state.

---

① Liu, S. The core status and method misplacement of rational choice studies in economic sociology [J]. *Sociological Studies*, 2003(6).
② Brubaker, R. *The Limits of Rationality: An Essay on the Social and Moral Thought of Max Weber* [M]. Boston: George Allen and Unwin, 1984: 1-2.

Regarding an economic man as rational does not mean that every act of an economic entity is made after a precise and rational calculation. In real life, all economic entities are embedded into the social and cultural network and all have experienced the process of socialization. Therefore, as Weber put it, the valuing of rational, traditional and emotional actions was generally controlled by the beliefs, habits, imitations, emotions and instinctive pulses from a non-logical level, and cannot be analyzed by the calculation principles of instrumental rationality or purposive rationality. In fact, people's pursuit of economic interests in real life is not simple. It is always subject to the constraints of ethics, customs, cultural tradition, social institutions, and social relations. Merely pursuing economic interests without considering the influence of other factors is an ideal state that can only be formed under an abstract condition. Of course, stating that an economic man possesses the social, cultural and ethical attributes does not mean the denial of the most distinctive feature of the economic man in pursuing the maximization of interests, rationality, calculation, and pragmatism.

Since industrial and commercial activities are a typical type of economic activity, then it is only natural that handicraftsmen and businessmen should pursue the maximization of interests in a rational manner. That is to say, under the Darwinian survival mechanism, handicraftsmen and businessmen whose goal is to maximize their interests must be "rational," and are able to analyze, compare and calculate, or in other words, place an emphasis on utility and effectiveness. The natural disposition of striving for practical results and stressing utility will often challenge handicraftsmen and businessmen to break through the shackles of customs, prohibitions, and ideologies, thereby conduct pragmatic actions. This point can be demonstrated by the abundant cases throughout the history of industry and commerce in China and foreign nations.

The Venetian merchants of the Middle Ages were realistic people.

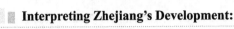
Venetians resembled the modern-day Italians, in the way that they spoke Italian and were Roman Catholics. In reality, the belief of a Venetian merchant (despite being a Roman Catholic) is a typical merchant belief. Christianity cannot bind these merchants against the disciplines of not borrowing and lending money for profits. Apart from trading with the Muslim community, the Venetian merchants would even dare to break through the restraints and prohibitions set by the ideologies of European Christianity, by trafficking weapon materials to the Muslim community and gaining profits. Although timber is used to build ships and steel is used to make weapons, these ships and weapons would be used against the Christians or sometimes against the sailors of Venice. However, just like any other merchant, pragmatic Venetian merchants do not concern themselves with these matters, for all they think about is how they can satisfy their commercial interests and make a good deal.

Wandering merchants of Europe in the Middle Ages were also realistic people. Driven by profits, they would continuously alter their identities. For instance, they may have been mercers to begin with, but upon arriving at a certain destination and discovering that the wine there is very famous, they would immediately change to vintners; they may have been merchants who traveled by land, but upon discovering that sea transportation would bring bigger profits, they would become a shipowner or seaman without hesitation.[1] This demonstrates that wandering merchants are results-oriented and put their interests as a top priority.

Similar to the Venetian merchants and wandering merchants of medieval Europe, Shanxi and Huizhou merchants of the Ming and Qing dynasties were also results-oriented. During the Ming and Qing dynasties, many Shanxi merchants once taught their disciples about the "books of the Hundred Schools of Thought," with an aim that the

---

① Zhao, L. *The Formation of the Merchant Class and Social Transformation in Western Europe* [M]. Beijing: China Social Sciences Press, 2004: 139.

disciples would take in the essence of all kinds of traditional cultural classics and eventually be able to "make money even in difficult times." Among these books, the spirit of "humanistic pragmatism" has been the common theme. The scholars of Shanxi took into account that "a good education can lead to greater prosperity" and step into the commercial world with their heads held up high in a society that places greater importance on education than trade and where the commercial industry is only a minor industry. A key reason for this was that their thoughts had not been constrained by the "hypocrite Taoism ideologies" that had prevailed for hundreds of years in the Northern Song Dynasty, instead, they always viewed the world with a rational and realistic mindset. To some Shanxi merchants, Confucianism and trade are connected, while education and trade follow the same principles. Confucianism was transformed into an ethical concept that was beneficial to commercial activities.

As previously mentioned, Huizhou merchants of the Ming and Qing dynasties were also very realistic. On one hand, Huizhou merchants stood firm in casting away the unrealistic ideas in Cheng–Zhu School of Neo-Confucianism; on the other hand, out of a need for their own commercial activities, the unrealistic ideas would add aspects of utilitarianism to the fundamental ideologies of the Cheng-Zhu School or even Confucianism. In the eyes of Huizhou merchants, even the concept of "righteousness" in the Cheng–Zhu School which was an absolute priority over "interest" was subject to achieving the business goal of gaining long-term interests. Here, compliance to "righteousness" is obviously not acted upon the moral principles set by practical rationality as put forward by Kant, that is, to not comply and execute the "categorical imperative" of moral principles, but is rather a result purely driven by commercial interests. To some Huizhou merchants, only by acting upon "righteousness" could they ensure that benefits can be brought in continuously. Therefore, just as Tang Lixing had said, "In Huizhou, scholars and merchants are not only connected, merchants who righteously pursue interests are better than scholars who

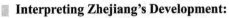
indulge themselves in books. It can be said that 'there is a heavenly principle of existence in human desires', as demonstrated by the link between interests and the ethics of filial piety and fraternal duty in Confucianism, as well as the connected values of good faith and honor. Neo-Confucianism's contribution to the rebirth of merchant culture is obvious."[1]

The well-developed industrial and commercial activities in the history of Zhejiang have clearly created the social mentality of "striving for practical results" and "stressing utility" in the Zhejiang. At the same time, with this social mentality, these activities have certainly played an important role in cultivating the cultural spirit of "striving for practical results" and "stressing utility" in the Eastern Zhejiang Practical Schools. It can be said that the birthplace of the Schools, whether it is the Yongjia School, Jinhua School or Yongkang School, all lie in regions which were once relatively developed in terms of traditional folk industry and commerce. Since the Song Dynasty, there has always been a lack of cultivated land in Wenzhou, due to the increasing concentration of people which could not be compensated by the increase in production scale and productive forces. Under the pressure of survival, people of Wenzhou gradually formed the idea of "looking up to the rich" and would strive to become one of the rich when the opportunity arises. As a result, "people spent most of their time engaging in trade."[2] At that time, Wenzhou people who engaged in trade either "woke up early or worked till late"[3], or set up street stalls to make small profits, or transported goods domestically or internationally. In comparison, in the birthplace of the Jinhua and Yongkang Schools, "handicraft productions were scattered across the cities and townships,

---

① Tang, L. *Social and Economic Research of Huizhou Since the Ming and Qing dynasties* [M]. Hefei: Anhui University Press, 1999: 212.

② Zhu, M. *Overview of Scenic Spots*: vol.9 [M]. Beijing: Zhonghua Book Company, 2003.

③ Dai, X. *Collection of Huanchuan*: vol.5 Records of Shenggai Pagoda [M].

handicrafts were becoming more and more varied and the flow of goods continued to increase. The speed of the flow was increased. All in all, the product economy was becoming more prosperous."[1] Therefore, the cultivation of the cultural spirit of "striving for practical results" and "stressing utility" is not a coincidence. The fact that the proposition for the values of "engaging in practical work and being results-oriented," "staying realistic and pragmatic," as well as "coexistence of utility and righteousness" took shape only in regions where industrial and commercial activities were relatively developed showed that regional commercial activities that were rational and "emphasizes pragmatism" would definitely be reflected in the traditions of the Eastern Zhejiang Practical Schools.

It needs to be clarified that if there was no continuation and expansion of the corresponding social culture and mentality after the Southern Song Dynasty, with the passage of time, the tradition of "striving for practical results" in the Eastern Zhejiang Practical Schools might have only become a fixed tradition sealed within the cultural classics rather than a vivid and continuous regional and cultural spirit that exists in Zhejiang's civil society. Historical evidence clearly shows that, from the Yuan, Ming and Qing dynasties to the period of the Republic of China, industrial and commercial activities in Zhejiang's civil society have been relatively active. This point will be specifically addressed in the other chapters of this book. The emphasis in this section will be placed on how as previously mentioned, industrial and commercial activities create the best environment for the growth and continuation of the spirit of rationality and pragmatism.

At the same time, through the unique social mechanisms of human society, the spirit of rationality and pragmatism will gradually become a regional social mentality or a regional social habitus. Bourdieu

---

[1]   Bao, W. *Studies on Zhejiang Regional History* [M]. Hangzhou: Hangzhou Publishing Group, 2003: 237.

believed that habitus was formed by the series of historical relations deposited in a person and that it was the internalization of objective yet common social norms and community values. Habitus embodies in the form of the unconscious and lasting dispositions to think, feel and act with unique cultural characteristics. Habitus possesses the following characteristics: First, in terms of its nature, it is a complete disposition system, or in other words, a system that distinguishes perception, judgment, and action. Second, in terms of its form, it is as stable as it is rooted within our mind or body and creates effects that go beyond the specific situations that we encounter. As our subjective construction, habitus on the one hand internalizes external constraints and possibilities by means of social conditions or regulation, that is to say, it builds our social cognition, perception, and actions; on the other hand, as a constructive structure, it provides individuals with a form and continuity to their activities in all spheres of the world, enabling actors to acquire the purpose and reason for their actions. Habitus is based on certain resource conditions and actions that will most likely lead to success in our past experience and drives the actors to choose their own practice according to the expected outcomes. Thus, habitus includes the subconscious calculation of what is possible or impossible.[①] In this sense, the "pragmatic" spirit demonstrated by the people of Zhejiang during the planned economy period and after the reform and opening-up is a direct manifestation of the "constructive structure" function of the traditional social mentality or habitus in the region.

2.3.2 The Folk Social Psychology and the Spirit of "Striving for Practical Results"

As mentioned, the cultural spirit of "striving for practical results" and "stressing utility" of the Eastern Zhejiang Practical Schools is not only rooted in the social existence such as relatively developed industrial and commercial activities in the history of Zhejiang, but is

---

①   Zhu, G. *Cultural Logic of Power* [M]. Shanghai: Shanghai People's Publishing House, 2004: 166-167.

also present in the small traditions of Zhejiang, namely "the traditions of the largely unreflective many." Plekhanov once made a brief summary of all levels of social structures and their relations: the state of productive forces; the economic relations constrained by the productive forces; the socio-political institution that sprouted from a certain economic basis; the mentality of the people that is in part directly determined by the economy and in part determined by all the socio-political institutions that sprouted from the economy, and various kinds of ideological systems that reflect such psychological characteristics. Plekhanov's theoretical summary uncovered the positions that folk traditions and mentality enjoy in social life and the intermediary roles they play among economic foundations, political institutions and forms of social consciousness. The folklorist Sumner also pointed out that: "It can be said that philosophy and ethics were the products of folklore, which were abstracted from morality and were by no means original concepts; they were the products and derivatives."[1] Therefore, if the social mentality bases of emphasizing the effectiveness and utility did not exist in the search for the source of water from the Great Traditions to the Little Traditions, it would still be hard to imagine how the cultural spirit of "striving for practical results" and "stressing utility" would be formed. It is especially noteworthy that this traditional social mentality is a kind of undercurrent that ran throughout the civil society of Zhejiang in different historical periods. They constitute the direct source of the "striving for practical results" spirit of contemporary Zhejiang society.

In *History of the Song Dynasty: Geography Records*, it is noted that Zhejiang people were "gentle and intelligent in nature, advocates Buddhism, knows how to enjoy life, are enterprising, good at making money, and stands out for their skillfulness." This indicates that the cultural spirit of "striving for practical results" and "stressing utility"

---

① Gao, B. *Folk Culture and Folk Life* [M]. Beijing: China Social Sciences Press, 1994: 86-87.

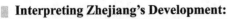

had already manifested in the Zhejiang civil society during the Song Dynasty. In real life, this enterprising and money-making spirit will undoubtedly be demonstrated in different ways. One particular method is the realistic religious attitude and behavior of "never burn the incense when all is well, but clasp Buddha's feet when in distress." The reason why folk religious attitudes deserve attention is that it is a projection of the value of the real world in the civil society. The 19th-century philosopher Schleiermacher believes that the starting point for religion is the "feeling of absolute dependence." Peter Berger believed that all humans in society were undertaking world-building activities and that religion had a special place amongst such activities. "It can thus be said that religion has played a strategic part in the human enterprise of world-building. Religion implies the farthest reach of man's self-externalization, of his infusion of reality with his own meanings. Religion implies that human order is projected into the totality of being. Put differently, religion is the audacious attempt to conceive of the entire universe as being humanly significant."[1] However, Simmel pointed out that "social phenomena and religious phenomena were so similar that social structures are bound to possess religious characteristics, while religious structures appeared to symbolize and legitimize those social structures."[2] Robert Neelly Bellah argued that religion provided individuals and groups with a sense of identity, such as the definition of self and the environment, in the sense that religion was a set of social perceptions and that it provided an interpretation of the reality, as well as a guide to self-definition and life. Paul Tillich believed that the most fundamental human experience that can serve as a starting point for theological discussions was the "ultimate concern" common to all mankind. The innermost nature of religious belief is the human soul and emotional state. Religion assumes that there is another world

---

[1] Berger, P. L. *The Sacred Canopy Elements of a Sociological Theory of Religion* [M]. Trans. Gao, S. Shanghai: Shanghai People's Publishing House, 1991: 36.

[2] Simmel, G. *Modern People and Religion* [M]. Trans. Cao, W. et al. Beijing: China Renmin University Press, 2003: 101.

outside the human world where divine beings that differ from humans are. These assumptions cannot be confirmed within human experience. No matter what they are in the ultimate respect, in terms of experience, they are merely the product of human activities and the projection of human beings. In this sense, it is fair to say that the traditional religious belief of Zhejiang is a revelation (or projection) of the true thoughts and mentality of the traditional Zhejiang civil society. It is for this reason that knowing the attitudes of traditional folk religions naturally becomes a key to understanding the true thoughts and mentality of the traditional Zhejiang civil society.

According to Allport's religious taxonomy, religion can be divided into intrinsic religion and extrinsic religion. Intrinsic religion means that the believers live their lives as their religion preaches that they should without reservation. Such believers serve their religion more firmly rather than letting religion serve themselves. Extrinsic religion is self-serving, utilitarian and self-protecting, offering consolation and salvation to the followers at the sacrifice of external interests. Following Allport's logic, Fang Wen, a scholar of China, expanded the taxonomy of intrinsic-extrinsic religion into one of the followers' religious orientation, that was, intrinsic (religious) believers-extrinsic (religious) believers.[①]

The faith of intrinsic believers is absolute. They find their most satisfied motives in religion, while the other needs, no matter how intense they are, are only seen as minor. They attempt to include these needs in the context of religious belief and rules. After accepting a creed, intrinsic believers would often attempt to internalize the creed and regard it as a moral law of conduct. Luther believed that "faith" in God was to live as God wants us to live. Hence, Luther's "faith" is

---

① Fang, W. How to form group symbol boundary? Take the Protestant Christian group in Beijing for example [J]. *Sociological Studies*, 2005(1).

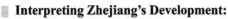
composed of three parts.[①] First, faith is not only historical, but also relational. "Faith" does not merely refer to believing in the authenticity of the deeds of Christ and the reliability of its history as recorded by the Bible, but more about believing that Jesus died for the salvation of each individual. His death is more personal than that of an individual. Second, "faith" includes trust. "Faith" is not only about believing that God is real but more about trusting his promises, conservativeness, faithfulness and leaving oneself to the hands of God. Therefore, the effect of "faith" does not take in mind of the strength of human confidence, but rather the trustworthiness and dependability of the object of faith. The things that we believe in will control our attitudes and actions to a great extent, that is, whether we are willing to show that we are depending on the matter through our actions. Lastly, Luther believed that "faith" would unite the believers and Christ. Faith means not only allowing us to understand that the words of God is filled with grace, freedom, and holiness but also connecting our souls with Jesus, just like how the bride and groom are attached to each other. In the eyes of Luther, faith merges the two parties into one and each is committed to the other. In leaving themselves to the hands of God, the Holy Spirit would dwell deep within their hearts and are justified and forgiven of all sins. They are also given the hope of eternal life. At the same time, the Holy Spirit would bring in increasing confidence and allow the believer to gain more knowledge in the faith.

In *The Protestant Ethic and the Spirit of Capitalism*, Weber mentioned that Catholic Christians would use diaries to record their sins, struggles and progress of faith. Of course, the main purpose of recording these is to ensure the "integrity of repentance" and to enlighten the other disciples. Protestant Christians would use diaries to "measure" their "pulses," that is, to keep an eye on their piety, use the diaries to observe and reflect their progress in gaining virtue, and

---

① Xu, Z. *Introduction to Christian Theological Thoughts* [M]. Beijing: China Social Sciences Press, 2001: 8-9.

reminding themselves of their obligations as "voters." Needless to say, the understanding of Protestantism in the eyes of figures such as Luther and Calvin can be regarded as the typical attitude that intrinsic believers have to "faith."

Contrary to intrinsic (religious) believers, extrinsic (religious) believers are utilitarian. They tend to use religion for their own means. Extrinsic believers may find religion useful in many aspects, such as providing security and comfort, communication and entertainment as well as status and self-expression. They are seldom serious when it comes to believing and accepting the creeds, or they would adapt certain creeds to the fundamental needs. According to the above classification, traditional Chinese folk religions can be generally categorized as "extrinsic religions," while its believers are classified as "extrinsic believers."

The sociologist Edward Ross pointed out that at the beginning of accepting a faith, the Chinese were just as practical as in any other aspects of life…the Chinese saw the Buddha as the source of satisfying interests. They prayed that the Buddha would grant them good health, a good harvest, success in the imperial examination, a profitable business, and a smooth career.[①] Whereas Christian Jochim, an American religious sociologist, pointed out that the belief in a spiritual system of ideas was by no means the driving force of ordinary Chinese people's religious behaviors…Chinese people do not pay much attention to religious creeds and they rarely believe that putting faith into a particular creed— and rejecting all other creeds—is a matter of life and death in China, there seems to be something of a contractual nature between God and man, and are often accompanied by promises of repaying favors.[②] The

---

① Sha, L. *Foreigners' View of the Chinese in the Past 100 Years* [M]. Taiyuan: Shanxi Education Press, 1999: 272.

② Jochim, C. *China's Religious Ethos* [M]. Trans. Wang, P. Beijing: The Chinese Overseas Publishing House, 1999: 163.

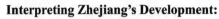
Chinese-American anthropologist Xu Langguang claimed that Chinese people treated the supernatural world in the same way they did to the mundane things in the world. They searched for the Buddha or other gods or spirits who could timely attend to victims, rather than look for gods who could guide people or bring salvation at all times.[1] Tang Junyi agreed and believed that "In China, there was no concept of an absolute God with absolute power who was isolated from the people. Thus, God was regarded the same as any other human being and so should be treated in the same way that humans interact with one another." [2] All of the scholars mentioned above have uncovered an important characteristic of Chinese folk religions, namely, having the features of being realistic, utilitarian and contractual. This characteristic of Chinese folk religion is particularly evident in the traditional civil society of Zhejiang. Zhejiang's traditional folk religions clearly demonstrate a kind of "pragmatic" and "utilitarian" cultural spirit.

Historically, Zhejiang was a region with relatively developed folk religions. Buddhism and Taoism are the most influential religions in the traditional civil society of Zhejiang. Although there are fewer Taoist temples than Buddhist temples, they hold similar status in society. The Buddhist and Taoist faith of the civil society embodies characteristics of Allport's "extrinsic religion." People worship Buddhism and Taoism mainly because they were "useful." Sacrificial activities were mostly held by Taoist priests with a very notable "utilitarian" orientation, though they are sometimes presented by both Taoist and Buddhist priests. In the people's eyes, The Taoist priests and Buddhist monks possess divine power so people would feel more relieved if both sides send their prayers. Therefore, the spiritual world of Zhejiang's civil society is very ambiguous, and especially so after the introduction of

---

① Sha, L. *Foreigners' View of the Chinese in the Past 100 Years* [M]. Taiyuan: Shanxi Education Press, 1999: 326.

② Tang, J. *Comparative Study of Chinese and Western Philosophy* [M]. Taipei: Taiwan Student Book Office, 1988: 235-248.

Buddhism into China. People did not differentiate the local deities from the foreign deities, nor did they mark the boundary between the gods of different religious systems. On frequent occasions, the gods of all the religions would live together harmoniously and the people would use these deities to serve their own ends. The people may go to a Buddhist Taoist temple to pray for heirs or go to a Taoist temple and pray for the recovery of health, or they may go to a Mazu temple to pray for safety. This concept of folk religious belief forms a stark contrast to the two most prevalent religions of the West, namely Christianity and Judaism. As Xu Langguang put forth, Christianity and Judaism "are basically personal religions that stress there is only one God that directly connects to people's hearts. The stronger the believer's faith in self-attachment, the firmer his faith in believing that there is an omnipresent, omnipotent or even omniscient (as part of the principles of Christian scientists) God. This situation thus determines that all the other gods are false and evil and should be eliminated at any cost."[①] Monotheism believes that there is only one God who is good and that his followers are carrying out good deeds by engaging in uncompromising struggles against the other gods. However, in the traditional folk religion of Zhejiang, no matter what kind of gods there are, as long as they are useful, they would become the objects of "worship."

There are a large number of deities in the civil society of Zhejiang throughout history. There are many kinds of gods, such as gods of myths and legends, gods of historical figures, gods of a certain profession, and gods of laborers. These different deities are worshiped in accordance with the different needs of the people of Zhejiang. Therefore, the faith in these local Gods also demonstrates very strong practical and utilitarian characteristics. For example, Zhejiang is often plagued by floods, so the flood-control hero King Yu is much adored by the people. Temples of King Yu are scattered throughout Zhejiang,

---

① Hsu, F. L. K. *Americans and Chinese: Passages to Differences* [M]. Trans. Peng, K. & Liu, W. Beijing: Huaxia Publishing House, 1989: 240.

covering a vast area from Hangzhou Bay, Ningshao Plain to the Taihu Lake Basin. Local officials who worked on constructing weirs and irrigated fields, building embankments to defend the seas or rivers, as well as opening up lakes and dredging rivers were also worshipped and enjoyed the treatment of a god. An example of this is the Temple of Prefecture Chief Ma in Shaoxing and the Temple of Tiancao in suburban Hangzhou, which worships Prefecture Chief Ma Zhen and County Magistrate Chen Hun. These two figures are worshipped for their efforts in building Jinhu Lake and opening up the roads to Nanxiang and Xixi. County Magistrate Lu Nanjin was ordered to build Dongqian Lake during the reign of Emperor Xuanzong of the Tang Dynasty, while Prefecture Chief Li Yigeng was ordered to continue building the lake during the reign of Emperor Zhenzong of the Song Dynasty. To commemorate their efforts, the Jiaze Temple was constructed beside Dongqian Lake for worships.[①] In 1146, during the reign of Emperor Gaozong of the Southern Song Dynasty, "people cherished the old times and restored the shrines and temples and put up statues."[②] For Zhang Xunxing's efforts in building Guangde Lake, a temple was built in his name, and sacrifices were offered to the "deity of this lake and he who has contributed to the well-being of this lake."[③] There is also the Fenghui Temple at Wangchun Mountain in the Guangde Lake area which worships the Prefecture Chief Lou Yi. In the beginning, these temples were built to commemorate officials who have made contributions to the region. However, as time passed, they were turned into realistic, utilitarian and contractual local protection deities that possess the divine power of "answering to the prayers no matter what they are." In some parts of Zhejiang, apart from humans, some animals have also been worshipped as protection deities that would help defend against droughts and floods. An example of this is when the sign

---

① Fang, W. *Records of Simin in the Baoqing Era*: vol.13 Records of Yin County: Temple [M].
② Ibid. vol. 13 Records of Yin County: Water.
③ Zeng, G. *Drafts of Master Nanfeng*: vol.19 Records of Guangde Lake [M].

of drought appears in Taizhou after autumn. During the worship period which lasts for 10 days, it is forbidden to slaughter pigs, cattle and other large livestock.[1]

Historically, Zhejiang is home to hundreds of craftsmen and its handicraft industry is relatively developed. The ancestral god is the god of industry protection, who is very useful and thus it forms a major branch of Zhejiang's folk deity system. In Zhejiang, almost every handicraft industry has its own ancestor. The well-known ancestral gods of each industry include: Lu Ban as god of the carpentry, masonry, brick and tile industries, Li Shizhen as god of Chinese medicine, Du Kang as god of brewing, Lu Yu as god of tea, Ge Hong as god of the dye industry, Luo Zu and Lü Dongbin as gods of hairdressing, Xuanyuan Shi (Huangdi) as god of tailoring. There are three main sources for these deities: First is that they are the founders of an industry, second is that they are the skilled workers and craftsmen or well-known figures of the industry. And third is that they possess magical power in the legends and myths. The statues of ancestral gods are usually placed at the workplace. Worships are made during the four seasons and eight solar terms or when receiving apprentices, finishing apprenticeship and when issues arise. There are also dedicated temples and guild halls for the same industries, and worships are made according to the seasons and solar terms.[2]

Western religious sociologists believed that religion is a form of social consciousness and an external social force that governs people's daily lives. It is a system of beliefs and practices in which people interpret and respond to the things they consider divine and

---

① CPPCC Taizhou City Cultural Information and Learning Committee & Zhejiang Taizhou Folk Literature and Art Association. *Grand View of Taizhou Folklore* [M]. Ningbo: Ningbo Publishing House, 1998.
② Chinese Confucius Society Editorial Board. *Integration of Chinese Regional Culture* [M]. Beijing: China Mass Publishing House, 1998: 244-245.

supernatural. Religions are collectively represented as divine and supernatural concepts or simply religious concepts. A religious concept has seven characteristics: Sacredness is a kind of power or force. It has two abstract features, such as nature and morality, life and universe, and beauty and ugliness, it does not feature utilitarian aspects, it is super-empirical, it does not involve knowledge, it can promote and support worshippers, and it can increase the moral needs of worshippers. A religious concept that can possess these seven characteristics is in fact in line with what Allport referred to as an "intrinsic religion." The folk religious concept of Zhejiang forms a stark contrast to the characteristics of religious concepts as described by Western religious sociologists in at least two aspects, namely "without utilitarianism" and "is super empirical."

As demonstrated above, the relationship between gods and men is a purely practical and utilitarian one. Most of the local gods of Zhejiang are relatively close to the people and are closely integrated with the lives and productive activities of the civil society. In other words, there is no clear boundary between the spiritual world and the folk world. People would treat the supernatural world in the same way they would to the mundane things in the world. People would usually search for deities that can provide timely help to those in need rather than deities that would guide people in various ways and bring salvation to the people at all times. Since folk gods are mainly established by the people themselves, it seems that even the gods cannot stand on their own feet and are dependent on the offerings that people make. Therefore, in the imagination of the folk world, many deities, such as the god of water and god of plague, would warn people of their disrespect by creating periodic catastrophes on earth. People may bribe these deities by celebrating their birthdays and even offer them brides. They rely on the deities to overcome disasters such as flood, drought, wind and rain, lightning and thunder, insects, as well as diseases to ensure a year of peace. For example, during the reign of Xuanhe of the Song Dynasty, there was a fish pond in the south west of Cixi and located between the townships of Songlin and Jinxi. There were many irrigated fields in the area and the pond was said to be the home to the eel spirit that holds divine power. People from the townships then built a shrine next to the pond and enshrined a statue of the god of rain. During the dry seasons, the "townspeople would come together to hold a ritual and drummers would welcome the eel spirit." The legend of the eel spirit made the fish pond famous throughout the region. Believers from Taizhou and Mingzhou would travel for hundreds of miles for a glimpse of the pond.[①] According to the *Shaoying Temple Records*, a stele in Huangyang County: "A drought hit the region in June 1116, the lands became barren and people were greatly concerned," the County Magistrate and his subordinates then went on to pray for rain at Bailongao, and eventually the "drought was overcome and harvests were brought back...but much of these was owed to the god of rain." Afterwards the county records also noted how in the 16th year of the reign of Emperor Kangxi of the Qing Dynasty, the County Magistrate Zhang Siqi "walked out of the east gate with straw shoes on and dressed in white," and climbed up Bailong Mountain from Jiufeng to pray for rain. It was claimed that "three prayers were made and three heavy rains were brought" this year. In some areas of Zhejiang, deities are even coerced to obey the utilitarian purpose of mankind. For example, when the drought season hits, people of Taizhou would place (the statue of) Master Daquan, the nephew of the Jade Emperor, under the scorching sun to pray for the heaven's pity and bring rain. Sometimes, the god of rain and the god of towns would also be placed under the scorching sun. Thus, there is a common saying in Taizhou: "No luck with the four seasons and eight solar terms, praying for rain is an arduous task."[②]

---

① Bao, W. *Studies on Zhejiang Regional History* [M]. Hangzhou: Hangzhou Publishing Group, 2003: 119-120.

② CPPCC Taizhou City Cultural Information and Learning Committee & Zhejiang Taizhou Folk Literature and Art Association. *Grand View of Taizhou Folklore* [M]. Ningbo: Ningbo Publishing House, 1998.

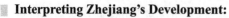
This folk religious concept is undoubtedly different from the concept of "conversion" in religious studies. Religious psychologist George Coe believed that religious "conversion" has four characteristics: First, conversion is a profound change of self. Second, the change of self is not a simple and mature matter, but rather it is the most typical and decisive sense of self-identity that, whether sudden or gradual, is a decision of a new self-perspective that is to be acknowledged. Third, this self-change constitutes a complete paradigm shift in human life— with a set of new interests, hobbies, and behaviors as the center. Lastly, this transformation is seen as the "supreme" liberation or the liberation from previous confusions and lives with little value.[①] The famous Doomsday Model of John Lofland shows that the fulfillment of conversion requires satisfying seven conditions, three of which are "continuation of intense experiences," "be immersed in the problem-solving viewpoint featuring religious inclinations" and "defining oneself from here onwards as a religious seeker." Conversion is not a sudden and instantaneous experience, but an ongoing process that involves many stages and progressing from one extent to another. Lofland's "model of conversion" pays particular attention to the integration of meaning and identity in the process of conversion, that is, to integrate the construction of meaning into the conversion process and highlight the trigger of life crisis for conversion. People who have undergone religious conversions generally experienced mental stress and anxiety.[②] "Conversion" has a deeper connotation in Christianity. It refers to the emotional experience of acknowledging Jesus as the Savior and having the feeling of being "born-again." In this sense, religious conversion is undoubtedly an unforgettable experience in the depth of the soul or even a radical reorganization of life.

---

① Liang, L. *Religious Psychology of Chinese People—Theoretical Analysis and Empirical Study of Religious Identity* [M]. Beijing: Social Sciences Academic Press, 2004: 18-19.

② Ibid. 21-22.

However, the religious beliefs held by Zhejiang's folk religions are not "complete reorganizations of identity, meaning, and life," nor are they "processes that transform the reality of the lowest level."[①] Zhejiang's traditional civil society does not regard deities as emotional supports to people's sense of loneliness, fear, depression, and pain, nor are they objects of repentance when individual feel that they have sinned, nor do the people treat their faith to the deities as an investigation and reflection of their souls. Zhejiang's traditional civil society neither "immerse itself in the problem-solving viewpoints featuring religious inclinations," nor are the people sincere in converting to the gods and showing their respect and admiration for the gods, thus "defining themselves from here onwards as religious seekers." Due to the vast number of gods, the worshipers' dedications to the religions must be divided. As a result, the solemnity of the gods is reduced and it would be impossible for worshipers to find out whether they hold an irresistible attachment to a certain deity. The motives of participating in religious activities are not "free of utilitarianism" and not out of devotion and reverence to the object of worship and supernatural powers, but more to satisfy a secular requirement and to pursue interests. "As gods are not regarded as role models or transcendental beings, the purpose of worshiping them is only because of the 'magic power' that they possess, just like how people try to please the officials simply because of the power they hold and not because of their charisma. People usually do not care about the existence of these deities, as Confucius once said to keep "at arm's length." To achieve a certain goal, people would sometimes 'abuse' the deities, just like how humans would hold uprisings."[②] This religious concept with realistic, utilitarian and contractual characteristics undoubtedly demonstrates the cultural spirit of "striving

---

① Lofland, J. & Skonovd, N. Conversion motifs [J]. *Journal for the Scientific Study of Religion*, 1981, 20(4): 373-383, 375.

② Sha, L. et al. *Chinese Social and Cultural Psychology* [M]. Beijing: China Social Press, 1998: 13-14.

for practical results" and "stressing utility" in the traditional civil society of Zhejiang.

As products of history and as the internalization of objective structures, the cultural spirit of "striving for practical results" and "stressing utility" also possesses the "constructive structure" put forward by Bourdieu. They are not only important social and psychological bases formed by the Eastern Zhejiang Practical Schools but are also linked to the cultural spirit of "striving for practical results" and "stressing utility" of contemporary Zhejiang that is passed down from generation to generation. Therefore, when studying the development of contemporary Zhejiang's spirit of "striving for practical results," the focus does not necessarily have to be placed on the Great Traditions of the Eastern Zhejiang Practical Schools. In fact, the "pragmatic" spirit has already been fully accumulated in the traditional Zhejiang civil society.

It should be further clarified that although the above discussion does explore the development of the cultural spirits of "striving for practical results" and "stressing utility" to a certain extent, we still cannot come up with a complete and reasonable explanation as to the reason why these spirits were formed in Zhejiang's civil society. Nevertheless, it can be said that the reason is not a single one, but rather a multi faceted one.

First, as Zhuo Yongliang puts forward, Zhejiang has better climatic conditions to cultivating cultural spirits such as "striving for practical results." He believes that if you do not make the effort, in a place surrounded by forests and swamps and with a not so high temperature all year round, it would be impossible to obtain food and therefore difficult to survive. As long as you make the effort, you will be awarded correspondingly or even enjoy a prosperous life because you have suitable temperatures and sufficient amount of rain water. For most of the years, farmers of Zhejiang will receive returns that are corresponding to their labor input. The suitable climate prompted the farms to form the rational expectation of "no pain, no gain." On the other hand, Zhejiang's superior climate has also contributed to the rapid population growth, offsetting the small amount of labor surplus created by the fragile agricultural industry, so the once affluent Zhejiang became poor. This gave rise to two basic incentives: "The positive feedback incentive between labor input and land output formed by positive rational expectations of labor and climate; and the incentive of improving land output and monetary income as population pressures prompted the farmers to pay more attention to their small plots of arable land."[①] The complicated causal relationship has formed between the rational expectations of labor and climate, and population pressure has fostered social temperaments such as the Zhejiang people's spirit of "striving for practical results."

Second, as a central region for Confucianism, Zhejiang is bound to be extensively influenced by the Confucian value of "humanistic pragmatism." As mentioned, throughout the history of Zhejiang and especially since the Song, Yuan, Ming, and Qing dynasties, Zhejiang's relatively developed industry and commerce may also be an important reason. The economic rationality of industrial and commercial activities determined that handicraftsmen and merchants must be "practical" and "utilitarian." This kind of pragmatic spirit must have been first manifested in the civil society, then later reflected in the Great Tradition of the Eastern Zhejiang Practical Schools. Of course, the Great Tradition can in turn have an impact on the mentality of the civil society, and reinforce the spirits of "striving for practical results" and "stressing utility" to a certain extent. On the other hand, as Yang Nianqun put forward, the historical changes since the Qing Dynasty, especially internal struggles and foreign aggression in modern times, have forced Confucian students in Jiangsu and Zhejiang to complete

---

① Zhuo, L. Challenging the Swamp [A] // Zhejiang Philosophy and Social Sciences Planning Office. *Zhejiang's New Ideas for Development and Countermeasures:* vol.1. Hangzhou: Zhejiang People's Publishing House, 2004.

the psychological transition from scholars to practical people. Rulers of the early Qing Dynasty once devised cultural policies that included the creation of a marginal Confucian class in Jiangsu and Zhejiang. These people used their special knowledge and skills that are beyond the scope of the imperial examinations as important resources for survival and social status. Apart from undertaking research and criticizing ancient texts as the basic means of self-entertainment or making a living, some of these "culturally marginalized people" were skilled at calculating and making things. "Prior to the mid-Qing Dynasty (circa 1750), the Confucian doctrine of moral governance was prevalent throughout the nation and so there was no room of development for 'trivial ideas' in society. As a result, it was only when China began to clash with the West and the Qing court realized that they needed to pay attention to 'clever tricks and wicked craft' that this group of talented individuals stood out, and became the backbone of the self-improvement movement."[①] It needs to be further clarified that the reasons why Confucian scholars in Jiangsu and Zhejiang were able to complete their transitions from scholars to practical individuals quicker than those at the other regions are not only limited to the cultural policies implemented at the beginning of the Qing Dynasty or changes in national situations. Another important influence may be the distinctive regional mentality of "striving for practical results." At the same time, in traditional Chinese society, the Confucian class is the elite and leading class which bears the responsibility of "enlightening" the society. Hence, the thoughts and behaviors of the Confucian class in Zhejiang since the early Qing Dynasty, which were oriented toward "practicality" and "making a living," will undoubtedly influence on the civil society.

Third, since the Song Dynasty, the ever-increasing population of Zhejiang and the resulting contradiction between man and land might

---

① Yang, N. *Modern Forms of Confucianism Regionalization—A Comparative Study of Three Knowledge Groups* [M]. Beijing: SDX Joint Publishing Company, 1997: 287.

have also been an important reason for the formation of the cultural spirits of "striving for practical results" and "stressing utility" in Zhejiang. During the Ming Dynasty, the per capita arable land in the Jiangnan region was 5.6 Mu(a unit of area in China, 1 Mu=666 m²). However, due to population increase, the per capita arable land in Zhejiang during the reign of Emperor Yongzheng of the Qing Dynasty dropped to 3.3 Mu and that of the following Qianlong reign down to 2.9 Mu.① This was also the general situation in Zhejiang, though in some places, the population growth rate and the rate of decline of per capita arable land exceeded this average. According to a simple principle, people can engage in other activities only after they have solved the basic problems of eating and living. Faced with a lack of land and under intense pressure for survival, people would inevitably become very pragmatic. It should be said that it was not a coincidence that the spirit of "striving for practical results and stressing utility" was formed in eastern Zhejiang, but rather it may be linked to the natural environment of Zhejiang where there is a large population with relatively little arable land. Ye Tan believed that "when studying the regional history of Zhejiang, it seems worth noting down the differences between eastern Zhejiang and western Zhejiang."② Eastern Zhejiang is mountainous while western Zhejiang is filled with marshes. Wang Bai said: "The poor in eastern Zhejiang cannot be compared to those in western Zhejiang."③ The mountains in eastern Zhejiang are barren and the backside is close to the sea so they are not suitable for farming. Under such circumstances, if the people of eastern Zhejiang do not become pragmatic, it would definitely be difficult to survive.

---

① Duan, B. & Shan, Q. *Modern Jiangnan Countryside* [M]. Nanjing: Jiangsu People's Publishing House, 1994: 57-58.
② Ye, T. Study on economic thoughts of real learning in the Eastern Zhejiang Practical Schools in the Song Dynasty—Centered on Ye Shi [J]. *Researches in Chinese Economic History*, 2000(4).
③ Wang, B. *Collection of Luzhai*: vol.7 Book on the Advantages and Disadvantages of Disaster Relief [M]. Beijing: The Commercial Press, 1936.

Of course, the aforementioned discussions may not be able to fully explain why the cultural spirit of "striving for practical results" and "stressing utility" was formed in Zhejiang's civil society. Hopefully, in addressing the issues that we have discussed, the arguments are sufficient as long as we can show that the civil society of Zhejiang indeed embedded with the spirit of "striving for practical results." The spirit of "striving for practical results" and "stressing utility" of contemporary Zhejiang people indeed stemmed from the little folk traditions. Rather than saying that this pragmatic spirit of contemporary Zhejiang people stemmed from the Great Traditions in the history of Zhejiang, it is much better to say that it stemmed from the little folk traditions. This is not a process of transition from the Eastern Zhejiang Practical Schools to the folk cultural mentality, but rather from the folk cultural mentality to popular belief. Of course, saying this does not deny the fact that the Practical Schools may also exert a certain degree of influence on the social psychology of the people. However, this kind of influence is not decisive. The decisive role is still played by the cultural mentality of civil society itself.

Chapter 3

The Cultural Tradition of Industry and Commerce and the Economic and Social Development of Contemporary Zhejiang

The regional cultural tradition of industry and commerce has played an important role in the economic and social development of Zhejiang since the reform and opening-up. As Zheng Yongjun said, "Since the reform and opening-up, Zhejiang people had shown talent in setting up factories and doing business. And more importantly, they enjoyed doing it. The formation of mercantile society was closely connected to regional business culture."[1] According to Fei Xiaotong, the Wenzhou Model is summarized as "Small Commodity, Big Market," and this model, furthermore, is closely associated with its historical tradition. "The historical tradition in Wenzhou is usually called 'Eight Immortals Crossing the Sea', which means that handicraftsmen who work on stone-carving, bamboo-weaving, cotton-fluffing, bucket-hooping, tailoring, hairdressing or cooking and vendors who sell sugar or small commodities travel around and later return to their hometown to settle down with their earned money." This culture has been extended since the reform and opening-up, "The connection between the scenes fifty years ago and today's market can be seen as necessary in history."[2] Allen Liu conducted a comprehensive and in-depth study on the secrets, enlightments and significance of the Wenzhou Model's success in *Advantage and Disadvantage of the Wenzhou Model*. He believed that the Wenzhou Model was the most famous, representative and typical model in the development of a regional economic society in China and

---

① Zheng, Y. Endogenous civilian power promoting economic development: Zhejiang experience [J]. *Zhejiang Social Sciences*, 2001(2).
② Fei, X. Small commodity, big market [M] //He, F. *Overview of Zhejiang*. Hangzhou: Zhejiang People's Publishing House, 2003: 350.

that its success relied on the combination of 3Ms and 1I (3Ms refer to mass initiative, mobility and markets and 1I refers to interstices in China's economic structure). Allen Liu emphasized the significance of the regional economic tradition of Wenzhou in his study, and he believed that the formation of regional tradition was related to how Wenzhou people reacted to environmental and political pressures in history. Therefore, the development of Wenzhou economy after the reform and opening-up can be regarded as a continuation of Wenzhou people's regional tradition .[①] In fact, such inherit relationship between contemporary industrial and commercial activities and the cultural tradition of industry and commerce can be found not only in Wenzhou but also in other parts of Zhejiang including Ningbo, Shaoxing, Taizhou, Yongkang, Yiwu, and Dongyang. The regional cultural tradition of industry and commerce influences the development of both contemporary Zhejiang economy and society.

3.1 Great Cultural Tradition of Industry and Commerce of Ideologists

Robert Redfield's view that cultural tradition can be divided into Great Tradition and Little Tradition serves as an effective theoretical reference frame. In his view, Great Tradition refers to the tradition of "the reflective few" and Little Tradition refers to those of "the largely unreflective many." People first think of the Great Tradition, namely the tradition of the reflective few, which refers to tradition of thinkers and cultural elites in the study of the influences by regional culture of industry and commerce on Zhejiang's economic and social development. It should be noted that some thoughts and views about industry and commerce created by thinkers or cultural elites in Zhejiang history are closely connected to the interests and spirits of Zhejiang people today.

---

① Zhu, K. *The Change from the Bottom—A Case Study of Longgang's Urbanization* [M]. Hangzhou: Zhejiang People's Publishing House, 2003: 21.

3.1.1   Industry and Commerce Being Equally Important

Regional culture of industry and commerce has long been rooted in Zhejiang Province. During the Spring and Autumn and Warring States Periods, the thought of being commercially successful had become an important part of the economic thoughts of Yue State. On the account of Fan Li's successful practice of fish-farming and his thought of "waiting for the best chance to do business and make profit," he was honored with the title "Shang Sheng" (Sage of Business) by later generations. The business theory proposed by Ji Ran that government should adjust grain prices by buying and selling foods and encourage cargo movement by goods trade, and that businessmen should buy unmarketable items cheaply and sell them at a higher price is the earliest commodity circulation theory in China. Since the Qin and Han dynasties, many famous statesmen and ideologists in Zhejiang have put forward many important economic thoughts and proposals, especially the Eastern Zhejiang Practical Schools after the Southern Song Dynasty, which becomes the spiritual heritage of "Industry and Commerce Being Equally Important."

Chen Liang from the Yonkang School and Ye Shi from the Yongjia School supported developing industry and commerce. The policy of encouraging agriculture and restraining commerce had always been in a dominant position since the Han Dynasty. In traditional Chinese society, the developments of agriculture and commerce were considered as mutually exclusive, since the flourishing of commerce was believed to make a large number of people abandon agriculture. Therefore, "restraining commerce" and "forcing people to engage in agriculture" had been a basic state policy since the Han Dynasty. In the Song Dynasty, Wang Anshi's idea that the government should regulate and control the commodity and currency circulation[1] reflects

---

[1]   Yang, S. & Huang, H. *Memorials from Famous Officials of Previous dynasties*: vol. 266 Financial Arrangement [M]. Shanghai: Shanghai Classics Publishing House, 1989.

the thought of "restraining commerce" and controlling industrialists and businessmen. Wang Anshi believed that people who engaged in industry and commerce should be punished with heavy tax, and those who were troubled with heavy tax would realize that doing business was useless and return to the farmland.[1] However, this method is not proper in Chen Liang and Ye Shi's minds. Ye Shi thought that such an approach would end with failure since setting price bureaus damaged businessmen's interests. They believed that agriculture and commerce were mutually dependent. Agriculture does matter, as Ye Shi stated. Attaching importance to agriculture was the foundation of a kingdom since the monarch would never govern his people well if he did not know the significance of agriculture. Similarly, Chen Liang thought that attaching importance to agriculture was a good way of governing a country. However, both Chen Liang and Ye Shi thought that there is no conflict between valuing agriculture and developing commerce. In Chen Liang's mind, agriculture and commerce were interdependent. If agriculture and commerce did not work hand in hand, they would be against each other until one caught the monopoly position.[2] Developing commerce will not only increase people's wealth and improve a country's financial resources and response to changes but also help prevent cheap prices from harming farmers' interests during harvest years and help farmers survive bad years. Therefore, Chen Liang's imagined ideal state assumes that officers, folks, farmers and businessmen all perform their own duties to create a cohesive society.

Ye Shi cited Confucian classics in order to support his arguments. As recorded in *The Book of History*, "Goods trading is exempt from taxation, and in the Zhou Dynasty, trade is under the supervision but still exempt from taxation." As recorded in *The Spring and Autumn Annals*,

---

① Wang, A. *Linchuan Collected Works*: vol.69 Custom[M]. Changchun: Jilin Publishing Group, 2005.
② Chen, L. *Longchuan Collected Works*: vol.11 Four Disadvantages [M]. Hangzhou: Zhejiang Ancient Books Publishing House, 2004.

the ancient authorities before the Spring and Autumn Period all agreed that "the country should support the development of commerce and currency circulation."[①] Hence, the policy of "encouraging agriculture and restraining commerce" started from the Han Dynasty. Restraining commerce would undoubtedly result in the malfunction of businessmen and business society. In Ye Shi's mind, the business had irreplaceable social value, which was shown in the way that people were called from all over the country to sell and buy goods in center markets in the afternoon and then returned to normal after trading.[②] All businessmen have made great contribution to society and the whole country, and rich people were the foundation of prefectures and counties. "Transferring the power of managing civilians from officers to rich people was not completed in one generation. Ordinary people who have no lands had to rent land first from rich people and even borrow money from them for farming. They later turned to them for help when they face. difficulties, and some even became maids serving rich people, and furthermore, some performed acrobatics, songs or dances to entertain rich people. Rich people, as the foundation of prefectures and counties, was relied on by both upper and lower classes. They paid taxes to the higher classes and helped support the lower classes, and made certain contributions to the whole society by earning a large amount of land and wealth. Those who misconducted should be punished by officials, or be supervised until they make corrections."[③] Hence, Ye Shi believed that the theory of "valuing agriculture and restraining commerce was incorrect. Later generations might engage in business for self-interest, which was against the theory of valuing agriculture and restraining

---

① Ye, S. *Xishui Records*: vol.19 The Historical Records [M]. Shanghai: Shanghai Classics Publishing House, 1992.

② Ye, S. *Xishui Records*: vol.2 Yi [M]. Shanghai: Shanghai Classics Publishing House, 1992.

③ Ye, S. *Shuixin Collected Works*: vol.2 Civil Affairs II [M].

commerce."[1] The ideal society in his thought, rather than valuing agriculture and restraining commerce, instead, would unite people from all kinds of life to improve society, which was similar to the belief Chen Liang once described that officers, peasants, and businessmen all performed their own duties to create a cohesive society.

A comparison between Chen Liang and Ye Shi's thought and Mandeville and Adam Smith's thought surprisingly uncovered something common. Mandeville believed that the universal motive of human nature stemmed from self-love, which promotes public interests, and Adam Smith, with a stricter theory, proved the same conclusion that people's hard efforts to maximize self-interest would ultimately help enhance public interests. According to his view, a person who pursues self-interest usually has no intention of promoting social interests. However, an invisible hand guided him to achieve a purpose which he did not intend before, and his economic activities for self-interest finally brought prosperity to the whole society. The unintentional effect of which is even greater than an intentional one. As previously mentioned, Chen Liang thought that developing commerce would not only increase people's wealth and improve a country's financial resources and response to changes but also help prevent cheap prices from harming farmers' interests during harvest years and help peasants survive bad years. Ye Shi believed that rich people, who earned a large amount of wealth and land, paidtaxes to the higher classes and helped support the lower classes. The above views proposed by Chen Liang and Ye Shi, though not as systematic and strict as those of Mandeville and Adam Smith, seemed to contain one proposition in modern economics that there was an internal connection between the individual behavior with purposes to pursue self-interest and the achievement of public interest.

Chen Liang and Ye Shi's thought of valuing industry and commerce

---

[1] Ye, S. *Xishui Records*: vol.19 The Historical Records [M]. Shanghai: Shanghai Classics Publishing House, 1992.

is further developed by later generations. Chen Qiqing, the student of
Ye Shi, on the basis of Ye Shi's thoughts of valuing both agriculture
and commerce and uniting people from all works to improve society,
formally put forward his idea that "it is unchangeable that scholars,
farmers, artisans, and businessmen have all been the backbones of
people's daily life since the beginning of human society"[1], and both
industry and commerce were the foundation of the national economy. In
the late Ming and early Qing dynasties, Huang Zongxi wrote in his book
Ming Yi Treated Visits Record: "The scholars do not understand and
consider both the country's situation and people's feelings. They think
that industry and commerce are of least importance, trying to suppress
the development of these two parts. However, the industry provides
the emperor with whatever he wants and the commerce enables him
to buy all he desires. Therefore, both industry and commerce are the
foundation of the national economy," which clearly clarified that it was
wrong to restrain commerce. Huang Zongxi's ideal that "Industry and
Commerce Being Equally Important" and Chen Qiqing's thought that
"Scholars, Farmers, Artisans, and Businessmen All Being Backbones
of People's Daily Life" say the same thing. However, the latter lived in
the Southern Song Dynasty, which shows that such a phenomenon has a
long history.

Since the Han Dynasty, businessmen have always been linked with
something evil in traditional morality, and as a result, the social status
of businessmen has always ranked the lowest among the four traditional
social classes. In the early Han Dynasty, Chao Cuo once said: "Both
big businessmen and small traders manipulate the market and earn
huge profits by hoarding. Consequently, many males and females
will give up farming and weaving respectively and pursue to live an
extravagant life, which makes them forget about farmers' hard work.
What's more, they will pay bribes to officers to gain greater power, ride
tall horses, wear expensive clothes, and collude with higher officials.

---

[1]   See *Records of Chi City (Taizhou)* in Jiading Reign.

Hence, businessmen have more power to merge farmers' lands, leading to the displacement of more farmers."[①] This reflects the social reality and people's disgusting attitude towards businessmen at that time, for businessmen were considered as the chief culprits of society, who disrupted public order and custom. Based on such an understanding, the emperors of the Han Dynasty carried out the policy of restraining commerce, which stipulated that businessmen were not allowed to wear silks and satins, or to become government officers, or to bear arms, or to ride on horses, or to own lands and houses. Since then, although some specific regulations have been changing, particularly in some periods and areas like Huizhou and Shanxi in the Ming and Qing dynasties, the social status of businessmen has always been the lowest among the four traditional social classes (namely scholars, farmers, artisans, and businessmen). Even by the fourteenth year of Hongwu Reign of the Ming Dynasty, the court still stipulated that farmers were allowed to wear satins, yarns, thin silks and ordinary clothes, while businessmen were only allowed to wear thin silks or ordinary clothes. In addition, if there was one member of farmers' family living on commerce, the whole family was not allowed to wear satins and yarns. The book *Collection of Qing Dynasty* notes the value of agriculture and restraining commerce.

In traditional Chinese society, the policy of restraining commerce worked in conjunction with the social idea of devaluing businessmen. The main content of the ancient *Family Instructions* is that the elder's inculcations is passed on to the younger generations, including family rules, family ethics and family requirements of being successful. Though the ancient scholars might say some empty words at different occasions, they never put useless words into *Family Instructions*, because its purpose was to keep the prosperity of the traditional family, which clearly reflected the mainstream values of the age. Therefore,

---

① Ban, G. *Han History: Shihuo Records* [M]. Beijing: Zhonghua Book Company, 2007.

there are several provisions cited from *Family Instructions* of different ages to demonstrate the honest views toward businessmen in traditional society.

Ye Sheng copied Lu You's instructions and here was one instruction: "Although later generations may be limited to talents, they should always keep learning. Even when living in poverty, we should provide enough food, clothing, and education to our children to make sure that the seeds of learning continue growing. It would be great if the later generations would engage in farming, being commoners and never go to the center cities. There is no regret being farmers since the career of officials can be unstable and rough. One thing worth noticing, however, is that the later generations must not engage in business deals for food and clothing."[①] We can see that Lu You's view about the social statuses of scholars, farmers, artisans, and businessmen is in accordance with the traditional theory of four social classes. As a result, he told his children that they could only make a living as scholars or farmers instead of businessmen, which showed his disgusting attitude towards businessmen and commerce. Yuan Cai, who lived during the same dynasty as Lu You, held a similar view. He wrote that: "The younger generations of scholars or officers, who inherit no official positions and salaries and have no fixed assets, should devote themselves into education in order to serve their parents and raise a family. Those who are highly talented could gain an official rank and a great wealth in the imperial examinations, and those who are less intelligent could make a living as teachers to impart knowledge and educate people. Those with mediocre talents could engage in document writing and those who are least intelligent could read some books and teach little kids. Other occupations including wizards, doctors, monks, Taoist priests, farmers, businessmen, and artisans are all acceptable since people can live a life decently out of these occupations. However, being beggars

---

① Ye, S. *Shuidong Record*: vol.15 Lu Fangweng Family Instructions [M].

or thieves would disgrace a whole family."[1] Compared with Lu You, Yuan Cai took on a more relaxed view. But he still insisted that the scholar was in the highest social class and in his mind, the social status of businessmen always ranked last, only higher than that of beggars and thieves. In the Qing Dynasty, when it came to career choices for descendants, Wang Fuzhi stipulated that "the best choice is to be scholars, followed by doctors, farmers, artisans, and businessmen, people can choose their job according to their own characteristics and abilities." "Being businessmen can be listed as a way to keep living."[2] Wang Fuzhi required that his descendants should, according to their own characteristic and ability, choose proper occupations. Although being businessmen was viewed as a decent job for Wang Fuzhi, it was the last choice.

Therefore, it is challenging for ideologists of the East Zhejiang Practical Schools to defend businessmen and commerce in consideration of the traditional Chinese social conditions and mainstream ideology.

3.1.2 Four Social Classes Engaging in Different Work Share the Same Purpose of Being Conscientious

In addition to the Practical Schools, Wang Yangming, a master of the Eastern Zhejiang School of Mind in the Ming Dynasty, revalued the social status of businessmen in another sense. Although Wang Yangming did not agree with the view that the primary task was to make a living, he said that "there is no conflict between doing business and being sages, as long as people value the cultivation of mind."[3] Doing business, as a daily routine, also helps people distinguish between right and wrong, but we still cannot imagine that Zhu Xi would connect doing business with being sages at his time. Besides, it is worth

---

[1] Yuan, C. *Yuan Family Instructions*: vol. Middle Later Generations should Study Confucianism [M].

[2] Wang, F. *Fourteen Commandments for Long-living Family* [M].

[3] See Wang Yangming, *Chuanxi Records*.

noting that Wang Yangming proposed the theory of "New Four Social Classes." An epitaph written by Wang Yangming for the businessman Fang Lin (Jie'an) in 1525 can be viewed as a remarkably document of Confucianism on the theory of "Four Social Classes", which means scholars, farmers, artisans, and businessmen.

Wang Yangming wrote in *Epitaph for Fang Jie'an*: "Fang Lin (Jie'an) used to be a scholar living in Kunshan, Jiangsu. After marriage, he lived with his wife Zhu's family and started to do business. His friend was surprised that he chose to be a businessman instead of a scholar, while Fang Lin thought that there was no essential difference between them... Wang Yangming said: 'Although the four social classes engaged in different work, they shared the same purpose of being conscientious; scholars for governance, farmers for land cultivation, artisans for technological development and businessmen for cargo movement, all four social classes took advantage of their own resources and power to make achievements for the same goal of staying good-hearted and benefiting all people. Hence, there was no essential difference between these four social classes. The social phenomenon of people preferring to be scholars and officials, while despising to be farmers and businessmen was because people were lost in their own world. In fact, in my opinion, what Fang Weng did showed the concept of Four Social Classes.[①]"

The historical significance of *Epitaph for Fang Jie'an* is shown as follows: first, Fang Lin was living in the second half of the 15th century, and his behavior of abandoning being scholars and engaging in business became an early typical case for future generations. Second, since Fang Lin used to be a scholar influenced by Confucianism, he brought Confucian values into the business world, as a result of which the letters he wrote to his two sons were all about loyalty, filial piety, chastity, and righteousness. It provides a concrete example to explain the connection between Confucian ethics and businessmen class. Such a connection,

---

① Wang, Y. *Yangming Collection*: vol 25 [M].

though not the only way, was one of the important channels. However, the most significant part of the epitaph is Wang Yangming's new ideas on the Confucian theory of "Four Social Classes," and the epitaph could represent Wang Yangming's final thoughts since it was written only three years before his death. The statement that the four social classes engage in different work but share the same purpose is the most novel part, which affirms that scholars, farmers, artisans and businessmen are on an equal footing. In addition, he promoted his idea of being conscientious into the four social classes. Businessmen who always stay kind-hearted in his work could also be viewed as sages, not lower than scholars, which was the theoretical basis of the theory of "All People Being Sages." Otherwise, as pointed out in the epitaph, the thought that being scholars was better than being businessmen was caused by prejudice.

Wang Yangming's statement that the four social classes engage in different work but share the same purpose affirmed that scholars, farmers, artisans and businessmen were on an equal footing, which objectively helped improve the social status of businessmen and benefited the development of industry and commerce. However, the implication of the epitaph was viewed as an example of the theory that the commercial development after the 16th century required the Confucianists to reevaluate the social status of businessmen and he believed that Wang Yangming's conclusion was out of the social phenomenon that the boundary between scholars and businessmen became more indistinct and could be further discussed. If Wang Yangming's statement helped in improving the businessmen's status, it would be more appropriate to view such a phenomenon as an unexpected result than one caused by the commercial development after the 16th century, which could be explained by Weber's elaboration on the relationship between protestant ethics and the rise of capitalism. According to Weber's view, because the subjective starting point of Protestant reformation is religious, it is impossible for protestant reformers to advocate for the so-called "capitalist spirit." They are concerned with one thing: soul-saving and the actual impact of their ethical goal and moralization are religiously motivated. However, the religious pursuit that aims at the afterlife promotes the professional efforts of the secular world, since the inner-worldly asceticism shown in Protestant ethics unconsciously promoted the formation of reasonable capitalism and the deployment of reasonable economic activities. In Fact, Wang Yangming's objective motive is ethical, not economic. The statement that the four social classes engage in different work but share the same purpose does not justify the deployment of reasonable economic activities, but provide a theoretical basis for theories of "All People Being Sages" and "Learning for Being Conscientious." In Wang Yangming's mind, conscience is one trait that everyone has. It is the same for both talented and untalented people, for all scholars, farmers, artisans and businessmen from the ancient times till today. Therefore, Wang Yangming's statement is not the result of "commercial development" or the increasingly blurred boundary between the scholars and businessmen, but a natural evolution of the mind's philosophy system which will be discussed later. Wang Yangming's statement that the four social classes engage in different work but share the same purpose objectively helps promote the businessmen's status and then benefits the development of industry and commerce. However, it is an unintentional outcome, since there is no evidence showing that Wang Yangming intended to make such a conclusion. It would be appropriate to use the saying that "those who carefully planted flowers do not get the intentional result, while those who optionally planted willow trees get the unintentional result" to describe such a phenomenon.

Certainly, it is worth noting that the practice of Protestant ethics in daily life unintentionally promoted the formation of European rational capitalism and the deployment of rational economic activities, which has become an experimental and historical truth. As previously mentioned, in the first chapter of *The Protestant Ethic and the Spirit of Capitalism*, Weber first used an example of occupation statistics to interpret the theme, and he clearly pointed out that if we looked

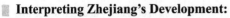

through the occupational statistical tables investigated by countries of different religious beliefs, we could find one truth that most capitalists, enterprise operators, senior skilled artisans and technical or business specialists were Protestants. Weber particularly listed several examples to note that it was possible to connect the capitalist spirit with the strong religious faith and make the connection exist in one person or a group of people. The situation was more than an isolated phenomenon, but a typical feature of many Protestant churches and denominations. In his mind, these examples indicated that Protestants usually had the spirits of diligence and progress, and they could build the connection between firm religious faith and career achievements. Weber believed that after the Protestant reformation, for most Calvinists, finding the salvation confirmation, namely to make the Calvinists believe that they are on the voter list, became a very important thing. And Calvinism provided two ways to help the believers in finding the salvation confirmation: First was that everyone had the obligation to believe that he has been chosen by God, and lacking confidence was the result of the lack in faith, namely the lack of God's grace. Therefore, we must treat all doubts as the temptation of the devil and fight against them. Those who have accepted such advice were no longer humble sinners whom Luther respected, but confident believers, which Weber saw in hardworking Puritan businessmen in the heroic age of capitalism. Second was to make people believe that doing "intense professional work" was the most appropriate way to gain confidence, since only "intense professional work" could remove religious doubts and help obtain God's grace. In other words, hard work could be viewed as the basis of the chosen people's recognition, which improved the sanctity of work and encouraged believers to manage themselves in a reasonable and systematic manner in order to achieve an ethically healthy personality. Without this, the Western rational process would be inferior. Hence, Weber believed that there was "elective affinity" between protestant ethics and capitalist spirit. The protestant ethics in the religious domain and the capitalist spirit in the economic field, after a long time of consideration and historical chances, selectively combined with each other to jointly promote the evolution of the Western culture and economic society. By contrast, we cannot find the "elective affinity" between Wang Yangming's thought and the economic evolution process from empirical and historical facts. Deducing the argument above that Wang Yangming's thought is an unexpected outcome is just a theoretical supposition and further discussion is needed to determine whether Wang Yangming's statement that "the four social engage in different work but share the same purpose" improves businessmen's status in social life and promotes the development of industry and commerce particularly in Zhejiang. The discussion needs reliable factual materials as its basis. It is regrettable that it is still hard to find materials to prove the "elective affinity" between Wang Yangming's thought and the economic evolution process. Although, the traditional theory of the four social classes has been changing since the Ming Dynasty, and businessmen in Huizhou and Shanxi proposed many views similar to Wang Yangming's statement, we still cannot find persuasive materials to prove that their thoughts were influenced by Wang Yangming's idea. Wang Gen of the Taizhou School inherited Wang Yangming's theory of "New Four Social Classes" and once said, as his student Wang Dong recalled, that "although scholars, farmers, artisans and businessmen engage in different work, they are on an equal footing and all people can freely choose what they like do." However, we don't find the evidence to prove that Zhejiang businessmen in the Ming and Qing dynasties inherited Wang Yangming's theory that "the four social classes engage in different but share the same purpose." In terms of likelihood, the conclusion that Wang Yangming's statement that "the four social classes engage in different work but share the same purpose" objectively helps improve businessmen's status and promotes the development of industry and commerce remains valid.

3.2   Little Traditions of Folk Industrial and Commercial Culture

In Husserl's philosophical language, the "tradition of the reflective

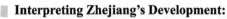

few," namely the Great Tradition of ideologists, refers to how "we measure the life-world—the world constantly given to us as actual in our concrete world-life—for a well-fitting garb of ideas (*Ideenkleid*)."[①] In contrast, the "tradition of the largely unreflective many," namely the Little Tradition in the folk world, constitute a self-evident world, namely the life world itself. Husserl pointed out that "[we] try to bring 'original intuition' to the fore—that is, the pre- and extrascientific life-world, which contains within itself all actual life, including the scientific life of thought, and nourishes it as the source of all technical constructions of meaning."[②] In his perspective, the unreflective life world is the world that naturally surrounds ourselves. This world is existing, and in the process of gaining experience, this is a world that can be directly understood and observed. In the absence of an ideology system, life is considered as something that is meaningful and has been validated by practice. The life world is the foundation of understanding since it is a starting point and something that has been preset. Therefore, studying the impact of regional industrial and commercial culture on the Zhejiang's economic and social development requires paying attention to both the Great Tradition, namely "the tradition of the reflective few," and "the tradition of the largely unreflective many," namely the Little Tradition of Zhejiang industrial and commercial culture in the folk living world.

3.2.1 Little Folk Cultural Traditions as Life Policy

The Cultural Materialist, Marvin Harris believed that "Infrastructure, structure, and superstructure constitute a sociocultural system. Change in any one of the system's components usually leads to a change in the others." "It does not deny the possibility that emic, mental, superstructural, and structural components may achieve a degree of autonomy from the etic behavioral infrastructure." "Structure and

---

① Husserl, E. *The Crisis of European Sciences and Transcendental Phenomenology* [M]. Trans. Zhang, Q. Shanghai: Shanghai Translation Publishing House, 1988: 61.
② Ibid. 88.

superstructure clearly play vital system-maintaining roles in the negative feedback processes responsible for the conservation of the system."[①] On one hand, as a type of mental superstructure, spiritual legacies such as the Eastern Zhejiang Practical Schools' view of "industry and commerce being equally important" and Wang Yangming's view that "although the four social classes engage in different work, they share the same purpose of being conscientious," regardless of those scholars' original intention, are likely to exert certain effect on the folk social psychology through the history accompanied by the spread of Eastern Zhejiang spiritual culture. Yang Taixin found that from the Southern Song Dynasty to the Ming and Qing dynasties, charitable schools, private schools and schools founded by a certain clan lay all over the towns and villages in eastern Zhejiang. Most scholars who once taught folks and students that went to schools for lectures spent their whole life teaching and giving lectures, except for the few who passed the imperial examinations and entered the court as officers. Students who were influenced by the Eastern Zhejiang schools helped popularize the essence of Confucianism and deliver the values of Eastern Zhejiang academics to the public after entering the folk world. Furthermore, the Eastern Zhejiang scholars contributed to transforming the traditional social customs as well. For instance, with the aim of removing people's sufferings and cultivating moral codes, besides setting up charitable country estates and charitable schools, they even revised genealogies and domestic disciplines, drafted regulations in towns and villages and established rules in various professions, so that unity and mutual assistance were strengthened and excellent civil customs were established. When the Eastern Zhejiang cultural spirits affected the folk social psychology, spiritual legacies about industry and commerce proposed by scholars of Eastern Zhejiang, more or less, had the same effect on folk society as well.

---

① Harris, M. *Cultural Materialism* [M]. Trans. Zhang, H. Beijing: Huaxia Publishing House, 1989: 76, 83, 85.

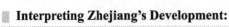

On the other hand, the Eastern Zhejiang cultural spirits have not only influenced the folk social psychology through the methods mentioned above but also reached the other regions of Zhejiang Province beyond their birthplaces. Taizhou is a perfect example in this case. Taizhou is not the cradle of the Yongkang School, Yongjia School or Jinhua School, and it was even treated as an uncivilized region before the Tang Dynasty. It was not until Zheng Qian went to Taizhou in 757 did its culture and education get started. When Liu Ao served as prefecture chief of Taizhou during the Ming Dynasty, cultural cultivation and education prevailed, and Taizhou was even renowned as Zou Lu in the south (Lu is the hometown of Confucius, and Zou is the hometown of Mencius). Although Taizhou is not where the Eastern Zhejiang mainstream culture originated, it is worth noting that demoted officials from other regions were the main force in spreading Taizhou's elite culture.[1] Taizhou boasted few native-born Confucian masters, but it was still influenced by the Eastern Zhejiang cultural spirits in ways of listening to and giving lectures, exchanging letters full of ideas and doubts, asking fellows and teachers, debating and so on. For instance, Chen Fuliang, a scholar of the Yongjia School once gave lectures in Guoqing Temple on Tiantai Mountain, and after hearing this, his students and friends came to follow him one after another.[2] Ye Shi, after being disposed and coming back to his hometown, once gave lectures in Huangyan, Wenling and nearby areas. Chen Qiqing, Wang Xiangzu, Wu Ziliang, Ding Xiliang, Xia Tingjian and Dai Xucai were all his students, and thus Qi Xuebiao, a scholar in the Qing Dynasty, praised him as one of the two origins of Taizhou culture (the other person is Wang Shipeng).[3] Huang Zongxi, a scholar of the Eastern Zhejiang Practical Schools during the late Ming Dynasty and early

---

[1] Gao, F. & Ni, K. "Grass-roots culture" and social and economic development in Taizhou [M] // *Eastern Zhejiang Schools and Zhejinag Spirit*, Hangzhou: Zhejiang Ancient Books Publishing House, 2006.

[2] Wu, Z. *Casual thoughts in Jingxi* [M].

[3] Qi, X. *Records of Taizhou* [M].

Qing dynasty, lived in Taizhou for several years as well. Under the unconscious impacts of Practical Schools, the Taizhou Practical School with regional characteristics gradually took shape locally, represented by Chen Qiqing and Wu Ziliang. All these were solid evidence to illustrate that the Eastern Zhejiang Practical Schools was introduced into Taizhou. Another instance is the cross-region spreading and mutual effect of the Yongkang School and Yongjia School. Chen Liang, a representative of the Yongkang School, paid multiple visits to Yongjia, and figures of Yongjia, like Chen Fuliang and Ye Shi, visited on Chen in Yongkang as well. Lü Zuqian, a close friend of Chen, commented that Chen's visit to Yongjia gathered scholars together and enlightened each other. In addition, letters, poems, mourning orations and epitaphs in Chen's collections are demonstrations of frequent communication and close discussions between him and scholars of the Yongjia School.

It is difficult to be absolutely certain as to what degree the ideas like "industry and commerce being equally important" and "different jobs sharing common goals," influenced other regions of Zhejiang Province in the process of spreading the Eastern Zhejiang cultural spirits, because as mentioned above, it is hard to find related materials. But in general, there are two points that deserve attention. First, since the thought of laying emphasis on industry and commerce plays a asignificant role in the ideology of the Eastern Zhejiang Practical Schools, and the thought of "different jobs sharing common goals" is a natural corollary of Wang Yangming's mind philosophy system, so it is hard to assume that these two important thoughts would not impact other regions with the cross-regions spreading of the Eastern Zhejiang cultural spirits. Second, a few out-of-town students of the Eastern Zhejiang thinkers inherit and develope the thoughts of valuing both industry and commerce. As noted, Chen Qiqing, a student of Ye Shi, developed his teacher's thoughts and was the first who theoretically stated that "scholar, farmer, artisan and merchant are fundamental occupations for common people, and no one can change this since the presence of people." And that is a strong evidence to demonstrate that the thought of "industry and commerce being equally important" has spread cross regions along with the Eastern Zhejiang Practical Schools.

However, as this book illustrates, it is still not enough if we only analyze the impacts of cultural traditions on the economic and social development of Zhejiang Province since the reform and opening-up in 1978 from the perspective of Great Traditions (cultural elite traditions), because in that case, a reasonable explanation to the fact that the contemporary economic miracle of Zhejiang is created by folk men of humble origins cannot be given. It can be asserted that after the "Cultural Revolution" and the movement of "abolishing outdated thoughts, cultures, customs and practices," most members who made brilliant economic achievements were unlikely to read the works of Chen Liang, Ye Shi, Wang Yangming, Huang Zongxi and other thinkers of Eastern Zhejiang before starting up business, and may have never even heard of the thinkers' names, let alone being influenced by their thoughts. In fact, we have not found strong evidence so far to illustrate that contemporary Zhejiang merchants are directly influenced by the great industrial and commercial traditions of Eastern Zhejiang thinkers.

Therefore, as important as Great Traditions are, studying merely from the perspective of Great Traditions is not enough. In that case, it is of necessity to introduce Little Tradition (namely a kind of folk tradition) into our views. The significance of analyzing from Little Traditions or folk traditions is revealed in the following aspects:

Firstly, Little Traditions, or folkways, are the dominant power of social life which all the social members are forced to conform. In other words, before ideology and laws had taken shape, humans had already been surrounded by folkways. Just as William Graham Sumner said, "The real process in the great bodies of men is not one of deduction from any great principle of philosophy or ethics." Instead, "World philosophy, life policy, rights, and morality are all products of the folkways."[1] From the basic significance, Little Traditions do not originate from great ones, but great ones are deeply rooted in little ones. Great Traditions first appeared in the little ones where world views, religions and philosophy were rough and ambiguous and "they seem true and right, and arise into mores as the norm of welfare in little traditions." With the development of civilization, the extension of humans' minds and the birth of thinkers, thence are produced faiths, ideas, doctrines, religions, and philosophies, according to the stage of civilization and the fashions of reflection and generalization. Therefore, "it can be seen that philosophy and ethics are products of the folkways. They are taken out of the mores, but are never original and creative; they are secondary and derived."[2]

Secondly, rather than a single structure, culture is a large and complex synthesis. According to the definition, Edward Burnett Taylor proposed in *Primitive Culture*, "Culture or civilization, taken in its wide ethnographic sense, is a complex whole which includes knowledge, belief, art, morals, law, custom, and any other capabilities and habits acquired by man as a member of society." And Ian Robertson even expanded its content. In his mind, culture includes all the products shared by human society. These products are divided into two basic forms: material and immaterial. Material culture includes all the things that human beings create and endow with meanings, or we can say tangible things, such as wheels, clothes, schools, factories, cities, books, spaceships, totem poles, etc. And the immaterial culture includes more abstract creations, such as language, thoughts, faith, norms, customs, myths, technology, family patterns, and political institutions. Ian Robertson's definition of culture combines the spiritual and material forms of culture, and classifies the social system as an important part of culture. According to this, culture refers to not only humans' excellent

---

[1]   Gao, B. *Folk Culture and Folk Life* [M]. Beijing: China Social Sciences Press, 1994: 86.

[2]   Ibid. 86-87.

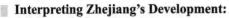

thought and speech but also other forms of knowledge, institutions, customs, habits, etc. Culture is not only the culture of elites but also the culture of folks. Obviously, this understanding of culture helps correct the bias of cultural elitism. As Raymond Williams puts it, only in this way, can we better comprehend the development of society and culture as a whole.①

Thirdly, the culture created by thinkers, the so-called "Great Traditions," is undoubtedly important, but it is the social and cultural environment in which they live, that is, the so-called "Little Tradition" or folkways, that has more direct impact on the ideas of the general public. As William Sumner said, "If now we form a conception of the folkways as a great mass of usages, of all degrees of importance, covering all the interests of life, constituting an outfit of instruction for the young, embodying a life policy, forming character, containing a world philosophy, albeit most vague and unformulated, and sanctioned by ghost fear so that variation is impossible, we see that with the coercive and inhibitive force, the folkways have always grasped the members of a society."② Folkways, or we can say "Little Traditions," exist because they are "appropriate," as the crystallization of the past or the experience of the elderly, and the "correct" life policy among folks that makes folk life regulated. "The folkways are the 'right' ways to satisfy all interests because they are traditional and exist in fact. They extend over the whole life. There is a right way to catch game, to win a wife, to make one's self appear, to cure disease, to honor ghosts, to treat comrades or strangers, to behave when a child is born, on the warpath, in council, and so on in all cases which can arise. The ways are defined on the negative side, that is, by taboos."③ The reason

---

① Luo, G. & Liu, X. *Cultural Studies: An Essential Reader* [M]. Beijing: China Social Sciences Press, 2000: 126.

② Gao, B. *Folk Culture and Folk Life* [M]. Beijing: China Social Sciences Press, 1994: 93.

③ Ibid.

why folkways or "Little Traditions" are important is that everyone who lives in reality must first accept social culture, learn the skills of life, and master the way of social life through socialization in order to adapt to society and survive in a specific social environment. Through socialization, folkways (customs) are internalized into humans' habits. Pierre Bourdieu believes that habit theory is superior to rational theory, because the former rejects all conceptual dualism and considers both individual and society, the present and history. He said that talking about habits equated to declaring that units, individuals, and subjects were all social and collective. Habit is a kind of socialized subjectivity. Rationality is restricted not only because the available information is shrinking, but more importantly because humans' thinking is socially restricted. Social actors are the products of history. Habits are chosen and expanded with the whole history of habits it breeds.[①] Folkways or social cultural environments ("Little Traditions") exert an unconscious influence on every member through the process of humans' socialization, and thus make people identify with and accept the norms and ways of life which are transmitted by this cultural value, and infiltrate into people's thinking structure, psychological models, moral ideas, values and behavior patterns through the inherent radiation and dissemination of culture.

Under the guidance of the viewpoint and methodology above, to study the influence of regional industrial and commercial culture on the economic and social development of Zhejiang, we should not only analyze the concept of industrial and commercial culture put forward by the thinkers of Eastern Zhejiang but also study the social and cultural environment of folk industry and business, namely the Little Tradition of folk commercial culture. In the regional industrial and commercial cultural traditions, only the latter constitutes the life world of folk industrial and commercial activities in Zhejiang, that is, what Husserl

---

① Bourdieu, P. *Cultural Capital and Social Alchemy—Interview with Bourdieu* [M]. Trans. Bao, Y. Shanghai: Shanghai People's Publishing House, 1997: 173-174.

said, the life world as the only one that exists, actually given through percipience, experienced and able to be experienced, namely the world of our daily life (Unsere alltaglich Lebenswelt).[①] The life world is the basic field of humans' world, where the whole practice of mankind takes place, and where the folk industrial and commercial practice of Zhejiang takes place as well.

3.2.2 Little Cultural Industrial Traditions of Zhejiang Folks

Among the little cultural industrial and commercial traditions of Zhejiang folks, the first thing to notice is the folk handicraft culture. In history, Zhejiang was the hometown of various craftsmen, with a relatively developed handicraft industry. Fixed handicrafts workshops were thriving, such as the textile industry, ceramics industry, paper industry, and wine-making industry, while craftsmen who engaged in carpentry, lacquering, cooking, stone-carving, bamboo-weaving, cotton-fluffing, sewing, haircutting also flourished endlessly. Most of them carried the burden and left the counties and provinces they used to live, which was commonly known as "going out." This type of craftsmen comprises the largest proportion of craftsmen in Zhejiang Province. They are able to endure hardship and they would go everywhere, even to mountain tops or the remote countryside and knock on doors to offer processing and repairing services. Even after 1949 when the People's Republic of China was founded, a large number of craftsmen were still carrying out their livelihood. In the history of Zhejiang handicraft industry, there were famous artisans like cementers and carpenters from Dongyang, blacksmiths from Yongkang, maltose entertainers from Yiwu, female embroiders from Taizhou, leather shoe makers from Wenzhou and cotton-fluffing lads from Yongjia. These various types of handicrafts, which have been passed on by generations, constitute the special professional human resources advantage of Zhejiang Province, so that though natural resources and industrial bases were not dominant,

---

① Husserl, E. *The Crisis of European Sciences and Transcendental Phenomenology* [M]. Trans. Zhang, Q. Shanghai: Shanghai Translation Publishing House, 1988: 58.

Zhejiang people were able to call on thousands of households and create tides of entrepreneurship at the beginning of the reform and opening-up. Distinctive local industries were also formed in many areas, laying an important foundation for Zhejiang's regional characteristic economy.

Hangzhou's handicraft industry developed from an early period. As early as the late Neolithic period, the ancestors of Hangzhou people had lived together in Liangzhu, the northern suburb of the present Hangzhou, and engaged in primitive farming, animal husbandry, fishing, and hunting. Moreover, their skills in making products of clay, jade, bamboo, wood, and handicrafts of silk and flax had reached a high level. In the Western Jin Dynasty, rattan paper was produced in the area of Quanshan in Yuhang County. By the Tang Dynasty, the paper making technology had further development, and the rattan paper produced by Youquan Village was of the best quality. According to the documents of Tang and Song dynasties like *The Book of Worlds of Peace*, Hangzhou kept paying rattan paper as tribute and became an important setting of paper production across the whole country from the Kaiyuan Period in the Tang Dynasty to the Northern Song Dynasty. Lin'an, a county in Hangzhou also boasted a kind of cheap but high-quality paper. According to *New Book in the South,* "The paper produced in Lin'an has a short diameter. Its color is yellow and its shape is like a tooth of humans. If you write something wrong, it can be removed by licking with tongue without leaving splodges. It is hard to find because they are sold out as soon as they are made for their low price."[①] From the Tang Dynasty to the Northern Song Dynasty, in addition to the paper industry, Hangzhou's ceramic, textile and wine industries also developed to a considerable extent. To be more specific, it has formed the earliest neighborhood to develop the silk industry in Hangzhou. When Hangzhou was the capital of Wuyue Kingdom, there

---

① Qian, Y. *New Book in the South*: vol. 9 [M].

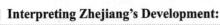

were more than 300 weavers in its government offices.[①] Additionally, the ceramic industry in Hangzhou became famous for its large scale of production and low price. According to *The Book of Worlds of Peace,* in Yuhang County, "Residents of Tingshi Village of Yushi Town all make big urns, which is called Zhejiang Urn."[②] After Lin'an was appointed as the capital of the Southern Song Dynasty, on the one hand, various craftsmen with different professionals migrated there, on the other hand, due to the rise in the number of residents in city, the demand for industrial products increased, thus opening up a huge market of handicraft products and creating favorable conditions for the rapid development of the handicraft industry in Hangzhou. At the same time, large-scale official handicraft workshops which directly offered services to the royal family and government moved to Lin'an from Kaifeng, and greatly changed the structure and proportion of the private handicraft industry against the official ones, which exerted great influence on the development of the handicraft industry in Lin'an. From the perspective of attribution, the handicraft workshops of the Lin'an government in the Southern Song Dynasty could be divided into three categories: the Shaofu Bureau, the Jiangzuo Bureau, and the Junqi Bureau. Among them, the Shaofu Bureau was in charge of the production of the emperor's daily necessities, the Jiangzuo Bureau in charge of the civil constructions for the royal family and government offices, the Junqi Bureau was in charge of the production of the military industry. The government handicraft industry was featured with large scale, fine division of labor, and ingenious technology. Each "courtyard, bureau, field, or storehouse" was equivalent to a large handicraft workshop, with hundreds of craftsmen or even thousands more. The products of the official workshop were more delicate and exquisite. Generally speaking, before starting, a pattern was first given, and then processed according

---

① *History of the Southern dynasties*: vol. 70 Biography of Honest and Lofty Officials [M].

② Yue, S. *The Book of Worlds of Peace*: vol. 93 One of the Five Regions in Jiangnan–Hangzhou [M].

to procedure. After the product was made, it would be inscribed with the name of the craftsman, the year when it was made and its color number of the utensils. After this, it had to be sent to "Zuotou" to make sure that its quality had met the standard. Only after that could it be taken into the storage.[1] As the official handicraft workshops were rapidly increasing, the private handicraft industry in Lin'an during the Southern Song Dynasty also witnessed a great progress, especially in silk-weaving, printing, porcelain, shipbuilding, fan making, and military equipment manufacturing, and all of them had important positions in the whole country.

Wenzhou's folk handicraft tradition is long-standing. After comparing the industrial and commercial cultural traditions between southern Jiangsu and Wenzhou, Fei Xiaotong pointed out that "The historical tradition of southern Jiangsu is supplemented by agriculture and industry. Men plough in the field and women weave at home. It is a traditional Chinese pattern, which can be said to be 'the Cowherd and the Weaving Maid,' but the historical tradition in Wenzhou is like 'eight immortals soaring over the ocean,' which means everyone takes advantage of their strengths. Craftsmen with skills such as stone carving, bamboo weaving, cotton fluffing, bucket hooping, tailoring, hairdressing and cooking, and traders who sell sugar and commodities go across the nation to earn money so that they could support their family and establish their business after returning to their hometowns. The combination of those migrant wandering craftsmen or traders and country women who plough at home is the combination of artistry and agriculture. On these two different old foundations, what grows in southern Jiangsu is the commune industry, and later, the thriving village and township industries. And what developed in the south of Zhejiang is a professional market for family industry and a professional processing market. Southern Jiangsu comes from agriculture and sideline industry

---

[1]   Lin, Z. *Lin'an—The Capital City of the Southern Song Dynasty* [M]. Hangzhou: Xiling Seal Engravers Society, 1986: 233-235.

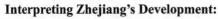

to supplement agriculture with labor, while southern Zhejiang bred industry from traders to expand business."[1] As early as the Eastern Jin and the Southern and Northern dynasties, the mulberry garden in the suburbs of Wenzhou could raise silkworms eight times a year, thus known as "silkworms of eight generations." Moreover, the porcelain of the "Dong'ou Kiln" was famous all over the country. By the time of the Sui and Tang dynasties, Wenzhou was renowned in weaving cloth. At that time, salt fields in the coastal areas of Wenzhou had also been developed, and the salt industry had become an important industry as well. To add, a place named Rui'an also began to refine copper. During the Song Dynasty, especially after the Song Dynasty moved south, Wenzhou's overseas trade, handicraft industry and commercial industry flourished, and its ceramics, shipbuilding, paper making, engraving, lacquer ware, embroidery, paper umbrella, leather, and weaving silk became famous all over the country. Although Wenzhou produced few lacquers, the lacquer ware produced in Wenzhou had a long history and exquisite appearance. As early as the Northern Song Dynasty, Kaifeng had a shop specializing in Wenzhou lacquer ware. And Lin'an, the capital of the Southern Song Dynasty, owned more shops selling such goods, such as "Peng Jia Wenzhou Lacquer Shops," "Huangcaopu Wenzhou Lacquer Shop," "Pingjin Bridge Riverside Wenzhou Lacquer Shop," etc.[2] Wenzhou was one of the nine regions that paid paper as tribute in the Song Dynasty, and at that time, Wenzhou Juan paper was a famous product. Youquan rattan paper, as mentioned above, was produced by Youquan Village of Yuhang County, and it still could not be compared with the Juan paper. During the reign of Zhenghe in the Northern Song Dynasty, 500 pieces of paper were paid as tribute each year. In the Southern Song Dynasty, its capital Lin'an even bore a profession that sold the Juan paper specially. Zhou Hui, who lived in

---

① Fei, X. Small commodity, big market [M]//He, F. *Overview of Zhejiang*. Hangzhou: Zhejiang People's Publishing House, 2003: 350

② Wu, Z. *The Book of Dreaming Liang*: vol. 13 & Nai, D. *Records of Scenic Spots in the Capital City: Shops*.

the Southern Song Dynasty once said, "in the Tang Dynasty, anyone who maked this paper could spare themselves of strenuous servitude, so the paper was named with Juan. The paper was produced in Yongjia, the scholar officials liked it because the work of calligraphy written on it was clearer, so they argued for a good price to purchase. Since the paper has been favored throughout history, it could be compared with Chengxintang paper."[1] Chengxintang paper was a famous product of Huizhou and was made by the Li family in the Southern Tang Dynasty. Wenzhou Juan paper could be compared to it, and its quality was undoubtedly excellent. In addition, Ke silk and Ou silk were also famous products at that time. "Wenzhou Ke silk was renowned southeasterly, and those who spoke of clothes would have to invest in it."[2] And the Ou silk produced in Wenzhou was as famous as the Hangzhou Textile, Huzhou Crepe, and so on. In the Ming Dynasty, the Wenzhou government set up a weaving and dyeing bureau. At the end of the Ming Dynasty, Wenzhou folk produced exquisite "cross cloth," and there were exports of Ou silk, embroidery, leather, wine, and so on. In the Qing Dynasty, Wenzhou's handicraft industry took Ou silk, leather, and paper umbrella as the three representative products. In the early stage, Ou silk became highly reputed as the main specialty of Wenzhou. After the mid-Qing Dynasty, the leather and paper umbrella industries gradually became prevailing. As Wenzhou became established as one of the "Five Ports of Commerce," Wenzhou's handicraft industry has also developed greatly. Ou embroidery has entered the European, American and Southeast Asian markets as an oriental art, and Wenzhou scissors were well known throughout the country and exported to Southeast Asia as well. To add, the firework and firecracker industries were also thriving. In this period, there were also some specialized handicraft villages in the rural areas of Wenzhou. For example, the village of Wanyao in Cangnan County was a fairly large-scale specialized village of ceramics. From 1912 to 1949, modern factories of industries such

---

① Zhou, H. *Records of Qingbo*: vol.1 [M]. Beijing: The Commercial Press, 1939.
② See *Records of Wenzhou* in Hongzhi Reign.

as textile, chemical engineering, food and light began to appear in Wenzhou one after another, though on a limited scale. During this period, the leather industry in Wenzhou also developed greatly. In the urban areas, there were tanning streets, leather shoes streets and leather goods streets. Tanning workshops were scattered intensively, and the shops linked with each other, forming a sheet of market and basically following the layout of "shop in front and factory at back." Besides, in the countryside, there even appeared a number of grass-mat towns and grass-mat villages.

According to textual research, in the Neolithic Age, there was already a pottery industry in Taizhou. Since the Sui and Tang dynasties, the handicraft industries of Taizhou, such as pottery, brewing, carving, salt making, and paper making, have been relatively developed and had a very long history of production, and a number of "one place, one product" professional handicraft villages have taken shape. From the Five Dynasties to the Northern Song Dynasty, celadon production had spread throughout the counties of Taizhou. So far, more than 70 ceramic kilns from the Five Dynasties to the Song Dynasty have been found in Wenling and other places. In the early years of the Northern Song Dynasty, green bamboo, mulberry, and bamboo shell were used in making Yuban Paper, Huajian Paper, Nanping Paper, small white paper and leather paper, etc. Mi Fu hammered Huangyan Rattan Paper in high temperatures until it was hot and then wrote or painted on it, and thus Huangyan Rattan Paper was praised as "smooth, clean, soft, processed." According to *Chicheng City Records During the Reign of Jiading* in the Southern Song Dynasty, "those who came out of Linhai were called Huangtan, Dongchen, those who came out of Tiantai were called Dadan, those who came out of Huangyan and were made of bamboo roots were called Yuban." It can be seen that at that time, all the counties in Taizhou produced paper, and there were a variety of products, and the quality of each was excellent. During the Southern Song Dynasty, the textile industry in Taizhou developed to a considerable extent. There were many kinds of textiles, including Hua Gauze, Du Gauze,

Jin Gauze, crepe yarn, spinning yarn, and Jin Thin Silk. "Tai silk" was a local famous product, juxtaposed with Yuban Paper, Taizhou mushroom, and dried ginger as tributes to the court. In addition, during the Southern Song Dynasty, Taizhou's wine, stone carving, mining, and metallurgical industries also developed to a certain extent. In the Ming Dynasty, Taizhou's handicraft industries, such as paper making, mining, and metallurgy as well as aquatic products processing, were further expanded. During the period of the Republic of China, Shuicheng, Zhusong and Louxia were villages specialized in the production of rough paper, and the farmers who engaged in production accounted for more than 90% of the whole village's population. In Jiangyang Village, more than 60% of the farmers specialized in the production of bamboo strips, and their main products including bamboo baskets, square baskets, and dustpan were sold to Shanghai, Ningbo and other places. In addition, almost every household of Qiaowu Village made stick incense (later developed into health incense).

Shaoxing's handicraft industry has a wide distribution and complex occupations. During the Spring and Autumn Period and the Warring States Period, the farming and aquaculture industries in Yue Kingdom were already in a fairly large scale, and handicrafts, such as textiles, metallurgy, and brewing, also witnessed a rapid development. By the time of the Three Kingdoms Period, Shanyin became the most important trading center of bronze mirror and Yue Cloth. In the Tang Dynasty, the celadon and silk market of Yuezhou were even famous overseas. As for the textile industry, the development level of the flax textile industry was similar to that in Hangzhou. According to the *Six Code in Tang Dynasty* written in Tianbao's reign, the imperial court divided the linen cloth from all over the country into nine grades according to texture, among which Yuezhou and Hangzhou cloths both ranked the fourth. What's more, the ceramics industry in Yuezhou was also famous for its technology. In the early years of the Southern Song Dynasty, Zhao Gou, Emperor Gaozong of Song, lived in Shaoxing for a while, and the residents of the north moved in in large numbers. This

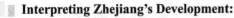
was the second time that the population of Shaoxing had increased dramatically, and thus the development of the handicraft commercial industry was stimulated. When it came to the Ming and Qing dynasties, there was a further increase in the number of handicraft categories in Shaoxing. For example, in the 13th year of Qianlong in the Qing Dynasty (1748), Chai Changhao, a Cixi native, set up a dyeing shop in Shengzhou. Since then, there were more traders and craftsmen coming to Shengzhou from other places. Cixi people were mostly engaged in the Chinese medicine industry, and Fucheng people were mainly engaged in the production and trading of cotton cloth, commodities, groceries and brewed wine. People setting up sauce shops were mostly from Shangyu and Yuyao; Zhuji people engaged wok-making; Tiantai people did haircutting; Yiwu people sold sugar; and Shengxian people were mostly engaged in the copper, tin, iron, bamboo, wood and other handicraft industries. In the third year of Xuantong in the Qing Dynasty (1911), there were 325 brewing workshops in Shanyin and Kuaiji County, and most brewing workshop owners opened their own wine houses, which took both production and sales into consideration with the shop in front and workshop at back. The prosperity of Shaoxing's handicraft industry lasted until the beginning of the Republic of China and the founding of the People's Republic of China. According to statistics in 1949, the workshop industry in Shaoxing accounted for 36.76% of the whole handicraft industry while the individual industry accounted for 56.81%. The rural handicraft industry was divided into two types: professional and part-time. Professional craftsmen managed production by opening shops or mobile operations, while part-time craftsmen did farm work during the busy season and traveled outside to other villages to do craft work during the slack season. The handicraft industry only required simple production tools, and it mainly relied on manual labor instead of a high level of technology with features such as multiple categories, decentralized operation, combination of production and selling. According to the investigation and registration in 1952, there were 25,074 handicraft households with 59,681 employees in Shaoxing, and the annual output value (price at that time) was 33.64

million yuan. The occupations mainly included carpenters, bamboo craftsmen, blacksmiths, plasters, stonemasons, sewers, etc. Shaoxing boasted as many as 85 industries and 80 in Shangyu, 45 in Xinchang. In 1952, among the 8,988 handicraft households in Shaoxing County, 661 were engaged in metal processing, 588 in construction, 2,762 in wood processing, 1,188 in textile, 944 in sewing, 22 in leather, 1,632 in food processing and 1178 in cultural and educational art supplies processing. According to its production and processing content, the handicraft industries in cities and towns mainly provided daily necessities and consumer goods, and repaired the old equipments and recycled the waste for residents, while few provided services for industrial and agricultural production. The rural handicraft industry mainly provided agricultural production services, as well as farmers' daily means of livelihood. For example, among the 2,572 handicraft households in Shaoxing, 72 households served industrial means of production, accounting for 2.8% of the total; 24 households served agricultural means of production, accounting for 0.93%; 1,023 households served the daily means of living for the residents, accounting for 39.77%; and 1,453 households were engaged in repairing consumer goods for daily use, accounting for 56.5%. According to the scale and mode of handicraft operations, there were more factories, workshops and shops in cities and towns, and their owners and masters took apprentices or hired helpers to organize production and operation. The labor scale ranged from a single family to dozens or even hundreds of employees.

Jinhua was called "the hometown of workers of all kinds," where pottery was produced in as early as the Neolithic Age. Industries related to ceramics, silk weaving, printing, cotton spinning, iron, paper making, hardware and foundry were gradually developed in the Tang and Song dynasties, and by the Ming and Qing dynasties they developed into a variety of handicraft factories: Craftsmen who engaged in processing metal, stone, clay, wood, bamboo, palm, cloth or brewing wine and businessmen who sold porcelain, pottery, paper, oil, cloth, silk, sugar, and wine all gathered in Jinhua. Fan Jun, who lived during the turn

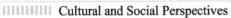
of the Northern and Southern Song dynasties, met a blacksmith in his hometown, Xiangxi of Lanxi County. The blacksmith started his career with casting agricultural tools such as ploughs, hoes and so on. However, because of the depression in agriculture, "The result of one day's exhaustion was only one tool, and in half or a whole month, the tool could not be sold," the worker was down and out. When the war started, people begged him for weapons such as knives, swords, arrowheads, and so on. A year later, the blacksmith already became rich.[1] Zhu Xi also reported that Tang Zhongyou had "called on more than a dozen craftsmen in Wuzhou with inscription and Buddha carving skills" and used the money of the minister's storehouse to support them. At that time, Wuzhou (Jinhua)'s craftsmen of all kinds were able to produce not only ordinary daily goods but also make weapons, engraved monuments, clay statues of Buddha and other arts and crafts products.[2] The hardware of Yongkang was most famous. Starting from the casting of tripod in Shicheng mountain of Yongkang during the legendary reign of Huangdi, to the forging of swords in the Spring and Autumn Periods, to the invention of the crossbow machine in the Han Dynasty, the industrious Yongkang people had long set foot on a hard but glorious road of hardware. "The burning fire reflects the sweat, and the lanes and streets witnessed their courage." According to *Yongkang County Chronicles* in the reign of Guangxu, Volume 1, "Earth, stone, gold, silver, copper, iron, and tin are all made by craftsmen, but the craftsmanship is natural and simple, rather than being exquisite." In 1929, Yongkang County carried out an investigation and found that the number of hardware craftsmen was 4,827, later in 1936, 5,931, in 1948, 9,295 and later in 1949, 9,606. They were mainly engaged in blacksmithing, filing, processing copper, tin, silver, and steelyard, and casting iron, copper, and tin. In 1937, Yongkang County owned

---

① Fan, J. *Works Collection of Fan Xiangxi*: vol.18 To Lü Yunshu, Man of Letters[M].

② Bao, W. *Studies on Zhejiang Regional History* [M]. Hangzhou: Hangzhou Publishing Group, 2003: 196.

1,059 iron, 850 copper, 822 tin, and 31 silver workshops. Additionally, the hardware craftsmen of Yongkang also moved to alien places in large numbers, "acquiring more skills in other places," or setting up workshops.[1] Wood artisans of Jinhua in the Ming and Qing dynasties were mainly engaged in manufacturing furniture, farm tools, and wood artifacts inside buildings. Wood carvings were often used to decorate furniture and buildings, such as the construction of shrines and dowries for marriage, which was most prevailing and renowned in Dongyang. By the mid-Qing Dynasty, Dongyang wood carving was fully developed and improved, and by the end of the Qing Dynasty, a large number of Dongyang carpenters flowed into cities, specializing in processing handicrafts. The artistic style also changed from the quaint and simple "ancient body" to the exquisite and elegant "new style."[2] Historically, there has also been considerable development in the handicraft products industry of Jinhua region, such as mat weaving, straw weaving, bushy shoes, leather, palm, rattan, and other handmade products. According to the third volume of *Dongyang County Records Newly Revised* in the reign of Kangxi, "Lisheng Rattan is mostly used to produce bamboo articles, and can also be used as a big rope. Another kind of rattan, known as Shu Rattan, can be used to build a house." "The mat grass has a three-edged body, which is brittle and easy to decay, but the mat made out of it with excellent craftsmanship can even reach the half price of Su mat." In the early years of the Republic of China, Dongyang introduced and planted Chinese Alpine Rush from Huangyan to promote the development of the straw mat weaving industry, and the annual output was 80,000. Those could also be used to make straw mat, straw hat, etc. In addition, straw mat from Jinhua, Pujiang was famous for its durability, and in Xueqianlou Village of Puyang Town, almost

---

[1]   Ibid. 198.

[2]   Xu, W. Wood carving of Dongyang in the Qing Dynasty [J]. *Cultural Relics World*, 1989(3).

every family weaved straw mats.[①] Besides, straw weaving also includes straw shoes. For instance, in *Pujiang County Records* in the reign of Guangxu, it was written that "the straw of Wumangnuo is flexible and can be utilized to wave shoes." And in some other counties in the Jinhua area, the production scale of bush-shoes was also quite considerable. For example, *Lanxi County Records* in the reign of Guangxu recorded, "For their livelihood, women in the countryside, in addition to textile, also make bush-shoes and sell in Suzhou and Hangzhou, the number of which often reaches millions upon millions." Pu shoes were also produced in many places in Dongyang. In addition, there were many craftsmen with skills of processing palms in the Jinhua area, such as those who processed palm in Lanxi and Longyou were mostly from Yiwu.

3.2.3 Little Cultural Traditions of Commerce of Zhejiang Folks

In history, Zhejiang was not only the hometown of a relatively developed handicraft industry but also one of the regions where the folk commerce were relatively developed and the folk industrial and commercial culture traditions was relatively profound.

The local chronicles of dynasties, especially during the Song, Yuan, Ming and Qing dynasties, recorded a large number of regular markets in Zhejiang. In *Market and Social structure in Rural China*, G. William Skinner made a deep analysis of the economic function of the market phenomenon. According to his opinion, the market that opens every day in cities can be called the "central market," and it is the highest level of the market system. The scattered trading markets, which are widely distributed in various villages, are the most basic "primary markets," while the "intermediary market," which is the regular market, lies between the central market and the primary market. In his opinion, to

---

① Bao, W. *Studies on Zhejiang Regional History* [M]. Hangzhou: Hangzhou Publishing Group, 2003: 199.

support a central market that opens every day, there must be sufficient demand, that is, "threshold demand." If there is a shortage of threshold demand, only "periodic markets" that open intermittently can survive. Within this range, the larger the demand, the more frequent and denser the opening days of the market will be, or vice versa. Of course, a natural corollary of this is that when the demand exceeds the "threshold," the intermediary market will develop into a central market. The natural evolution of the Zhejiang bazaar has undoubtedly confirmed Skinner's view.

The first recorded Zhejiang bazaar is "Yueda Market" in the Qin and Han dynasties, which was located in the south of Duting Bridge in Shaoxing. However, besides this one, there must be markets in other places which cannot be found in written books. It can be inferred that the earliest market in Zhejiang was the "primary market," a set of scattered trades in villages. For example, mountain people brought mountain goods in exchange for grain and cloth from farmers who lived in the plain areas by the road or the stream, and both parties agreed to congregate a few times within 10 days. This kind of "primary market" then gradually evolved into a regular market that opened a few times within ten days of the lunar calendar, that is, "regular market" or "intermediary market." An interesting phenomenon of the regular market is that since there were markets on the 3rd, 6th or 9th day, there must be markets on the 2nd, 5th, or 8th day. This means that the market days of adjacent intermediary markets were staggered. This is because each intermediary market has its own coverage area, and the range of the area is usually the maximum radius for a vehicle driven by a person who is going to the market or a person who walked from the morning and arrived home at evening. When the market closes, the mobile suppliers at the scheduled bazaars (many of which are street vendors) would have the opportunity to do business in other adjacent intermediary markets. Setting different market days for neighboring markets is a satisfactory arrangement for both the supply and requisitioning parties.[1] The formation of bazaars is of great significance. As an important institutional arrangement, bazaars play an essential role in providing information. As North said, on a growing scale, bazaars replaced the occasionally-used and costly ones where people bargained with only one trading partner in each transaction, trying to get more market information. Bazaars "reduce the cost of individual search for market information" and play a pioneering role in capital markets by developing effective information tools. The bazaars, like "other institutional innovations, are the source of productivity growth."[2] As information spreads among an increasing number of people, the average trading cost for every businessman decrease.

Although Yueda Market of Kuaiji was scrapped in the Song Dynasty, it was recorded as an "ancient abandoned market" in *Kuaiji Records*, "The ancient abandoned market was in Lixun Place, south to the Duting Bridge, where Jizixun was said to sell medicines." In the Eastern Han Dynasty, Yue cloth, Yue porcelain, bronze mirror and other products were famous both at home and abroad. As the imperial court carried out the policy of reducing tax and advocating "equal emphasis on food and goods," commercial activities in Kuaiji became more frequent, and folks who sold silk and cloth for livelihood spread throughout urban and rural areas. In the Eastern Jin and Southern dynasties, Shaoxing's markets were prosperous, with a reputation of "the present Kuaiji, the past Guanzhong." Folks alongside Shanyin Road were rich in products, and both goods and grains were traded, and many traders and businessmen traveled here, as a result of which it later became the trading center of Jiangdong silk and rice. At the same time, regular bazaars appeared in Yongjia County in Wenzhou. During the Sui Dynasty, with the opening of the Beijing-Hangzhou Grand Canal,

---

① Zhejiang Province Market Editorial Department. *Annals of the Markets in Zhejiang Province* [M]. Beijing: Local Records Publishing House, 2000: 2-3.
② North, D. C. & Thomas, R. *The Rise of the Western World* [M]. Trans. Li, Y. & Cai, L. Beijing: Huaxia Publishing House, 1999: 72.

Hangzhou formed a trade market of rare and precious things where merchants were converged. After the mid-Tang Dynasty, Hangzhou was not only a place selling various goods but also a place that attracted merchants coming from all around the world. In the first year of the Yongtai reign, Li Hua wrote *The Wall Records of Hangzhou's History Hall,* saying that Hangzhou "was a key link between Wu and Yue, and it boasted even more imposing momentum than the lakes and sea, with 20 miles of parallel bulwarks and 30, 000 rooms opening."[1] By the end of the Tang Dynasty, Hangzhou "had great lakes to its east where numerous boats soared over, and cities to its north where rare goods were traded," with a prosperous scene that "every market you fond must light on fires and every building you fond must be filled with musical instruments playing and singing."[2] "Where fish and salt gather was a market, and where wisps of smokes and fire rise was a village," and "fires were lighted on the side of bridges on night market, and boats are berthed compactly outside the temple in vibrant spring." During the Five Dynasties, Wu Yue State expanded the city wall many times, and Hangzhou gradually formed the pattern of the city proper in the north and the palace in the south. With halls in the front and market at the back, shops were built along the streets. Markets were expanded, and domestic commercial and trade bazaars flourished. During the Northern Song Dynasty, the development of market trade and the prosperity of the commodity economy in Zhejiang could be measured by commercial taxes. According to *The Draft of the Song Dynasty's Convention Changes,* before the tenth year of Xining in the Northern Song Dynasty (1077), the Hangzhou tax collection scope including the markets of Hangzhou city proper, Longshan, Zhejiang, Beiguo, Fanpu, Yuhang, Baikan, Lin'an, Yuqian, Changhua, Fuyang, Xincheng, and Nanxin had a tax revenue of 120,303 *guan*. At the same time, the Yuezhou commercial tax collection scope including Yuezhou city

---

① Dong, H. *Entire Donovan*: vol. 316 [M]. Beijing: Zhonghua Book Company, 2013.

② Luo, Y. *Notes on Hangzhou and Luocheng* [M].

proper, Shangyu, Xinchang, Yupu, Zhuji, Yuyao, Xixing, Xiaoshan, and Shanxian had a tax revenue of 27,577 *guan*. In the tenth year of Xining in the Northern Song Dynasty (1077), the Hangzhou commercial tax collection scope included six counties of Hangzhou city proper, Fuyang, Xincheng, Lin'an, Yuqian, Changhua and Yanguan, and Zhejiang Market, Longshan Market, Fanpu Town, Jiangzhang Bridge Town, Waixian Market Town, Nanxin Market, Baikan Market, and Caoqiao Market, which had a tax revenue of 173,813 *guan* and 523 *wen*. In the same year, the Yuezhou tax collection scope included six counties of Yuezhou city proper, Xiaoshan, Shan, Zhuji, Shangyu, Yuyao and Xinchang, and Xixing Town, Yupu Town, Cao'e Town, and Sanjie Market, with a total tax revenue of 64,002 *guan* and 77 *wen*.[①]

Braudel believed that there was a discontinuous contact surface between a self-sufficient material life and a mutually reinforcing economic life, which was made up of bazaars, stalls, stores and thousands of other tiny spots as material embodiment. On both sides of the "contact surface" are the material life of "self-sufficiency" and the economic life of "exchanging necessities." Exchanging is the way to span from "material life" to "economic life."[②] Since Lin'an (Hangzhou) became the capital of the Southern Song Dynasty, there has not been (and cannot be) a fundamental change in the dominance of Zhejiang's natural economy. However, the commodity economy did have a further development. Ye Shi pointed out that "the land of Wu and Yue... with forty years of prosperity, drifted from the four directions have all moved together within a thousand mile, while people of the highest rank did not know the number of rich people. Therefore, with a population as many as that of 15 states which equal to half of the national population, there was insufficient land to support even half of the existing

---

① Revenues of Hangzhou and Yuezhou are cited from *The Draft of the Song Dynasty's Convention Changes*.

② Braudel, F. *Civilization and Capitalism, 15th-18th Century* [M]. Trans. Gu, L.& Shi, K. Beijing: SDX Joint Publishing Company, 1993: 1, 4.

population. The value of rice, millet and silk was three times that of the old, and the price of chicken, pigs, vegetables and firewood was five times that of the old, and it became more convenient, while the number of people who did not engage in trade were a hundred or so times that of those who did."[1]

Shiba Yoshinobu said, "without quoting Marco Polo's testimony, the capital of the Southern Song Dynasty, Lin'an (which is now Hangzhou), was a typical example of business and urban revolution that took place in China from 9th to 13th century."[2] After Lin'an became the capital of the Southern Song Dynasty, "the people of all directions gathered in Zhejiang." The population of Lin'an grew rapidly. According to *The Book of Dreaming Liang*, Volume 18, *Residence Registration*, within 100 years or so, the population of Lin'an has doubled. The rapid growth of urban population has expanded the demand for all kinds of consumer goods, thus creating favorable conditions for the prosperity of commerce. In addition, a large number of industrialists and businessmen from the north went southwards, bringing more abundant commercial capitals and flexible means of operation from places such as Kaifeng, thereby playing a role in promoting the business development of Lin'an. According to Shiba Yoshinobu, the market circle of Hangzhou in the Southern Song Dynasty can be divided into three levels: First, a long-distance commercial transportation circle composed of the largest hinterland with Hangzhou as the center. Hangzhou was a rare national market for the distribution of medicinal materials and spices. Imports from the southeast coast and the South China Sea were unmistakable, and they also attracted merchants from Shu (Sichuan Province, in the southwest of today's China). Second, a commercial circle composed

---

① Ye, S. *Separate Collection of Shuixin*: vol. 2 Folk Lives[M]. Beijing: Zhonghua Book Company, 1960.

② Shiba, Y. *Study on the Economic History of Regions South of the Yangtze River in the Song Dynasty* [M]. Trans. Fang, J. & He, Z. Nanjing: Jiangsu People's Publishing House, 2001: 321.

of a small-scale hinterland with Hangzhou as the center which was a medium-distance commercial transportation circle formed to meet the daily living needs of 1.5 million people in Hangzhou. Third, a commercial circle composed of Hangzhou and its suburbs, where you could find a distinctive feature of the division of labor, "vegetables near the East Gate, water near the West Gate, firewood near the South Gate and rice near the North Gate." According to Wu Zimu's *The Book of Dreaming Liang*, "During the one hundred or so years after Hangzhou became the capital, the number of households increased, and the number of traveling merchants and traders was ten times larger than that of the past." "There was no such day when the streets would be empty and no vendors were seen traveling about." "From the main street and other lanes, shops of various scales were connected and none of them is vacant." *The Book of Dreaming Liang* also recorded that in Lin'an, there were more than ten types of shops selling various products including tea, liquor, noodle, fruit, colored silk, knitting wool, incense candles, oil sauce, rice, fish, meat and so on. Lin'an, at that time, boasted more households which were engaged in markets than those simple shops. For example, the Wushan area in the south of the city was the home of out-of-town merchants and businessmen. Among the merchants, a group of great ones who were good at drilling for profits also took into shape. Many "industrial markets" were also formed inside and outside the city proper, that is, shops in the same trade. The stalls which were relatively concentrated in one street or lane were referred to as "Hang" (firms), "Tuan" (groups) or "Shi" (markets). According to *Lin'an Records During Xianchun Years in the Song Dynasty, Records of Dreaming Liang* and so on, there were mainly pharmaceutical markets, flower markets, pearl markets, rice markets, meat markets, vegetable markets, fresh fish firms, fish firms, pig firms, cloth firms, crab firms, green fruit groups, citrus groups, salted fish markets, book stores, etc. Everything was gathered here—all kinds of markets, scales of groups—the place never run short of buyers and sellers. There were morning markets and night markets, and in the outskirts there was also Zhejiang Market (now Nanxing Bridge area), Beiguo Market, Jiangzhangdong Market, Huzhou

Market (namely Hushu), Jiangzhangxi Market, Bandaohong Market, Xixi Market (Liuxia Town), and Chishan Market, etc. In the early Yuan Dynasty, Hangzhou was a place for foreign businessmen to gather, and trade was flourishing, almost as prosperous as the Song Dynasty. According to *The Travels of Marco Polo*, in the Yuan Dynasty, there were ten big markets in Hangzhou and countless small markets along the streets. Every week, there were three days for opening markets. 40,000 to 50,000 people would come to trade with commodities, and there was an abundance of all kinds of food. Afterwards, as the natural and man-made disasters continued, the market gradually declined. During the Ming and Qing dynasties, the business and trade industry in Hangzhou was gradually restored and developed. According to *The Official Records of Hangzhou* in the Ming Dynasty, there were the Shou'an Square Market, Zhong'an Bridge Market, Huiji Bridge Market, East Garden Market, Bushi Market, and Chunxi Bridge Market, Qingchun Bridge Vegetable Market (Caishi Bridge) in the territory of Hangzhou. These markets were concentrated on fruits and vegetables, fish and meat, sugar, rice and noodles, cloth compatible with different seasons and regions, livestock, clothes, utensils, etc. In the Qing Dynasty, Hangzhou had Daojiang Market, Qinghefang Street, Siqian Market, Ta'ertou Market, Naoshi Market, Yangshi Street Market, East Garden Market, Shou'an Square Market, Zhong'an Bridge Market, Huiji Bridge Market, Eastern Street Market, etc.

In addition, a relatively deep folk commercial tradition has also taken shape in other regions of Zhejiang Province, especially since the Southern Song Dynasty. A few regions have been cited as examples in the following.

According to Shiba Yoshinobu's research, the market organization of Mingzhou (namely Ningbo today) in the Southern Song Dynasty "took shape with the development of such social division of labor and

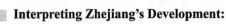
played a regulating role in balancing demand and supply."[1] This has been specifically shown in the following aspects: organizations for the supplementary exchange of surplus and insufficient supplies in villages, wooded and hilly lands and fishing areas, organizations of goods distribution for the supply of the city, in particular the central market, Mingzhou; organizations with the purpose to expand the market and increase regional consumption that exchange local specialties and imported goods transported by sea. These organizations ultimately supported the prosperity of the central market of the city of Mingzhou. During the Baoqing reign of the Southern Song Dynasty, there were 22 fairs in Ningbo. In the Ming Dynasty, famous fairs in Ningbo included Great Market, Middle Market, Back Market, Yongdong Market, Xiguo Market, Xiguo Eight Markets, Dongjin Forty-Nine Markets, etc. The fairs outside the four gates opened once every ten days, and the markets outside the west gate were held on every 8th, 18th and 28th day; those outside the south gate held on every 7th, 17th and 27th day; those outside Dongdu Gate held on every 9th, 19th and 29th day; and those outside Lingqiao held one very 4th, 14th and 24th of the month. By the time of the reign of Qianlong in the Qing Dynasty, the number of Ningbo market was up to 113 and the markets opened once every five days or three days instead. By the end of the Qing Dynasty, the forms of Ningbo's bazaars became more diversified. For instance, the Yuyao County Great Bazaar had various forms such as an everyday market, odd-number day market, even-number day market or markets that opened three to four days within every ten days. The small bazaar, also known as the open-air market or half day market, usually opened in the early hours of the morning and closed near noon. When the weather was smooth and the harvest season was good, the bazaars were crowded with vendors and thousands of merchants gathered in the bazaars, where the north and south commodities competed for sales. People came and went with unstoppable bustling, while the trading was booming and the market was in full swing.

---

① Shiba, Y. *Study on the Economic History of Jiangnan in the Song Dynasty* [M]. Trans. Fang, J. & He, Z. Nanjing: Jiangsu People's Publishing House, 2001: 493.

In the late Qing Dynasty, a notable phenomenon of Ningbo's trading markets was the choice of the opening day. In analyzing the overall market situation in China, Skinner said that when choosing the opening days, no special attention was paid to avoiding time clashes among the neighboring markets. Instead, people focused on the trading day of the lower market and tried to avoid conflict with the trading day of the upper market. According to a study by Shiba Yoshinobu, the western plain of Ningbo City in 1877 can be used as an annotation of Sinner's point of view which has been mentioned above. At that time, there were three central markets for the commodities distribution in the area, one of which was Maimian Bridge Market, located on the bank of Zhongtang River, which had a straight road connecting with the west gate of Ningbo. Another one was Shiqi Market, located next to Nantang River, which was opposite to the south gate of Ningbo. And the other was Huangguling Market, which was located between Zhongtang and Nantang. It served as a link between the above two bazaars. All the other markets in the middle of Ningbo and the western plains were either primary markets or intermediate markets. Shiba Yoshinobu also reminded that the opening days of the subordinate markets under these three central markets were all corresponding to the opening days of the central markets. The opening time of the three central markets was three days per every ten days, while in the western plains none of them was open for three days per every ten days. According to Shiba Yoshinobu, "the choice and adjustment of the opening day of the central market was mainly decided by the merchants according to the requirements of the orderly trading of commodities. The shopkeepers who ordered goods from the wholesalers in the central market had an impact on the choice of the opening day, and so do the dentists, the weighers, and the rental owners. The above central market organizations actually overlaped with each other. This means that most intermediate markets belonged to more than one central market, and most commodities in the primary market also came from two or three central markets. On the contrary, the form of goods-delivering was

the same as above. Even the central market, which had only indirect links to Ningbo, has its own selectivity in commodity transactions."① Because market organizations are closely connected and are toothed and intertwined in time and space, the competition between these markets is very fierce, which also promotes the adjustment of uniform price in Ningbo's commercial circle.

In the Jiatai reign of the Southern Song Dynasty, Shaoxing's archways increased from 36 to 96. Shaoxing became one of the three major cities in the country and enjoyed equal popularity with Jinling. It also set up Zhaoshuifang Market, Qingdaqiao Market, Dayun Bridge East Market, ancient abandoned market (that is, Yueda Market), Dayun Bridge West Market, Longxing Temple Front Market, Yidi Market, etc., and they formed a commercial network within the city. In the 8th year of Chunxi (1181), Zhu Xi held the post of Changping Tea Salt Official in eastern Zhejiang, and he divided Shaoxing's rural households into two types: one was "property households"; the other was tenants who ploughed in the fields and open shops.② It can be seen that in the Shaoxing countryside at that time, the fourth and fifth class households of the lower class have quite commonly used the town market to engage in small business and hawker business. During the Ming and Qing dynasties, the Shaoxing market developed to become better, since the number of markets increased and a number of professional markets with various features appeared. According to *Shaoxing Official Records* in the reign of Qianlong, the bazaars at that time included Zhaoshuifang Market, Liquor Shop Market, Dayun Bridge East Market, Yueda Market, Qingdao Bridge Market, Longxing Temple Front Market, Dayun Bridge West Market, Yidi Market, Jiangqiao Market and so on, which mainly managed agricultural and sideline products. In addition,

---

① Shiba, Y. *Study on the Economic History of Jiangnan in the Song Dynasty* [M]. Trans. Fang, J. & He, Z. Nanjing: Jiangsu People's Publishing House, 2001: 530.

② *The Draft of the Song Dynasty's Convention Changes—Food Goods; The Whole Collection of Zhuxi:* vol. 99 Charitable Granary[M].

due to the thriving of the brewing and tin foil industry and the large food consumption, liquor companies, tin foil, tea markets, Rice Street and other professional markets gradually formed. During the period of the Republic of China, Shaoxing served as a consumer city. Most mountain products markets were located in the south of the city near the Kuaiji Mountain area with a higher topography; most aquatic products markets were located in the north of the city, a low-lying region connected to the plain's water system; some markets were located in urban and rural traffic arteries such as side gates around the city, Xiguo Gate, Chang'an Gate and Wuyun Gate; while inside the city, according to the traditional pattern, there were Changqiao Bridge Market in the east, Beihai Bridge Market in the west, and Dajiang Bridge Market in the north, most of which were selling agricultural produces. The Dashan Temple, located at the center of the city, had not been repaired for a long time. The ruineded temple house and the open space prompted many traders and quack artists to gather there and gradually opened hotels, snack shops, miscellaneous jigger shops, barber shops, needle and thread shops, tobacco shops, tea rooms, opera houses and so on. The local products, such as Shaoxing wine and tin foil, also had their own marketing methods. Shaoxing's wine businesses were mainly managed by brewers and retailers. In 1936, Shaoxing had 367 hotels that sold Shaoxing wine, with an annual sales volume accounting for two or three tenths of the total Shaoxing wine sales. The tin foil shops in the city and the tin foil produced from workshops relied on being sold to foreign ports, foil shops, etc. Negotiations for trade between the tin foil businesses were often held at teahouses, thus giving rise to the name "tinfoil tea market."[1]

In the early days of the Southern Song Dynasty, Wenzhou was well known for its commercial prosperity and numerous businessmen. In the Southern Song Dynasty, when Cheng Ju, a scholar, wrote about

---

[1]   Zhejiang Province Market Editorial Department. *Annals of the Markets in Zhejiang Province* [M]. Beijing: Local Records Publishing House, 2000: 250-251.

Wenzhou, he said like this: "its goods were fine and extravagant, and most natives engaged in business." At that time, merchants in Wenzhou "got up with birds although the morning bell did not ring yet."[1] Because of the prosperity of the state-regulated commerce, in the Northern Song Dynasty, the commercial tax of Yongjia County had reached as much as 25,391 *guan* and 6 *wen*, which was seven times the national average. Of course, the tax revenue of Yongjia in the Southern Song Dynasty is more than that in the Northern Song Dynasty, but it is a pity that the official materials in this respect are still lacking. However, Ye Shi once wrote in his poem that three million wen were levied every day. Though it may be exaggerated, we can still see that Yongjia County of the Southern Song Dynasty received a large amount of business tax revenue. Not only did some counties in Wenzhou had a lot of commercial tax, the commercial tax in some towns in Wenzhou was quite considerable as well. According to *Food Goods* from *The Draft of the Song Dynasty's Convention Changes*, the annual commercial tax in Rui'an was 6,287 *guan*, Yong'an 4,703 *guan*, Liushi Town 2,049 *guan* and 794 *wen*, Qiancang Town 1,512 *guan* and 130 *wen*. In addition, since the Southern Song Dynasty, the internal division of labor in the commercial industry of Wenzhou has become more and more detailed. By the end of the Ming Dynasty, Rui'an was already home to pawnshops, satin shops, cloth shops, garment shops, fruit shops, fish shops, wine shops, paper shops, rice shops, and bowl shops, pie shops, Chinese fir shops, chicken and goose shops, casting copper shops, etc.[2] Since the Qing Dynasty, Wenzhou has been "filled with fish and salt, and merchants have converged." The business has become more and more prosperous, and the city has formed a commercial network with four pillars including the Chinese medicine industry, sauce industry, south goods industry and satin industry. At that time, Wenzhou had already become the place where merchants would meet. "Wenzhou is good, attracting merchants

---

① Dai, Y. *Collection of Huanchuan*: vol. 5, Shanghai Tower in Jiangshan [M].

② Cited from *Rubbings of Stele to Commemorate Official* Hou in the 6th year of Tianqi in the Ming Dynasty (1626), collected by Wenzhou Museum.

and folks from all directions, it is where ships from Wuhui reach after one night of sailing, and where specialties and products from Fuqing are updated quickly, and Tianjin is located to its north."[①] Wenzhou attracted a lot of foreign businessmen to do business, who often carried rare and precious goods.[②] The Ningbo group and Fujian group were both at the pivotal position of merchant groups in the commercial sector of Wenzhou. Besides, the market trade in the Wenzhou area has a long history as the stronghold for Wenzhou people to "exchange rice and other commodities for daily use." During the Ming and Qing dynasties, Yueqing County had "Xinshi Market on the 3rd and 8th, Lakeside Market on the 1st and 6th, Furong Market on the 2nd and 7th, Baixi Market from December 20th to 29th, Dajing Market on the 3rd, 6th and 9th, and so on."[③] At the juncture of the Ming and Qing dynasties, there were 13 places in Pingyang County which were called market or town, and six were called as such in the present county. In the early period of the Republic of China, in Pingyang's urban-rural market towns such as the county town, Aojian, and Shuitou, there were specialized markets selling aquatic products, firewood, piglets, cattle, bamboo, tea, fruit, and other products. *Pingyang County Records* in the Republic of China divided Pingyang's towns and markets, according to their scales, into "markets" and "small markets." Among them, there were 17 called "markets" for being located in thoroughfare or densely populated villages and 27 called "small markets" for having inns and stalls.

The commercial industry of Taizhou also has a long history. Linhai has been where Taizhou's government was located since the 11th year of the Sui Dynasty (591), and its commerce was well developed. In the Ming Dynasty, it had the reputation of "opening markets every day." Baita Bridge and Cross Street were the downtown areas of the city. Due to the reliance on water transportation on Lingjiang River, the trading of

---

① See *Annals of Yongkang County* in Guangxu Reign.
② See Fang Dingrui, "Wenzhou Zhuzhi Poem."
③ See *Annals of Yueqing County* in Guangxu Reign.

bamboo, wood, firewood, charcoal, fruit and other agricultural products were mostly distributed along the streets at the river's lower reaches. In the Song Dynasty, Wenling included towns such as Quanxi (now Chengguan), Zhengzhuang (now Zeguo), Qiaoling (now Wenqiao), Shilang (now Daxi). By the 19th year of Jiajing in the Ming Dynasty, the county already had 19 market towns to gather goods to trade, and by the 15th year of Jiaqing in the Qing Dynasty, the main market towns in this county were more than 30. Thus, a system in which markets opened on non-overlapping days was formed. According to *The Outline of Wenling County Administration* in 1935, in the early period of the Republic of China, "The most commercially prosperous town among all key towns in this county was Zeguo, followed by the county town, Xinhe, Songmen and Wenling Street, and then places such as Ruoheng, Daxi, Panlang, Aohuan, Dalü, Qiaoxia, Changyu, Tangxia. To add, there was also a market day in other rural towns. Merchants dealt in cotton cloth, silk and satin, goods from Beijing, Guangdong or foreign countries, soy sauce, cigarettes, goods, Chinese medicine, mixed specialties, dried and fresh aquatic products, pig meat and poultry eggs, grain, oil, teahouse, inns, etc." The market trade in Zeguo of Wenling began in the Five Dynasties and took its form in the Song Dynasty. By the Yuan, Ming, and Qing dynasties, it gradually developed and scaled up, and things traded were various daily necessities. From the sixth year of Guangxu to the second year of Xuantong in the Qing Dynasty, there were 13 markets in Yuhuan County, such as Huangqi, Xiqing, and Houwan. During the period of the Republic of China, there were nine markets, such as Xia'angong, Lao'aoqian and so on. These markets, except for the few that were no longer in existence, are still being used today. In the Song Dynasty, Zhangan Town was one of the three major towns in Linhai County. It had an official wine store and tax office for the collection and management of goods. It was the earliest professional beverage and spices market in Jiaojiang. During the years of Qianlong and Jiaqing in the Qing Dynasty, Jiepai, Shuidou, Xiachen, Hengtang, Shadian, Sanjia, Henghechen, Huangjiao, Daogantang and other

prefectures all developed into a certain scale. By the end of the Qing
Dynasty, the Jiaojiang River has gradually formed a market network
with different market days. In the Ming Dynasty, Huangyan County had
Dajingtou Market and Tianchang Market, as well as ten markets in the
countryside, such as in Xianqiao Village (Yuanqiao) and Luqiao Village.
In the Qing Dynasty, there were 39 markets including Dajingtou Market
and Shitanggang Market, and in the Republic of China there were 64
markets. At each market, stalls were set up at the doorstep of the street-
facing shops, and people often said to each other, "You should go to
Dajingtou for fish and meat, to Caoxiangkou for chicken and duck, and
to Qiaotingtou for rice and firewood."

3.3   Cultural Tradition of Industry and Commerce and Path of Zhejiang's Economic and Social Development

According to Neoinstitutional Economics, path dependence refers to
the mechanism of returns-increasing and self-reinforcing in institutional
changes. After the establishment of such a unique development path, a
series of externality, organizational learning procedures and subjective
models would reinforce the path. In other words, the initial institution
choice would strengthen the stimulation and inertia of the existing
system, since it is easier to follow the changing path and certain
direction of the original institution than to find a new path. On one
hand, the underlying causes for the formation of path dependence first
relate to interest. The formation of one institution would result in an
organizational interest group closely connected to the existing system.
They have a strong demand for such a institution (or path). On the
other hand, cultural factors including values and beliefs, moral ethics,
customs and ideology arranged by informal institutions also greatly
influence the institutional innovation and changing path of economic
society. It is true that economic activities, economic procedures and
economic systems have their own natural order. However, such natural
order is undoubtedly the result of a combination of various constraints

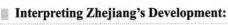
determined by the material and spiritual culture. In this sense, culture, as a public article shared by one country, one nation and one interest community, is the human capital that would produce great external effects. The reason why human's social life and trading activities differ from that of animals is that the former operates under certain social environment and specific constraints. Such constraints are formed by both formal and informal institutional arrangements in and throughout the entire span of human history. The function of culture is to influence and form these restraints through its own genetic mechanism. As Buchanan pointed out, "The cultural evolution had formed or produced abstract regulations for non-instinctive behaviors. Although we depended on these abstract regulations, we did not understand them. The rules of cultural evolution would always be constraints on our behaviors, though we did not understand and cannot clearly construct these rules."[1] North believed, that cultural factors including values and beliefs, moral ethics, customs and ideology arranged by informal institutions had a great impact on the institutional innovation and changing path of economic society. "Informal constraint plays an important role on the progressive evolution of institutions, which is the source of path dependence. We still have a long-term pattern relating to cultural evolution. However, we do know that the viability of cultural beliefs is strong and most cultural transitions are progressive."[2] In his speech at Peking University, North further pointed out that in today's society, our cultural traditions and belief systems were all fundamental constraints. We must take these constraints into consideration. Therefore, we could clearly understand what constraints and choices we may face in the future. In economic society, people always consciously or unconsciously follow certain customs and rules and pursue their own interests under certain social, institutional and cultural mechanism.

---

[1] Buchanan, J. M. *Liberty, Market and State* [M]. Trans. Ping, X. & Mo, F. Shanghai: SDX Joint Publishing Company, 1989: 115-116.

[2] North, D. C. *Institutions, Institutional Change and Economic Performance* [M]. Trans. Liu, S. Shanghai: SDX Joint Publishing Company, 1994: 133, 61.

Hence, the cultural traditions have a great impact on traditional social and economic activities as well as on social and economic development.

3.3.1   Regional Cultural Tradition of Industry and Commerce and Contemporary Zhejiang Economic Evolution

The relatively developed private industry and commerce throughout Zhejiang in history reflects the fact that the cultural tradition of the private industry and commerce in Zhejiang is deep and profound. The deep cultural tradition of the private industry and commerce constitutes the "genetic factor" of Zhejiang people throughout history and has a deep impact on the economic evolution of Zhejiang since the reform and opening-up. After the reform and opening-up, various regions in Zhejiang, particularly Wenzhou and Taizhou, adopted many institutional innovation models. For instance, these districts organized streets with specialized markets featured by front shop and back factory, and promoted industry by developing commerce to form the interaction between specialized market and massive economy and between industry-revived markets and share-holding cooperative system by promoting industry. They also collected funds to increase social welfare, and established private finance and mutual benefit associations, and supported the interest floating system. These models are not newly invented, and instead, all of them have existed in the development history of Zhejiang's industry and commerce. To some extent, they can be regarded as the follow-up effects of the relatively developed institutions and traditions of industry and commerce in Zhejiang history after thirty years' silence, or the inheritance, variation, innovation and development of historical institutions and traditions of industry and commerce in the Zhejiang civil society. The relatively developed industries in contemporary Wenzhou and Taizhou, including aquatic products processing industry, fruits processing industry, clothing industry, plastics industry, and small-scale electromechanical and chemical industry, are to some degree linked up with traditions.

Wenzhou and Taizhou are regions with relatively developed private finance and share-holding cooperative system. The proportion of deposits and loans in private financial institutions in Luqiao District of Taizhou reached 40% and the fund-raising inside enterprises in Wenzhou started in 1980. According to the statistics of June 1985, there were 2,887 enterprises raising funds in both rural and urban areas with a total amount of 15,970 accounting for 30% of the working capital of those fund-raising enterprises. And the fund raised inside enterprises was about 300 million yuan in 1990. Therefore, a key feature in Wenzhou's and Taizhou's development model of economic society is the establishment of various industries relies on private financing instead of government investment. The civil tradition "Cheng Hui"(rotating savings and credit association) and other derivatives, including Ping Hui, Tai Hui, Yao Hui, and Pai Hui, were original forms of the private finance and share-holding cooperative system in Taizhou and Wenzhou. Before 1949, financial institutions in Wenzhou, such as private banks, numbered 38, and the private credit had a longer history. In the early Qing Dynasty, private banks, pawn shops and private lending were exceptionally active. During the Qing Dynasty, it was a common phenomenon that "Cheng Hui" and other derivatives, including Ping Hui, Tai Hui, Yao Hui, and Pai Hui, widely existed in both Wenzhou and Taizhou. Such a phenomenon even survived during the planned economy times and later evolved into a contemporary economic model after the reform and opening-up. In Ye Dabing's opinion, the civil tradition of "Cheng Hui" which has lasted for hundreds of years is exactly the initial form of the contemporary practice of Wenzhou that establishes various industries by depending on private financing. "The share-holding cooperative system developed during the economic tide contains the extension, variation, reformation and development of the 'Cheng Hui' tradition. During the economic transition period, it effectively works on fund-raising."[1] Ye Dabing thought that the transition from the civil tradition of "Cheng Hui" to the development model of economic society featured by crowd-funding and share-holding cooperative system could be divided into three stages.[2] The first stage is a purely civil mutual aiding type with main two forms of Lun Hui and Yao Hui. Lun Hui, also known as "Zuo Hui," means collecting membership fees in accordance with the scheduled order, and Yao Hui means that the sequence of collecting membership fees is determined by shaking dice. The second stage is a new debit and credit type, developed from the purely civil mutual aiding type and featured by the combination of mutual-aiding and interest-bearing. In addition to the original forms of "Lun Hui" and "Yao Hui," new forms include "Yu Qing Hui," "Ren Qing Hui" and "Biao Hui." The third stage is a type of fund-raising inside society during the economic transition period. The fundraisers are various enterprises and the money is used by the share-holding cooperative system.

Sumner believed that the motivation for civil construction was demand. People started their careers by real action instead of mental activity. Demand is the first experience for human beings. Various urgent demands appear constantly and people must fulfill them, and then these demands bring about interest problems. "Life is composed of activities that fulfill interest requirements since in a society, life is a course of action and effort that expands to both the material field and social scope."[3] Considering that life is promoted by demand (interest), the activities that constitute life are motivated by demand

---

[1] Ye, D. Traditional borrowing form and modern stock ownership—The relationship between economic development and folk culture in Zhejiang [M] // *Eastern Zhejiang Schools and Zhejiang Spirit.* Hangzhou: Zhejiang Ancient Books Publishing House, 2006.

[2] Ibid.

[3] Gao, B. *Folk Culture and Folk Life* [M]. Beijing: China Social Sciences Press, 1994: 83.

(interest) and folk customs as standard activities of life are naturally motivated by demand. The evolutionary process from the civil custom of "Cheng Hui" to crowd-funding and the share-holding cooperative system reflects the rules of Wenzhou's economic development and civil demands. The economic folk custom "Cheng Hui" first emerged with the demand for smallholder economic and social life, featured by purely civil mutual aiding. With the development of cottage industries and small commodity economy, "Cheng Hui," while keeping the original function of mutual aiding, gradually developed into a supplementary form of gathering social production funds and developed from a mutual-aiding type into and interest-bearing type. "Folk customs are set for all living demands in certain time and place."[①] The inheritance of folk customs is not invariable, because the folk customs may vary with changes of objective conditions, and it is the same for "Cheng Hui." Since the reform and opening-up, with changes of the social and economic society, Wenzhou has used the form of "Cheng Hui" to transform the original type of mutual-aiding private debit and credit into a new type of developing social production collection and fund accumulation, "finally integrating into a modern operation form of fund-raising, namely the share-holding cooperative, to satisfy the needs of modern economic development, and becoming a new economic action and form to create the 'Wenzhou Model'."[②]

Shaoxing County has a profound cultural tradition of textile, and the "silk town" Huashe Town enjoys a high reputation for producing a great amount of silk every day. Since the reform and opening-up, such profound cultural tradition of textile has continued under a new policy

---

① Gao, B. *Folk Culture and Folk Life* [M]. Beijing: China Social Sciences Press, 1994: 83.

② Ye, D. Traditional borrowing form and modern stock ownership—The relationship between economic development and folk culture in Zhejiang [M] // *Eastern Zhejiang Schools and Zhejiang Spirit.* Hangzhou: Zhejiang Ancient Books Publishing House, 2006.

background and gradually developed into a complete textile industrial cluster including chemical fiber, textile production, textile dyeing and clothes-making after the textile machine revolution in the 1990s. Shaoxing Textile District has rapidly developed into the largest textile distribution center with complete equipment and most varieties of textile products in China and is the largest textile specialized market and cloth distribution center in Asia as well. Since the Tang and Song dynasties, Jiaxing has been one of the most developed areas in nationwide silk production. And in the Ming Dynasty, Jiaxing, as the home of silk, gained a high reputation for producing clothes for the whole nation. Since the reform and opening-up, with the rapid development of township enterprises, the cultural gene of "Silk House" has been reactivated and all counties and villages in Xiuzhou District of Jiaxing have started to open chemical fiber weaving factories. After the system of household contract responsibility was carried out in rural areas in 1983, farmers living in the north of Xiuzhou District started to develop individual and private chemical fiber weaving factories to enrich themselves. In the following twenty years, Xiuzhou District organized a large-scale chemical fiber weaving industrial cluster. The further spatial conglomeration of enterprises inside the industrial cluster promoted the urbanization process in Xiuzhou District. In addition, Wenzhou has the well-developed shoemaking industry, and the development of this industry in contemporary Wenzhou is closely related to its profound history and culture. According to relevant research, the traditional skill of shoemaking can be traced back to the Southern Song Dynasty. Shoes made in Wenzhou were listed as royal shoes during the reign of Chenghua in the Ming Dynasty, and through the efforts of generations of Wenzhou people, the shoemaking skills in Wenzhou became more advanced. After 1900, a tanning street, a leather street and various shoemaking workshops appeared.

The phenomena mentioned above add credence to one of the economists' views: innovation, in a sense, is an activity that destroys the old and establishes the new, or a creative destruction, which means to boldly abandon nonfunctional factors and turn to functional ones that lead to success. However, in addition to the contradiction between tradition and innovation, there is also a relationship between compatibility and inheritance. The functioning of one organization or individuals' conventions can contribute to the emergence of innovation, since the problems resolved by innovation are usually related to current conventions. Those current-convention-relating problems usually lead to the reflection and then the occurrence of great issues. Nelson and Winter even viewed the innovative activities as conventions, which is similar to Schumpeter's view. Schumpeter viewed the innovation as a new combination, which means that the innovation in the economic system is largely composed of existing concepts and materials. Similarly, most of the innovation in organizational conventions is a new combination of existing conventions. Whether traditions and conventions could be inherited, and that to what extent they would be inherited depends on how much these conventions would help people adapt to new environments. If the existing conventions are successful, people are likely to replicate that success; if the existing conventions fail to be profitable, people are likely to contract the conventions. Replication is an alternative response to the success, while contraction is an imperative response to the failure.

The rise of Taizhou specialized markets is undoubtedly the most convincing evidence of innovation and convention as well as traditional relationship. After two decades of development since the reform and opening-up, in 2002, Taizhou owned 585 commodity exchange markets, of which 67 held a trading volume over 100 million yuan and four held a trading volume over one billion yuan. Luqiao China Daily Commodity City, Luqiao Small Commodity Wholesale Market, Zhejiang Songmen Aquatic Product Wholesale Market and other specialized markets sell their products to over 20 provinces and cities in China and some countries overseas. To be more specific, the trading volume of Luqiao China Daily Commodity City has been over 10 billion yuan for years since 1994. In the late 1990s, professional transportation groups that hired 200 thousand people and hundreds of professional production bases featured by "One Village, One Product" and "One Place, One Product," are closely connected with these markets. Nearly half of the raw materials and electromechanical equipment required by rural industries in Taizhou are sold through these markets. There are multiple factors contributing to the rapid development of Taizhou's professional markets, and one is the function of the civil cultural tradition of industry and commerce in Taizhou. Taizhou is a region with relatively developed specialized markets in history. For instance, in Zeguo Town of Wenling, the markets were established in the Song Dynasty and further developed in the Ming and Qing dynasties. According to *Zeguo Town Records*, during the Republic of China period, there were specialized markets selling different products including rice, porker, bran, tree, cloth, firewood, fish, chick, vegetable, and straw-hat. After the reform and opening-up, Zeguo, with such historical endowment, naturally started to develop specialized markets of 25 different types and scales, including the Zhejiang Zeguo Shoe Mall, Zhejiang Zeguo Electrical Appliance Trading Center, Zeguo Hardware Bearing and Electrical Appliance Trading Center, Motorbike Sales Market, Bamboo Product Market, Timber Market, Fruit Market and Moso Bamboo Market. As recorded in *Huangyan City Records*, in the Ming Dynasty, the specialized markets were well-developed. For instance, firewood and forestall product markets were set in Toutuo and Yuanqiao; fragrant thoroughwort and straw mat markets were set in Hengshantou; silk market was set in Yangyudian; cotton gauze market was set in Xialiang; and daily commodities were sold in Wuyan, Sanjia, Yangfu temple and Shiqu. In the late Qing Dynasty and the Republic of China period, the specialized markets in Huangyan sold various products including orange, fish, silk, tobacco, straw mat, used steel, bamboo, timber, small commodities, cattle, and egret. Most of these specialized markets, except silk and tobacco, recovered and gradually prospered after the reform and opening-up. In the late Qing Dynasty and the Republic of China period, Tianyangwang Village of Luqiao used to take blacksmithing as a vocation, since boat nails and hooks were needed to supply the fishery industry. Therefore, Maizhiqiao set up specialty

stores to sell boat nails and hooks, which gradually formed a used steel market. The markets twice flourished in 1951 and 1960. However, the markets were banned in the "Great Leap Forward" and "Cultural Revolution" periods and transferred into remote areas. In 1980, the used steel specialized market in Xiayangdian occupied an area of 2000 square meters with over 100 fixed booths and an output of about 500 tons. After several years of development, by 1987, the trading volume in the used steel market reached 133,779 tons and 28.71 million yuan, and by 1988, the trading volume reached 16 thousand tons.

Therefore, as North said, the choices people made in the past decide the choices they may make today. To some extent, the rise of Zhejiang's specialized markets is an inevitable result of the traditional industrial and commercial thought and practice as well as the specialized market tradition in Zhejiang's history. Other measures to develop Zhejiang's economy are more or less connected with historical and cultural traditions since people are usually influenced by traditions. Zhejiang Province has always been the first one to respond to the marketization policies carried out by the central government or the provincial government since the reform and opening-up and was able to quickly obtain significant results. Prior to this, Zhejiang people may have already gained a lot of successful experiences from practices.

3.3.2 Regional Cultural Tradition of Industry and Commerce and the Development of Contemporary Zhejiang Society

The regional cultural tradition of industry and commerce has an impact on both the development of contemporary Zhejiang economy and society. After the reform and opening-up, the urbanization process in most regions of Zhejiang had an internal connection with the regional cultural tradition of industry and commerce. In other words, it is an inevitable accompaniment for the evolutionary process from the regional cultural tradition of industry and commerce to the contemporary Zhejiang economy.

Compared with rural areas, one important feature of the cities is concentration. A large population and various industries, capitals, technologies as well as buildings were concentrated in cities. A high density of population, constructions, wealth and information has been a common characteristic of cities. Marx and Engels once pointed out that "the cities indicated the concentration of population, production tools, capital, entertainments, and requirements, while rural areas indicated the opposite, isolation and decentralization."[1] The British scholar, K. J. Barton also defined cities from the view of concentration: "The basic feature of all cities is the special concentration of population and economic activities. To clarify using economic terms, city is a network interweaving housing, manpower, land, transportation and other economic markets in a limited region. Urban economics called the large-scale geographical concentration of various acting factors as the city."[2] In Barton's definition of cities, one thing worth mentioning is that the concentration, as one important feature of cities, is achieved by the establishment of a network interweaving housing, manpower, land, transportation and other economic markets in a limited space, which means that the development of regional market or commodity economy is an intermediary agent or bridge for concentration, the basic feature of cities. Mackenzie emphasized the impact of commercial development on the "concentration" and he believed that such a phenomenon always existed in cities of the early stage. The distribution of cities is actually determined by the business model, and villages, towns and cities would first be the space forms for the process of commodity distribution. In addition, business activities and types are largely expanded due to the improvement of production rate and people's living standard, while many business functions have been geographically concentrated

---

① *Karl Marx and Frederick Engels*: vol.3 [M]. Beijing: People's Publishing House,1995: 57.

② Barton, K. J. *Urban Economics* [M]. Trans. Research Office of Urban Economy in Institute of National Economy in Shanghai Academy of Social Science. Beijing: The Commercial Press, 1984: 14.

because the improvement of transportation and communication tools accelerated the growth of large-scale organizations.[1]

Harvey shared similar views with Barton and Mackenzie. Harvey believed that the production and establishment of a city, namely a built environment, contained logic about the market economy and commodity economy. "Built environment" is one of the most important concepts of Harvey's urban theory. The term refers to a complex commodity containing different factors and a material structure that contains road, wharf, ditch, port, factory, warehouse, sewer, housing, school, culture and entertainment organization, office building, shop, sewage treatment system, parking lot, and other facilities. In Harvey's mind, "built environment" is an extremely simplified concept, the purpose of this concept is to further study the process of production and utilization. City is a human material landscape made up of various human environmental factors and it is a man-made "second nature." The urbanization process is the process of producing and establishing various built environments. The production and establishment process of the city, the built environment, is the result of capital control and functioning, as well as the consequence of satisfying the need of capital development that requires establishing a human material landscape to meet the production purpose. In other words, the commodity economy, in accordance with its own logic, establishes various human material landscapes, including road, housing, factory, and shop.[2]

The views of Barton, Mackenzie, Harvey and other scholars are sufficiently verified in the urbanization process of contemporary Zhejiang. As mentioned before, the contemporary Zhejiang economy, to some extent, is the result of the natural evolution of the regional

---

① Cai, H. *Urban Sociology: Theory and Vision* [M]. Guangzhou: Sun Yat-sen University Press, 2003: 10.

② Cai, H. *Urban Sociology: Theory and Vision* [M]. Guangzhou: Sun Yat-sen University Press, 2003: 176.

cultural tradition of industry and commerce. Such a result has a great impact on Zhejiang's urbanization. Since the reform and opening-up, one distinctive characteristic of Zhejiang's urbanization is that the prosperity of one town or one city relies on business development. Experiences gained in the process of the reform and opening-up indicate one universal law for Zhejiang's urbanization that with the development of regional industry and commerce, various markets, as commodity circulation bases, would become regional economic centers, while the development of commodity economy and market would significantly promote the development of various local industries. Therefore, in Zhejiang, most cities and towns chose to develop both commerce and industry instead of being purely commercial cities and towns. The development of markets usually leads to the increasing number of guests and commodities, and then helps to improve the development of the tertiary industry, including the hotel industry, catering industry, transportation, warehousing industry, financial industry, tourism industry and entertainment industry, at the same time stimulating the development and optimization of infrastructure including transportation, telecommunication as well as communication.

The urbanization phenomenon where the prosperity of towns and cities relies on the development of business in contemporary Zhejiang is similar to the urbanization process of Europe. As P. Boissonnade said, "the first result of recovering industrial and commercial activities in the Middle Ages was the partial renaissance of city life, and many cities were rebuilt on the ruins of ancient Rome." "The development of industry and commerce brings forth industry, city, town, transport port, market, and ports in the Western Europe plains or on both sides of roads and rivers that attract a large population and forms some important cities."[1] In the early Middle Ages, after suffering the invasion from barbaric ethnic groups, most cities of the Western Roman

---

[1]   Boissonnade, P. *Medieval European Life and Work (5th to 15th Century)* [M]. Trans. Pan, Y. Beijing: The Commercial Press, 1985: 113.

Empire were destroyed or abandoned, and only few survived. The city recessions differed with the different districts in Western Europe. The city life around the Mediterranean Sea, though showing signs of decaying, did not end. In most parts of Spain, Gaul and in Britain and Rhineland, some cities were abandoned, while some still had inhabitants. However, the government system originating from Rome disappeared in most cities and towns, and under most circumstances it was the church that ensured the cities' normal functioning. At that time, the cities and towns became consumption centers instead of production centers and the source of poverty instead of the source of wealth. Since the cities and towns were supported by rural areas, when all the landowners stepped back to their own lands, the purpose of the cities and towns being economic entities became under threat. The emergence of the self-sufficient economy also added to this threat. Although the cities at that time were only in the prototype stages and were like empty shells, they provided businessmen with the bases for initial development. "The fact was that businessmen living in the Middle Ages did not develop themselves by building new cities in a new land. They used their commercial awareness and business actions to transform the original cities and to create the commercial atmosphere. The combination of businessmen and cities led to the renaissance of cities, while the renascent cities guaranteed the existence and development of the business class."[①] Although the initial combination of businessmen and European cities of the Middle Ages had the nature of housing and being housed, the characteristics of both parties did not change. The businessmen chose these cities and the cities accepted them, though the cities they moved into had different origins and functions. "A common characteristic that emerged from the cities' combination with the business class was that all cities, no matter what origins or structure they had, were gradually enveloped by the commercial atmosphere. The coming of businessmen had changed the staff composition of cities as

---

① Zhao, L. *The Formation of the Merchant Class and Social Transformation in Western Europe* [M]. Beijing: China Social Sciences Press, 2004: 163.

well as the original city life itself. These nascent cities were thus called commercial cities, and businessmen became a major part of the urban population."[1]

Since the reform and opening-up, the renaissance of business in cities and towns has changed the situation that the development of cities and towns lagged behind under the planned economic system. The changing process of Zhili Town of Huzhou could be viewed as an epitome of the contemporary Zhejiang phenomenon in which the prosperity of towns and cities was dependent on the development of business. Zhili used to be a poor small town with only one narrow street. The embroidery, a regional cultural tradition of industry and commerce in Zhili's history, has been inherited and further developed since the reform and opening-up. The evolution of embroidery skill brought forth a large-scale embroidery market, heavily influencing the small town. Zhili Town now has broad new streets, on both sides of which comprise high-rise buildings. In addition, there are newly-constructed water works, power substation, gas stations and other facilities that make Zhili Town an emerging commercial center. The most typical example is the development of Choucheng Town in Yiwu. The Yiwu small commodity market derives from "Feather for Sugar," a cultural tradition of industry and commerce. After the reform and opening-up and with the rapid development of Yiwu's small commodity transactions, Choucheng Town gradually increased the number of booths, expanded the specialized streets and built many new markets. Driven by the development of Yiwu's small commodity market, the largest one nationwide, the urbanization process of Choucheng Town has greatly accelerated. It could be found from the comparison between the construction land area of Yiwu and the expansion history of the small commodity market that every expansion of the construction land area was the result of every expansion of the small commodity market.

---

[1]   Zhao, L. *The Formation of the Merchant Class and Social Transformation in Western Europe* [M]. Beijing: China Social Sciences Press, 2004: 165.

Therefore, the expansion of the small commodity market became the driving force for the urban development of Yiwu. Choucheng developed from an average small county into a city of tremendous vitality over the past two decades. The construction land area of Yiwu City has seen an annual increase of four to five square kilometers and the urbanization rate has seen an annual increase of over three percentage points since 1998. At the end of 2002, the construction land area reached 38 square kilometers with a population of over 430 thousand and an urbanization rate over 55%, which laid the foundation for the construction land area reaching 50 square kilometers and population reaching over 500 thousand in 2005.

After the reform and opening-up, there are countless examples similar to Zhili and Choucheng where the prosperity of cities and towns relies on the development of business in Zhejiang. Shaoxing's China Textile District is one of the largest textile product specialized wholesale markets in China. Datang Textile Market in Zhuji is the largest textile raw material terminal market nationwide. The China Technology Hardware City in Yongkang is the national hardware distribution center. The Luqiao China Daily Commodity Market is one of the largest daily commodity specialized markets in China. The evolutionary process of these specialized markets has an inheritance relationship with the historical regional cultural tradition of industry and commerce. In the meantime, the emergence of various specialized markets, together with the concentration of urbanization factors including local capital, technology, information and population, accelerates the process of local urbanization.

3.4 Differences in Traditional Business and Contemporary Relations with Economic and Social Development in Zhejiang, Huizhou and Shanxi

As mentioned above, an important reason why Zhejiang Province has quickly obtained economic and social development since the reform and opening-up is that Zhejiang boasts profound industrial and commercial cultural connotations and tradition, which is firmly backed up with a large number of historical materials. However, what should be further considered is why the economic and social development in contemporary Zhejiang Province inherits the traditional industrial and commercial cultures while in history, other Chinese regions where such culture had once emerged did not develop further influence in current society. There is no doubt that the ways to answer this question are through comparison and analysis.

3.4.1   Comparison of Traditional Commercial Culture in Zhejiang, Shanxi and Huizhou

From history and reality, profound commercial culture and connotations flourish where industry and commerce thrive. Therefore, industrial and commercial activities are often combined with regional culture, thus cultivating a unique regional industry and commerce cultural tradition. The business groups formed in these areas share a lot of similarities in modes of industrial and commercial activities which reflect distinct regional features. Even if the regional activities spread to other areas, the local features still remain. Zhang Haipeng and Zhang Haiying think that before the Ming Dynasty, most commercial activities by Chinese businessmen were conducted in person, individually and separately, thus not giving rise to any characteristic business groups; that is, there were businessmen but no faction. However, since the Ming Dynasty, commercial factions, or commercial groups, which feature regional culture, have been formed. The commercial factions, that aimed to help each other, are based on region, blood and friendship. These factions, acting spontaneously as close yet incompact business groups, used guild halls and public halls as places for liaison and discussions in foreign lands.[①] The inter-regional remote trade they initially deal with is different from the senior market transactions

---

① Zhang, H. & Zhang, H. *Ten commercial groups in China* [M]. Hefei: Huangshan Publishing House, 1993: 2.

in community-based primary markets, and this in turn nurtures big businessmen groups which are unlike the traditional dealers. Among the numerous commercial factions during the Ming and Qing dynasties, Huizhou merchants and Shanxi merchants were the most typical ones.

Compared with Zhejiang Province, Huizhou and Shanxi in the Ming and Qing dynasties have more aged commercial cultural traditions. As mentioned before, since the Song Dynasty, in the context of "encouraging agriculture but restraining commerce," thinkers in Zhejiang have brought about philosophies that benefit the development of industry and commerce in the region, which forms a general social mood of stressing commerce in some certain districts, to some extent. For instance, thinkers have put forward the ideas that industry and commerce should be of equal importance, and that although the four social classes (scholars, farmers, artisans, and merchants) engaged in different jobs, they shared the same pursuit. However, Huizhou and Shanxi thinkers in the Ming and Qing dynasties thought deeper in the acquaintance with commerce than those in eastern Zhejiang Province. Plus, in real life, both regions had a more profound social climate of emphasizing business than in Zhejiang. Merchants in these two regions during the Ming and Qing dynasties not only enjoyed the same status as the other three social classes, but also surpassed the other social classes in reality to some extent.

As mentioned before, ideologists of the schools of eastern Zhejiang have raised a lot of valuable viewpoints which benefit the development of industry and commerce in history. However, Huizhou thinkers were shown to be more eloquent than those in eastern Zhejiang in being more assertive towards approaching merchants and commerce. To illustrate this, it is necessary to make a further comparison between the relevant points of Wang Daokun, a thinker from Huizhou, and those of Ye Shi and Wang Yangming, whom are both thinkers from eastern Zhejiang.

As mentioned before, Ye Shi claimed that stressing agriculture but restraining commerce was not correct because scholars, farmers, artisans and merchants exchanged what they wanted with currency and then boosted the economy. However, Wang Daokun, born in the home of merchants in Huizhou in the Jiajing Period of the Ming Dynasty, took a step further on the same issue. Ye only realized the one-sidedness of the policy of physiocracy and restriction of business, while Wang directly opposed to the tradition of agriculture-orientation and business-decentralization, and raised that agriculture and commerce should weigh the same instead of unbalancing them.

In *The Stele of Discussing Politics by Chen Shijun*, Wang Daokun wrote, "I heard that the deceased monarch gave priority to commerce rather than agriculture, so he cut the taxes on farming but stressed on business taxes. However, I do not agree and I consider that we should balance agriculture and commerce. After the Patron of Agriculture engaged in business, commerce, along with agriculture, became more and more important, and finally they shared the same status. At that time, only one out of ten was a farmer. However, the Emperor did not neglect the significance of agriculture, which reflected his sight. And if the government monopolizes the business and raised taxes, the government is not good. But in reality, the taxes are not quite heavy. Therefore, there is no close relationship between merchants and farmers."[1] Compared with Ye's notions that stressing agriculture but restraining commerce was incorrect and that agriculture was the foundation of an empire, it can be said that in Wang's opinion the businessmen were not inferior to farmers, as a kind of voice from Huizhou merchants, raised the status of merchants whose state used to be ranked lowest among the four traditional social classes. Ye's notion, subjectively, not only stands for the government and imperial court (the rich play the roles of providers for the people and taxpayers

---

[1]   Wang, D. *A Study of Economy of Anhui and the Ming Dynasty*: vol.65 The Stele of Discussing Politics by Chen Shijun[M]. Hefei: Huangshan Publishing House, 2004.

to the government) but also inherits the philosophy of "external king" (pragmatism) in traditional Confucianism, especially Xun Zi's thought of enriching people. Although Ye's view objectively does good towards businessmen, its starting point does not speak for the stratum of industry and commerce, specialized in production and logistics. Therefore, Ye's view resonated greatly with people in the Ergonomic circle of eastern Zhejiang but did not have a deep influence among businessmen in Zhejiang Province. However, compared with Ye's view, Wang's opinion that businessmen were not inferior to farmers spoke for the businessmen. As a result, it had strong resonance in businessmen and officials born in merchant families in Huizhou. During the Hongzhi and Mingde periods of the Ming Dynasty, Xu Daxing, a businessman in She County, said, "I've heard that merchants with virtues are respectful, while those with bad qualities are not. Therefore, some people say that merchants are not as good as farmers. In my hometown which is located in the valley of Baojie Mountain, there is even no land for rich men who want to be engaged in agriculture to do farming. Therefore, they have no choice but to do business. What's more, one out of ten farmers may have good virtues. So does the merchant. From this aspect, are there any differences between farmers and merchants?"[1] Xu Chengxuan, an official working in the imperial government and born in a merchant family, once wrote a memorial to the throne in order to address the heavy taxes placed on agriculture and commerce, "Please ban extra taxes to farmers and merchants, and reduce corvee to people so as to revive agriculture and commerce."[2] He thought that of the four social classes, "only one out of ten are scholars while the rests are all farmers and merchants." What should we notice is that Xu mentioned "reviving agriculture" and "saving merchants" in the same breath, inclining that he placed commerce and agriculture at the same level. In the Xianfeng

---

[1] See *Genealogy of Xu's Family of East Branch in the North of She County, Xin'an.*

[2] Xu, C. *A Memorial to the Throne on Tax Reform, Works in the Qing Dynasty*: vol.28 [M].

Period of the Qing Dynasty, Wang Maoyin, the right assistant minister
of the Ministry of Revenue in feudal China and another official born in
a merchant family, once wrote in his memorial to the throne, "Nowadays,
workers in pawn shops have no choice but to receive the ingots given
by those who redeem their treasure. However, the ones who impawn
their treasures rarely use ingots. Therefore, there are seldom ingots in
the shops. Thus, there is no capital left, but only ingots. Then the shops
cannot operate well and finally turn to bankruptcy. Poor people have
no approaches to solving the problem."[1] Surprisingly, Wang's advice
irritated Emperor Xianfeng. He rebuked Wang for being prompted
by the merchants.[2] Wang Daokun's view, along with Xu Daxing, Xu
Chengxuan, and Wang Maoyin, is interlinked logically and fix each
other exactly in asserting merchants' interests.

Not only did Wang Daokun think that businessmen were not
inferior to farmers who ranked second in terms of traditional social
status, but that businessmen were not less than scholars who ranked first
in terms of social status. In *The Epitaph of Min Yiren Written by Cheng
Gongji, Vice Director of the Ministry of Revenue in Feudal China*, he
said, "To the south of the Yangtze River, the new capital is famous for
its relics. The custom passing from generation to generation in this
region is that one who is not capable of studying Confucianism can
become a merchant. Therefore, the status of fine merchants is not lower
than scholars."[3] In volume 168 of *The Genealogy of Wang's Family* in
the Ming Dynasty, "In ancient time, our ancestors did not classify the
four classes. Therefore, it did not really matter what you did. The status

---

① Wang, M. *A Memorial to the Throne by Official Wang*: vol.6 Argument Again
on Monetary [M].

② Zhu, S. *Donghua Records in Guangxu Reign*: vol.26 [M]. Beijing: Zhonghua
Book Company, 1958.

③ Wang, D. *A Study of Economy of Anhui and the Ming Dynasty*: vol.55 The
Epitaph of Min Yiren, Written by Cheng Gongji, Vice Director of the Ministry of
Revenue in Feudal China [M]. Hefei: Huangshan Publishing House, 2004.

of merchants was not lower than scholars. In later years, the social system is different, but people still pay little attention to the different states of merchants and scholars. These two groups of people share the same position. Scholars are good at improving themselves. So do merchants. As a result, whether you are a merchant or a scholar matters little. Scholars and merchants do different jobs, but the essence of their life is the same. Life is not limited by occupations."

In the Ming Dynasty, Wang Yangming from eastern Zhejiang once brought about the opinion that although four social classes did different jobs, they shared the same pursuit, which was quite similar in literal meaning to Wang's thought that good merchants were not less than Confucian masters and merchants were not inferior to scholars. However, with further observation, there are still differences in positions and starting points existing in Wang Yangming's and Wang Daokun's views. Wang Daokun was born in a family of merchants. His grandfather started the family business in the salt industry, and the Wang family also developed affinity relationships with the Wu, Huang, Cheng, Fang families and so on that were all famous merchant families in Xin'an. Therefore, Wang Daokun can be said to be a favorable salt businessman in Xin'an. Although some of his views were similar to Wang Yangming's, such as the belief that "although scholars and merchants do different jobs, the essence of their life is the same," his starting point was to defend the merchant class and raise the social status of merchants, which is subjectively the same as declaring that businessmen were not inferior to farmers.

However, unlike Wang Daokun, Wang Yangming, a Neo-Confucianism philosopher in the Ming Dynasty, advocated mixing the substance and function together, and that the mind alone is the source of all reason and no reason exists outside the mind. Therefore, the mind of a sage is strong enough to seek the truth in his own heart, not helped by others. "Intuitive knowledge" is in everyone's mind, no matter what your gender, age, and job is. Therefore, Wang Yangming advocates that "though the four classes have different jobs, they share the same pursuit." Although objectively it may elevate the social status of businessmen and have affinity with businessmen and business activities, his starting point is not to defend for the businessmen like Wang Daokun, but to illustrate the mind philosophy that everyone can be a sage.

As for merchants appreciating great profits, Wang Daokun gave sufficient affirmation. He thought that merchants who rightly made profits were worthier of praise in moral than those who were greedy. However, Wang Yangming did not share the same perspective. He did not negate business and admitted that buying and selling were means of livelihood, but he advocated not giving business priority and illegitimately seeking profits.[①] In other words, Wang Yangming held a negative attitude towards merchants who improperly and continuously sought fame and profits. In fact, an ideal merchant, in Wang Yangming's perspective, is a moral person whose behaviors are led by individual moral consciousness or the philosophy of "sageness within" referred to by Confucians rather than an economic person whose behaviors are driven by interests. Wang Yangming said, "If one can be both moral and economic and does not feel tired at the same time, one is still able to be a sage though he does business all day,"[②] but the untiring state of the body and mind means the sense of consciousness without any slight of desire.

As mentioned before, though Wang Yangming claimed that people did different jobs but shared the same pursuit, his original intention was not to assert for merchants. Instead, he called for merchants to become saints according to his ideal that all the people in the world were saints. As a result, Wang did not raise specific suggestions to advance the status of merchants and commerce in ancient China. Unlike Wang Yangming, Wang Daokun argued for the businessmen. With the merchants' interests

---

① See Wang Yangming, *Chuanxi Records*.

② Ibid.

in mind, he asked the government not to restrain commerce, but to take the merchants' convenience into account. Wang Daokun said, "The demand for salt is not as large as rice. The price of rice depends on people, not the government. The reason why salt is in bad demand is not that of money. The source of money comes from people, not the government. Why? Just be considerate. Considering the people's life will enable them to live and eat in content, whereas, considering the merchants' life will make them willing to sell their stock and develop the market. This is a truth."[1] Most of the wealthy businessmen and moguls in Huizhou were salt producers. The hope of taking merchants' convenience into account is akin to offering a piece of advice to the government on behalf of the salt producers. Therefore, Wang Yangming spoke for the Confucian sage, while Wang Daokun spoke for the merchants.

Honestly speaking, during a certain period in history, the concept of attaching more importance to commerce than to education and agriculture was formed in a minority of districts in Zhejiang. For example, the education level in Pingyang, Wenzhou was once not as good as districts in the west of Zhejiang. "Scholars there were satisfied with few achievements in their academic career and got into the habit of doing business." "Having hardly passed the examination and entered the state school, these students would put books on the shelf and engage in making small profits."[2] During the Ming and Qing dynasties, in terms of Zhejiang Province, stressing commerce had already been a part of social concept in some districts, to some extent. However, what we can conclude is that the social morality of commerce-orientation did not overwhelm the importance of Confucianism. The imperial examination acceptance rate in Zhejiang was well above the other regions, which can substantially demonstrate the former point. According to the statistics in

---

① Wang, D. *A Study of Economy of Anhui and the Ming Dynasty*: vol. 64 The Stone Tablet Recording the Political Achievement of Wang Mingfu [M]. Hefei: Huangshan publishing House, 2004.

② See *Records of Pingyang County* in the Republic of China.

Geographic Distribution of Jinshi in the Qing Dynasty written by Zhang Yaoxiang, the total number of *yijia* (the *jinshi*, or advanced scholar, who ranked first overall nationwide), *bangyan* (the *jinshi* who ranked second overall) and *tanhua* (the *jinshi* ranked third overall) was 342, of which 119 were from Jiangsu Province (34.8%), 81 from Zhejiang Province (23.7%) and 18 from Anhui Province (5.2%). The statistics were done only in the narrow sense of talents in the imperial examinations.

According to *The Geography and Distribution Table of Celebrities in the Qing Dynasty by Zhu* compiled by Zhu Junyi on the basis of *Brief Biography of Ministers, Craftsmen, Scholars and Civilians from 1616 to 1850* written by Li Heng, there were 19 types of people in the Ming Dynasty, among which the numbers of 16 types of talents in Jiangsu and Zhejiang were among the top three. These 16 types include: chancellors, second- and third-class officials, literature attendants, advisers, langshu's who were officials chosen from Xiaolian to help the king in administrative work, commanders of border-provinces, inspection officers, filial people, Confucianism scholars, Confucian classics learners, well-educated people, people living in seclusion, prefectures and magistrates, assistants in a government office, talented and brave people, as well as craftsmen. [①] Thus, it shows that the distribution density of talents in the imperial examinations in Zhejiang were far higher than the other regions, except for Jiangsu. It is hard to imagine the high imperial examination acceptance rate which was well above the other regions without the strong social morality of worshiping Confucianism, which matches with the sayings that Confucianism in eastern Zhejiang was quite developed after the Song and Yuan dynasties.

However, in Huizhou and Shanxi during the Ming and Qing

---

① Yang, N. *The Modern Morphology of Confucianism Regionalization: A Comparative Study of the Interaction of the Three Knowledge Groups* [M]. Beijing: SDX Joint Publishing Company, 1997: 270.

dynasties, weighing Confucianism and commerce the same or stressing more on commerce than on education and agriculture had become popular in some districts.

Indeed, the Confucian spirit was well-developed in Huizhou during the Ming and Qing dynasties. According to *A Brief Introduction of Custom, Imperial Examinations, Official System and Laws in the Qing Dynasty* written by Zhu Pengshou, Anhui ranked third in the number of *zhuangyuans* in the imperial examinations from the Shunzhi period to the Guangxu period, nine in all. Anhui had eight offices and five townships, among which the Huizhou office alone boasted four *zhuangyuans*. This number was the same as the ones in Guangxi and Zhili, but bigger than the ones in Jiangxi, Fujian, Hubei, Hunan, Henan, Shaanxi, Sichuan, Guangdong, Guizhou, Shanxi, Gansu, Yunnan and so on, which reflected that people in Huizhou respected Confucianism from the side and complemented the saying that Confucianism was quite popular in Xin'an. However, what we need to further explain is that though people in Huizhou loved Confucianism, they paid more attention to commerce. Merchants in Huizhou were Confucianism lovers. As Wang Daokun once said, "Our ancestors revered Confucianism but despised commerce, but in my township the contrary is the case. One who is incapable of business will go to learn Confucianism, while talents who are not satisfied with Confucianism come back to commerce."[①] In addition, he said, "In Xiu and She Counties, people there stress more on business than on Confucianism. They even replace the Confucian classics with math books."[②] In Xindu (Huizhou), three out of four were merchants, and only one of them was a scholar. "If people apply Confucianism to everything in their lives, then they pay more attention to Confucianism. However, if they think

---

① Wang, D. *A Study of Economy of Anhui and the Ming Dynasty*: vol.54 The Epitaph of Wu Chang in the Ming Dynasty [M]. Hefei: Huangshan Publishing House, 2004.

② Ibid. vol. 77 Jinyuan Garden.

about their children and grandchildren's future, they will pay more attention to wealth. The changes of their views on Confucianism and commerce make merchants more reasonable when they do business."[1] In *Textual Research of Custom and Ritual in Xi County*, "Merchants are the lowest in the ranking of the four classes, but this ranking does not apply in Huai. Most rich people who do business to the north and south of Huai River come from Huizhou. Although many merchants pursue immediate profits, there are also many scholars whose reason for learning Confucianism is fame and fortune. In addition, good merchants are good scholars, too, in Huizhou." Huizhou is not only a home to merchants and commerce but also another cradle of Confucianism. Merchants were scholars as well. The argument above fully shows that merchants and scholars generally shared the same social position in Huizhou during the Ming and Qing dynasties. However, in real life, people in Huizhou regarded business as the most important means of livelihood.[2] "Seven or eight out of ten were merchants."[3] "Even the scholar-bureaucrats earn a living by doing business so as to pay for their traveling."[4] That is to say, people in Huizhou paid more attention to commerce than to education. According to the research conducted by Chong Tiande, in the Qing Dynasty there were 40 to 50 cases of abandoning study for business in Wuyuan, Anhui alone.[5] Not only is the scholar social stratum's view of scholars and merchants different from the past, but the attitudes of other people have also changed deeply and subtly. According to *The Records of Xi County* written in the Wanli

---

[1] Wang, D. *A Study of Economy of Anhui and the Ming Dynasty*: vol. 52 The Epitaph of Mrs. Dai, Zhong Wengpei's Wife, in Haiyang [M]. Hefei: Huangshan Publishing House, 2004.

[2] Ling, M. *Slap the Table in Amazement, Part II* [M]. Beijing: Zhonghua Book Company, 2009.

[3] Wang, D. A *Study of Economy of Anhui and the Ming Dynasty*: vol.16 Fucheng [M]. Hefei: Huangshan Publishing House, 2004.

[4] Wang, S. *Four Works of Mine*: vol.61 Fifty Letters Sent to Mr. Chen [M].

[5] Shigeta, A. *Research on the Social and Economic History of the Qing Dynasty* [M]. Tokyo: Iwanami Shoten, 1975.

Period of the Ming Dynasty, commerce "now has become the most important one, unlike in the past." *The Biography of Lord of the Sea in Liaoyang* written by Cai Yu in the Ming Dynasty describes the social concept at that time, "The custom in Anhui is that whether a merchant is good and filial enough depends on his wealth."

Compared to Huizhou, Shanxi stressed more on commerce during the Ming and Qing dynasties. According to *Emperor Yongzheng Edict,* on May 9, 1724, Liu Yuyi, a minister, said to the emperor, "People in Shanxi have formed a concept that wealth is more important than fame. Most of the talents would start doing business and trade, and the rest of them would rather be officials. Only those who are not so gifted are willing to go to school and sit the imperial examination." Three days later, Emperor Yongzheng responded to him, "I am aware that merchants in Shanxi enjoy the top of the social ladder, the second is farmers, then officials and the last is scholars." Meanwhile, on February 12, 1730, Shi Lin, another official, reported the same situation to the emperor, "Most of the people in Shanxi choose to work in business."[1] This concept of ranking merchants in the first place among all social classes went on until the end of the Qing Dynasty. Liu Dapeng, a scholar in the end of the Qing Dynasty, once said, "Recently in my hometown (Taigu County), there is a bad tendency that people attach much importance to commerce but despise education. Those who have great talents all do business. Few of them choose to go to school. Even some scholars who give up studying and then begin doing business say that scholars have to suffer hunger and cold, while merchants can make enough money to support their families."[2] Under such circumstances, some children could not even afford to take the examinations. "Nowadays, people often persuade their

---

① Zhao, R. An analysis of Shanxi merchants in history [M]//Mu, W. *Research on Historical Materials of Shanxi Merchants.* Taiyuan: Shanxi people's Publishing House, 2001: 6.

② Liu, D. *Diary in Tuixiang Study* [M]. Taiyuan: Shanxi People's Publishing House, 1990.

sons and brothers not to study but to do business because study makes you poor, whereas business brings you wealth. Therefore, Shanxi is the province that has the highest numbers of children who cannot afford to take the examinations. The situation in the other provinces is unknown."[1] Some folk songs also reflect this phenomenon. For example, "One who has a son that does business is as powerful as a county magistrate," "A penny in wallet is better than a field with harvest," "Farmlands with stores make you wealthy" and "I would rather do business and earn thousands of money than be a county magistrate."

There were also many people who shifted to do business in Shanxi during the Ming and Qing dynasties because they failed to pass the imperial examinations or their families could not afford them money to study further.[2] For instance, Xi Ming from Pingyang, Shanxi, failed to pass the examination when he was young, and he did not like farming. So he said, "If a man cannot make huge contributions to the world, does it mean that he cannot support his family?" He then traveled to Jiangsu, Zhejiang, Hunan and many other places to do business and became a wealthy merchant that everyone admired.[3] Yang Jimei, another businessman in Shanxi, did not pass the imperial exam either when he was young. He thought that though people did different jobs, they shared the same pursuit. Therefore, he did business in the regions along the Yangtze River and Huai River with thousands of money. Although Shanxi people sometimes stressed education in the Ming and Qing dynasties, they thought that education should work for business. A good scholar will make a merchant. For example, in the history of business and education investment of the Chang family in Chewang,

---

① Ibid.

② Yu, Y. *Religious Ethics and Merchant Spirit in Modern China* [M]. Hefei: Anhui Education Press, 2001: 213.

③ Ge, X. Modern Chinese merchant ethics and its modern value [M]//Mu, W. *Research on Historical Materials of Shanxi Merchants*. Taiyuan: Shanxi people's Publishing House, 2001: 308-309.

Yuci, the number of *xiucai* (one who passed the imperial examination at the county level), *juren* (a qualified graduate who passed the triennial provincial exam) and *jinshi* was 170, but only one of them became a government official and his term was quite short. So we can say that all the students of the Chang family stepped into the commercial life.

After Chang Lixun, one of the Changs was accepted as a *xiucai* and *bagong* (a recognized scholarly achiever who passed the triennial national exam), he still chose to succeed his father as a merchant. He said, "Business is hard work, but it can support your life and is suitable to what Confucius teaches." After Chang Qilin, another *bagong* who was quite proficient in Confucianism in the Chang family became a merchant, other people of the same generation persuaded him to change his career to a scholar. He said, "Zigong is a sage, so he is my model." After graduating from the Imperial Academy, Chang Weifeng, son of Chang Qilin, enjoyed a brilliant career as a government official because of his great talent in literature. However, his father told him, "As a saying goes, when a country is well governed, poverty and a mean condition are things to be ashamed of, therefore, you should succeed our family career."[1]

All the examples of the above show that the culture and the custom of stressing commerce in Huizhou and Shanxi were more profound than those in Zhejiang during the Ming and Qing dynasties.

In addition, in the Ming and Qing dynasties, the influence of merchants in Zhejiang, Huizhou and Shanxi obviously cannot be named in the same breath. According to the research conducted by Yoshinobu Shiba, it remains unknown whether Xin'an commercial groups existed in the Song Dynasty. However, according to the fact that merchants and businessmen all over

---

[1] Yang, H. &Lin, W. A brief analysis of the phenomenon of the mixture of Confucianism and merchants in Chang's Family in Chewang, Yuci [M]//Mu, W. *Research on Historical Materials of Shanxi Merchants*. Taiyuan: Shanxi people's Publishing House, 2001: 326-328.

the nation gathered together on April 8 every year to celebrate *Wutong God (Wuxian God*: God of Wealth in Wuyuan) in Wuyuan, which was an obligatory stop to every merchant in southern China (*Notes on Si Rivers in Yangdoulin, Wuyuan County*, Volume VI of *The Works of Shan Yuandai*), it seems to conclude that Huizhou merchants had already been influential in the business world in the Song Dynasty[1], to some extent. In the Ming Dynasty, Huizhou merchants were quite active. This phenomenon is depicted in *Records of Xi County* in the Wanli period, "They stock different kinds of products. They travel all over the world to conduct business. Their time is precious. They count accurately, concerning much about their profits and enjoying great power in hand. Salt merchants in the downstream areas of the Huai River and Yangtze River have the most privileges." In *Records of Xiuning County: Custom* in the Wanli period, "Huizhou merchants travel around the capital with little money. Their trades depend on landform, and their profits and loss on seasons. They travel to almost all over the world to do business, such as to islands and deserts." Moreover, in *Records of Huizhou Government: Custom* in the Kangxi period, "Rich merchants in Huizhou will move their whole family to counties, like Yiyang, Suzhou, Huai'an, Wuhu, Hangzhou, Nanchang, and Hankou. They even move to as far as Beijing. Sometimes they even remove the remains of their ancestors far away from their hometowns, without any shame." According to *Records of Xi County: Geography & Custom*, written in the Republic of China, "Although Huizhou merchants do business almost all over the nation, such as Yunnan, Guizhou, Fujian, Guangdong, Shaanxi, Beijing, Shanxi, and Henan, Anhui, Zhejiang, Hunan, and Hubei are the nearest places they will go." It is because of the broad scope of Huizhou merchants' business activities that sparked a saying that "Huizhou people are in every town" along the river. The capital that Huizhou merchants owned was quite huge. Small merchants owned 200 or 300 thousand, medium ones 400 or 500 thousand, and the big ones owned millions. It was difficult for Zhejiang merchants in the same period to compete with Huizhou merchants, and

---

[1]   Shiba, Y. *Study on the Economic History of Jiangnan in the Song Dynasty* [M].
Trans. Fang, J. & He, Z. Nanjing: Jiangsu People's Publishing House, 2001: 414.

even the European traders at the time were unable to catch up.

Shanxi was more prosperous than Xin'an. Records of the active Shanxi merchants can be found in most ancient documents. By the Ming Dynasty, Jin merchants had enjoyed a reputation in the country. During the Qing Dynasty, the currency capital of Shanxi merchants gradually formed, which not only monopolized the whole northern trade and capital scheduling but also got involved in all parts of Asia and even extended its vast tentacles to Europe. Similar to the saying "no town without Huizhou people," there are also "Cao family first, Chaoyang County after," "first there are Fu Shengxi, then Baotou City," "first Jin Yilao, then Xining City," "where there are crows and dogs barking, there are Shanxi businessmen," and so on. In *Records of Yunzhong County*, written in the Shunzhi period of the Qing Dynasty, "Merchants were all born on the right side of the mountain and those born in Fenjie County were the majority. They lived at the border of the mountains from generation to generation, and they were free to decide whom to marry." Emperor Kangxi once said, "I visited seven provinces every year, but only people in Shanxi and the land of Qin were slightly well-off."[1] This indicates that he had begun to notice the brilliance of Shanxi merchants. In Ningwu County, "Decades ago, women in rich families could only afford to wear clothes in bad texture and simple colors. Since Emperor Yongzheng enlisted soldiers in the northwest of China, those who went there to trade goods or mastered one of the skills came back to their hometowns with wealth which they used to please the women they adored. Because of this, many women began to wear beautiful clothes made in silks and in different colors."[2] In the second year of Daoguang (1822), Gong Zizhen wrote in *Argument of Establishment of Government Officials in the West of China*, "Shanxi is known as the richest province in the world." In the Xianfeng Period of the Qing Dynasty, Mian Yu, Prince Hui, said, "In this wide world, many

---

① Yan, S. *Raises and Falls of Shanxi Merchants* [M].

② See *Records of Ningwu* in Qianlong Reign.

rich people live. But the richest provinces, in my view, are Guangdong and Shanxi. I have heard that in recent months, Shanxi merchants who had previously traded in Beijing have already left for their home while carrying tens of millions of money, from which one can see the prosperity of Shanxi."[1] According to *Military Records* in the Xianfeng period, Zhang Siheng, supervisory censor in Guangxi, described the prosperity of the central part of Shanxi in his memorial to the emperor, "Sun's family in Taigu, Shanxi, owns 20 million, Cao's and Jia's four million and five million respectively. Hou's family in Pingyao County and Zhang's family in Jiexiu County owns four million and five million respectively. Xu and Wang, living in clans in Yuci County, own 10 thousand respectively. There are almost ten millionaires in Jiexiu County, dozens of millionaires in Qi County." In Shanxi, the Qiao, the Cao, the Qu, the Wang and the Chang families in their heyday owned millions of silver ingots. However, during the Opium War, the Qing Government's annual revenue was only 70 million silver ingots. Even during the Sino Japanese War in 1895, the total tax revenue of the Qing Government was only 90 million silver ingots. It was precisely because of the brilliant achievements of Shanxi merchants that Liang Qichao said, "For more than a decade I have been abroad, I often could not say anything against the criticisms made by the foreigners on my country's commercial ability. But now we have a history and a foundation to develop the business in Shanxi continuously. So now I would often boast before the people of the world.[2]"

Undeniably, like Huizhou and Shanxi, Zhejiang has also historically been a relatively developed region with industrial and commercial activities, thus forming a long tradition of folk industrial and commercial culture, and giving birth to the Eastern Zhejiang Practical

① Zhang, Z. & Xue, H. *Selected Information of Shanxi Merchants in Ming and Qing dynasties* [M]. Taiyuan: Shanxi People's Publishing House, 1989: 29.
② Liang, Q. A welcome speech to ticket merchants of Shanxi [M] // Liang, Q. *Works in Yinbing*. Beijing: Zhonghua Book Company, 1989.

Schools which advocate the development of industry and commerce. As mentioned above, during the Ming and Qing dynasties, Hangzhou, Ningbo, Shaoxing, Taizhou, Wenzhou, Huzhou, Jiaxing, Jinhua, Quzhou and other places in Zhejiang Province all had relatively developed market trade and handicraft activities in varying degrees. However, during the Ming and Qing dynasties, the protagonists were not Zhejiang merchants, but Shanxi merchants and Huizhou merchants. As people in the Ming Dynasty said, "The most renowned merchants in our nation are Huizhou merchants living in the south of the Yangtze River and Shanxi merchants living in the north of the Yellow River." Neither the scale nor the influence of Zhejiang businessmen can be compared with the Huizhou merchants and the Shanxi merchants. Even in the hometown of traditional Zhejiang merchants, it was Shanxi and Huizhou merchants that excelled in the Ming and Qing dynasties. According to *The True Records of Emperor Kangxi*, Emperor Kangxi wrote in February 1689, "I have heard that the business tycoons of the Southeast are gathered together. I traveled to Wuyue County this year to check its city and trade and I found that many people came from Shanxi Province. The life of native people was used to be simple and poor, but after Shanxi people came, the standard of people's life gradually developed." However, the influence of Huizhou merchants in Zhejiang is much greater than that of Shanxi merchants. *Records of Jianzhi* which recorded the Chinese commodities needed by Japan in the Ming Dynasty pointed out, "The porcelain of Rao County, the silk of Hu County, the yarn of Zhang County and the cotton cloth of Song County were the most important."[1] The important producing areas of Chinese handicraft products such as Raozhou, Huzhou, and Songjiang are precisely the areas where Huizhou merchants are most concentrated. The activities of Huizhou merchants in the areas of Suzhou, Songjiang, Hangzhou, Jiaxing and Huzhou were recorded in as early as the Song Dynasty. However, the important position of Huizhou merchants in these areas was established during the Jiajing and Wanli periods of the Ming Dynasty, along with the rise of

---

① Yao, S. *Records of Jianzhi* [M]. Beijing: The Commercial Press, 1936.

the towns in the south of the Yangtze River. For example, the towns in the Taihu River Basin were rich in lacustrine silk. These towns were all places of convergence for Huizhou merchants. According to *Records of Jiashan County*, "The merchants of the past went back to their villages, but now they also go far away from their hometown. However, almost all of those who bear heavy capital and make heavy profits are Huizhou merchants, not native people."[1]

According to *Records of Hangzhou*, "Huzhou was the name of the market where all the goods from Huzhou gathered. This Qiantang River shore where Huizhou traders landed is also known as Huizhou Tong."[2] According to the description in *Records of Tangxi*, which cited *Records of Geography & Custom in Tangxi* written by Hu Yuanjing at the end of the Ming Dynasty, "The town is 22.5 kilometers away from Wulinguan and is surrounded by the Yangtze River. Chongde, in the east of the town, is 27 kilometers away, which you can take a boat to get there. Since the town is located in the central part and enjoys convenient transportation, lots of government and merchant ships can be seen traveling about on the river day and night. And then it gradually became a big town where goods and products gather. As a result, rich merchants from Huizhou and Hangzhou regarded the town as a place with big profit potential and began to gather there, opening stores and trading silk."[3]

However, times have changed. Shanxi merchants and Huizhou merchants today are no longer brilliant, while contemporary Zhejiang businessmen have gained the reputation of "no business without Zhejiang." Since the reform and opening-up, new investors and businessmen with Zhejiang accent are everywhere, not only in big cities such as Beijing and Shanghai but also in every corner of China

---

[1]   See *Records of Jiashan County* in Jiaqing Reign.
[2]   See *Records of Hangzhou* in Qianlong Reign.
[3]   See *Records of Tangxi* in Guangxu Reign..

and even cities in Europe and the United States. According to a survey conducted the Zhejiang Provincial Government, as early as 2003, more than 300,000 Zhejiang residents have set up businesses in Shanghai, with a registered capital of 90 billion yuan and actual operating capital of more than 300 billion yuan. Of the 400 rich people listed in the first domestic media list of the rich in China published in the *New Fortune*, 63 are from Zhejiang, accounting for 15.75%. The All-China Federation of Industry and Commerce announced that among the 500 top private enterprises in China in 2003, Zhejiang, ranking first, accounted for 183, occupying nearly two-fifths of all the enterprises in the nation. As for the top 20 in the total business income, Zhejiang enterprises were the majority. According to *The Blue Book of China's Private Enterprises* in 2004, on the list of "the most competitive private enterprises in China," Zhejiang enterprises occupied 26 seats in the top 50. According to *The Blue Book of the Top 50 Competitiveness of Private Enterprises in China's Manufacturing Industry* in 2005, 23 Zhejiang enterprises entered the top 50. According to the "Survey List of the Top 10 Brands Known by Consumers in the Zhejiang Market in 2005" and "The Top 50 Competitive Markets in China's Commodity Specialty Market" announced at the Third China Private Enterprises Summit, 18 Zhejiang markets were selected in all and all of them ranked in the top 20. Zhejiang Yiwu China Commodity City topped the list, followed by Hangzhou Sijiqing Clothing Market, Haining Leather City, China Cocoon and Silk Trading Market (Jiaxing), Zhejiang Yigao Digital, Zhejiang BMW Auto parts, etc. In 2003, 30 of the 67 counties in Zhejiang Province were on the list. In recent years, many indicators of Zhejiang ranked first in the country, such as the individual and private economic output value, total sales, retail sales of social consumer goods, export volume of foreign exchange and the number of private enterprises in China's top 500 enterprises. In the "2016 List of the Top 500 Private Enterprises" published by the All-China Federation of Industry and Commerce, there were 134 Zhejiang enterprises. Although the number is slightly lower than in 2015 (138), in terms of the total number of enterprises listed, Zhejiang Province has maintained its number one position for the 18th consecutive year. Geely Holding Group and Hailiang Group were ranked in the top 20, at 12 and 13 respectively.

In a sense, it can be said that since the late Qing Dynasty when the influence of Huizhou and Shanxi merchants declined, the Great Traditions (such as the business spirit, business philosophy, organization management, qualities etc. of Huizhou and Shanxi merchants) have been recorded in the books and became the objects of study by scholars. However, the Little Traditions (folk commercial culture traditions), which are the methods subsistence and lifestyle of a specific group, have gradually disappeared. In particular, after 30 years of practicing the planned economy, the folk commercial cultural traditions of Huizhou and Shanxi can be said to have almost vanished. As a Shanxi scholar said, "The enterprising spirit of Shanxi businessmen who have the courage to open up and dare to break into the world has been worn out, and then came the ideas that 'it is better to be at home than to go out' and 'east or west, home is best'."[1] There is not much connection between the economy of Anhui and Shanxi and the traditional culture of Huizhou and Shanxi merchants. It is not the continuation and development of traditional Huizhou merchants' economy and Shanxi merchants' economy. In contrast to this, Zhejiang's industrial and commercial traditions and culture have been sharply impacted in the course of the 30-year planned economy practice, but as has been shown above, the economic development of Zhejiang Province today and its development in history have a clear inheritance relationship. In a sense, Zhejiang's economy, nowadays, is a result of the natural evolution of traditional industry and commerce.

---

[1]   Zhao, R. An analysis of Shanxi merchants in history [M]// Mu, W. *Research on Historical Materials of Shanxi Merchants*. Taiyuan: Shanxi People's Publishing House, 2001: 22.

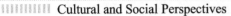
3.4.2 Cultural Traditions of Businessmen in Zhejiang, Shanxi and Huizhou, and the Contemporary Political Environment

To explore the reasons for the continuation or non-continuation of the cultural traditions of Zhejiang, Shanxi and Huizhou businessmen, first of all, it is necessary to make a comprehensive and comparative analysis of the national macroeconomic environment in the early stage of the reform and opening-up, as well as the different characteristics of traditional merchants in Shanxi, Huizhou and Zhejiang.

As mentioned earlier, there are mechanisms of increasing returns and self-strengthening in institutional changes. Once a unique development trajectory is established, a series of externalities, organizational learning processes and subjective models will strengthen this trajectory. That is to say, the choice of the initial system will strengthen the stimulation and inertia of the existing system, which is the so-called path dependence. In traditional society, merchants in Shanxi, Huizhou and Zhejiang have remarkable regional characteristics and the inheritance of economic activity paths or occupations and skills in their regions. In the political environment at the beginning of the reform and opening-up, these kinds of characteristics and skills, undoubtedly, play different roles in the economic and social development. During the Ming and Qing dynasties, Huizhou merchants operated in a variety of industries, as "they stored different kinds of goods." But among them, "salt, classic, tea and wood were the most important."[1] Chen Qubing also said, "Four main kinds of business of the commercial industry in Hui County—salt, tea, wood and pawn broking."[2] Among these four commodities, the salt industry ranked first. For example, according to *Records of Xi County* written in the Wanli period of the Qing Dynasty, Huizhou merchants "were not as

---

① See *Records of She County* in the Republic of China. "The most popular industries are the salt, pawn broking, tea and woods, with salt being the most flourishing in the past."

② Chen, Q. *Five Stones* [M]. Nanjing: Jiangsu Phoenix House, 1999.

big as those salt sellers in the districts at the Huai River and Yangtze River." Huizhou people also said, "The biggest merchants in our hometown engaged in the trade of fish and salt, followed by cloth and silk. Those selling fabrics are small merchants." Huizhou pawnshops in the Ming and Qing dynasties were most famous for their large scale, wide distribution and profit-making. There was a saying in the folk, "no Huizhou merchants, no pawn broking." According to *Records by Ming Shenzong*, "Huizhou merchants opened pawn stores all over the north of the Yangtze River. They earned thousands of ingots but only had to pay a tax of no more than ten ingots." According to volume three of *Shanxi Travel Diary* (1795) written by Li Sui, a Shanxi government staff, "Pawn stores in the south of the Yangtze River were all set by Huizhou people." Even the word "Chao feng" which is used to describe the shopkeeper of pawn stores came from the common sayings of Huizhou merchants. During the Ming and Qing dynasties, the Huizhou tea merchants' scope of activity and their commercial networks covered almost half of China, even abroad.[①] The timber industry of Huizhou merchants was in great condition in the Southern Song Dynasty. According to *Records of Xin'an County* in the Southern Song Dynasty, "Good woods came from the mountains in Xiuning County."[②] In the Ming and Qing dynasties, "Wuyuan merchants first sold woods."[③] Huizhou timber merchants were no longer limited to selling woods from Huizhou. Their footprints had spread throughout the major timber producing areas. Similar to the Huizhou merchants, the trades operated by Shanxi merchants varied, not only in specialty products such as salt, iron, wheat, cotton, leather, wool, wood, and tobacco but also in silk, silk fabric, tea, and rice from the region in south of the Yangtze River. As *Notes of Everything* wrote, "The richest district in the south of the Yangtze River was Xin'an County, in the north of the Yangtze River was Shanxi. Shanxi merchants

---

① Tang, L. *A Study on the Social Economy of Huizhou Region Since the Ming and Qing dynasties* [M]. Hefei: Anhui University Press, 1999: 160.

② See *Records of Xin'an County* in Southern Song Dynasty.

③ See *Records of Wuyuan County* in Kangxi Reign.

sold salt and silk, traveled to different places to vendor and store rice and food. Shanxi is richer than Xin'an." However, since the Qing Dynasty, Shanxi merchants have been most famous in dealing with the exchange business of the financial industry. Shanxi's exchange shops during the Xianfeng and Tongzhi period of the Qing Dynasty almost monopolized the national exchange business, becoming the country's leading financial business groups, thus having the reputation of "linking the world."

Undeniably, in history, the business operations of merchants in Zhejiang, Shanxi and Huizhou have overlapped in many aspects. For example, in the business components of Ningbo business groups during the Ming and Qing dynasties, there were also the silk cloth, tobacco, and grain industries. Among the business contents of Longyou commercial groups, there were timber, tobacco leaves, bamboo shoots, paper, sugar cane, tea, and so on. However, the traditional industries of Zhejiang merchants which can best reflect the characteristics of Zhejiang and have an inherited relationship with the economy since the reform and opening-up were not the same as those of Huizhou and Shanxi merchants, like salt, pawn broking, timber, tea, and exchange, but are what Fei Xiaotong described as "the 'eight Immortals crossing the sea', which include stone carvings, bamboo carvings, flowers, hoop buckets, sewing, haircuts, cooks and other art crafts. Those selling sugar and working in small department stores would travel everywhere to earn money and support the family."① In the Ming and Qing dynasties, what salt, pawn broking, timber, tea and exchange nurtured in Shanxi and Huizhou were business tycoons with hundreds of thousands of assets and whom can be considered as the richest merchants, as well as powerful commercial groups that exerted a great influence on finance across the nation and played a role of "linking the world." However, artistries like stone carvings, bamboo weaving, flowers, hoop buckets,

---

① Fei, X. Small commodity, big market [M] // He, F. *Overview of Zhejiang*. Hangzhou: Zhejiang People's Publishing House, 2003: 350.

sewing, haircut and cooking as well as selling sugar and goods in small department stores in Zhejiang in the Ming and Qing dynasties only gave birth to people whose goal was simply to make a living, including some small businessmen and craftsmen whom were the so-called "artisans."

Therefore, the answer to the above question, that is, "Why has the cultural tradition of Zhejiang merchants been continued and gradually developed since the reform and opening-up, but the traditional culture of Huizhou and Shanxi merchants has not," must be translated into an answer to the following questions: Since the reform and opening-up, why has not the tradition of Huizhou and Shanxi merchants, which took salt, pawn broking, timber, tea and exchange as the business content and which nurtured the traditional culture of commercial groups in Huizhou and Shanxi, been continued in Anhui and Shanxi Provinces, while the industrial and commercial traditional culture in Zhejiang, characterized by small sized business, such as selling sugar and goods in small department stores, and artistries, such stone carvings, bamboo knitting, elastic flowers, hoop buckets, sewing, haircuts, and cooking, has been continued and developed, eventually forming the contemporary economy in Zhejiang Province? Obviously, when the latter question is answered, the former one will be solved.

At first glance, the questions raised above seem to be of no great significance because Shanxi merchants and Huizhou merchants had already declined in as early as the end of the Qing Dynasty and the early years of the Republic of China, not to mention their continuation and development. However, from a broader historical background, in fact, under the planned economic system which lasted for 30 years, all the regional commercial cultural traditions in Chinese history have declined to vary degrees in the macro social environment of "industrial and commercial transformation" and "cutting off the tail of capitalism." Therefore, the above questions are still relevant. What really matters is not the "decline," but the phenomenon that some regional commercial cultural traditions are no longer "prosperous" after the "decline," while others are reviving after the fall. In order to facilitate the understanding of this problem, we have to accept the decline of Zhejiang, Shanxi and Huizhou merchants before the reform and opening-up as a necessary prerequisite and assume that their traditions and culture still exist in the cultural memory or "convention" of the people in the corresponding regions. Although, as mentioned above, facts show that after 30 years of planned economic practice, the folk commercial cultural traditions of Huizhou and Shanxi can be said to have almost disappeared. But the above assumption is still necessary for understanding the phenomenon in Zhejiang. Here, the assumption is to provide a simulated environment and a theoretical model. Although it may not correspond to reality, it helps to illustrate the issues to be studied.

Many terms in modern evolutionary economics theory are borrowed from the concepts and ideas of biological evolution, and the theory holds that "daily routine" is the gene of economic change, which plays the same role as the genes in biological evolution. This is a repetitive behavior, a cultural process and a standard behavior determined by individual experience accumulated before a certain point of time, which control, replicate, and imitate the path and scope of economic evolution. Schumpeter believed that no one could survive, even one day, without the help of habits. In evolutionary economics, like biological systems, evolution is driven mainly by two mechanisms: One is the innovation mechanism which produces diversification through systematic innovation and the other is the selection mechanism which conducts systematic screenings within these diversifications. Innovation is reflected in practice and is associated with the mechanism that triggers it. The selection mechanism refers to how the institutional context of the economic system (a more general basic operating environment) may favor certain practices over others, so the choice will change the spread of habits and the behavior of individuals and organizations.

According to the evolutionary economics theory, the commercial activities of selling salt, pawn broking, selling timber, selling tea and operating exchange shops by Huizhou and Shanxi merchants can be regarded as the cultural memory or "convention" of people in Huizhou and Shanxi. Meanwhile, the commercial activities of doing some artistry such as stone carvings, bamboo, flowers, hoop buckets, sewing, and haircuts or selling sugar and goods can be regarded as the cultural memory or "convention" of people in Zhejiang. Although during the Ming and Qing dynasties, some people in Huizhou and Shanxi might have been engaged in the same activities as Zhejiang people did, and Zhejiang people might have also been engaged in what Huizhou and Shanxi merchants did, these activities were not representative and typical in the corresponding commercial culture tradition at that time. Hence, the foregoing view can still be established. As Durkheim said, "The initial origin of all social processes must be found in the composition of the social internal environment."[1] Anything must be manifested in a certain field, and the "field" of social phenomena is the social environment which consists of two factors: human beings and things. Things include matter and law, custom, architecture, art, etc. What relates to human beings' social capacity and social dynamic density? These two changes will profoundly influence the basic conditions of social existence. "Social environment is the determining factor for social evolution"[2], especially for the human environment. "The main reason for historical development is not outside the social environment, but within the environment, and the same applies to all kinds of social phenomena."[3] Therefore, the reasons for any social phenomenon must look within the inner society. Whether it is the commercial cultural memory or "convention" of Huizhou, Shanxi or Zhejiang people, all are associated with a certain incentive mechanism, which is what Durkheim called "internal environment of

---

① Durkheim. *Sociological Research Methodology* [M]. Trans. Hu, W. Beijing: Huaxia Publishing House, 1989: 90.

② Durkheim. *Sociological Research Methodology* [M]. Trans. Hu, W. Beijing: Huaxia Publishing House, 1989: 92.

③ Ibid. 93.

society," or to be more precise, with the institutional background of the economic system (a more general basic operating environment) in the evolutionary economics theory. The institutional background of the economic system is the policies launched at the beginning of the reform and opening-up and other institutional environments. The state policies launched at the beginning of the reform and opening-up and other institutional environments are not specially designed and arranged for Zhejiang people. What intriguing, however, is that the practice of the reform and opening-up has fully demonstrated that the economy of Zhejiang Province has a sharp contrast to the economy of Anhui and Shanxi Province. Zhejiang's economy is described as "When there is sunshine, it sprouts, and when there are rain and dew, it sprouts." That is to say, the policies since the reform and opening-up are conducive to stimulating the cultural memory or "conventions" of contemporary Zhejiang people, like the artistry mentioned above, but are not conducive to stimulating the cultural memory of Huizhou and Shanxi people.

In order to analyze this contrasting result, it is necessary to link the cultural memory or "convention" of different regions with the policy and other institutional environments of the early stage of the reform and opening-up and make a comprehensive investigation. At the beginning of the reform and opening-up, the Communist Party of China affirmed that the individual economy was a complement to the socialist public economy in the policy of treating the individual economy and its positive effects, such as addressing unemployment, meeting the needs of social diversity and providing funds for the state, etc. As stated in the report of the Thirteenth National Congress of the Communist Party of China, "Practice has proved that the development of the private economy to a certain extent is conducive to promoting production, enlivening the market, expanding employment, and better meeting the needs of the people in all aspects of life, and is a necessary and beneficial supplement to the public ownership economy."[①] This showed that in the first ten years of the reform and opening-up, the policy of the Communist Party of China was to take the individual and private economy as a "necessary and beneficial supplement to the public sector of the economy" and a definition of "remedying defects" because of its effects to the national economy. The traditional industrial and commercial activities carried out by Zhejiang people, can be used as necessary and beneficial supplements to the public sector of the economy. Under the situation of shortage economy and the coexistence of the planned economy and commodity economy in the external economic environment, the activities of "artisans" can make up for the gap in the system and remedy defects of the national economy. Therefore, it is permitted and encouraged by the state policy. Hence, although the state policy at the beginning of the reform and opening-up was a shining light, Zhejiang did not enjoy special preferential policies. However, in reality, it is especially helpful to stimulate the cultural memory or "convention" of Zhejiang people. Especially in the serious shortage of daily necessities caused by the long-term planned economy, the cultural memory or "convention" of Zhejiang people not only seems to have a natural affinity with the "institutional background of the national economic system (a more general basic operating environment)" at the beginning of the reform and opening-up, but also helps meet the needs of Zhejiang people who do not benefit from the state-owned economy. Therefore, Zhejiang has a special advantage.

However, as cultural memories or "conventions," the business contents of Huizhou and Shanxi people such as salt, pawn broking, wood, tea, and exchange shops are not in compliance with the national policy at the beginning of the reform and opening-up. The exchange shops of Shanxi merchants, in a way, are "private banks" in modern society, which are neither allowed at the beginning of the reform and

---

① Zhao, Z. *Advance Along the Socialist Road with Chinese Characteristics* [M]. Beijing: People's Publishing House, 1987: 32.

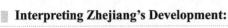
opening-up when private economy was regarded as "a necessary and beneficial replenishment" or "remedy" to public-owned economy, nor at present when we advocate "a multi-ownership economic system with public-owned economy as its main body." Therefore, it is difficult for these exchange shops to thrive according to the national policy, though now they are still alive. What's more, the other business contents of Huizhou and Shanxi merchants either declined in importance in modern society or were restricted by the policy at the beginning of the reform and opening-up as well.

Take the business of salt, tea and wood as examples, in the Ming Dynasty, it was the government that controlled the production, transportation and sale of salt while the merchants usually supplied goods and materials like grain to border counties. Thus, the government offered the right of monopoly to the merchants who exchanged the goods and materials for Salt Yin (a certificate that allows merchants to sell salt). Then they got salt with Yin at designated saltworks and sold it to designated districts. As Zhang Mao, a litterateur in the Ming Dynasty remarked, "Emperor Zhu Yuanzhang decreed the merchants to transport grains to the borders and gave them the Salt Yin in return because it would waste a lot of money and manpower for the government to transport the grains to the far and dangerous borders. The merchants were also pleased to do this for they could get many profits from this trade, thus it was a win-win policy."[1] Because of the control of the government, the right of monopoly meant a chance to get substantial profit. That was why Miyazaki Ichisada believed that "Salt served an important role among those initial goods in the origin of China's business."[2] Like salt, the right of monopoly of tea was also controlled by the government in the Ming and Qing dynasties. As a result, there was also a substantial profit that was made in the tea

---

[1] Zhang, X. *West Garden Records:* vol. 35 [M].

[2] Miyazaki, I. *Collection of Miyazaki Ichisada's papers* [M]. Trans. Institute of History, Chinese Academy of Sciences. Beijing: The Commercial Press, 1965.

business. Only when merchants exchanged money for Tea Yin, were they allowed to trade in tea. As Zhang Han (a government official in the Ming Dynasty) remarked, "Only great merchants could trade in salt and tea as they generated huge profit."[①] However, salt and tea are not so important as before because they are no longer monopolized by the government in modern society. Therefore, they do not generate as huge of a profit as before and even ordinary merchants can trade them. On the other hand, wood trade was hardly limited by the government except some exorbitant taxes and levies were required to be paid in the Ming and Qing dynasties. As *Records of She County* notes, "A lot of merchants trading in wood in Huizhou got wood from Sichuan and Guangdong then gathered it in the upper reaches of the Jiangning River. These merchants had at least ten thousand wealth."[②] In the Ming and Qing dynasties, wood trade was a double-edged sword— on one hand, it would get you a large amount of wealth; on the other hand, it came with a huge risk. However, the government had already forbidden excessive deforestation and closed hillsides to facilitate afforestation before the reform and opening-up, and this policy will definitely continue now and in the future when we advocate sustainable development. Thus, the wood trade mode of "cut, transport and sell wood" in the Ming and Qing dynasties has been limited by the policy since the reform and opening-up.

To conclude, on the aspect of business contents, the cultural memories or "conventions" of Zhejiang merchants have a kind of affinity with the policies since the reform and opening-up, thus they could be activated by "the institutional background of the economic system (a more general basic background)" according to evolutionary economics. However, the cultural memories or "conventions" of Shanxi

---

① Zhang, H. *Records of the Ming Dynasty in a Pine Studio*: vol. 4 [M]. Shanghai: Shanghai Classics Publishing House, 1986.
② Xu, C. *Records of She County*: vol.18 Customs and Ethical Education of She County [M].

and Huizhou merchants do not have affinity with the policies since the reform and opening-up, and could not be activated. This is the reason why the cultural traditions of Zhejiang merchants have been sustained since the reform and opening-up while those of Huizhou and Shanxi merchants have not.

3.4.3 Features and Subsequent Effects of Zhejiang, Huizhou and Shanxi Merchants' Cultural Traditions

The feature of Huizhou and Shanxi merchants' cultural traditions is that their commerce is unmixed, while that of Zhejiang merchants is that they combined the handicraft industry with commerce, namely that they are "art businessmen" who are both handicraftsmen and businessmen according to Fei Xiaotong. Because of this difference, they left different subsequent effects in their areas.

The analysis above is based on the conclusion that the influence of all these three merchants declined before the reform and opening-up with the assumption that the cultural traditions still exist in the folks' cultural memories or "conventions." However, the truth is that after the 30-year practice of the planned economy, almost nothing remained of the commercial cultural traditions of Huizhou and Shanxi merchants, while plenty of evidence show that the cultural traditions of "art businessmen" in Zhejiang have been alive continuously like a string without a break.

In the light of Max Weber's "elastic explanation system," it is obvious that we need to take a multi-angle view on the relations between traditional Zhejiang, Shanxi and Huizhou merchants and contemporary economic development. It is believed by Braudel that the development of the handicraft industry and modern industry requires the promotion of multiple factors, and among these, poverty usually leads to pre-industry. Besides, he also listed plenty of examples to prove this. Landi Ortensio wrote in his book *The Frugal Life: A Paradox* that the silk city, Lucca, was called Ant Republic in the 13th Century because its field (referring to the rural areas belonging to the city) was not enough for specializing in industry. "Textbooks talk of Colbert as if he persuaded a reluctant and undisciplined France to go to work, whereas the economic situation and increased taxation alone would have been sufficient to push the kingdom into industrial activity. Modest though such industry might be, was it not a life-raft, a 'second providence'? Savary des Bruslons declared: 'It has always been noted that the prodigies of industry [note that he uses the word unhesitatingly] spring from the heart of necessity.' This remark was worth remembering. In Russia, the poorest land fell to the 'black' peasantry—free peasants who sometimes had to import grain to survive. And it was among them that craft industry tended to develop. The mountain dwellers around Lake Constance, in the Swabian Jura or in the Silesian hills, were linen-workers from the fifteenth century, in order to compensate for the poverty of their agriculture. And in the Scottish Highlands, the crofters who could not make a living from their meagre crops, survived either by working as weavers or as coal-miners. The market towns where the villagers of north-west England brought their cloth, woven at home and still greasy, provided a large proportion of the products collected by the London merchants who under-took to finish them before selling them in the Cloth Hall."[1] Undoubtedly, the marginal status in the planned economy and insufficient lands made Zhejiang people bear heavy stress, thus they were more eager to transform into the non-agricultural fields and more impulsive to make a living and innovate independently. This point has been fully expounded elsewhere in this book. In the period of the planned economy, the low investment rate of the country and the livelihood that cannot be maintained simply by agriculture made it necessary for Zhejiang people to find their way out of agriculture. In addition, the Yangtze River Delta region, which is one of the most economically active areas in contemporary China, also provides special geographical opportunities for Zhejiang people. These are the stimulating factors that can extend

---

[1]   Braudel. *Civilization and Capitalism: 15th to 18th Century*: vol. 2 [M]. Trans. Gu, L. & Shi, K. Beijing: SDX Joint Publishing Company, 1993: 322.

the traditional industrial and commercial activities, cultural memories or "conventions" that Zhejiang people have engaged in.

However, a more important secret as to why Zhejiang merchants' cultural memory or "conventions" continued, while that of Shanxi and Huizhou merchants did not, lies in their differing features, namely that Zhejiang merchants combined "industry" with "business" yet Shanxi merchants only worked on business. As mentioned earlier, the distinctive characteristics of the traditional Zhejiang merchants are stone inscription, bamboo knitting, cotton fluffing, sewing, hairdressing, hardware, chefs, coopers, cobblers, and man selling sugar and other small things of daily use, and these commercial activities more or less have some connection with handicrafts. But for traditional Shanxi and Huizhou merchants, their tradition is "purely commercial." Not only were the merchants themselves handicraftsmen, their activities were basically confined to the field of commodity circulation. As the Shanxi scholar Zhang Zhengming said, "Although Shanxi merchants were rich, only few of them invested their capital into industry, which happened mostly in the late Qing Dynasty. Thus, there was no big trend of transformation from commercial capital to industrial capital, and commercial capital still remained in circulation."[1] Like Shanxi merchants, Huizhou merchants' capital basically stayed in commercial circulation. Qin Peiheng has said clearly on this point: "the activities of Huizhou merchants were a kind of commercial labor which serves as a connection between production and consumption in the process of commercial circulation."[2]

It should be said that after hundreds of years of history, Shanxi and Huizhou merchants' cultural tradition—"pure commerce," is

① Zhang, Z. *History of the Rise and Fall of Shanxi Merchants* [M]. Taiyuan: Shanxi Ancient Books Publishing House, 2001: 270
② Qin, P. *The Social and Economic History of Ming and Qing dynasties* [M]. Zhengzhou: Zhongzhou Ancient Books Publishing House, 1984: 173.

quite mature. Both Shanxi merchants and Huizhou merchants have
formed a very complete set of business management ideas as well as
an organization and management system, which are quite advanced,
not only in China but also in the world at that time. However, from
the point of view of Chinese modern history, compared with Zhejiang
merchants' traditional culture that combined "handicrafts" with
"business," Huizhou and Shanxi merchants' "pure commerce" cultural
tradition is more likely to decline or is more vulnerable to be lost in
the contemporary social environment of China. There is no doubt
that during the 30 years of the planned economy period, the social
environment that was good for commerce and industry was no longer
existed in China. In order to continue a business culture, there must be
a learning environment. Commercial knowledge is a kind of practical
knowledge, and some parts of it are "tacit knowledge," which means
the basic knowledge of things that need to be completed skillfully, to
a great extent, cannot be spoken. Michael Polanyi believed that tacit
knowledge occupied a central position among all the human knowledge.
It is not only a logical possibility but also an ordinary situation that
people can do something, but cannot explain how it is done. Nelson and
Winter pointed out that language was an imperfect tool for transmitting
information, and the degree of imperfection was directly proportional to
the difficulties experienced by people in achieving goals. Language can
convey a framework, but after the exhaustion of language resources,
there are still many things to be filled in, which involve many laborious,
wrong and retrying searches. "In short, much practical knowledge
still cannot be explained in words, because people cannot clear it
fast enough; because it is not possible to clearly explain everything
necessary for a successful completion of the work, and also because the
language cannot simultaneously describe the various relationships, and
explain the characteristics of things."[1] Therefore, in order to acquire
practical knowledge of business, though indirect experience from

---

[1]   Richard, R. N. & Sydney. G. W. *Evolution Theory of Economic Changes* [M].
Trans. Hu, S. Beijing: The Commercial Press, 1997: 90, 93.

predecessors and knowledge from books is an important way, it is more important to learn from practice. To a great extent, practical knowledge is tacit knowledge, and the key way to understand it, is that individuals engage themselves in the practice of commodity economy, and that is to say, we can learn to swim only when we swim.

To master and improve the level of business knowledge, reading books is a way, but it is more important to learn through practice. Since the cultural tradition of Shanxi and Huizhou merchants is "staying in circulation," the learning (especially the "tacit knowledge") and the continuation of this tradition must be done in the real commodity circulation. That is to say, only in the process of managing an "exchange shop" can we learn the management of it; only in the process of selling tea, salt and wood, can we learn the trade of tea, salt and wood. If the knowledge from books is not combined with business practice, it is likely to be a useless. This is due to the complexity of Huizhou and Shanxi merchants. For example, since the implementation of the Zonggang system in the salt business, salt drawing and transportation was conducted by "Gang" as a unit. Each "Gang" had general merchants and scattered traders. The general merchants were ruled by the salt commission and ruled the scattered traders. According to their own wishes, the scattered merchants choosed the general merchants that they want to follow. The management in this Gang system was quite complicated: In the process of transportation, merchants needed to be questioned, examined and taxed several times, besides they needed to go through numerous formalities and even use money to pass through the joints easier. Wood or tea selling all involved many steps such as purchase, transportation, sales and so on. The management of exchange shops not only requires a set of rules and methods of hospitality but also required management systems such as a manager responsibility system, an apprenticeship system, a share-holding system, an affiliate system, an account system, a gauge system, etc. As a precondition for the continuity of the "purely commercial" culture of Shanxi and Huizhou merchants, the learning environment is bound to be a large class of social commodity economy. However, as mentioned above,

during the 30 years of the planned economy, the social environment that
was good for commerce and industry no longer existed in China, which
meant that the social commodity economy that was beneficial to the
learning and continuation of Shanxi and Huizhou merchants' cultural
traditions also no longer existed. Memory needs to be recalled through
learning so that it will not be forgotten. In the absence of a learning
environment, the cease of cultural traditions and cultural memories of
Huizhou and Shanxi merchants seems to be a historical fate.

In contrast to the fate of Huizhou and Shanxi Merchants' "purely
commercial" cultural tradition, the cultural memories or "conventions"
of Zhejiang still has the learning and continuation environment, even
in the period of the planned economy when the beneficial social
environment for business activities no longer existed in China. If the
condition for the learning and the existing environment for Shanxi and
Huizhou merchants' "purely commercial" cultural traditions must be
the social commodity economy, then the combination of "handicrafts
industry" and "business" of Zhejiang merchants' cultural tradition, can
not only be learned in society, but also in the family. P. Boissonnade
has described craftsmen' features in the Middle Ages' Europe. He
said that these people had technical knowledge and lived off of their
craftsmanship, which, in the Middle Ages, were called "art workers"
or artisans, sometimes worked alone and sometimes gathered a few
assistants in their workshops. He was the head of business and chose
his career freely according to his talents. Their professional skills were
manifested in many ways. Occasionally, artisans worked at home in
certain jobs that were not highly specialized, either individually or
with the help of his family members. "Artisans work for orders, getting
paid on pieces or days, in his own room or in someone's home, using
other's raw materials but his own tools, requiring neither capital nor
intermediaries."[1] Craftsman's skills and knowledge of business can

---

[1]   Boissonnade. *Medieval European Life and Work (5th to 15th Century)* [M].
Trans. Pan, Y. Beijing: The Commercial Press, 1985: 184.

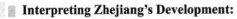

obviously be learned and passed on through family. The characteristics of "art businessmen" are similar to those of the "craftsmen" of medieval Europe described by Boissonnade, that they can also be learned and transmitted through family. From the perspective of "business," all are individual and easy-to-learn, because they simply need to deal with the customers and not be concerned with the staff management and establishing a sound organization management system. From the perspective of "handicraft," stone carvings, bamboo knitting, coopering, sewing, hairdressing, hardware, cooking, can all be passed on in the family environment from father to son and from son to grandchildren. Therefore, even if the social environment conducive to industrial and commercial activities no longer exists, the cultural tradition of Zhejiang merchants' "handicrafts" and "business" combination can still be continued through the family.

3.4.4 The Evolution and Expansion of the Cultural Tradition of Zhejiang Merchants in the Contemporary Era

The cultural tradition of Shanxi and Huizhou merchants produces great merchants, however, the cultural tradition of Zhejiang merchants produces handicraftsmen, small business hawkers, or small businessmen. It is ironic that the tradition of Shanxi and Huizhou merchants was interrupted in contemporary China, while the creation of the handicraftsmen, small business hawkers, or small businessmen tradition, has been continued, and continues to flourish. What is even more intriguing is that the creation of the handicraftsmen, small business hawkers or small businessmen cultural tradition has become a tradition of producing great businessmen in contemporary society after the reform and opening-up. Ninety percent of Zhejiang's richest people in the 1980s and 1990s were from poor families and were referred to as "grassroots Zhejiang merchants," and a significant part of them started their career as the "handicrafts-business-combined" merchants or small business hawkers at the beginning of the reform and opening-up. In the first generation of new Zhejiang merchants that emerged in the 1980s and 1990s, there were endless examples: for instance, Lu Guanqiu used to be a blacksmith, Qiu Jibao and Nan Cunhui were former cobblers, Hu Chengzhong used to be a tailor, Zheng Jianjiang used to be a car mechanic, and so on.

The "handicraft-business-combined" cultural traditions of the handicraftsmen, small business hawkers, or small businessmen have also become a tradition of producing great businessmen in contemporary society, which can only be fully understood in the special socio-economic environment of contemporary China. Needless to say, the formation of a large number of contemporary Zhejiang businessmen is not an isolated social phenomenon, but an inevitable accompaniment in the process of a large number of Zhejiang laborers transferring from agriculture to the industrial and commercial fields since the reform and opening-up. Schulz believes that the migration of labors from one department to another occurs because individuals expect to get more profits than cost from the migration. Todaro's model of population migration shows that people make decisions for relocation on the basis of the "expected" (rather than realistic) urban-rural real wage differentials and the possibility of employment in cities, and that the urban unemployment rate may have a restrictive effect on population migration. Lewis's unlimited supply of labor under the dual economic conditions has seen the traditional sector (sustaining the livelihood sector) as a "reservoir" for the modern sector's workforce. For those in the low-income sectors of the economy, all other people must do their utmost to squeeze into the high-wage sector when the required capital and technical level of high-pay sector has been identified. However, all of these theories must be based on the premise of the free flow of labor, which was not available to the Chinese society before the reform and opening-up, as well as the Chinese society at the beginning of the reform and opening-up. As pointed out by Liu Jingming and other scholars, since the 1950s, in order to make sure that the capital and resources of heavy industry are guaranteed, and that the cost of heavy industry development is reduced, under the absolute authority condition, the state has, on the

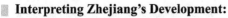
one hand, began to form an all-social-resources-concentrated planned economic system controlled by it; on the other hand, established the division boundaries of the social resources that agriculture was less important than the industry, and rural areas were inferior to city. Through a series of institutional arrangements, this boundary ultimately separates the peasant groups from urban residents. The major urban-rural division system is the "identity system." Although the "identity system" was established during a certain period of economic development, it developed along the logic of its "equitization" and was relatively independent. In this way, in the process of modernization, the increased labor demand for industrialization is not based on the comparative advantages of departments, because under the identity system, the Chinese employment system with its household registration system and welfare guarantee constitute a trinity system. In terms of specific operations, "measures like household registration, grain rations, and arrangements for temporary workers which were required to be handled with the commune's commercial office, have impeded the migration to the city."[①] In this situation, a large number of surplus rural labor forces refrained from free movement. They lost the right to choose their profession freely according to "comparative interests."[②]

This also means that before and at the beginning of the reform and opening-up, not only the peasant groups had difficulties to move freely to the cities, but also a person without a craftsmanship felt that it was hard to leave his homeland and survive in an unfamilier land. The planned economy implements a special employment system, that only those who have the "social status" of the urban *hukou* can become employees of local enterprises and institutions. For a non-craftsmanship

---

① Rozman, G. *The Modernization of China* [M]. Trans. National Social Science Fund "Comparative Modernization" Research Group. Nanjing: Jiangsu People's Publishing House, 1995: 470.

② Liu, J. Transferring non-agricultural occupations: A study of farmers' life history [J]. *Research on Sociology*, 2001(6).

foreigner, the only possible way to make a living in a foreign land is to become a temporary worker in enterprises and institutions. Needless to say, under such circumstances, becoming a temporary worker is not an easy task. This is not only because the arrangement of temporary workers should be handled with the commune's commercial office but also because the number of positions for temporary workers is small and there is a high threshold for temporary workers. So, people must make use of relations to get a position. Therefore, at the initial stage of the reform and opening-up, although the national policy has already advocated the individual economy as a "necessary and beneficial supplement to the public economy," and regarded the process of the reform and opening-up as a deregulation process, or more directly a process of delegating rights to individuals, the institutional arrangement of the long-term planned economy, including the household registration system and the employment system, in fact is a restriction and discrimination on the livelihood activities or economic activities of foreigners. However, the "handicrafts-business-combined" craftsmen and small business hawkers may find a way to break through this restriction of the planned economy. A craftsman can use cotton fluffing, shoe cobbling, goldsmithing, and tailoring skills to integrate into the city's urban division of labor system and survive outside of the country's formal system.

In fact, in the initial stage of the reform and opening-up, handicrafts were not simply a means of earning a livelihood for Zhejiang people in a foreign land but also an important means for them to enter the foreign market. The formation of the "Zhejiang Village" in Beijing illustrates this point. In the words of a sociologist, the reason why the "Zhejiang Village" was able to squeeze on the "table of poker" in Beijing at the beginning of the reform and opening-up was that it entered Beijing in a clearly different way from other later migrant workers. The people of "Zhejiang Village" is different from Anhui people, they do not have to work for the family in the city. "Zhejiang Village" is also different from the people of Nantong, Jiangsu, because they did not work on

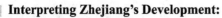

contracted projects in the city. The "Zhejiang Village" people do not enter the state-owned or collective, foreign-funded, or even individual companies like most migrant workers from all provinces. "Zhejiang Village" is a unique way of entering the city in a self-employed manner. The "villagers" here were not simply wage earners, but labor force operators who had certain technology, capital, commodity information about the market, and upper-class fellowships.[①] After the 1980s, the demand for social services from Beijing residents had been increasing. In order to solve the problems of "difficulty in eating," "difficulty in getting dressed," "difficulty in service," and employment of urban youth, Beijing relaxed the restrictions on individual economy and a number of individual industrial and commercial households developed. However, the self-employed households in this city of Beijing were mainly concentrated in the circulation field and the catering industry. The problem of "difficulty in clothing" was still prominent. Therefore, there was a demand for the garment processing industry in Beijing. This provided an opportunity for Zhejiang craftsmen who had traditional skills in garment processing. However, at the time, although Beijing allowed for the existence of individual economies, the obstacles to foreign businesses were not removed. Beijing supported business operators with local accounts. They were called "self-employed individuals" while foreign businesspeople were called "farmers from other provinces to do business" and did not have the full market access rights. The garment processing skills that are difficult to replace by the locals in Beijing have become an important means for Zhejiang people to enter the Beijing market. Therefore, the pressure of surviving more people and less land has enabled Zhejiang people to leave their homeland under the drive of self-reliant living. With a certain set of handicraft skills, they have important means of earning a living after leaving their homeland and make it possible to survive.

---

① Zhou, X. *Tradition and Transformation—The Social Psychology of Farmers in Jiangsu and Zhejiang Provinces and Their Transmutation in Modern History* [M]. Beijing: SDX Joint Publishing Company, 1998: 258.

At the beginning of the reform and opening-up, Zhejiang's craftsmen, small business hawkers or small businessmen, may survive in a foreign land, which is undoubtedly very important for the formation of new Zhejiang merchants. The history of Chinese and foreign commerce shows that many people leave their hometowns and become professional traders and even big business people after having relations with strangers and different customs. Early European businessmen were almost all foreigners. From the middle of the 10th century to the middle of the 14th century, except in certain regions such as Italy, the southwest and the north of France, Flanders, Rhineland, and the Danube region, the Western world has had no native businessman class which acted as an intermediary between producers and consumers. In the beginning, the merchant class consisted almost exclusively of adventurers and foreigners, and even non-Christians, or Jews who were on the brink of feudal society. They were particularly engaged in the trade of luxury goods and precious metals or engaged in currency lending to meet the needs of nobles. These businessmen were not usually settled in one place. They acted as peddlers, sold on a large scale along the way, or as a peddler group, from one country to another to go to the market. "But despite these commercial rallies being given various privileges, businessmen are still seen as intruders, like all foreigners."[①]

Max Weber pointed out: "Initially, business is a matter between disparate groups. It does not exist between members of the same tribe or the same group. It is the oldest kind of social community, and an external phenomenon targeted at unorthodox people, but the business can also be the result of the specialization of production between the unorthodox groups. In this case, it is either the trade of a producer between the unconventional groups or the production of the products of other ethnic groups. However, in any case, the oldest business is usually

---

① Boissonnade. *Medieval European Life and Work (5th to 15th Century)* [M]. Trans. Pan, Y. Beijing: The Commercial Press, 1985: 163.

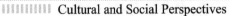

only the exchange relationship between the alien tribes."[1] Braudel also believed that "The political quarrels and religious passions of medieval and modern Europe excluded from their communities of origin many individuals who then formed minorities in the foreign countries to which they were exiled...They were forced to leave their homes and stay away from their hometowns to make their fortunes prosperous."[2] Similar to Western Europe, during the Ming and Qing dynasties, most of the Chinese business people started business activities in other places. Large businessmen operating in different parts of the country were mainly foreign merchants like the Huizhou, Shanxi, and Shaanxi merchants. Therefore, the question that needs to be answered further is: Why would leaving one's hometown lead to great fortune?

Yin Haiguang believed that traditional interpersonal relationships had the effect of limiting economic transactions within the scope of traditional relationships. When they conduct economic transactions with each other, "All heads are calculating the depth of human relations, and all are involved in personnel implications. It is the pros and cons of interpersonal relationships that are carefully watched all day long."[3] This leaves traders in a "dilemma," always facing the clash between profit targets and the moral responsibilities for families, neighbors, friends, relatives, etc. Therefore, large-scale trading activities require a very important social distance. As Wang Su said, "Trading in traditional societies required that businessmen and customers maintained a certain social distance, while members of mainstream society were trapped within each other's close interpersonal relationships. In close interpersonal relationships, it was impossible to operate according to

---

① Weber, M. *Weber's Collection:* vol. 2 Types of Economic and Historical Domination [M]. Trans. Kang, L. & Wu, N. Nanning: Guangxi People's Publishing House, 2004: 126.

② Braudel. *Civilization and Capitalism: 15th to 18th Century:* vol. 2 [M]. Trans. Gu, L. & Shi, K. Beijing: SDX Joint Publishing Company, 1993: 160.

③ Yin, H. *China Cultural Outlook* [M]. Beijing: China Peace Press, 1988: 136.

business principles. Therefore, only the 'special identity person' or 'outsider' recognized by people within the community can maximize profits and become a professional businessman."[1] Fei Xiaotong also believed that there was an intimate kinship society where business was difficult to exist. It does not mean that such society does not trade, but rather that transactions are maintained by human relations and are mutual gifts. The closer the social relations are, the less the exchange of reciprocity, and the common situation is to build a commercial foundation outside the blood relationship. "Outsiders who are on the brink of a consanguineous community have become a medium for commercial activities. The people in the village can talk about the price with him and do the spot sale. They do not have to consider the dependency between them and feel embarrassed. Therefore, in addition to the embarrassing nature of the elderly people who open stores in the village I know, most of them are 'new guests' from the outside. Business is developed outside of bloodlines."[2] "Outsiders" and "foreigners" can break the shackles of traditional interpersonal relationships. This is an extremely important reason why they can become professional traders.

On the other hand, there are huge differences in the natural conditions of climate and landforms in various regions of the world. The economic development in different regions is uneven, and different property prices and price differences between the same properties are formed. According to the principle of economics, "the specialization of functions allows everyone and each region to use the benefits of their particular skills and resources most effectively."[3] Therefore, "the two

---

① Wang, X. *Cultural Traditions and Economic Organization* [M]. Dalian: Dongbei University of Finance and Economics Press, 1999: 175.

② Fei, X. *The Native China* [M]. Beijing: SDX Joint Publishing Company, 1985: 76-77.

③ Samuelson, N. *Economics I* [M]. Trans. Gao, H. Beijing: China Development Press, 1992: 92.

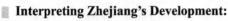

markets that are quite far away may have different prices." [1]Usually, economic people tend to exchange products that are produced with relatively inferior resources for those with produced relatively superior resources, which bring them the concept of "comparative cost." The exchange led him to discover that there is a clear gap between the unit production costs of some products and other products, and it is advantageous to exchange products with relatively low unit production cost (that is, with relative resource advantages) for products with high unit production costs. Therefore, there is a mutual exchange of needed goods in different regions, where products produced by a region's relatively advantageous resources are used to exchange for products produced by relatively inferior resources in another region. Thus, a business opportunity is formed. Such fortunate business opportunities, when the means of modern media have not yet been fully developed, can only be discovered by strangers who have left their hometowns, and will never come to a person who lives in his homeland for life. So, only strangers can know what differences exist between the "hometown" and "exotic land" in property and price. A person who lives in his native land for life and who is "born and always at home" cannot compare the "hometown" with "outside of town." Braudel therefore believed that "Long-distance trade certainly made super profits; it was after all based on the price difference between two markets very far apart, with supply and demand in complete ignorance of each other and brought into contact only by the activity of middleman...Remote trade, of course, took risks, but it was often possible to obtain excess profits, just as it was for winning lottery prizes." [2]

Therefore, the significance of stone carving, bamboo knitting, bullets, hoop barrels, sewing, haircuts, chefs, hardware, shoe repair, and

① Samuelson, N. *Economics II* [M]. Trans. Gao, H. Beijing:China Development Press, 1992: 816.

② Braudel. *Civilization and Capitalism: 15th to 18th Century*: vol. 2 [M]. Trans. Gu, L. & Shi, K. Beijing: SDX Joint Publishing Company, 1993: 437.

selling sugar, selling small articles of daily use, etc., far exceeds the arts and crafts activities of small businesses and hawkers themselves. If Zhejiang people continued to engage in the activities of handicrafts and small business hawkers themselves, then there could be no brilliant Zhejiang private economy today. The significance of handicrafts and small business hawkers' activities in the history of Chinese business and industry is that these activities enable Zhejiang people to survive in the difficult environment at the beginning of the reform and opening-up as "foreigners," thus allowing them to find different properties in different regions as well as the price difference between the same property and the huge business opportunities it contains. Under this circumstance, Zhejiang's industrial and commercial cultural tradition will spontaneously undergo fission and innovation. Driven by the motive of pursuing profit maximization, flower hitters, hoops, sewers, hairdressers, goldsmiths, shoemakers, as well as those who sell sugar and sell small articles of daily use are digging the first sheet of gold. After accumulating a certain amount of seed capital, it may be possible to choose to go home and set up a family factory related to the original industrial and commercial activities. For example, a shoemaker may set up a leather shoe factory, and a goldsmith may set up a hardware factory, etc. A person may not continue to engage in hooping, sewing, haircutting, goldsmithing, shoe repairing, selling sugar, and selling small articles of daily use, but will instead choose to engage in new businesses found in other places that can bring greater profits.

In this regard, the rise of Beijing's "Zhejiang Village" has been very persuasive. The founder of the "Zhejiang Village" in Beijing is said to be the Lu brothers, Lu Bize and Lu Biliang, farmers of Yanfu Township near Hongqiao Town who had previously engaged in the clothing business in Baotou, though some others believe the founder is Mr.Qian of Nanyang Township, Hongqiao District (now part of Hongqiao Town). In 1983, the Lu brothers who had been forced to return to Zhejiang due to bankruptcy changed their minds when transferring cars in Zhejiang. They rented a house of a local farmer in Haihu Tun and

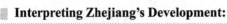

laid down a sewing machine and set up a cutting platform. In Beijing, they resumed their old business and quickly established their footing. At almost the same time, Mr.Qian, who had previously set up a cobbler's shop at the entrance of the Tianqiao Shopping Mall, also decided to operate a clothing stall instead after finding out that the supply of rayon in the mall always fell short of demand. After this, the news of the Lu brothers and Mr.Qian pursuing the "treasure" to make a fortune continued to spur Hongqiao and Wenzhou people who were "naturally" sensitive to the market. They began to rush to the Beijing City in the form of "chain migrations," like a snowball effect.[①] The prosperity of the Yongjia Bridge button market is equally persuasive. In 1979, it was said that a cotton-fluffing lad with the surname Wang found a business opportunity whilst engaging in cotton fluffing in Jiangxi: a batch of disposed buttons. From then on, he no longer fluffs the cotton, but brings the buttons back to the bridge and puts up button stalls. This business actually became a very profitable one. A year later, there were more than 100 button stalls in the town. In early 1983, the county government approved the town of Qiaotou as a button professional market. In 1986, there were more than 700 button shops and booths in the whole town, and 1300 varieties of buttons produced by more than 300 button factories throughout the country were sold here. In 1985, people in Qiaotou Town were no longer satisfied with simply buying and selling. They began to use the funds accumulated in the operation to set up factories to produce buttons. In 1986, there were 430 button factories in the region, of which 300 were home factories.[②] The rise of the button market in Qiaotou can be seen as a microcosm of the path of contemporary industrial and commercial development in Zhejiang. Since the reform and opening-up, the rise of a company and the rise of

① Zhou, X. *Tradition and Change: Social Psychology of Farmers in Jiangsu and Zhejiang Provinces and Their Transmutation in Modern History* [M]. Beijing: SDX Joint Publishing Company, 1998: 260-261.

② Fei, X. Small commodity, big market [M] // He, F. *Overview of Zhejiang*. Hangzhou: Zhejiang People's Publishing House, 2003: 348.

a professional market may all have some correlation with handicrafts and hawker activities. The rise of Yiwu China Commodity City and Yongkang China Science and Technology Hardware City will become difficult to understand without knowing Yiwu's people's history of chicken feathers for sugar exchange and Yongkang people's history of goldsmithing.

Hayek believed that some innovative practices were adopted at the outset for other reasons, or even entirely accidental, and these practices are then extended because they enabled the groups that emerged to outperform other groups. That is to say, when a party responds to a particular environment and accidentally or for some other reason adopts a rule that leads him to gain an advantage in later competition, the rule is then continued as a result of survival of the fittest; at the same time, other parties will increase its own competitiveness by imitating the rule and allowing it to be widely spread. Evolutionary economics also believes that in the innovation phase, if the laws of large number play a role, innovation may be stifled; but if the system is open and far from equilibrium, innovation will rise through the system due to the effect of self-enhancement (positive feedback). The drop is amplified so that it crosses an unstable threshold and enters a new organizational structure. In this mutation process, the law of large numbers fails. However, when the new structure is formed, self-enhancement will start the law of large numbers, while new ideas and new ways of doing things will enter the proliferation stage, and will gradually become a socially popular state.

The above theories of Hayek and evolutionary economics can be used to explain the contemporary Zhejiang phenomena. At the beginning of the reform and opening-up, most craftsmen and small business hawkers in Zhejiang moved to a foreign land. They did not aim to become big businessmen. Their motives were actually very simple. However, one factor that may be very accidental has changed their traditional path. Innovation activities had already taken place quietly and new practices had begun to take shape at the same time when

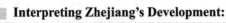

craftsmen and business siblings living in the fields discovered new business opportunities and no longer engaged in activities involving cotton fluffer, barrels, sewing, haircuts, gold, shoe repairs, sell sugar, and selling small articles of daily use, and instead shifted their attention to the more profitable activities. Needless to say, not all contemporary Zhejiang merchants have direct experience in craftsmanship and hawker activities. At the same time, because human rationality is limited, people are faced with bounded rational constraints and a decentralized environment of knowledge. The heterogeneity of individuals and the differences in the distribution of knowledge lead to differences in the discovery and acquisition of profit opportunities. Some of them obtain success. However, the innovative practices of the craftsmen and business siblings who make a living in the outside world will rapidly spread to other groups under the effect of making money. Due to the effect of self-enhancement (positive feedback), the innovations of craftsmen and traders who make a living in the outside world will be amplified through systematic fluctuations, so that they will cross a certain unstable threshold and enter a new organizational structure. In other words, when those wealthy people make a fortune and prosper, the other parties in Zhejiang will try to maximize their interests and increase their own competitiveness by mimicking them. The new ideas and new ways of doing things of those who ventured into foreign lands will then become proliferated and gradually become popular in society. This can not only explain the reasons for the formation of Zhejiang's "One Town One Product" and "One Village One Product" special characteristic industrial zone but also explain the formation of the professional market in Zhejiang to some extent. As a Zhejiang scholar puts it, the "Zhejiang Characteristic Industrial Area," which originates from the neighborhood effect and has a village and a product, is a "learning community" and "innovative organization" where many participants share information, teach each other, learn from each other, and improve overall competitive skills. "On the surface, Zhejiang's characteristic industrial districts seem to have developed from small products and simple products, but their essence lies in the farmers who stepped out of their farmland to engage in trading these small and simple products, which then with the help of the neighborhood effect became prevalent and led to the formation of various One Village One Product commodity circles."[1] Obviously, not every trader in Yiwu China Commodity City and Yongkang China Science and Technology Hardware City has "feather-sugar exchange" or "goldsmithing" experience, but new ideas and new ways of doing things of the "goldsmith" undoubtedly produced a "demonstration" effect on them, thus the "new ideas and new ways of doing things" entered a stage of rapid proliferation. Therefore, a single spark can start a prairie fire, and the inconspicuous "feather-sugar exchange" will evolve into a magnificent "international trade city," and a trickle of "hardware" will evolve into a turbulent "China Science and Technology Hardware City."

In fact, the influence is reflected not only in its huge demonstration effect but also the extensive learning effects it has caused. What's more significant is that the art businessmen who travel to the north and the south also expand the market space in Zhejiang to promote division of labor and specialization. It is difficult to underestimate. To a certain extent, it can also be said that in the initial period of the reform and opening-up, art businessmen are the bridges and links between the Zhejiang market and the national market. The activities of the art businessmen are of great significance to the breeding of the Zhejiang market and the expansion of the market. According to economic theory, the expansion of market scope and the development of division of labor have a close relationship. In this regard, Adam Smith made a clear statement in the title of Chapter 3 of *The Wealth of Nations*. Smith pointed out that "When the market was very small, no person could have any encouragement to dedicate himself entirely to one employment, for want of the power to exchange all that surplus part of the produce of

---

[1]   Yan, C. Zhejiang private economic development and characteristic industrial zone [M]//He, F. *Overview of Zhejiang*. Hangzhou: Zhejiang People's Publishing House, 2003: 239.

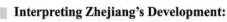
his own labor, which is over and above his own consumption, for such parts of the produce of other men's labor as he has occasion for." [1] On the contrary, only when the demand for a certain product or service grows to a certain extent with the expansion of the market scope, can specialized producers actually emerge and exist. With the expansion of the market scope, the degree of division of labor and specialization will improve continuously. Therefore, the expansion of market scope is a necessary condition for the development of division of labor. Smith's point of view shows that the expansion of the market comes first and the division of labor develops later; that is to say, the market expansion can explain the development of division of labor, but not vice versa. As Sheng Hong said, "Although the decline in production costs brought by the development of division of labor would further promote market expansion, it was clear that the development of division of labor cannot explain the initial expansion of the market since market expansion was a necessary condition for the development of division of labor." [2] In this sense, it can also be said that the division of labor and specialization in the "One Town One Product" "One Village One Product" throughout Zhejiang stems not only from the "neighborhood effect" and "learning effect," but also from the effect of the activities of art businessmen who traveled the south and the north on the expansion of the market space. The activities of art businessmen have undoubtedly played a crucial role.

---

① Smith, A. *An Inquiry into the Nature and Causes of the Wealth of Nations*: vol. 1[M]. Trans. Guo, D. & Wang, Y. Beijing: The Commercial Press, 1981: 16.
② Sheng, H. *Division of Labor and Transactions—A General Theory and Its Application to China's Non-Professional Issues* [M]. Shanghai: Shanghai People's Publishing House, 1995: 150.

Chapter 4

Trust, Social Network and Zhejiang's Economic and Social Development

Trust and social networks include implicit knowledge, a collection of networks, accumulation of reputation and organizational capital. In the context of organizational theory, trust and social networks can be seen as ways to deal with moral traps and motivations. Stiglitz stated: "When a society developd its economy, its social capital must be adapted as well so that interpersonal relationship networks could be partially replaced by a formal system of market-based economy, for example, a structuralized legal system imposed by the dominant representative form. The process might start with social capital loss on an overall level, but eventually a different type of social capital would be created, in which social relations were rooted in the economic system rather than the opposite."[①] In a cooperative economic exchange, both formal and informal relations, including the relationship between the inside of the company and the outside of the company, determine the economic process. If corporations and covenants can be considered as formal mechanisms to reduce the volatility of economic affairs, then networks like trust and social networks can be said to provide a paradigm for analyzing informal paths through which trust and social networks resolve economic risks through informal relations and rules. Historically, Zhejiang was a region deeply influenced by the family culture of purely personal, familial and semi-familial relationships. On this basis, Zhejiang has formed a model of trust, network and social capital with distinctive regional characteristics. Since the modern

---

① Stigilitz, J. Formal and informal institutions [M]. Trans. Wu, X. // Cao, R. *Prisoner's Dilemma—An Analysis of Social Capital and Institutions*. Shanghai: SDX Joint Publishing Company, 2003: 113.

times, especially since the reform and opening-up, along with the rapid change of economy, politics, and society, Zhejiang has also experienced profound changes in its trust, social network and social capital model, which have distinctive regional and cultural features. The model played a very important role in Zhejiang's economy and society development since the reform and opening-up.

4.1 Particularistic Trust and Family Culture in the Region of Zhejiang

By common sense, the so-called trust refers to expectations of credit and goodwill. Hosmer argued that "trust was an irrational choice behavior when an individual faced an unforeseen event where loss might be greater than gain."[①] According to Gambetta, trust "is a particular level of the subjective probability with which an agent assesses that another agent or group of agents will perform a particular action…when we say we trust someone or that someone is trustworthy, we implicitly mean that the probability that he will perform is an action that is beneficial or at least not detrimental to us is high enough for us to consider engaging in some form of cooperation with him."[②] Since trust is a kind of anticipation of the behavior of others around or a subjective expectation of probability acquired in nurtured social activities, it, of course, cannot escape from the constraints and influences of the cultural traditions and social structures of a particular society. The establishing mechanism of trust, the means of assurance, and the mode of operation are deeply embedded in the concrete social operation and cultural background. On the one hand, the problem of trust is diffused in every corner of social life, touching on the individual actors at all times, and thus has a very strong individuality; on the other hand, as a

---

① Yang, Z. & Peng, S. Conceptualization of interpersonal trust in China: A Human relationship perspective [J]. *Sociological Studies*, 1999(2).

② Chu, X. & Li, H. Trust and the growth of family business [J]. *Management World*, 2003(6).

social relationship, it is soaked with social and cultural factors such as values, systems, and structures. Different social modes of operation and cultural modes will inevitably evolve different establishing mechanisms of trust. The trust of Chinese people, including people from Zhejiang, is based on purely personal familial and semi-familial relationships and is a particularistic trust formed and sustained by the blood relationship within a family and a clan. This, obviously, is determined by the special status of "family" and "clan" in Chinese society and culture.

4.1.1　Family Culture, Particularistic Trust and Differential Mode of Association

According to Maslow's view, human beings have five basic needs: physiological, safety, belonging and love, esteem and self-realization. Xu Langguang believes that these needs are first met in the primary group, or family. If not completely met, these needs will be met in the secondary group. Different ways of meeting people's needs constitute different cultures. The so-called secondary groups, also known as "societies," include all groups that are artificially established between relatives and national groups, or for a certain purpose, such as the military, political parties, schools, factories, companies and various amateur groups. In any society, plenty of secondary groups can be found, but there must be one of them which possesses a dominant position. According to Xu Langguang's explanation, in a traditional society, the most important secondary group of Chinese people is their family. When forming a family group, the "kinship principle" is followed. Under this principle, the distance between people tended to be measured by the distance between paternal kinship. "An individual is subject to seeking interdependence, that is, he depends on others as though others depend on him, and he fully understands the obligation to repay his benefactor, no matter how long it would take."[1]

---

① Hsu, F. L. K. *Clan, Caste and Club* [M]. Trans. Xue, G. Beijing: Huaxia Publishing House, 1990: 2.

In traditional Chinese society, family and clan are the most important social institutions, and the region of Zhejiang is no exception. Lu Zuofu said: "Family life was the most important social life for Chinese people while the relationship with relatives, neighbors and friends is the second. This dual social life centralized the demands of Chinese people, set the range for their activities, and stipulated the moral conditions of their society and the political legal system."[1] Li Yiyuan pointed out that Chinese culture was a "family culture"[2], while Yang Guoshu pointed out that "family had not only become the core of Chinese people's social, economic and cultural life, but had become the dominant factor in political life."[3] Wang Dingding also believed: "What passed down from that most profound cultural level was the core of the Chinese people even today, the concept of 'family'."[4] Fei Xiaotong advocated paying attention to the role of the family by saying "this cell has a strong vitality."[5] This kind of culture under the family and clan system is first manifested by a high degree of emphasis on consanguinity. Traditional Chinese interpersonal relationships are based on the sequence of blood relationship and the three-dimensional network with father and son as the longitude and brothers as the latitude. Almost all acquaintances can be included in this network, but the relationships between different people are different just like there is a difference of distance between different knots in this three-dimensional network. It is actually "self-centered,"

---

① Lu, Z. Development of China and training of people [M]//Liang, S. *Sum and Substance of Chinese Culture.* Shanghai: Xuelin Press, 1987:12.

② Li, Y. Chinese families and family culture [M]//Wen, C. & Xiao, X. *The Chinese: Perceptions and Behaviors.* Taipei: Taiwan Juliu Books, 1988: 113.

③ Yang, G. Familization, pan-familism and its organization and management [M]//Huang, G. *Organization and Management of Cross-Straits.* Taipei: Taiwan Yuanliu Publishers, 1998.

④ Wang, D. *Economic Development and Institutional Creation* [M]. Shanghai: Shanghai People's Publishing House, 1995: 21.

⑤ Dialogues between Fei Xiaotong and Li Yiyuan [J]. *Journal of Peking University (Philosophy and Social Sciences)*, 1998(6).

like a stone thrown into the water, and the social relations with the other people…are like water ripples, launched in concentric circles and getting pushed outward and becoming thinner.[①] This is the "differential mode of association" that Fei Xiaotong refers to as the basic feature of the social structure of China. Fei Xiaotong believes that there is a "self" at the center of this scalable and differentiated pattern, which is not individualism but egoism.

"Differential mode of association" determines a person's relationship, attitude and trust to the same person on different occasions, or to different people on the same occasion. Therefore, "differential mode of association" sets particularism as the value orientation, that is, the value of the object and its behavior is determined according to the special relationship between the actor and the object. This obviously differs from the universalistic values in which the value of the object and its behavior is independent of the object's special identity relations between the actor and the object. According to Fei Xiaotong, the "ten relations" in the ritual part in *The Book of Rites*: ghosts and gods, monarchs and courtiers, fathers and sons, the rich and the poor, wages and awards, husbands and wives, politics, the elderly and children, the superior and the inferior, all refer to orders. "Unfailing Ethics" is to differ from father and son, close and distant. Ethics is an order with hierarchy. It is a path from self to home, from home to the country and from the country to the world. Doctrine of the Mean set up Five Ethics as the world's doctrines, for in a society with such a structure, there are several levels from self to the world. In the particularistic-oriented "differential mode of association," "self" stays in the center while the family is only the smallest in the social circle. After leaving the "family circle," "relative circle" or "kinship network," the important social circles include "neighborhood circle" or "private networking circle." In other words, although Chinese people attach great importance to the consanguineous and familial relations that they were born with,

---

① Fei, X. *Earthbound China* [M]. Beijing: SDX Joint Publishing Company, 1985.

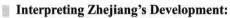

the relationship is not limited to consanguineous or familial relations preordained by people; rather, it can be artificially operated and constructed. "Blood relationship can also be extended to other people who are not actual blood relations through a variety of ways and means of 'operation of relationship'." Therefore, trust built on the relationship with retraction and accommodation will not only point to their families, relatives, and clan members but also to other social members who have a close relationship.[①]

In these particular exchanges and organizations formed on the basis of familial or semi-familial "circles," a "credit card of favor" is created. Such a comprehensive and strong relationship of trust within established (familial and semi-familial) groups reduces the cost of bargaining among group members, while the conscientious belief in the ethical conviction of working for the family greatly reduces the transaction costs of internal management. However, the particularistic differential mode of association is always limited to a certain circle. When people exchange with "outsiders," they have a strong sense of distrust and more bargaining is needed to reach certain kinds of exchanges, so the transaction costs are higher. Therefore, the boundary between self and others under the differential mode of association is between "self" which includes "one's own" and others who are regarded as "outsiders." The self-boundary under the differential mode of association is not used to distinguish between self and others and the society, and thus it cannot become the boundary between "individual self" and "group self" or "social self."[②] In fact, it is a boundary of trust. For this reason, intimacy and alienation, as well as trust and distrust, have become two indivisible features of interpersonal relationships in a differential mode of association. In the words of Liang Shuming, "Lack of group life and reliance on family life

---

① Li, W. & Liang, Y. Special trust and universal trust: Structure and features of Chinese trust [M] // *Trust in Chinese Society*. Beijing: China City Press, 2003: 192.

② Yang, Y. An analysis of interpersonal relationships and their classification—A deliberation with Mr. Huang Guangguo [J]. *Sociological Studies*, 1995(5).

are the two sides of one thing, not two things. ... Why is family especially important for Chinese people? Family is not unique to Chinese people, but if we lack group life in which the relationship between the group and the individual is invisible, then the family relationship will naturally become particularly visible—and it has to be visible. ... As one side loses attention the other will be seen; as one catches attention, the other disappears from the eyes."[①]

With the changes of Chinese society, the connotation, scope and characteristics of the particularistic differential mode of association based on familial and semi-familial relations have all changed. Some sociologists believed that changes were mainly manifested in the following aspects[②]: the center of the differential mode of association has changed; with the industrialization, the acceleration of population mobility and the change of families, most of the social members have been integrated into the professional network system and have gained status, power, interests and personal status and legitimacy from it. With the awareness of "family" still deeply rooted, many Chinese people, therefore, have dependence on a professional network system and "family" at the same time, interests have become a factor that affects the intimacy of interpersonal relations in the differential mode of association. The range of interpersonal relations in the differential modes of association are enlarged, and marriage relationships and fictive kinship relationships emerge as differential modes of association. Human networks composed of differential modes of association have characteristics of being both fixed and flowing. It means that when an individual encounters a special event in his social life, his attachment to his inner group will render his particular needs unmet because the relationship and resources are very limited at any rate. As a result, he will have an inner group (kinship or "circle") as a basis to temporarily form his network

---

① Liang, S. *The Essence of Chinese Culture* [M]. Shanghai: Xuelin Press, 1987: 75.

② Bu, C. Theoretical explanation and modern connotation of "Differential Pattern" [J]. *Sociological Studies*, 2003(1).

of relationships, that is, he will try to seek flowing relationships on the basis of fixed relationships during interpersonal communication. Although the connotation, scope and characteristics of the differential mode of association have changed, the social conditions that fostered the differential mode of association still exist. Therefore, it is still appropriate to apply the "differential mode of association" in explaining the contemporary Chinese society.

4.1.2 Family Culture and Particularistic Trust Pattern in the Region of Zhejiang and Their Revival

Historically, Zhejiang was a region deeply influenced by consanguineous family culture and its extended forms. Just as Qian Hang and Cheng Zai said in *Social Life in Jiangnan during the 17th Century,* eastern Zhejiang had always been an area where lots of strong clans stayed in throughout history. "The 'strength' of a clan is not only reflected in its economic prowess over the other clans in its village and the political power that comes from the aid of the imperial court, it is also manifested in its effective management of the internal order of the clan. These two sides may be uniform on most occasions, and especially in eastern Zhejiang, the unity was already realized in the 17th century and, to a large extent, the degree of unity was higher than those in the other regions."[1] Zhou Xiaohong's research showed that since modern times, due to various factors, there had been a progressive weakening of clan kinship from southern Jiangsu to northern Zhejiang and then to southern Zhejiang. In other words, until 1949, the importance attached to clan kinship in the Wenzhou area was still stronger than that in northern Zhejiang, and especially stronger than that in southern Jiangsu.[2] Although the weakening of blood

---

[1]　Qian, H. & Cheng, Z. *Jiangnan Social Life in the 17th Century* [M]. Hangzhou: Zhejiang People's Publishing House, 1996: 118.

[2]　Zhou, X. *Tradition and Change: The Social Psychology of Peasants in Zhejiang and Jiangsu and Its Evolution since Modern Times* [M]. Beijing: SDX Joint Publishing Company, 1998: 290.

relationships in the rural areas of Jiangsu and Zhejiang has been quite evident since the Western powers entered China in 1840, the degree of laxity of clan blood relatives is highest in southern Jiangsu, second in northern Zhejiang and lowest in southern Zhejiang. For example, in the rural areas of Zhouzhuang in Kunshan of southern Jiangsu, there was basically no public land and no ancestral hall. This phenomenon was already widespread in the mid-19th century. In Zhouzhuang, at least since the mid-19th century, people of the same ethnic group no longer gathered together at the ancestral halls to worship their ancestors, and although family worships were made to all "ancestors following the first ancestor," they were mostly dedicated to the generations of parents and grandparents only. In most parts of southern Jiangsu where Zhouzhuang was located, patriarchs ceased to exist since a long time ago. In some parts of southern Zhejiang, patriarchs still existed in the 1930s and 1940s, though apart from mediating inter-family conflicts or family conflicts, the constraining force that they exert on members of the family have been greatly reduced. ①

The Hangzhou-Jiaxing-Huzhou Plains in northern Zhejiang can be seen as a transitional state between southern Jiangsu and southern Zhejiang. Similar to southern Jiangsu, although clan blood relations in northern Zhejiang continued to exist in modern times, there are also signs of gradual laxity, but the degree of laxity is weaker than that in southern Jiangsu and stronger than that in southern Zhejiang. According to studies conducted by Cao Jinqing, Zhang Letian and Chen Zhongya, villages of "combined families" were spread throughout northern and western Zhejiang in the 1930s and 1940s. The clan organization inside these villages has already been dissolved, with the kinship ties of the clan greatly relaxed, the sense of clan being quite indifferent, and the individualization and independence of the family being completed.

---

① Zhou, X. *Tradition and Change: The Social Psychology of Peasants in Zhejiang and Jiangsu and Its Evolution since Modern Times* [M]. Beijing: SDX Joint Publishing Company, 1998: 130.

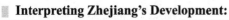

The village has become a settlement of independent families and the geographical relation of the village is higher than its blood ties. Clan activities are mostly limited to big events such as weddings and funerals, while mutual support for family production and living is mostly limited to immediate family members, relatives and their neighbors. According to the local elderly, in the 1930s and 1940s, most clans did not have any genealogies and only a few kept the "genealogy of the rich clans," whose latest revision was done in the period of the late Qing. In Sheng County of Zhejiang Province, before 1949, some clans generally revised their genealogies every 30 years. After the revision, people would brew wine to sacrifice while farewell dramas would be performed in some villages. In 1985, after preliminary visits, there were 520 pedigrees such as Wang and Zhang that remained in the county, of which one was from the Ming Dynasty, 142 from the Qing Dynasty, 197 from the Republic of China and 180 from unknown eras. In addition, in the villages of northern Zhejiang in the 1930s and 1940s, "The vast majority of clans did not have any clan property. Even if a few clans did own clan property, the number could be negligible. The profits from their lands were just enough for one annual joint sacrifice, or each household needed to share the cost of it, or it needed to be funded by people who became rich by doing business." [1] In stark contrast to the laxity of the external organizational form of northern Zhejiang clan culture, until the beginning of land reform in 1949, Hongqiao in Wenzhou of southern Zhejiang still possessed 1,078.41 acres of clan land, which accounted for 13.4% of the total 8,044.51 acres of land in the town, and ancestral shrines could also be seen everywhere. [2] In Tiantai County of Taizhou Prefecture in southeastern Zhejiang, until 1949, even before the reform

---

① Cao, J., Zhang, L. & Cheng, Z. *Social and Cultural Changes of the Villages in Contemporary Northern Zhejiang* [M]. Shanghai: Shanghai Far East Publishers, 2001: 500.

② Zhou, X. *Tradition and Change: The Social Psychology of Peasants in Zhejiang and Jiangsu and Its Evolution since Modern Times* [M]. Beijing: SDX Joint Publishing Company, 1998: 129.

and opening-up, most people in the town lived together with people of the same family name. The same applied to people in the city, such as the Chen family who lived near the east gate, the Jiang family who lived near the brook, the Wang family near the bridge and the Cao family who lived along Housi Street. The countryside was composed of numerous households which constituted natural villages. The vast majority of villages were formed by people from the same clan. There were also cases where large clans that divided themselves and lived in two or more villages, or where more than two clans lived in one village. People living in the village must have ancestral shrines. Shrines could also be either large or small. The county's oldest ancestral shrine was the East Gate Zheshan Chen ancestral shrine; the most ambitious one was that of Yuan who lived in the county. *Chorography of Tiantai County* wrote: "People in Tiantai mostly lived with their clans, imposed emphasis on friendship and were good at staying united," and "they were aggressive and ruthless and often made fighting appointments due to little conflicts." If people in the clan were insulted by people from other clans, then all the clan members would gather and fight with them. Disputes often included territory conflicts or small issues which evolved into big fights. Sometimes because of bullying from the big clans, the small clans would unite and fight back, or the big clans would fight with each other in order to show strength. Clan fighting was mostly caused by minor problems.

After 1949, as in other parts of the country, Zhejiang's economy and society have experienced unprecedented social changes. Social changes will inevitably have a great impact on the family system and culture. Due to the changes in social, economic, political and fertility systems, the living space of traditional families which came into being from the Song Dynasty, marked by genealogies, clan land, rules and patriarchs, has been extruded on an overall level and lost the external organizational appearance, not only in the north of Zhejiang, but also in the areas of central Zhejiang and southern Zhejiang. The land reform confiscated clan land, which served as clan property, and the land was reassigned to farmers. Groups tied together through blood no longer had the power to control their kinsmen. Defeating the leaders (such as patriarchs) who belonged to the landlord class also deprived the former family (clan) of some of their administrative and judicial powers. Cooperation and consequent communalization solved the problem of public land ownership. Ancestral halls became public properties and could be collectively disposed by groups which did not follow the blood tie principle. The People's Commune system attempted to abolish the traditional community and family identity; the implementation of production teams transformed the original clans and settlements into units of production and work under unified state administration. The division between groups broke the principle of internal integration and mutual assistance within the settlement. The exclusion of mutual help in traditional social relations created new social relations.[①] Since the reform and opening-up, urbanization, globalization and the establishment of a modern fertility system as well as the vertical and horizontal flow of population in the context of institutional transition and social transformation have created a new impact on traditional culture which includes family culture.

It needs to be further explained that although the traditional family clan, marked by genealogies, clan land, clan rules and patriarchs, has gradually lost its external appearance in different historical periods since modern times, in many parts of the country, the kinship (the complex of blood and marriage), which constitutes the prerequisite for the existence of the family culture, has not been fundamentally shaken throughout its history, whether be it in northern, central, or southern Zhejiang. The tradition of living in groups, which constitutes the objective condition for family continuity, has not been totally damaged, therefore, the family as a social group has never been destroyed. The concepts of family and the remnants of family consciousness thus have

---

① Wang, M. & Wang, S. *Order, Justice and Authority in Rural Society* [M]. Beijing: China University of Political Science & Law Press, 1997: 71.

the possibility of becoming reality. In the 1930s and 1940s, kinship and geographical relations were still familiar to the villagers and were made use of. The original interpersonal relationships established by marriage, childbirth and living in groups were still the foundation of social relations of villagers. All kinds of family needs that can be met by non-single families can only be met through the familial or semi-familial networks. All villagers are living in a relation network interwoven by kinship and geographical relations. In addition, friendship in northern Zhejiang in the 1930s and 1940s also demonstrated its importance.[①]

After 1949, not only the organizational appearance of the family culture but also the family concept and family consciousness, were criticized and suppressed as feudalism to some extent in northern, central and southern Zhejiang. However, it is interesting to note that following the reform and opening-up, people observed that, as in many other parts of the country, although some of the external organizational forms of family culture (such as clan lands) have not regrown in Zhejiang, the family concept and family consciousness have been revived to a large extent.

According to a survey conducted by Xu Jialiang in the South Village of Sancan Street, Cixi City, Zhejiang Province in the late 1980s, although the traditional family structure of Sancun Street South Village in Cixi has been damaged and differentiated to some extent since modern times, even with its authority in the village society weakened, the network of relationships still enveloped the village society. The network of relationships refers to family, affinity, cousinship. The chain formed by the network of relationships in village society cannot be broken or removed, thus creating a situation where the development of family structure and family authority has to coexist with other relations.

---

① Cao, J., Zhang, L. & Cheng, Z. *Social and Cultural Changes of the Villages in Contemporary Northern Zhejiang* [M]. Shanghai: Shanghai Far East Publishers, 2001: 508.

Although the village party branches, village committees and other organizations have become veritable authoritative centers that handle all the public affairs of the village community, they are still heavily constrained by the network of relationships.① According to Ren Xiao's investigation into Xiaoyi Village, Xiangshan County, Zhejiang Province in the late 1980s, Xiaoyi's family concept was stronger in the old society and gradually weakened. However, the custom of family culture still remains. Where there is a marriage relationship or a succession relationship, the contacts are very close. Not only do they visit one another at major events such as marriages, funerals and building construction works but also during "monthly and seasonal festivals". "Relatives help relatives" and "neighbors help neighbors" have become social norms. The more relatives there are in the neighborhood, the more the power one holds and the easier it will be to do things. Therefore, there has been a tendency toward marriage within villages to prevent from being infringed by others in recent years.② From the South Village of Sanzao Street and Xiaoyi Village, we can look into the village community in eastern and northern Zhejiang, or we can also say that the South Village of Sanzao Street and Xiaoyi Village are to some extent the epitome of a rural community in northern and eastern Zhejiang, which bears a certain degree of representation.

In Wenzhou, southern Zhejiang, the revival of the awareness of clan culture has even affected all aspects of social life. In some parts of Wenzhou, including Yueqing, there have been incidents where clans would disrupt the general election of towns and villages by pulling votes through force or tearing up votes. With the revival of clan consciousness, rebuilding temples, ancestral shrines and graves, rewriting genealogies, observing Feng Shui, sacrificing ancestors and

---

① Wang, H. *Village Family Culture in Modern China* [M]. Shanghai: Shanghai People's Publishing House, 1991: 354.
② Wang, H. *Village Family Culture in Modern China* [M]. Shanghai: Shanghai People's Publishing House, 1991: Addendum: Case 4 Xiaoyi Village in Zhejiang.

worshipping gods have become a trend in places like Yueqing and Yongjia. In Hongqiao, not only were the temples which were destroyed in the early liberation or "Cultural Revolution" period mostly restored, but new temples and even several Christian churches were also built in many of the villages. There were several shrines that were rebuilt in Hongqiao as well. In Yongjia where the trend is more widespread, Huangtian Township rebuilt 33 ancestral temples in 1989. There are more than 1,000 ancestral shrines in the southern part of Cangnan County. Among 25 surnames in three townships and eight administrative villages, 68% have ancestral shrines. The revision of genealogies has also become popular in Taizhou, Jinhua, Wenzhou, Shaoxing and even Zhejiang as a whole. In Qiaotou Town of Yongjia, in the four years from 1980 to 1983, 17 big families including the Ye have reprinted 53 genealogies.[①] In Hantian Village of Rui'an, Wenzhou, families such as the Han, Chen, and Cao have resumed their revision of genealogies after 1978. The other 33 families rebuilt their genealogies at the present village or the original village where they emigrated from.[②] In addition, after 1978, activities of worshipping ancestors and sweeping the tombs of ancestors in many places in Zhejiang were also changed from underground to open, and as the economic strength of households increased, the units of offering sacrifices began to expand from family to clan with higher expenses and larger scale.

There are many reasons for the revival of family culture in Zhejiang since the reform and opening-up. The important points are as follows: First of all, since 1949, as in other parts of the country, there have been a series of radical social movements in rural Zhejiang that forcibly cut off and downplayed the identity of people with the same surnames in the

---

① Zhou, X. *Tradition and Change: The Social Psychology of Peasants in Zhejiang and Jiangsu and Its Evolution since Modern Times* [M]. Beijing: SDX Joint Publishing Company, 1998: 291.
② Zhou, Z., Lin, S. & Chen, D. *Social Studies on Zhejiang's Clan Villages* [M]. Beijing: Local Records Publishing House, 2001: 266.

countryside and made a series of real changes in the actual interpersonal structure. On the other hand, however, this compulsory behavior cannot truly abolish the deep caring in the rural cultural tradition about the history of one's own and one's own blood community.[①] In fact, the measures taken by the government since 1949 were merely "to suppress the development of clan activities in rural areas for a certain period of time," but "the deep foundation of the patriarchal system in social structure and social consciousness has not been touched on enough. Therefore, although the effects of the clan and clan systems have nearly vanished in nearly three decades, their roots in the countryside, in fact, still exist and have long been running in a hidden way."[②] This is because "The base for a clan to survive is related to people's living conditions, relatives in daily life, psychological habits formed from tradition, as well as religious needs."[③] Clan organizations, family awareness and family activities in rural areas are surely manifested in areas such as family rituals like worshipping ancestors, genealogies, ancestral halls, symbolic symbols of the family and institutional norms, but more importantly, they are living things that flow, emerge and infiltrate farmers' daily life practices, thereby bringing themselves a long-lasting life in the cultural sense. For this reason, since the reform and opening-up, when the state relaxed the external coercion, the more family-conscious Zhejiang, especially the farmers in southern Zhejiang immediately started to rebuild the kinship community in various ways.

Second, apart from the relaxation of external coercion, the household responsibility system since the reform and opening-up

---

① Qian, H. The reconstruction and reconstruction environment of the contemporary patriarchal clan in China [J]. *Chinese Social Sciences Quarterly (Hongkong)*, 1994(1).

② Qian, H. & Xie, W. Clan problem: A perspective of contemporary rural studies [J]. *Social Sciences*, 1990(5).

③ Qian, H. Several issues concerning religious studies on contemporary rural China [J]. *Academic Monthly*, 1993(3).

has obviously also played an extremely important and stimulating role in the reproduction of the family system and family culture. To a certain extent, the household responsibility system rests on the power of family kinship. It restores and even reinforces the significance of clans and especially families as basic units of production and consumption, and this is precisely the important economic basis for the restoration of particularistic family culture. At the same time, the shift from production brigades and groups as the unit of production to families as the unit of production after the dissolution of the People's Commune led to the weakening of the grassroots political power in the countryside to a certain degree. The new administrative system of townships, administrative villages, natural villages and villager groups does not actually play a strong socio-economic role. "They are not a system of joint production but only a symbol of social control and state power. The real socialization of economic processes is done by the traditional family system and community identity. In other words, modernization has not had a destructive effect on the traditional network of family relatives, affinities and neighbors, but rather has facilitated the process of this series of informal local institutions to resume their original functions."[1] In this context, the traditional family kinship network began to emerge and, in a certain sense, replaced some of the functions previously undertaken by the rural grassroots political power.

Moreover, in Zhejiang, especially in southern Zhejiang, the highly intense conflict between population and land, combined with the high risk and uncertainty of the development of individual and private businesses after 1978, have undoubtedly imposed great pressure of survival on farmers. This pressure, on one hand, cultivates their

---

[1]　Wang, M. Tradition and modernization of Chinese folks–A case study of the Tangdong Village in Fujiang [M]//Jia, D. & Zhou, X. *Farmers in Modernization*. Nanjing: Nanjing University Press, 1998: 314.

independent and innovative spirit as well as willingness to earn an independent living, but creates a sense of isolation, helplessness, uneasiness, and anxiety of losing control on the other hand. Therefore, they "usually resort to the creative application of traditional wisdom and the reinforced utility of the remaining network of relationships,"[1] hoping to rely on their familiar old traditions to combat with the new impact from the social life. In Zhejiang, especially in southern Zhejiang, a large number of non-agricultural economic activities characterized by decentralized operations (such as individual transport, commerce, processing and sideline businesses) have emerged since the reform and opening-up. Coupled with the weak local collective economy, not only did the self-employed need to find blood groups such as clans as the basis to solve various problems in production and operation, but also the charity projects in rural communities often cannot help but rely on blood groups and clans as back up.[2]

Of course, although the family culture has revived to a certain extent since the reform and opening-up, its concrete cultural form has also transformed with the economic and social changes in Zhejiang since then. On one hand, in contemporary society, some aspects of family culture have been weakened, and their influence diminished. On the other hand, family relations and family culture have developed in a new direction. According to Wang Xiaoyi and Zhu Chengbao's survey in Cangnan County, Wenzhou, there are two main directions for the change of contemporary family culture. First, the sense of collectivity of the family is reduced. Family interests are given more attention with the differentiation of interests within the blood group. Second, the interaction between families increases and the social interaction

① Yang, S. Politics of families and selection, orientation and replacement of village-level political elite [J]. *Sociological Studies*, 2000(3).

② Zhou, X. *Tradition and Change: The Social Psychology of Peasants in Zhejiang and Jiangsu and Its Evolution since Modern Times* [M]. Beijing: SDX Joint Publishing Company, 1998: 322.

becomes frequent. Contemporary family culture demonstrates more complexity and diversity.[1]

The revival of family cultural psychology means that the contemporary Zhejiang people's trust pattern is particularistic. This also means that in the interpersonal communication, the closer to the blood relationship of the family, the more likely the center of the "self" is to be trusted and accepted by a considerable number of contemporary Zhejiang people and the easier it is to form a cooperative and intimate relationship. The further from the center of "self," the more they are easily excluded from them and the more likely for others to have psychological distrust. Since the reform and opening-up, with the transformation of the economic system and social transition, the influence of the universalistic trust model based on the "contract principle" is undoubtedly increasing. However, for a considerable number of Zhejiang people, particularism based on the "blood relationship" is still the dominant mode of trust. For example, a survey conducted by Chen Dongsheng on Hantian Village in Rui'an, Wenzhou in 2000 showed that when answering the question "What kind of relationship do you trust, kinship or contract?", of the 114 household samples, 61% chose "kinship," while "contract" accounted for 39%.[2] This shows that in the opinion of most villagers in Hantian village, the particularistic familial and semi-familial trust are higher in status than the contractual trust. The economy of Hantian village is rather well developed. In 1982, at the beginning of the reform and opening-up, most villagers have been engaged in the production of automobile and motorcycle parts. They have been involved in commodity economy activities rather early and have a strong sense of market economy and the modern times. Therefore, it can be said that the responses of

---

① Wang, X. & Zhu, C. *Nonstate Enterprises and Family Economy in Rural China* [M]. Taiyuan: Shanxi Economic Publishing House, 1996: 156.
② Chen, D. The influence of family culture on auto spare parts industry in the Hantian Village [J]. *Wenzhou Forum*, 2000(4).

villagers in Hantian Village are very representative in Wenzhou and even in Zhejiang.

4.2 Trust Pattern, Network of Relationships and Economic and Social Behaviors in Contemporary Zhejiang

Robert D. Putnam believed that a society which relied on generalized reciprocity was more efficient than a distrustful society, for the same reason that money was more efficient than barter. Trust lubricates social life. He also thought that stocks of social capital, such as trust, norms and networks, tended to be self-reinforcing and cumulative. Networks of civic engagement foster sturdy norms of generalized reciprocity and encourage the emergence of social trust. Such networks facilitate coordination and communication, amplify reputations, and thus allow dilemmas of collective action to be resolved. When economic and political negotiation is embedded in dense networks of social interaction, incentives for opportunism are reduced. Successful collaboration in one endeavor builds connections and trust—social assets that facilitate future collaboration in other, unrelated tasks.[1] Georg Simmel observed that trust came from a combination of knowledge and ignorance. Trust exaggerated information of the past psychologically and accomplishes a transcendence to define future and facilitate choice and action. Niklas Luhmann also pointed out, "Trust reduced social complexity by going beyond available information and generalizing expectations of behavior.[2] "The clues employed to form trust do not eliminate the risk, they simply make it less. They simply serve as a springboard for the leap into uncertainty."[3] Trust reinforces the existing ability to understand and simplify complexity,

---

① Zhang, W. Social capital: theoretical argument and empirical study [J]. *Sociological Studies*, 2003(4).
② Luhmann, N. *Trust and Power* [M]. Chichester: John Wiley & Sons, 1979: 93.
③ Ibid.

as well as the current situation which corresponds to the complex future. Trust increases the tolerance for uncertainty, adding the courage and possibility of action. That is why trust is one of the major tools to build social order. "Trust is able to perform this function because it can boost the certainty of a person's behavior. The increase in the certainty of behavior is accomplished by the role of trust in customary and reciprocal cooperation."[1] This is why trust, norms and network are commonly seen as the key factors of social capital that underpin economic relations and social process. Basically, trust is a common understanding of exchange rules, namely, actors hold expectations and follow the principle of "trust" when lacking in complete information and legal guarantee. Trust from an economic standpoint depends on the assumption of norms and forms through customary exchange.

As stated earlier, traditional trust of Chinese people (including Zhejiang people) "rests upon purely personal, familial, or semi-familial relationships," as well as a particularistic trust formed and sustained through based on bonds of family and clan in the community by blood. Nevertheless, this particularistic trust pattern resembles the universalist pattern, as they both increase certainty and reduce opportunist behaviors in networks of social interaction. Zhang Qizai argued that kinship and extended kinships like the relationship of friends, teachers and students, neighbors and acquaintances were "different from general social relations, but a form of social capital, and social relations that were multi-linear and lasting. The rights, responsibilities and obligations of both sides were determined not by laws or rules and clearly stated regulations, as well as mutual trust was not guaranteed by law, but by customs or traditions.[2]" This particularistic trust pattern established and guaranteed by customs or traditions and "rests upon purely personal,

---

① Zheng, Y. *Trust Theory* [M]. Beijing: China Radio and Television Publishing House, 2001: 73.
② Zhang, Q. *Social Capital Theory: Social Capital and Economic Growth* [M]. Beijing: Social Sciences Academic Press, 1997: 73.

familial, or semi-familial relationships" no doubt has a special economic social function which is deeply embodied in the economic activities and social behavior pattern of Zhejiang since the reform and opening-up.

4.2.1 Particularistic Trust, Network of Relationships and Performance of Regional Responsibility System in Agriculture

In accordance with the national reform which began with the introduction of the system of household contract responsibility in rural areas, Zhejiang's economic development also started out with agriculture. Against the macro-background of comprehensive national rural reform, in the spring of 1983, 94.7% of the production teams in Zhejiang Province implemented the household responsibility system. The transformation from the production team system with group as a unit to the household responsibility system with household as a unit had undeniably and tremendously improved the farmers' enthusiasm as well as facilitated comprehensive and rapid growth of Zhejiang Province. The agricultural output increased from 8.584 billion yuan in 1978 to 12.522 billion yuan in 1984 (before the reform), increasing by 45.9% (at the constant prices of 1980); the grain production achieved a breakthrough growth, with a 23.9% rise in total output from 14.672 million to 18.1715 million metric tons, setting a new record; and the average income of rural households experienced a 1.71 times increase from 265 yuan to 446.37 yuan.[①]

Why is the system of household contract responsibility able to increase efficiency rapidly? Lardy believed that the policy mandated of grain self-sufficiency in the period of the "Great Leap Forward" Movement had left local governments no choice; so they made collectives of production grow grain in lands with climate and

---

① CPC Zhejiang Provincial Party History Lab & Contemporary Zhejiang Institute. *Brief History of Contemporary Zhejiang 1949—1998* [M]. Beijing: Contemporary China Publishing House, 2000: 326.

soil conditions more suitable for growing other crops. Before the agricultural reform, there was no relaxation of this policy. The adoption of the policy and relaxation afterward directly correspond to the fall and growth of the possibility to utilize comparative advantage. Based on the above analysis, Lardy proposes a hypothesis: this change of policy leads to a remarkable change in agricultural productivity. Putterman, Dong, Dow and other scholars hold similar views.[①] Lin Yifu interpreted from another angle. He believed, under the system of People's Commune and production team, the sharp decline of efficiency in agriculture production was because the effort and remuneration are not closely connected. The income expectancy of each member of the production team is determined by his or her effort and the total output of the whole team. Due to the high cost of supervision of each member's labor and measurement of its input and output, the accordance of effort and remuneration cannot be reached. When effective stimulus and supervision are not in place, members of the production team with economic rationality must have the tendency to "take a free ride," which determines that the institutional arrangement of production team is of low efficiency. However, "Under the household responsibility system, the difficulty of supervision is generally surmounted. By definition, household system ensures full supervision, because a laborer knows exactly how much labor is contributed with zero supervision fees because it is not necessary to spend resources on measuring labor. The result shows that a laborer has the highest level of incentive under the household responsibility system, because he can not only reap all of the marginal return that he gained through effort, but also save on supervision fees."[②] Lardy and Lin Yifu's explanations are no doubt fully substantiated and reasonable. Their analysis mainly looks from a policy and economic perspective, however, a more complete answer

① Lin, Y. *Second Discussion on System, Technology and Agricultural Development in China* [M]. Beijing: Peking University Press, 2000: 235.
② Lin, Y. *System, Technology and Agricultural Development in China* [M]. Shanghai: SDX Joint Publishing Company, 1994: 55.

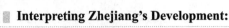
to these questions shall resort to the angle of cultural sociology and economic anthropology.

An important reason for the sharp growth of agricultural production in Zhejiang after the reform is that the contract responsibility system takes the household as a unit, which implies that it can effectively use the power of traditional family relations with the goal of generating economic profit to utilize traditional trust resource. As previously mentioned, according to Fei Xiaotong's theory of "differentiated mode of association," traditional interpersonal relationship, with its succession determined by consanguinity, is a three-dimensional network of relationships with relationship of the father and son as the vertical axis and that of brothers as the horizontal axis, along with all acquaintances included with different ties between one another. Among different links of this network, there are differences in distance, as well as the level of trust. During the time of People's Commune, like other parts of China, traditional communities and family identity in Zhejiang were abolished, because units of production and work were changed into "production teams and groups," which largely broke the principles of integration and mutual assistance within settlements based on consanguinity. Under the system of "production teams and groups," farmers communicated as neighbors, friends and partners of production, while family consanguineous relationship was repressed. However, "family life is the primary social life for Chinese people, while ties of relatives, neighbors and friends are the second."[①] According to the theory of "differentiated mode of association," the ties of neighbors, friends, partners of production and blood relationship vary in the level of trust in particularistic culture. Wang Feixue and Shan An used

---

① Lu, Z. *The construction of China and personnel training* [M]// Liang, S. *The Essence of Chinese Culture*. Shanghai: Xuelin Press, 1987: 12.

a questionnaire on special trust to conduct their survey[①]: "To what extent do you trust the following types of people?" The answers to this question show that in the context of particularistic culture, people mainly trusted family members with consanguineous and familial ties and various types of relatives; among which family members received the highest level of trust. Although close friends without blood and familial ties were included in the group of "relatively trustworthy," others like colleagues, neighbors and acquaintances were in the range of "difficult to determine" and "can be trusted." People without stable social relationships had the lowest level of trust. According to the level of trust, subjects could be classified into three types, namely, relatively trustworthy, difficult to determine whether to trust and cannot be trusted.

Under the system of People's Commune, since farmers communicated more frequently as neighbors, friends, and partners of production, there was clearly the problem of "lack of trust" in comparison with family and blood relations. If people lack trust in exchange activities, many resources will be spent on measurement and supervision to prevent being deceived. But the feature of agricultural production determined the high cost of effective supervision. Therefore, the problem of "lack of trust" was obviously a vital reason for the low efficiency of agricultural production in the People's Commune System.

In contrast, the household contract responsibility system is supported by family and blood relations, but in particularistic trust sequence, or in "differentiated pattern," family is in the nearest place to "self" in the sequence of "self, family, country, and world." Therefore, the highest level of trust is undoubtedly based on family and kinship. "Self" itself is not an individual, or person, but a social

---

① Li, W. & Liang, Y. Special trust and universal trust: Structure and features of Chinese trust [A] // *Trust in Chinese Society* [M]. Beijing: China City Press, 2003: 195-196.

individual subordinate to family and bound by "family and blood." "This 'self' is different from Western 'self', and can be well described as 'family oriented self', with a relative boundary present between people inside and outside the groups."[①] Therefore, the differential mode of "association centers on self," is in fact centered on familial and consanguineous relationships, so interpersonal relationships based on this are exclusive. In interpersonal communication, ties close to the center of "self" in familial and blood relations are generally easier for people to accept and form cooperative, intimate and trustful relations with one another.

For this reason, during the first half of 1982, all places in Zhejiang that had implemented the household contract responsibility system enjoyed increases in the yield of grain, both in spring-harvested grain and early-season rice. Senior officials and people generally gave feedback mentioning that "the contract household system was much better than the production team and groups system"[②]. Undeniably, it was a fairly objective judgment.

Peter Blau believed that particularistic values were characteristic attributed that distinguish collectivities, and simultaneously by uniting the members of each in social solidarity they created segregating boundaries between collectivities. "Particularistic values create integrative bonds of social solidarity in substructures but simultaneously segregating boundaries between them in the wider social structure.[③]" "Substructure," or "circle" as referred earlier, divided a society into many "substructures" or "circles" by particularism. "This raises the

---

① Bu, C. Theoretical explanation and modern connotation of "Differential Pattern" [J]. *Sociological Studies*, 2003(1).

② CPC Zhejiang Provincial Party History Lab & Contemporary Zhejiang Institute. *Brief History of Contemporary Zhejiang 1949—1998* [M]. Beijing: Contemporary China Publishing House, 2000: 325.

③ Blau, P. *Exchange and Power in Social Life* [M]. Trans. Sun, F. & Zhang, L. Beijing: Huaxia Publishing House, 1987: 308.

question of the compass of particularistic standards—how inclusive the scope of their unifying force is. As a matter of fact, the particularistic standards in a social structure often become universalistic standards in its substructures. On the contrary, universalistic value in certain social structures may be changed into the foundation for the tendency of particularism."① This is to say, "substructure" or "circle" varies in size but are related. According to Peter Blau's analytical framework, compared to production and communication activities with "production team" as a unit, "production group" is obviously a "substructure" or "circle" which is easier to establish intimate or relative kinship relations, and therefore leads to a higher degree of trust between people. However, compared to production and communication activities in groups, family business activities with the family, another "substructure" or "circle" based on blood ties as the unit, has a higher level of trust with one other. Interpersonal relationship built through "relativeness" or kinship is in fact guaranteed by trust. In family economy, there exists what János Kornai referred to as protective "paternalism." Family resource allocation is not dependent on supply-demand relationship, legal system or administrative orders, but on the role of non-economic factors such as blood and marital ties, as well as ethics. Among them factors like family ethics, kinship and relationship are decisive. Every person was a fixed position in the networks of relationships of family and kinship in family life. "The basic pattern of behavior is mutual dependence. That is to say, in kinship relationships, he is dependent upon other human beings as much as others are dependent upon him, and he is therefore fully aware of his obligation to make repayment, however much delayed, to his benefactors."② "Reciprocity" from this view has as much significance in the allocation of resource in family economy as "pursuit

---

① Ibid.
② Hsu, F. L. K. *Clan, Caste and Club* [M]. Trans. Xue, G. Beijing: Huaxia Publishing House, 1990: 277.

of profit" in that of the market.[①] Different interest bodies are competing and seeking self interest in the market, while in family economy, family members compete against outsiders, and adopt altruistic principles to pursue mutual and common benefit. Therefore, a "protective" network of mutual trust and benefit is formed among family members and even among other relatives.[②] In exchanges and organizations of families based on special blood relations, members have full and strong trust. With this exchange cost of economic operation, acts of "taking a free ride" within the organization can be effectively reduced, as can resources of measurement and supervision and cost of bargaining and arguments. Though it is not the only reason for the high production efficiency of the household contract responsibility system, nevertheless, it is definitely an important factor.

4.2.2　Particularistic Trust, Network of Relationships and Regional Social and Economic Activities

Since the reform and opening-up, the contents of Zhejiang economic pattern can be summarized as marketization + diversified investment (mainly private economy) + professional and characteristic industrial region.[③] This pattern is able to proceed and sustain because of its utilization of interpersonal familial and semi-familial relationships in which particularistic trust notions serve as the lubricator.

Zhejiang's scope of resource allocation gradually shifted from reliance on the provincial market, to the national market, and into the

---

① Li, P. *Transformation of China's Social Structure—A Sociological Analysis of the Economic System Reform* [M]. Harbin: Heilongjiang People's Publishing House, 1995: 90.

② Zhang, J. *Informal Institutions in the Process of Marketization* [M]. Beijing: Cultural Relics Press, 1999: 79.

③ Yan, C. Zhejiang private economy development and characteristic industrial region [M] // *On Zhejiang*. Hangzhou: Zhejiang People's Publishing House, 2003: 238.

great international market since the reform and opening-up. In other words, the "great market" in Zhejiang pattern not only refers to the numerous professional markets within the province, but also includes national and even international economic exchange networks. There is a saying in folk society: "Where there are Zhejiang people, there is a market; where there is a market, there are Zhejiang people." So how does the great market tie together with Zhejiang people?

Research on the social network has begun to attract the attention of Chinese scholars in recent years. As a microscopic research, the analytical framework of social networks inclines to the relational pattern that connects members together. Network analysis explores the deep structure—the fixed network pattern hidden under the complex surface of the social system, and applies this description to understand how network structure limits social behaviors and social changes. Viewing from this analytical framework, we can find there is an important phenomenon in the ways and directions of business that migrant Zhejiang people engaged in, namely, population concentrations of Zhejiang or certain regions of Zhejiang that frequently exist in certain large- or medium-sized cities, communities or industries, therefore forming large numbers of "Zhejiang Villages" and "Zhejiang Streets" at home and even abroad. "Zhejiang Village" is not a natural village, nor an administrative unit, but a term by convention that is beyond the administration and natural villages to address the concentrations of Zhejiang migrant workers who have left their hometowns and are living in Beijing. "Zhejiang Villages" across China are like a special loose group blended by familial and geographical networks and production and market networks, or a "migrant workers' town" taking shape.

The "Zhejiang Village" in Beijing has been the focal economic social phenomenon over the past decade. "Zhejiang Villages" and "Zhejiang Streets" are distributed in Chaoyang, Haidian and Fengtai Districts of Beijing. The Zhejiang people's "community" is the largest in Nanyuan Township of Fengtai District. Though the local government massively evicted migrant workers several times in name of "combat illegal business" and "Clean up the city for the Asian Games," more and more migrant workers have been coming to the villages. According to Zhou Xiaohong's survey, the area of "Zhejiang Village" in Fengtai District by 1995 has expanded to cover five townships and 24 natural villages, including Dahongmen and Nanyuan, and extending to places like Shawo, Xiju, Dajiaoting, and East Gate of Jinsong. Among the 100,000-plus migrant workers who live in "Zhejiang Villages," 75% of them are from Yueqing (of which 40%–50% are from the original Hongqiao District); some others are from Wenzhou and Taizhou (Yongjia, Rui'an and Wenling, etc.), and few come from Hubei, Sichuan, Anhui and Jiangsu Provinces. In the 1990s, Chinese medium- and large-sized cities had settlements of migrant workers from places called "X Village", respectively, for example, "Henan Village" in Nanjing with farmers from Gushi of Henan Province as the majority, where people moke a living by purchasing, collecting, processing and selling waste plastic, as well as "Xiaoshoudao Apartment" constructed by the government. However, settlements of migrant workers with a long history, large-scale and internal systems like "Zhejiang Village" are rare.[①] This "quasi-community phenomenon" with its own geographical boundaries and clear division of living and production zones can be found both inside and outside Zhejiang Province. "In this regard, taking Hangzhou as an example, Wenzhou people are the majority in the business of North Hangzhou Trade Mart, formerly just a place for doing leather business. They also built the Sijiqing Clothing Wholesale Center in Hangzhou. Xinchang people outnumber people of other places in the tea market. In the market of pearl and pearl manufactured goods,

---

① Zhou, X. *Traditions and Developments: Social Psychology of Jiangsu and Zhejiang Farmers and Its Development since Modern Times* [M]. Beijing: SDX Joint Publishing Company, 1998: 261.

Zhuji accent is the most common."[1] This indicates that the villagers of 'Zhejiang Villages' across the country are not scattered in the city, but concentrated in 'quasi-communities' that associate with the local residents but distinguish from them in ways of production and living. In these "quasi-communities," villagers have a relatively great sense of co-existence, belonging and self-identity.

Some scholars surveyed and analyzed this phenomenon. In sociological academia, Song Min and Xiang Biao have conducted panoramic reports on "Zhejiang Village" in the earlier periods. Afterward, Wang Hansheng and Xiang Biao and their students surveyed in-depth and left volumes of works and materials with theoretical and practical value. Then Zhou Xiaohong conducted household surveys, collected perceptual materials and interpreted the phenomenon from a creative sociological perspective in *Traditions and Developments: Social Psychology of Jiangsu and Zhejiang Farmers and Its Development since Modern Times*. There are multiple reasons for the phenomenon of Zhejiang Villages and Streets, and one of the key reasons is that the source of information of Zhejiang migrant worker's business is often their familial and quasi-familial groups. This is to say, the direction and distribution of migrant businessmen are limited by their network of relationships. An individual has a number of choices in the face of so many business opportunities: Where should he/she go? His/her choice of place is connected to people who have social relationship with him/her and do business there. Those people will offer information and try their best to give all types of help to him/her. For instance, a comparison and survey between "Zhejiang Village" in Beijing and "Wenzhou Town" in Paris showed[2] that the information of migrant businessmen

---

①   Zheng, Y., Yuan, Y. & Lin, C. *Interpretation of the "Great Market Province": Study on the Phenomenon of Zhejiang's Professional Market* [M]. Hangzhou: Zhejiang University Press, 2003: 98.

②   Wang, C. Social networks in motion: Wenzhou people's behavior patterns in Paris and Beijing [J]. *Sociological Studies*, 2000(3).

in the two places was often provided by their relatives, fellow villagers and friends. Wenzhou people (also other Zhejiang people) working and doing business in cities share one thing in common: In the beginning, without a definite destination, few people find a place to make money and then write a letter (then give a call thereafter) or send someone home to bring relatives, friends and neighbors, otherwise they would send home some money and the information attracts acquaintances. That is basically how "Zhejiang Village" in Beijing, "Wenzhou Town" in Paris and other Zhejiang migrant business settlements were formed. One helps others in this course, meaning when a person finds a market opportunity, his or her relatives, friends and fellow villagers will follow suit so as to grow the business. In the process of aggregation, social network and particularistic trust are the media to transmit information of movement and also its mechanisms.

Mark Granovetter indicated that economic behavior was embedded in social relations which were different in every society. Different social relations lead to varying economic behavioral patterns. In a particularistic society, people pay more attention to existing relations and prefer to associate with people who have a particular relationship with them, and hence enhance their ties. So, this tendency solidifies pre-existing relations and improves trust between members in the network of relationships. According to Peter Blau, particularism is the "media of solidarity and integration," but the media are limited between people with a particular relationship. The consequence of this process of dealing with interpersonal relations is categorized into two groups: Those with special ties and one of them that can be trusted; and those without a special relationship, whom particularistic actors often find are hard to trust.

Zhejiang people's information on business of migrant workers comes from familial, geographical and semi-familial relationships (relationships replicated or extended from familial relationships, for example, relationships between neighbors, friends, classmates, fellow soldiers, etc.) largely because these relationships have a high level of trust. Zhai Xuewei's research on Relationship Strength and Job Strategy of Migrant Workers showed,[①] in the cultural context of particularism or "differential mode of association", that trust did not refer to the authenticity of information transfer. It is possible that people with familial and semi-familial relationships give false information in real life; however, the receiver believes that it is true because of their ties, while he or she see the information given by people without familial ties as false. The reason is that the former is a strong tie, while the latter is a weak tie. Conspicuously, this view can be applied in the analysis of "Zhejiang Village" and "Zhejiang Streets" at home and even abroad.

Kinship and quasi-kinship (neighbors, classmates and friends) social networks offer information to Zhejiang migrant workers and build a chain of population movement. Wang Chunguang's study on Wenzhou people in Paris shows that social networks not only provide communication and transmission of information between Wenzhou and France but also set up a chain of population movement. "Every year some Wenzhou people would enter Paris with the help of this chain of migration. Nevertheless, this is not a novelty, but an existing practice, as where there are immigrants, there are social networks to underpin them. This phenomenon has already existed among Wenzhou people coming to Paris in the earlier periods."[②] Looking at Wang Chunguang's study, most Wenzhou people in Paris at present have immigrated to France since the 1980s; however, only a few applied to enter France for the purpose of family reunion, while most people failed to meet the requirements of legal immigration, so they were smuggled into the country in a process in which the social network of relationships plays the following roles: First, people from places with more overseas social

---

① Zhai, X. Social mobility and relationship trust—Relationship strength and job searching strategies of migrant workers [J]. *Sociological Studies*, 2003(1).
② Wang, C. *Wenzhou People in Paris—The Social Construction of an Immigrant Group* [M]. Nanchang: Jiangxi People's Publishing House, 2000: 63.

relations in China are more likely to migrate abroad, and if they cannot do so via legal channels, they will consider illegal immigration. These people think that they are able to survive there with the social networks as long as they steal into that country. Wenzhou people who are engaged in human smuggling are not distributed evenly. They are mainly from hometowns of overseas Chinese or neighboring places, such as Li'ao Town of Rui'an, Qidu Town of Yongjia County and Shankou Township of Qingtian. Second, the social networks determine the destinations of smuggling. The more social relationships one has and the more reliable and close these ties are in a country, the more likely he or she would steal into that country. For example, overseas Chinese of Li'an Town of Rui'an, Wenzhou mainly live in France and Italy, which then become the main destinations of stowaways from the town thereafter. Since most overseas Chinese of Qidu Town of Yongjia County are in the United States, more stowaways from this town would go to the United States. At last, the social network of relationships is the only path for stowaways to reach illegal immigration brokers. Without social relationships, one does not know where brokers are, how to negotiate the terms, and even reach some verbal agreement and promise to fulfill requirements and commitments in the agreement. "Of course, unless relatives and friends are reluctant to help people at home to smuggle, otherwise relationships such as relatives and friends are the main sources of reliance."[①]

Between "Zhejiang Villages" and "Zhejiang Streets" within Zhejiang and those across the nation, there are chains of population movement established by kinship and quasi-kinship social networks like those between Wenzhou and France as well. According to scholars such as Wang Hansheng and Liu Shiding, "Zhejiang workers and businessmen's migration for operation purposes often rest upon small communities based on traditional interpersonal networks, which

---

① Wang, C. *Wenzhou People in Paris—The Social Construction of an Immigrant Group* [M]. Nanchang: Jiangxi People's Publishing House, 2000: 66-67.

guarantee safety, reduce psychological cost of flow and help each other in life. At the same time, there is a need of coordination and division in production and business operation. This phenomenon had already appeared in small scale flows of the earlier stages."[1] Wang Hansheng, Liu Shiding's survey on Zhejiang Villages in Beijing showed that the social network of relationships built the base of common movement and the path and network of continuous movement between Zhejiang and Beijing. Common movement means the population simultaneously and coordinately moves to a destination, and continuous movement refers to the population successively moving to a destination. Both are dependent on networks of interpersonal relationships and can be seen as two forms of movement in the Zhejiang–Beijing network of relationships. Wang Hansheng and Liu Shiding stated, "The continuous movement based on rural interpersonal relationships came from the need of operators who had come to Beijing first, as they requires more labor force to expand production scale, while workers hired through the network of relationships were easy to manage with low cost of organization." After workers in Beijing learned the methods of business, they start their own and bring their family to Beijing to form new businesses and commercial households. This is a common phenomenon in "Zhejiang Villages."[2]

In addition, the survival, development and integration of migrant Zhejiang people since the reform and opening-up largely depend on kinship and kinship-like social network of relationships and trust on this basis. Graves believed that in the case of migrants, "In coping with the world around him, each individual had a variety of alternative

---

① Wang, H., Liu, S., Xiang, B. et al. "Zhejiang Village" of Beijing: A unique way Chinese farmers enter cities [M] // Jia, D. et al. *Peasants in the Process of Modernization*. Nanjing: Nanjing University Press, 1998: 313.

② Wang, H., Liu, S., Xiang, B. et al. "Zhejiang Village" of Beijing: A unique way Chinese farmers enter cities [M]// Jia, D. et al. *Peasants in the Process of Modernization*. Nanjing: Nanjing University Press, 1998: 314.

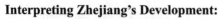
resources which he could call upon: his own, those of the nuclear family, those of his extended family, those of his friends and neighbors, and those of the wider society. In kin-reliance strategy, the individual called on resources of the wider circle of relatives beyond his nuclear family; in peer-reliance strategy, he turned to persons of roughly his own generation and social standing; whereas in self-reliance strategy, he depended on his own resources, those of his nuclear household, or the impersonal institutions of the wider society."[①] For Zhejiang migrant businessmen, leaving the familiar rural society for the unfamiliar urban society unquestionably means to alienate the rural social network of relationships where they were born and brought up or have gone through over the years. However, an individual has limited strength and resources in a new environment and cannot support his or her survival or development. As a result, it objectively requires the individuals to reconstruct their social support network so as to acquire resources from members of networks to resolve difficulties in daily life and management. Some scholars even believe that the significance of the social network to immigrants can never be overestimated.

A study on "Zhejiang Village" of Beijing indicates that social support network is truly of vital significance to Zhejiang people doing business outside their hometowns.[②] For example, private clinics operated by non-locals were banned by Beijing government, but clinics opened by some Wenzhou rural doctors were never shut down, though had been suppressed constantly. The reason is that once a clinic is closed, the news will spread to other clinics through the social network of Wenzhou people. So, the owners will soon transfer equipment and medicine to their relatives and friends for concealment, and temporarily close their clinics. In addition, since Beijing authorities collect fees

---

① Wang, C. Social networks in motion: Wenzhou people's behavior patterns in Paris and Beijing [J]. *Sociological Studies,* 2000(3).

② Wang, C. Social networks in motion: Wenzhou people's behavior patterns in Paris and Beijing [J]. *Sociological Studies,* 2000(3).

according to the number of people, many Wenzhou people manage to get rid of the fees by being unregistered. Social network provides multiple economic resources and social support for migrant Zhejiang businessmen. Remarks of Zhang Annai, manager of a shoe shop in "Zhejiang Village" of Beijing also confirmed this point. He said, "On one hand, we treasured our relations with fellow villagers, relatives and friends; we sought their help in business and we even tended to ask Zhejiang people working in government for favors when we met tough problems; on the other hand, our attitude towards relatives and friends was very simple: I could lead you a way if you come to me, but you had to chart your own path.[①]"

Barry Wellman and Scot Wortley found five types of social support in their study of East York's urban social networks[②]: 1. Emotional aid, provided by 61% of the network members, includes minor emotional aid, advice about family problems, major emotional aid and major services; 2. Services, provided by 61% of the network members, includes minor services, lending and giving household items, minor household aid, major household aid and organizational aid; 3. Companionship, provided by 58% of the network members, includes discussing ideas, doing things together, and joining an organization as fellows; 4. Financial aid, provided by 16% of the network members, includes small loans and gifts, large loan and gifts, housing loans or gifts; 5. Job and housing information, provided by 10% of the network members, includes job information, job contacts and housing information.

Social network is a social structure or a relatively stable system formed by social interactions among actors. Research on social network

① Zhou, X. *Traditions and Developments: Social Psychology of Jiangsu and Zhejiang Farmers and Its Development since Modern Times* [M]. Beijing: SDX Joint Publishing Company, 1998: 273.
② Zhang, Q. *Social Capital Theory: Social Capital and Economic Growth* [M]. Beijing: China Social Sciences Press, 1997: 64.

lays special emphasis on the relationship between people, people and community and communities, instead of research and survey on the nature and qualities of the individual and the community; it highlights the ability of actors to capture social resource rather than occupy a certain type of resource. Barry Wellman and Scot Wortley's study indicated that the city community network had an extremely important social function to indigenous city people. But in fact, social network is especially significant to non-local businessmen in cities. However, "non-local people", like Zhejiang people doing business outside their hometown, must rely on original social relations (i.e. blood relations, geographical relations) as a bond to receive support from the social network. Because in the case of migrant Zhejiang businessmen (mostly used to be farmers), previous social systems, especially the legacy of *hukou* system made urban management authorities and city dwellers "indifferent to" or "ignore" them. Moreover, factors including partitioned labor market, rigid household registration system and living structures obstruct their integration into existing local social networks. Under these circumstances, Zhejiang migrant businessmen cannot immediately find resources of social support in the local social networks. The only practical path for them is to use their original genetic and quasi-genetic social network of relationships and follow the principle of original relation construction (i.e. blood relations, marital relations and geographical relations) to expand their social relationships. This familiar principle of relation construction and social network of relationships offer them convenience, therefore reduce the cost of exchange and give them a high sense of security and trust.

The original social networks of relationships (or that of hometown) cannot remain entirely intact after migration, and instead the networks must adapt to the change of social surroundings at their destination. Wang Chunguang's research showed[1] that this change took place in

---

① Wang, C. Social networks in motion: Wenzhou people's behavior patterns in Paris and Beijing [J]. *Sociological Studies*, 2000(3).

"Zhejiang Village" in Beijing and "Wenzhou City" in Paris. First, many relatives without any contact in their hometowns are re-recognized and rebuilt, expanding their kinship. Second, many people barely have any contact with one another because of distance, but they would naturally have more chances to associate since they live closely together. However, Zhejiang people choose contact partners with their hometowns as the center, extending and expanding outwards. If they were in their hometowns in Zhejiang, some of them may never become possible contacts or never know each other. In this sense, the social network of migrant Zhejiang businessmen covers a much larger geographical area than previously in their hometowns. Third, the urban-rural relationship is greatly undermined than that in Zhejiang. Since the identity of a fellow villager is highlighted, former residents of the two areas become close, and the difference of identity is weakened. Apart from that, the common experience of smuggling abroad, doing business, working in factories, and joining the army together is gaining importance in the construction of social networks.

The impact of the network of relationships on social economic activities in Zhejiang since the reform and opening-up embodies in both the migrant businessmen's dependence on particularistic social network of relationships to acquire information and social support and also the local professional and characteristic industrial clusters of "One Village One Product" "One Town One Product" in Zhejiang. The industrial cluster of Zhejiang features thousands of family workshops and regional aggregation of the same industry based on these workshops, for instance, clothing from Ningbo, leather shoes from Wenzhou, polyester fabrics from Shaoxing, leather clothing from Haining, small ware from Yiwu, small hardware from Yongkang, ties from Shengzhou, fine chemicals from Huangyan, shirts from Fengqiao and small home appliances from Cixi. Particularistic culture and network based on kinship and geography serve as the media in the process. For instance, there are many professional households specializing in secondary and tertiary industries and families working in the same industry in the rural areas of Wenzhou. The phenomenon of economic diffusion with family as the center and blood and familial ties as the bond is even more conspicuous at the early stages of the reform and opening-up. Influenced by the living structure with the same clan and ethnicity in rural communities, industries are diffused by blood and familial relationships and the same industry is aggregated in a region in industrial distribution; this phenomenon is what Michael Porter referred to as "cluster phenomenon."[1] A typical example is Hantian Village's industry of automobile, motorcycle and auto parts. When the national policy allowed farmers to become professional and key households, more than 40 workers left No.57 Factory of Hantian, Rui'an of Wenzhou and started family workshops, then the industry spread from households to neighboring areas.[2] These family workshops are connected by various social relations, such as families, neighbors and friends into enterprise networks with professional division and collaboration of labor inside the network, as well as multiple weak or strong links between one another, transforming industrial clusters into a great invisible factory.[3]

This demonstrates that the characteristic industrial clusters in Zhejiang region, which are connected by relatives, friends, neighbors and classmates and based on tens of thousands of family workshops, enjoy a rapid development following the pattern of "a person leads a household, a village and then a township (town) to prosperity." Particularistic social network of relationships undeniably provides information, knowledge and social support in the process. At the initial

---

① Zhu, K. Family culture and Wenzhou regional economic development [M]// Shi, J. et al. *Institutional Change and Economic Development*. Hangzhou: Zhejiang University Press, 2002.

② Chen, D. Village family culture's influence on Hantian Village [J]. *Wenzhou Forum*, 2000(4).

③ Zhu, H. *Zhejiang Industrial Cluster—Industrial Network, Growth Trajectory and Development Motivation* [M]. Hangzhou: Zhejiang University Press, 2003: 76.

stage, once a person in a village makes a fortune in a certain industry, the information will spread and disseminate to other members of his or her social network of relationships, therefore introducing them to engage in the same industry, in turn they bring people that they share a close relationship with into the industry, resulting in a snowball effect in the number of workers and the size of the industry.

4.3   Particularistic Trust, Network of Relationships and Zhejiang's Business Organizations

Nelson and Winter have proposed the concept of "routine" based on limited rationality and the depressiveness of knowledge. Enterprises are based on routine practice, so things like production planning, price determination, allocation of research and development funds all follow a behavioral pattern based on routine, rather than calculating the optimal solution at any time. Every enterprise's routine can be seen not only as a carrier of knowledge and experience of the enterprise but also as a product growing from a specific socio-cultural environment. In the process of the formation of Zhejiang's enterprise routine, the particularistic trust culture, the family culture tradition, etc. clearly have all played their part. Yang Guoshu once proposed the concept of pan-familial process, believing that the ethical or role relations of the family would be assimilated into those of groups outside the family. According to this theory, through the pan-familial process, it is not surprising that interpersonal relations in business organizations share some similarities with those in the family. In Zheng Boxun's opinion, many private enterprises in Taiwan use the family as a metaphor for their businesses and show similar interpersonal relationships. Since the reform and opening-up, based on the purely personal familial or semi-familial relationships, the network of social relations and special trust formed and maintained by virtue of the kinship community's family strengths and clan ties have undoubtedly exerted a profound influence on Zhejiang's enterprises. A large number of cases show that Zhejiang enterprises since the reform and opening-up were not external to social relations but embedded in the particularistic social network of relationships. Both the effect of generalization or metaphor, have obvious expressions in the contemporary Zhejiang regional business organizations.

4.3.1　Particularistic Trust, Network of Relationships and Village and Township Collective Enterprises

In the early stage of reform and opening-up, like what happened in southern Jiangsu, the most unforeseen gain was a large number of township collective enterprises (most of which were subsequently restructured) that emerged during the rural reform in Zhejiang, especially in northern Zhejiang. The predecessor of township collective enterprises is the commune and production team enterprises. After the Third Plenary Session of the 11th Central Committee of the Communist Party of China, the CPC Central Committee put forward the policy of "great development in the commune and production team enterprises." In terms of policies, it is appropriate to reduce the tax burden of commune and commune enterprises, allow their product prices to fluctuate by a certain margin, take care of them in terms of bank loans and agricultural support funds, and so on. Zhejiang's commune and production team enterprises (renamed as township and village enterprises in 1984) have shown signs of vitality since the reform and opening-up. The development of township and village collective enterprises of Zhejiang led to the important innovation of the province's rural economic system—a system that can be placed on a par with the household responsibility system in agriculture.

Township and village enterprises (TVEs) developed under the collectivist cultural background were once regarded as having the of most "socialistic nature" and most contribution to the "socialist direction." The collective nature of the township and village collective enterprises seemed to determine that they were not family businesses in the strict sense. The original commune and production team enterprises were owned by the collective and were under collective management. Almost immediately after the full implementation of the household responsibility system, the commune and production team enterprises started to implement the responsibility system, meaning the commune and production team would be in the charge of some "capable people." These "capable people" were basically farmers, most of whom are grassroots leaders among farmers or former managers of commune and production team enterprises. They became the protagonists of the first step of institutional innovation in township and village collective enterprises. Clearly, the fact that capable people were able to become the protagonists of institutional innovation was because it was in coordination with the informal institutional arrangements or cultural atmospheres such as the ideology, values, and beliefs as well as moral ideals during the start-up stage of collective enterprises in villages and towns. At that time, capable people did not only refer to those who knew how to manage things, but they also had to possess a "strong sense" of ideology, that is, they had to be "red (being in line with Party principles) and professional." This widely-accepted sense of ideology was a precise reflection of the expectations and requirements that farmers had on what makes a capable person. "To improve the rural areas, the key is the Party branch"; "a village follows another village; a household follows another household; members follow leaders." Having a good Party secretary and a good team is crucial to the construction of rural grassroots organizations. With these arrangements in place, people would then be able to play a leading role in promoting economic development and driving farmers out of poverty. In the early stages of the development of township and village enterprises in Zhejiang, there were usually one or two people who played a key role. The primary task of entrepreneurs is to design and discover markets, evaluate products and product technologies, and actively manage employees' labor. Yet, these are all determined by the uncertainty of the economic environment, which refers to events that are completely unpredictable. These events are different from risks because risks can be smoothed by insurance mechanisms. When uncertainty occurs, innovation becomes necessary. To achieve these tasks, entrepreneurs should possess the relevant specialized knowledge, that is, to be "professional."

On the other hand, due to the collective nature of township and village collective enterprises, capable people have "a greater ideological endowment that is oriented toward collective goals." According to new institutional economics, a greater ideological endowment can reduce the shadow price of devotion, thereby reducing the possibility of individuals to "take a free ride" or violate rules. His ideological belief that the surrounding institutional arrangement and institutional structure should be ethical is rather strong, while his ideological beliefs about the current rational institutional arrangements can effectively undermine opportunist tendencies and behaviors. The strength of personal ideology shows that his ideological capital is so large that the shadow price of devotion is low. The marginal utility configured on devotion is high, and for this reason he will configure more time to devotion. In fact, in the early stage of the development of collective enterprises in towns and villages in Zhejiang, the "greater ideological endowment" of capable people is the most important source of spiritual motivation for their institutional innovation and management. As Weitzman and Xu Chenggang once put it, "township and village enterprises should be lazy because there was no clear property right and no business owner who was motivated by the greatest profit, and as a result township and village enterprises were bound to run poorly."[1] However, the efficiency of TVEs has actually been quite substantial for a long period of time. For example, in 1983, enterprises run by communes and brigades in 26 counties (districts) in Zhejiang Province showed a revenue of over 100 million yuan, of which the highest was Shaoxing County which reached

---

[1] Zhang, Q. *Social Capital Theory: Social Capital and Economic Growth* [M]. Beijing: China Social Sciences Press, 1997: 172.

958 million yuan. In the seven years from 1984 to 1991, the gross output value of Zhejiang's township enterprises increased by 6.67 times, from 12.07 billion yuan to 92.857 billion yuan (constant price). In 1991, Zhejiang's township and village enterprises accounted for 51.38% of the province's industrial output value, supporting half of the province's industry. To contrast between theory and reality, it is obviously difficult to make convincing explanations if social, cultural or spiritual factors are omitted.

However, under the context in which a particularistic social network of relationships still exists, the value orientation of collectivism cannot be pure, and the latter will inevitably be affected to a considerable extent by the former. If we carefully observe the development, organizational structure and management of collective enterprises in towns and villages in Zhejiang, it is not hard to find that they still have, to a considerable degree, the imprint of the particularistic family culture. In fact, in the initial stage of the development of TVEs in Zhejiang, those red and professional "capable people" had, to a certain degree, the characteristics of "parents" in the family culture. Moreover, the characteristics of such "parents" have been increasingly strengthened with the development of township and village collective enterprises and changes in the social environment. Correspondingly, the value orientation of collectivism gradually weakened. In the early stage of the development of township and village collective enterprises, the capable people won the approval and respect from members and other villagers due to their ability of using their outstanding talents to contribute to the goals of the collective and the members. Undoubtedly, the approval and respect from members and other villagers in the rural community, which has a heritage of thousands of years of family culture, will more or less have the features of a family culture, that is, to a large extent, the approval and respect of the "natural leader" of the family community—"parents." On the other hand, this kind of "approval" and "respect" with a tint of family culture will further reinforce the "parental awareness" of the capable people. According to Peter Blau's

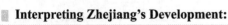
social exchange theory, "the collective approval of a power legitimates that power. If people think that when a superior exercises power, the benefits they receive outweigh the sufferings they bear for obeying him, then they would form a consensus by mutual exchange of views. The consensus manifests itself in the groups' pressures and in people's obedience to the orders of the ruler, thereby strengthening the ruler's control and legitimating his authority."[①] Capable people's contribution to the township and village enterprises eventually earns the members' obedience and they are then treated like family members'. Since the members recognize that the contributions made by capable people were for the sake of the collective goal, they must assume the corresponding obligations in return. Meanwhile, the only thing that a member can do is to obey the patriarchal authority for the capable person and listen to his arrangements. However, this will lead some "capable people" or village leaders down the path of patriarchal domination. Not only will members of village and township enterprises and other villagers become unable to confine their behavior, sometimes it is even harder for the state to control them.

In Zhejiang, the comparative advantages of a considerable number of township and village enterprises have weakened since the 1990s, especially in the mid- to late-1990s. To some extent, problems such as the shift to the "two state-owned assets," the deterioration of the mechanism and the degeneration of economic efficiency have emerged. The tendency could be shown through the comparison of development trends between northeastern Zhejiang where TVEs were relatively more concentrated, and the area of Wenzhou and Taizhou where there were relatively less TVEs in the same period. There were various reasons that led to the problems that TVEs faced after the mid-1990s. For example, the product mix was not adapted to new changes in the market; the pattern of "small and dispersed" industrial productivity

---

① Blau, P. *Exchange and Power in Social Life* [M]. Trans. Sun, F. & Zhang, L. Beijing: Huaxia Publishing House, 1987: 26.

seriously affected competitiveness, the technology and personnel did not adapt to the competition requirements, property rights organizations and operating mechanisms did not meet the requirements of the new situation and so on. Apart from these material reasons, spiritual factors cannot be ignored. In the initial stage of the development of TVEs, although the value orientation of collectivism was affected by the family culture to a certain extent, the dominant values of the society at that time and the values and beliefs of the capable people were generally compatible with the nature of TVEs. This not only provided a sufficient mechanism of spiritual motivation for the capable-people's institutional innovation but also promoted the rapid development of the TVEs. Subsequently, the social environment changed dramatically. Its most notable feature was that Zhejiang, like other parts of the country, underwent the transition from a planned economy to a market economy and a comprehensive social transition as well. However, the profit-driven mechanism of market economy will inevitably strengthen people's motives and desires of pursuing personal interests. It cannot help but have the effect of influencing the psychology of those capable people who deal with the market frequently. With capable people being highly sensitive to and extremely concerned about their own interests, it will undoubtedly decrease the weight of collective interests and goals of others in the objective function of some capable people. As some capable people would seek personal interests and strengthen patriarchal authority, the collective property nature of township and village enterprises would have a mismatch with their personal worth and goals. In other words, although the operators of township and village collective enterprises have been transformed from "red and professional" capable people with collectivistic values to the parents-like capable people with an idea of private ownership and self-interests, the initial institutional arrangements (both formal and informal) of township and village collective enterprises determined that they still needed to be developed on a collective basis, or that their development was already path-dependent. Under such circumstances, how do we ensure that capable people would have inexhaustible motivation for innovation? How do we ensure that Zhejiang TVEs in the fierce market competition would continue to have a good economic performance? The transformation of collective-owned township and village enterprises in the mid- to late-1990s was unavoidable precisely because it was difficult to effectively resolve such problems.

Of course, dialectically, it is not entirely negative to have the influence of the particularistic family culture on the development of Zhejiang's TVEs, while the positive side is also very obvious. What's more typical is the use of particularistic networks of relationships in the development of Zhejiang TVEs. Different from the original industrialization in Western developed countries and the large numbers of migrant workers entering Zhejiang after the 1990s, in the early stage of the development of Zhejiang TVEs, the employees of enterprises were often not immigrants from various places, but were people with various pre-emptive relationships from the areas where they had originally lived. In the context of the policy of "leaving the farmland without leaving the home village," if the newly established TVEs want to break through the barriers of self-development, the best or most economical way is to use blood or geographical relationship (village folks) and relationship of classmates and friends, etc. For example, historically, Ningbo and Shanghai had a natural connection with blood and geography (fellow villagers). In the course of the development of TVEs in Ningbo, such social network relationships were fully utilized. In the initial period of Ningbo's garment industry, on the one hand, through blood, familial, geographical and other relations, the local people of Ningbo continued to pour into Shanghai's garment enterprises to learn modern tailoring techniques and then returned to set up modern garment factories. On the other hand, Shanghai's technical staff who had blood, familial and geographical relations with Ningbo were often invited to Ningbo for technical guidance. These technical staff from Shanghai have not only brought technology and information to

Ningbo's township garment enterprises but have also established a close business relationship with Ningbo.

Cao Jinqing, Zhang Letian and Chen Zhongya's research[1] on the villages in northern Zhejiang further proved the importance of familial and semi-familial networks to the survival and development of TVEs in Zhejiang. From the nature of property rights, TVEs are undoubtedly "collective." However, from a broader perspective, the collective enterprises in the rural areas of northern Zhejiang can be seen as the central knot in the particularistic networks of interpersonal relationships. It is through the "network of relationships" that the remaining rural labor force in the family was able to enter the collective-owned enterprises. Managers of rural collective-owned enterprises often maintain close ties with township governments, credit cooperatives, tax offices, industry and commerce administrations through the "network of relationships." In order to obtain their support and protection, rural collective enterprises must extend the "network of relationships" to relatives and friends working in urban state-owned enterprises and commercial departments in the country, through which they can obtain raw materials, technologies or promote the sale of products. The establishment of the supply and marketing channels for the survival of TVEs is based on the "network of relationships" and "interpersonal relations." This way, unnecessary exaggeration and procrastination in the so-called "public affairs" procedures can be avoided, so as to improve efficiency and get a far lower price than the market price or raw materials that are not available in the market. For which reason, a small amount of "relationship investment" actually reduces the production costs. Therefore, in the official exchanges between TVEs and its staff, the higher functional departments, and the external enterprises and units, "the intricate network of relations and the subtle contacts between human beings can be found,

---

[1] Cao, J., Zhang, L. & Cheng, Z. *Social and Cultural Changes of the Villages in Contemporary Northern Zhejiang* [M]. Shanghai: Shanghai Far East Publishers, 2001: 521-525.

or, in formal contracts established through the 'public relations', it can be found that 'personal relationship' plays a decisive role." [1]

According to Peter Blau, the distinction between particularism and universalism is "whether the standard which dominates people's orientation is dependent on the particularistic relations between them... Therefore, the particularistic criteria for the distinction is whether the value of the standard dominating orientation and exchanges between people is independent of their social status."[2] In theory, the nature of collective property rights of the township collective enterprises determines that they should be based on collectivism. However, they advocate breaking the blood and geographical basis and establishing collectivism with "comrade-style" relations. The value orientation is similar to universalism in terms of value cognizance of the actor and object, which is independent of the particularistic relations between the actor and the object. However, in fact, the township collective enterprises in northern Zhejiang have shown both collectivism value orientation (especially in the early stages of development) and particularism value orientation, which means that the value orientation of the object and its behavior is identified by the particularistic relations between the actor and object. In the transitional period of economic system when the market system was not fully established, the segregation of urban and rural areas made it very difficult for township collective enterprises to get enough information, funds, raw materials and sales channels through formal institutional arrangements. Township enterprises have built necessary mutual trust with other socio-economic and political institutions through their own particularistic social networks. These networks of mutual trust can

---

[1] Cao, J., Zhang, L. & Cheng, Z. *Social and Cultural Changes of the Villages in Contemporary Northern Zhejiang* [M]. Shanghai: Shanghai Far East Publishers, 2001: 521.

[2] Blau, P. *Exchange and Power in Social Life* [M]. Trans. Sun, F. & Zhang, L. Beijing: Huaxia Publishing House, 1987: 305-306.

facilitate their identification, selection, use and other necessary social support. Translating the particularistic social networks in daily contacts into economic activities is conducive to saving the costs of building relationship networks. Therefore, it is clear that the particularistic social networks played an important role in the rapid growth of township collective enterprises in Zhejiang during the initial stage of reform and opening-up. However, on the other hand, it should also be seen that the so-called "collectivism" that is mixed with factors such as personal interests and family culture will inevitably cause irreconcilable contradictions with the collective property rights of those collective enterprises.

4.3.2   Particularistic Trust, Network of Relationships and Private Enterprise Organizations

Particularistic social networks and trust are important and sometimes even crucial resources for Zhejiang's private-owned enterprises. The development of private enterprises in Zhejiang shows, in particular, the imprint of a particularistic culture based on kinship ties. A survey of 31 large-scale employers in Wenzhou in 1985 showed that private entrepreneurs mainly came from salespersons, technicians and managers of commune and brigade enterprises, or captains of former production teams, production brigades, accountants and educated youths. Not only are they the elites in local rural communities, but they have also established extensive social networks over the years in their relatively frequent social interactions with the community and the outside world.[1] Since the reform and opening-up, most private enterprises in Zhejiang have acquired the ability to control scarce resources such as rights, status, capital, wealth, knowledge, opportunities and information through such social networks.

---

[1]   Zhu, H. *Zhejiang Industrial Cluster—Industrial Network, Growth Trajectory and Development Motivation* [M]. Hangzhou: Zhejiang University Press, 2003: 77-78.

In Zhejiang's private enterprises, the proportion of enterprises based on kinship or relative kinship networks is very high. To some extent, the majority of private enterprises in Zhejiang, particularly in Wenzhou, Taizhou, and Jinhua, developed on the basis of the kinship principle starting from household industry or family business. For example, in Wenzhou where the private sector was relatively more developed, in the early 1980s, along with the reform and opening-up, the cottage industry as a replica of the historical tradition was born in the form of family workshops with shop in the front and a workshop at the back. In the houses with street frontage, each family lives in a house and each house is a family production unit. On the ground floor of the house, the frontage is the shop where the products are placed while the back of the house consist of the plant (or workshop). According to statistics, as early as 1985, the total number of Wenzhou's household industries had grown to 133,000 with an output value of 1.13 billion yuan, accounting for 61% of the total output value of the rural industry.[①] Since then, the household industry has been growing and developing, some of which have grown into larger private companies. This fully demonstrates the role of kinship networks in the development of private enterprises in Wenzhou and the wider Zhejiang Province. According to Wang Xiaoyi and Zhu Chengbao, among Zhejiang's private enterprises, kinship or relative kinship network enterprises can be broadly divided into four categories: one is the home network type, which belongs to all family members and is jointly managed by the family members. Second is the family network type, which is composed of different families of the same clan cooperative enterprise. The family that forms the foundation of the enterprise is usually represented by one person in the enterprise who sees to the management and control of the enterprise. Third is the alliance type, which is based on the in-laws and co-funded by families with affinal relationships. The last category is the relative kinship network type. This kind of business is not co-financed by families. It is

---

① Wang, X. & Zhu, C. *Private Enterprises and Family Economy in Rural China* [M]. Taiyuan: Shanxi Economic Publishing House, 1996: 12-13.

based on the business relations, or on the friendships. There is almost no private enterprise in Zhejiang that was truly isolated from kinship and relative kinship social networks. Even if an enterprise was originally composed of economic ties, a group of social networks should be gradually developed for the development of the enterprise. More often is to first develop a social relationship, and then establish economic relations on this basis, or doing both at the same time.

In the growth of the private enterprises in Zhejiang, the kinship and relative kinship relations extended by the family or Fei Xiaotong's so-called "differential mode of association" of traditional Chinese family culture has indeed played an essential role. Colman believed that any interpersonal and organizational relationships were based on trust. The simplest trust relationship includes two actors: the principal and the client. Exchanging between individuals is a complex social interaction and organizational relationship. Blau believed whether in the micro or macro fields, exchange needed "common values" as the media.[①] Emerging in social activities, these values are gradually formed in the organization and internalized among members of society through socialization.[②] Jane Fortuin and Robert Atkinson pointed, "When scientific research institutions successfully cooperated with joint ventures, the 'glue' which bound them together was not the stipulated contracts which made this complex and dynamic relationship exhaustive (of course, contracts were also important) and not just information systems that linked the various agencies (of course, these networks promote information sharing). In the new economy, the factors contributing to such cooperation are mainly composed of the

---

① Zhang, J. Informal institutions in the process of marketization [M]//*Chinese Social and Cultural Psychology*. Beijing: China Social Sciences Press, 1998: 314-315.

② Zhang, J. Informal institutions in the process of marketization [M]//*Chinese Social and Cultural Psychology*. Beijing: China Social Sciences Press, 1998: 314-315.

mutual trust among policymakers within the network, the principle of reciprocity and the enlightened self-interest."[1] The so-called "common values," are included in the informal institutional arrangements. Therefore, if a society does not establish universalistic interpersonal relationships, and particularistic relationships are popular, then the particularism is likely to become an important part of Blau's "common values" and provide a basic standard for the exchange and social organizations of citizens. In the development of private enterprises in Zhejiang, the "common values" of exchanging and organizing trust relations undoubtedly include both people's identification of kinship and geographical relationship as well as the acceptance of "insiders" as Fei Xiaotong mentioned. Obviously, both these identifications are particularistic, and their significance for the growth of private enterprises in Zhejiang is very prominent.

In the particularistic network that takes self as the center, from "self" to "home," from "home" to "state" and from "nation" to "the world," owners' closest relatives including parents, brothers and sisters, relatives, friends, and fellows play an important role in the success of private enterprises. According to Wang Xiaoyi and Zhu Chengbao's investigation of Xiangdong Village, Cangnan County in Wenzhou, when asked whom they would cooperate with to set up a business, 10 out of 19 villagers (more than 50%) responded that they would choose their brothers and sisters, while six of them responded that they wanted to cooperate with their friends and three answered they wanted to cooperate with their relatives. In answering the question "Who do you trust the most," eight out of 15 people (more than 50%) responded that they trusted their brothers and sisters, three respondents trusted members of the family the most, and four trusted friends and relatives the most. When asked "who would you borrow money from,"

---

① Fortuin, J. & Atkinson, R. Innovation, social capital and new economics [M] // Li, H. & Yang, X. *Social Capital and Social Development*. Beijing: Social Sciences Academic Press, 2000: 213-214.

five out of 26 people answered that they would borrow from brothers and sisters, while 13 people responded relatives and eight people answered that they would borrow from friends.[①] Particularistic social networks are often the most effective channel to raise funds for private enterprises in Zhejiang since the reform and opening-up. The most typical example in this regard is the financing form called "*Chenghui*" (literally means presenting) that is prevalent throughout the province. Although the word "*Chenghui*" has different names across the province, they are all traditional economic cooperation folkways in Zhejiang. The operation of "*Chenghui*" often requires a particularistic social network and particularistic trust as a lubricant. After analyzing the evolution of Wenzhou's folk financing from "*Chenghui*" to private financing and stock ownership, Ye Dabing believed that the most pivotal point from the birth of "*Chenghui*" to the initial stock ownership was that it incorporated the invisible social ethics that have supported the formation and development of this folklore. "In its early stage, '*Chenghui*' is a form of mutual-aid lending based on traditional ethical beliefs (including morality, kinship, geography, etc.) and human relations in the peasant economy and society. When the planned economy is transformed into a market economy, on the one hand, people are more proactive in using ethical concepts to supplement their production funds under the market mechanism. Through the formula of 'ethics + interest', people's enthusiasm of participation has been mobilized."[②] Practices have proved that Zhejiang people who use and inherit the "*Chenghui*" custom, in fact, use particularistic social network as a means of financing. An example is a form of "*Chenghui*" in Wenzhou called "Yucheng Hui" or "Renqing Hui." This is a form of economic mutual

---

① Wang, X. & Zhu, C. *Private Enterprises and Family Economy in Rural China* [M]. Taiyuan: Shanxi Economic Publishing House, 1996: 83.

② Ye, D. Traditional Borrowing Form and Modern Stock Ownership—The Relationship Between Economic Development and Folk Culture in Zhejiang [Z] // Conference Proceedings of the Eastern Zhejiang School and Zhejiang Spirit Seminar.

aid that embodies solidarity, mutual assistance and equality. Each 50 yuan is called a "50 hui" and each 100 yuan is called a "100 hui." Most of the promoters of "Yucheng Hui" or "Renqing Hui" invite neighbors, friends and relatives to help them settle down difficulties in capital turnover. Since the reform and opening-up, with social relations as an intermediary, "*Chenghui*" has developed from a small amount of mutual aid loans into a new financial accumulation and business pattern to ease the financing difficulties and provide funds for social enterprises in the social and economic development of Zhejiang.

In the economic and social transformation period, if the dual track system and social discrimination against the private sector have not yet been completely eliminated, the relationship with friends, relatives, fellows, classmates in authorities are relatively more important to the success of the private sector. For example, when the "villagers" of "Zhejiang Village," composed of peasants from Wenzhou in Beijing, encountered troublesome things in Beijing, they would find Beijing officials who were born in Wenzhou or Zhejiang. Zhang Annai, manager of Southern Leather Shoes Wholesale Market in the "Zhejiang Village" in Beijing, admitted frankly that he even went to find a fellow who was a department-level leader for the sake of business.[①] Therefore, the non-economic social interaction and connection of enterprises and their operators are often the bridge between enterprises and the outside world to communicate and build trust with other enterprises. They provide capital for enterprises to survive and develop as well as an informal mechanism to obtain scarce resources and win over projects. As some private entrepreneurs in Zhejiang said, business operators should not only be open-minded and creative, but also need lots of friends.

Li Lulu once made a study in the late 1990s, apparently in a

---

① Zhou, X. *Tradition and Change: The Social Psychology of Peasants in Zhejiang and Jiangsu and Its Evolution since Modern Times* [M]. Beijing: SDX Joint Publishing Company, 1998: 55.

broader context, but it was undoubtedly meaningful for us to understand the significance of kinship and kinship-style social networks and family culture to Zhejiang private enterprises. First, an analysis of the social relations of owners who have obtained loans from institutions such as banks and credit unions makes it clear that over 50% of their closest friends are officials in urban state-owned and collective authorities, of which, more than 40% of the closest relatives are urban officials. Although the statistics do not directly reveal (perhaps never to be clear) that these owners' loans are made through their relatives and friends, particularly those who are officials, the fact that the network is so focused on specific groups of people who have particularistic social power explains the phenomenon to some extent. Second, the significance of establishing or maintaining a particularistic social network by private entrepreneurs lies in the fact that it is possible to link the planned economy with the private sector through friends or relatives. Through this channel, the resources and authorities within the system would then become influencing factors to the success of the private sector. Third, among the variables of the success of private enterprises, "relationship" exceeds the owners' original social status, which to a certain extent means that the structural advantages of the economy within the system do not appear in the private sector as direct inheritance and its advantages are not specific to a particular social group. Since the influence of the economy within the system on the private sector gradually became market-based, social groups that were not predominant in the traditional planned economy have also made use of this advantage in the private economy. In addition, this informal relationship is not merely a substitute to make up for the deficiencies in formal institutions, as formal institutional arrangements may never be able to meet the needs of a rich and varied socio-economic life, whereas private entrepreneurs who have accumulated more social capital may obtain more resources which are not available through formal institutional arrangements, or may be in a good position for competition through relatives and friends.[1] The above analysis clearly shows that the particularistic orientation of private entrepreneurs rooted in traditional culture and external society bears significance for the success of private enterprises under the particularistic institutional background.

Kinship and kinship-style social networks also have essential social functions for the innovation activities of the private sector. The connection between enterprises is often accompanied by the transmission of information and knowledge, and this transmission is usually achieved through interpersonal relationships. The particularistic linkages among private firms can provide enterprises with a more timely and accurate understanding of the potential needs and other information related to their industries, thus generating innovative inspiration. For example, Wenzhou Jun'er Polymer Co., Ltd. originally produced cable materials, but the operating efficiency has been poor; therefore, the company move into transfer to other related industries. In the initial stage of product transformation, the chief executive of the company learned from conversing with the shoe-making owners that there is a demand for materials with excellent wear resistance and elastic properties for making shoe soles. Therefore, the company has developed and produced various products that meet the needs of shoe factories. This brought the company back to life, and also promoted the upgrade of Wenzhou's shoe production technology.[2] With the kinship and kinship-style social networks, many private enterprises in Zhejiang not only obtain the inspiration of information and innovation, but also gain important technologies. For example, a private entrepreneur in Hantian Village, Rui'an, Wenzhou, after he made a fortune in automobile and motorcycle part factories, many relatives came to ask

---

① Li, L. The personal background of private entrepreneurs and the success of the Company [J]. *China Social Science*, 1997(2).

② Zhang, X., Liu, W. & Jin, F. The development of local traditional industry and China's entry into WTO—from the successful example of a private company in Wenzhou [J]. *China Economic News*, 2002-01-01.

him for assistance. The other two shareholders also encountered similar situations. As a result, all three shareholders reached an agreement. When relatives of shareholders came to the factory to learn technology, they arranged their positions in key posts so that the experienced worker would give careful guidance. However, ordinary workers were forbidden to have direct access to technical secrets. When the relatives of shareholders came to the factory to stock, they would make the first transaction on credit for him as the capital; and for the ordinary clients, they ought to pay at sight. In just a couple of years, this private entrepreneur helped his three brothers-in-law, two nephews and a niece run the automobile and motorcycle part plants for production and distribution through such an approach. Now they have all made great success. Among them, his younger nephew stayed in his factory to learn technology and management in 1987, and by 1999, the annual output value of his nephew's automobile and motorcycle plant in Changchun has reached over 50 million yuan.[1] So, through the kinship and kinship-style social networks, Zhejiang private business owners can save much time on learning market knowledge, management experience and business technology, and greatly reduce the market entry costs.

The particularistic orientation of private enterprises in Zhejiang reflects not only the relationship with external society but also the family-oriented tendency of the management organizations in private enterprises. Based on the social exchange theory, Huang Guangguo developed a theoretical model of "Face and Favor: The Chinese Power Game."[2] His model assumes that under the influence of Confucian ethics, individuals can roughly classify their relationship with each other into three categories and deal with each other according to different social rules. The three relationships are emotional (following

---

[1]　Chen, D. The influence of family culture on automobile and motor parts industry in Hantian Village [J]. *Wenzhou Forum*, 2000(4).

[2]　Huang, G. Face and favor: The chinese power game [M] // Huang, G. *The Chinese Power Game*. Taipei: Chuliu Publisher, 1988.

the law of demand), mixed (law of humanity) and instrumental (law of equality). The so-called emotional relationship refers to that between family members; mixed relationship refers to the various relationships, including relatives, friends, neighbors, classmates and fellows established by individuals outside the family; instrumental relationship refers to individuals contacting with others with only a little emotional component and the two sides do not expect the contacts will establish long-term emotional relationship. In a family business, entrepreneurs interact with family members who work in an organization based on the "law of demand," with their employees based on "law of humanity," and others outside the organization in temporary "instrumental relations."

The internal management and employment system of many private enterprises in Zhejiang is based on particularism and the differentiated "social rules" put forward by Huang Guangguo. Two sample surveys conducted by the Zhejiang Association of Industry and Commerce on private enterprises in Zhejiang Province in 1995 and 1999 showed that the decisions made by private owners and the board of directors on major issues accounted for 80.9% and 78.0%, respectively. The impact of family culture can be clearly seen in the employment system of many private enterprises. In the survey conducted by the Zhejiang Association of Industry and Commerce on the private sector in 1995, it was found that about 63.9% of the enterprise managers were close and trustworthy people after combining the answers to the questionnaire on the sources and requirements of business managers.[1] This shows that the management and organization system in Zhejiang's private enterprises is still largely based on kinship. The 1999 survey that the Zhejiang Association of Industry and Commerce of Zhejiang had conducted on private enterprises showed that, although initial changes have taken place, in terms of the sources and requirements of business managers

---

[1] Zhejiang Association of Industry and Commerce. Sample survey data and analysis on Zhejiang's private enterprises in 1995 [J]. *Practice and Seeking Truth,* 1999: 128.

and technical staff, there were still about 61.3% of the business
managers and 18.8% of the technicians who were closely related to the
owners. Around 79.2% of the technicians were professionals with more
appropriate skills.[①] This survey also showed that in the composition
of the leadership of private enterprises in Zhejiang, family members
as the majority accounted for 41.30%, while managers accounted for
28.64%, and technical personnel accounted for 21.49%.[②] According to
Yinghuan Hong's survey of 88 sample enterprises in Yueqing, Wenzhou
in August 2002, 59.31% of the managers were relatives, neighbors
or friends of the owners. Among them, in the finance department,
the highest proportion of family members was 98.43%; followed
by senior management, where the proportion of family members as
general manager, deputy general manager, foreign trade manager,
etc., was 95.65%. The reason why these two departments have a high
percentage of family members is that both departments are the core
of an enterprise.[③] According to Wang Xiaoyi and Zhu Chengbao's
survey in Cangnan County, Wenzhou, many private entrepreneurs often
start out not only as an investment project but also as a solution to the
unemployment of their own family. Therefore, they generally use their
children and relatives as their first choice. Other workers often enter the
company through relationships, especially through acquaintances, rather
than through labor markets. Among the surveyed enterprises, almost all
enterprises regard the owners' and employees' children and relatives
as their first choice for recruitment. Among the three enterprises
surveyed with 79 registered employees, only 18 of them have no

---

① Zhejiang Association of Industry and Commerce. Sample survey data and
analysis on Zhejiang's private enterprises in 1999 [J]. *Zhejiang Academic Journal*,
2000(5).
② Zhejiang Administration for Industry and Commerce. *Zhejiang Individual and
Private Economy Research Report* [R]. Beijing: China Workers Publishing House,
2000: 59.
③ Ying, H. *Institutional Innovation of Family Enterprises* [M]. Beijing: China
Social Science Press, 2005: 239, 265.

direct relationship with the owners of the enterprises. More than 75% of workers are relatives of business owners. In such enterprises, workers are linked by human relations, and in the private sector, human relationships are often an important link in maintaining relationships. Managers, workers and owners to a certain extent have particularistic relations, those particularistic managers are mainly distributed in the crucial positions for the enterprise, such as in the accounting, supply and marketing, personnel and other departments. This kind of differentiated management employment system of private enterprises in Zhejiang Province reflects, to some extent, the patriarchal, humanistic and defensive (due to insecurity) characteristics, showing their tendency to "exclude" or "distrust" the outsiders.

This kind of psychological tendency of "exclusion" or "distrust" to the outsiders is, in a certain sense, a natural feature of Zhejiang private entrepreneurs who have grown up in the cultural background of kinship network or particularism. In the entire analysis framework of S.B. Redding, Chinese entrepreneurs do not always trust the outside world, and this includes the distrust of the government, outsiders, and family enterprises with no relationship. The insecurity caused by distrust has made defensiveness an important part of the Chinese capitalist spirit. In answering the question "why Chinese family businesses in the enterprise use relatives or nepotism," S.B. Redding responded very simply that it is because Chinese entrepreneurs do not trust outsiders. Due to the lack of trust in outsiders, private entrepreneurs in Zhejiang need to create a family network or faction power around their own core family in the enterprise. On the other hand, the reason why they do so is that it also takes quite a long time and a large cost to build trust. At this point, trusted members such as family members, fellows and friends enter as a resource that saves transaction costs. The particularistic cultural constraints of family will undoubtedly help to simplify the supervision and incentive mechanism of enterprises and reduce the transaction costs.

4.3.3   Particularistic Trust, Network of Relationships and State-Owned Enterprise Organization

Due to their particularistic status and historical origins, compared with township collective enterprises and private enterprises, Zhejiang's state-owned enterprises obviously bear less imprint of family culture. However, in any society, any type of social interaction will be somehow affected by all sorts of interpersonal relationships, and the interpersonal relationships in daily interactions will affect the interpersonal relationship patterns in non-daily communication. Therefore, it is quite natural to fail in getting rid of the fetters of particularistic values out of respect toward the formation of state-owned enterprise organizations and the mode of human relations, in a region where the concept of clan culture is still deeply-rooted. In particular, for a considerable period of time, the state-owned enterprises in Zhejiang, similar to other parts of the country, have adopted internal employment and replacement, where children could take over their parents' jobs. This reinforced kinship relations in some enterprises. With the coexistence of various ownership patterns and the dramatic changes in the entire society, the family cultural psychology oriented by particularism is apparently further revived and presented in the evolution of the state-owned enterprises in Zhejiang. The market-orientation reform also causes the state-owned enterprises in Zhejiang to face the same challenges as other ownership enterprises. Therefore, it should also be reasonable to seek and maintain particularistic relationships to enhance the opportunities and efficiency of state-owned enterprises.

It can be observed that in the era of the planned economy, China's state-owned enterprises were like a "big family," and Zhejiang was no exception. Walder argued that the patronage relationship between leaders (such as workshop directors) and activists among workers in state-owned enterprises was an "informal relationship" embedded in the formal organization. The combination of public factors and private

factors is an important part of the formal organizational structure. In other words, it is a "small circle" affiliation that forms part of a formal organization based on a set of rules different from the principle of formal organization—"rules of exchange of humanity."[①] For workers, state-owned enterprises were the crucial bridge between the state and the family during the planned economy period. It provided an indispensable space for the individual's social and economic activities. It was an external sign of personal life, identity and political orientation, and at the same time it was the carrier and implementer of the state regulation and control system. State-owned enterprises were usually featured in appearance by a tall wall separating the inside and the outside of the institution, as well as guards and transmission rooms at the gate to check the "outsiders." Whether it is a light bulb factory, a cement plant or an oil refinery, it had its own kindergarten, infirmary, swimming pool, cinema, canteen, bath house and so on. Some large state-owned enterprises had everything except prisons. It even included courts, police stations and a large-scale crematorium. Such institutions were like a small country, a manor or a "big family in the city."

According to Kornai, state-owned enterprises were often in constant negotiation with the authorities. In order to win investment projects, get preferential credit and allocations, reduce or eliminate taxes, or to obtain state financial subsidies, it was necessary to establish and maintain good relationships with the authorities and even delight them. Therefore, the degree of softening of the budgetary constraints of state-owned enterprises depended on the outcome of bargaining between the enterprises and the competent authorities. As Kornai pointed out: "A very important factor in the soft budget constraint syndrome was that external assistance was a bargaining issue for more subsidies,

---

① Walder, A.G. *Communist Neo-traditionalism: Work and Authority in Chinese Industry* [M]. Berkeley and Los Angeles: University of California Press, 1986.

tax exemptions, allowable administrative prices, and so on—
not everything could be negotiated in the market, but in the
bureaucratic system of paternalism."[①] Kornai's analysis showed
that in the institutional environment of the patriarchal system,
state-owned enterprises tended to regard "following upper path"
as a kind of "production activity," but this production activity
took place not in the "production area" but in the "controlled
area." Thus, the search and maintenance of particularistic social
networks by state-owned enterprises (especially between superiors
and subordinates) was caused by institutional factors in the first
place. Of course, the state-owned enterprises in Zhejiang also
have the phenomenon above. On the other hand, it needs to be
specially explained that the sociocultural background oriented
by particularism undoubtedly strengthened the "relationship
investment" of state-owned enterprises. In this sense, the "contacts"
between state-owned enterprises and higher authorities in many
parts of Zhejiang since the reform and opening-up such as sending
gifts and giving New Year's greetings to senior officials were
caused by combination of institutional and cultural factors. At
the same time, the influence of the family culture characterized
by the particularistic orientation on Zhejiang state-owned
enterprises is not only reflected in the relationship between the
state-owned enterprises and the external society, but also in its
internal relations. To a certain extent, the internal management of
many state-owned enterprises in Zhejiang, particularly in terms of
employment, rewards and punishments, also have "particularistic"
features such as cronyism.

4.3.4   Particularistic Trust, Network of Relationships and Organizational Performance of Enterprises

The informal institutional arrangements of particularistic trust

---

① Kornai, J. Gomulka on the soft budget constraint: A reply [J]. *Economics of Planning*, 1985(2).

pattern and family culture based on kinship relations have created a deep imprint on the internal and external relations between Zhejiang's enterprises and organizations since the reform and opening-up. This is one aspect of the issue. On the other hand, this arrangement also exerts an essential influence on the institutional innovation and development of Zhejiang's enterprises.

Edward Hall divided cultures into "high context culture" and "low context culture." The so-called "high context culture" is a culture such as that of American society where clear and impersonal information dominates. People regulate their own behaviors through various contracts. While in the "low context culture," people prefer to make vague and indirect exchanges. Moreover, the exchange of information relies more on the consensuses formed by the *ex ante* people in a common cultural context. They can often understand each other within a few words, but the same exchange of information is very vague and inadequate for an outsider. Similar with Hall, Fukuyama divided societies into "low-trust society" and "high-trust society" according to different cultures. Fukuyama believes that "social capital" determines the costs of social interaction, thereby affecting the form and size of social organizations and economic organizations. The so-called "social capital" refers to the human resources assembly of mutual support, trust and cooperation established by members of the community when forming new collectives and new associations. This kind of "human resources" is not only limited to things such as law, contract and right at the institutional level, but also to a large extent is closely related to the "moral community consciousness" or "unwritten ethical principle" as the "irrational habits" of society. In a low-trust society, due to the relative lack of "social capital," the cost of social interaction between people is very high, and there are great difficulty and risk in cultivating trust between each other. As a form of compensation, such societies often make use of spontaneous forms of social capital, such as kinship, as a basis for strengthening trust relations. This has gradually formed a family-based culture, and social activities are also featured by family to some extent. Generally, a society with rich "social capital" is a high-trust society. Such societies often have a strong sense of social cooperation and commonwealth with higher density of mutual aid social groups and have developed a set of social arts for group communication relatively early. In a low-trust society, trust mainly exists in kinship, while in high-trust society, it transcends kinship.

It is clear that Hills and Parsons' division of interpersonal relationships into particularistic and universalistic and Fukuyama's perspectives are in consensus. According to Fukuyama, it is difficult for a low-trust society based on kinship relationships to establish a private sector that is not based on blood ties, whereas for family businesses based on blood ties, it seems that they are bound to experience "the three generations of demise" (establishing the business in the first generation, maintaining the business in the second generation and declining in the third generation). Therefore, the market of a low-trust society is generally dominated by small and medium enterprises. Fukuyama divided the existing family-based businesses in Asia into "familial" and "quasi-familial." Chinese enterprises fellow the traditional family style. Japanese enterprises, however, are "quasi-familial" based on the fact that Japanese families have historically been extended beyond blood ties.[1] Based on this, Japanese society undoubtedly lies between a "low-trust society" such as China and a "high-trust society" such as Europe and the United States, and between a "particularistic" society and "universalistic" society. Japanese family enterprises have apparently weakened blood relationships to a considerable extent, which has partly eliminated the difficulties for traditional

---

[1]   Li, X. China's family business and business organizations [J]. *Chinese Social Sciences Quarterly (Hongkong)*, 1998(3).

families in creating a non-consanguineous private sector.①
According to Japanese scholar Shiga Shuzo, to Japanese families, the
existence of a human group formed by kin or spouse is only a matter
of the home, above which there is an inherent sense of family business,
family name, etc. The purpose, that is, has nothing to do with human
life and death, requires people to strive for their dedication while
making people enjoy their eternal purpose. It is precisely because the
concept of home contains the value and purpose of such a home that it
was able to give rise to the concept of "leader" at the time. Of course,
it also gave rise to the term "inheritance of home," which is used to
indicate the alternation of the leader. Although the manifestations
of this consciousness have changed with the times, most of the civil
laws from the clan era to the pre-war period have not been lost in our
minds. If this "family" concept, which does not emphasize kinship, is
transformed into social organizations and manufacturing enterprises, a
way of accumulating wealth belonging to a certain name other than kin
inheritance will become possible. In the course of their development, the
family-oriented enterprises need to continuously enrich their manpower
and technologies to ensure succession in generations of people, money,
technology and social work. Because it cannot be maintained by their
own kinship, those who worked for generations with no blood relation
must be fully integrated into their system, and be regarded as one family
to make a life community. This kind of living community or "family
business" consisting of kin and non-kin employees, further strengthened

---

① The reason why we use "partly eliminated" is because the "yuanyue principle"
in Japanese family business is different from the "kinship principle" to unite
families and the "contract principle" to establish clubs. Japanese society is still in
the middle ground between "high-trust society" and "low-trust society" and the
family business is constituted by "quasi-particularistic" or "quasi-universalism"
interpersonal relations. Therefore, Japanese enterprises may possess the
advantage of "universalistic" interpersonal relations as well as the disadvantage
of "particularistic" relations. The impact of the Asian Financial Crisis has largely
explained this problem.

the Japanese people's sense of collectivism. At this time, the concept of collectivism came into being. Because there is no interference with kinship concepts, one can directly attribute oneself to his/her work group. This is obviously an extremely important internal mechanism for the rapid expansion of modern Japanese enterprises to the world.

However, family businesses linked by blood are undoubtedly made up of a typical particularistic relationship. According to this classification, family businesses are made up of particularistic relationships. Under the particularistic mode of interpersonal relationship, the costs of economic transactions between those "inside the circle" and "outside the circle" are quite different. Inside the "circle," a family business may preserve the same beliefs and values of internal members, reducing or even eliminating distrust and possible opportunistic tendencies among members. The comprehensive and intense interpersonal relationships inside the circle can reduce the transaction costs between the principal parties that have particularistic relationship with each other and lower the transaction costs under the universalistic interpersonal relationship. For example, there are many advantages to the socialized division of labor based on the cottage industry in Wenzhou and other parts of Zhejiang such as low management costs, lack of need for specialized management personnel with the owner as the factory manager, and lack of need for specialized financial personnel and detailed production and financial system. All the work is maintained and carried out by relying on kinship. This organization is more efficient. They work for themselves. Working overtime in tight production tasks will not bring about conflicts between labor and capital, with less investment in fixed assets and high utilization rates. Using their own housing as a place of business, so that production costs can be greatly reduced, you can win in the market competition by price advantage.[1] Translating the kinship and family ethics rules into operation, township enterprises use them as their

---

① Wang, X. & Zhu, C. *Nonstate Enterprises and Family Economy in Rural China* [M]. Taiyuan: Shanxi Economic Publishing House, 1996: 13.

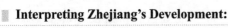

own organizational norms. As Li Peilin said, peasant workers do not need to adapt to the modern bureaucracy entering the factory and thus the costs of enterprise management could be greatly reduced.[①] Although all kinds of enterprises in Zhejiang are influenced by the family culture, they have shown remarkable achievements (especially in the early stage of reform and opening-up), which testifies this point. In the growth of contemporary private enterprises in Zhejiang, they dare not give any consideration to any risks and offered their helping hands to self-made starters. Most of them are relatives and friends. In a particularistic social network, people can get funds and manpower support at any time. Relatives and friends will also operate in the same industry or related industries, intentionally or unintentionally, in order to take care of each other. For example, within the operators of "Zhejiang Village" in Beijing, there is a capital market relying on local interpersonal relationships. There are usually two ways to borrow money. First is to borrow from relatives, where the rules of the market are still prevailing. Borrowers must pay interest to the lender even between immediate family members, but interest rates may be lower. The second is to rely on the help of "rural financiers."[②] After the establishment of Zhejiang Village, resources such as capital and manpower flow along the local interpersonal network between Beijing and Zhejiang. When the business scale expands, people often return to mobilize local resources; not only a considerable part of the capital and technology come from the original communities, but also a large part of the fabrics used in the production are resold from the markets in Zhejiang. The nationwide sales network also relies on the traditional blood and geopolitical relations. According to Chen Dongsheng's survey of Hantian Village in Rui'an in 2000, during the start-up period of the Hantian Village automobile and motorcycle parts manufacturing enterprises in 1982, the banks did not

---

① Li, P. Urban industry in China's countryside [J]. *Sociological Studies,* 1995(1).

② Wang, H. "Zhejiang Village" in Beijing: A unique way for Chinese peasants to come to cities [M]//*Chinese Peasants in Modernization.* Nanjing: Nanjing University Press, 1998.

issue any loans to these unplanned enterprises. At that time, the owner's savings were very limited. In this context, support from family members and relatives has become the only source of funds for business owners in the village. A sample survey of 114 households in Hantian Village showed that in the early 1980s, 92% of households borrowed money from relatives, families and friends for household auto and motorcycle parts businesses; 84% of households lent money to others. Han Yuming, Chairman of Zhejiang Ruiming Auto Parts Company, recalled: "I started my car and motorcycle parts store with 5,000 yuan borrowed from my mother-in-law."[①] Therefore, to some extent, it can be said that the economic ties based on kinship are both extensive and effective. The particularism-oriented networks save the organization transaction costs. In the face of high risks brought by the fierce market competition, you can form a reliable mutual support and mutual protection of strategic network organizations. At the same time, in the family-owned enterprises, the family culture oriented by particularism, which is the identification of kinship, has become an important mental force that brings together members of the enterprise and consciously serves the ethical conviction of family work, thus greatly reducing the transaction costs of internal management. The success of Zhejiang's contemporary family enterprise system in a certain period is to a great extent the result of the kinship of family culture, the trust resources, and the inward cohesion.

But at the same time, family businesses are also facing insurmountable growth barriers. Family enterprises based on the principle of kinship and particularism have always been facing the predicament of heirs. On the one hand, a successful entrepreneur, apart from his own efforts, should be in possession of talent and quality. However, the talents and some key qualities of the previous generation are not all passed on to the next generation through biological genes. On the other hand, the environment is also crucial for creating an

---

① Chen, D. The influence of family culture on automobile and motor parts industry in Hantian Village [J]. *Wenzhou Forum*, 2000(4).

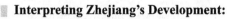
entrepreneur. Unluckily, the growth environment of the new generation is not the same as that of the successful entrepreneurs. The first generation of entrepreneurs need to struggle in the face of adversity, and when they succeed, their children tend to enjoy it. Striving in adversity undoubtedly gives birth to upward mobility and strong will. If one enjoys achievements, he will grow unambitious. However, it is difficult to eliminate an incompetent son when the succession selection mechanism of family enterprises is based on the "kinship principle." This is clearly a contrast to Japanese companies based on the "yuanyue principle." Although regarding some reliable and competent long-term apprentices as foster children is also a costly deal for the family organization, as Chen Qinan said, the Japanese view of the inheritance and son-in-law, "inadvertently provided them with a key set of preferences: in the private sector talent is seen as a criterion to choose heirs (foster sons or sons-in-law). There is no choice of sons, but sons-in-law can be carefully selected even in our society. It is a pity that the son-in-law that we have chosen carefully cannot replace the natural son to inherit the rising business. 'From clogs to clogs is only three generations' has become the iron law of the development of various sizes of enterprises in China since ancient times. Even in good families, unscrupulous descendants always appear in three or five generations. Much of the wealth and business accumulated in previous generations has therefore tended to decline."[1] Additionally, as Li Xinchun pointed out, under certain institutional and cultural value systems, only family trust could help reach an optimal cooperation (loyalty), but such cooperation was not the most efficient, because the most competent agents could not form a family. Family firms can reduce agency costs more effectively, but they cannot effectively stimulate their agency capabilities.[2]

---

[1] Chen, Q. *The Trace of Culture* [M]. Shenyang: Chun Feng Cultural and Art Publishing House, 1987: 139-140.

[2] Li, X. Trust, loyalty and the predicament that clannishness is in [J]. *Management World*, 2002(6).

Besides, the family businesses based on kinship and particularistic trust also face other barriers. The prominent problems are small size, low level of industry and loose organizational structure. From 2017 to 2019, Zhejiang Province plans to phase out more than 1000 enterprises with backward production capacity each year, eliminating and remedying over 10,000 "low-level, small and scattered" enterprises (workshop). "Low-level, small and scattered" enterprises will lead to many problems, the biggest of which is that it will restrict the improvement of technological innovation, which in turn will affect the domestic and international competitiveness of the products. Although many enterprises in Zhejiang have improved the technical content and quality of their products through "imitation," this low-cost, cost-effective way, compared with high domestic and international standards, leads to a processing accuracy is not high. Enterprises and group renowned for brand-name products are still not enough. There are many reasons for these problems. For example, Zhejiang has a poor industrial base and scarce resources; it takes a long time to develop one business, while most private enterprises in Zhejiang Province only have a history of about two or three decades, or even shorter. On the other hand, as Fukuyama said, the credibility of a region directly affects the size, organization, scope and form of transactions of the enterprises in the region as well as the size and intensity of indirect productive profit-seeking activities in the society. The influence of the family culture based on the kinship principle and the particularistic trust is undoubtedly a very important reason for the small scale of some enterprises in Zhejiang. The differentiated employment systems, nepotism and non-institutional management in family enterprises will affect the scale expansion and long-term survival of enterprises. Max Weber once determined Chinese family as a "blood economy shackle" that undermined "work discipline" and impeded "a universal commercial credit of beyond the kinship relations" as well as "a free labor market mode to select talents." "In China, all trust and the cornerstone of all business relations are clearly based on purely kinship

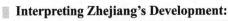

relations, which is of great economic significance. Ethical religion, particularly Protestant Ethic and the great performance of abstinence sects, is the advantage for the blood community torn apart by religious ties, to establish a community of faith and ethical way of life, which is to the advantage of the family in a large extent."[1] Fukuyama believed that "the extreme mistrust of outsiders in Chinese culture often hindered the institutionalization of companies, because Chinese owners did not allow professional managers to assume management responsibilities, preferring to reluctantly divide the company into several new companies or even completely disintegrate."[2] In societies such as China and South-central Italy, the family concept is so deep that it is often seen as a lack of a broader, general social trust beyond the family. This discourages groups to accept the beneficial effects of the external environment, and even worse, it can greatly trigger distrust, slackening or even hatred and violence against members of non-communal groups. Marion Levy also believed that the traditional Chinese family was of a "highly standard type of structure," which is a major obstacle to industrialization, "It has greatly complicated Chinese modern enterprise management from two aspects. One is on the employment; nepotism relationship has been extensively injected into the company. The other is on maintaining the external relations of enterprises, which involves buying, selling and servicing."[3] These criticisms are reasonable.

In light of Partha Dasgupta's view, social capital is a kind of private good, but full of positive and negative externalities. An example of a positive externality is the Puritanism specification Max Weber

---

[1] Weber, M. *Confucianism and Taoism* [M]. Trans. Hong, T. Beijing: The Commercial Press, 1995: 289.

[2] Fukuyama, F. *Trust—The Social Virtues and the Creation of Prosperity* [M]. Trans. Li, W. Hohhot: Yuanfang Publishing House, 1998: 296.

[3] Chen, Y. & Liu, L. The impact of familism on ethnic Chinese in Southeast Asia [J]. *Sun Yat-Sen University Journal (Philosophy and Social Science Column)*, 1998(5).

had described. This specification requires ethical treatment of all people, not just relatives and family members. Therefore, the potential of cooperation exceeds the direct group of people with puritanism specification thereof. In the meantime, negative externality also exists in large numbers. The realization of many internal aggregations is based on the losses of the non-group ("out of the circle"). The family business social capital formed on the basis of kinship and kinship-style relations undoubtedly has negative externalities. Although family enterprises are networks based on kinship and kinship-style relations where the relationship is very close and the internal transaction costs are very low, sometimes even free, they are quite "exclusive" to the outsiders, with only remote relations or even lack relationship. In other words, the trust formed on the basis of kinship is a kind of primitive natural trust. As a kind of social capital, it can only be used in a specific small group as "club goods." The principle of discrimination against outsiders and the "blind" loyalty to the interior may take away the general principles of a fair market. It is possible to sacrifice the interests of outsiders to meet their own interests. In some cases, it may even harm the interests of the majority of "outsiders," which may lead to immoral or illegal actions.[1] Under the "differentiated" principle, if any "outsider" wants to enter into a "circle" and conduct transactions, it is obviously necessary to break through the "relationship barriers." The identification of the kinship of contacts in the extended family trust, the identification of trust, and the interaction of different types of interaction all require extra costs, and the transaction costs are higher than that of the universalistic human relations model. In other words, interpersonal relationships have an adverse effect on economic transactions that go beyond the subgroups, which increase the transaction costs outside the network while saving the transaction costs within the network. Under such circumstances, the transaction cost saved within the network may not be able to

---

[1]   Li, X. & Zhang, S. *Family Business: Organization, Behavior and the Chinese Economy* [M]. Shanghai: SDX Joint Publishing Company, Shanghai People's Publishing House, 2005: 506-507.

offset the extra transaction costs outside the network. The quantitative relationship between the two is obviously determined by the relative position of the internal and external transactions of the network as well as the degree of saving and increasing of the transaction costs. In general, the transaction cost of particularistic interpersonal relationships saves more in economies where economic transactions mainly occur among acquaintances and vice versa.[1] As far as a society is concerned, the strong ethical ties within a group can actually reduce the trust of group members toward non-group members as well as the efficiency of cooperation. A well-disciplined, well-organized group of members can take coordinated and collective actions, but it can also become a social impediment.

Nathan Rosenberg and L.E. Birdzell, Jr. pointed out in *How the West Grew Rich,* "When the required trade scale exceeded what the family enterprises and joint ventures can afford, it was the only way for private enterprises to trade and invest on the basis of mutual trust beyond kinship. Without this kind of interpersonal relations which play a similar role as the family ties, there would be no development of non-governmental and secular trade and investment after the 16th century."[2] However, family enterprises based on kinship are difficult to break through blood "relationship barriers" to create non-blood-related business organizations, which will inevitably encounter insurmountable obstacles in the development. It is more difficult to show better economic performance especially in the face of global market competition. In marketing, they are often affected by the atomic competition, and can rarely evolve into an international brand. Although they may face a huge market, the market is often fragmented. So, the particularism-oriented enterprises are likely to result in "warlords'

---

[1] Wang, X. Interpersonal relations and economic transaction [J]. *Seeking Truth,* 1997(5).

[2] Rosenberg, N. & Birdzell, L.E, Jr. *How the West Grew Rich* [M]. Trans. Liu, S. Hongkong: SDX Joint Publishing (Hongkong) Company, 1989: 132.

separatism" and will ultimately not help to cultivate a large market that conforms to international standards. Practices since the reform and opening-up show that Zhejiang people pay close attention to particularistic family culture and its psychological orientation in the kinship network which is conducive to a certain period of economic and social development in Zhejiang. It conforms to Zhejiang's socioeconomic characteristics of "low-level, small and scattered," "family plant," "shop in the front and workshop at the back" and so on. However, it is unsuitable for the economic development of Zhejiang, that is to say, from the "low-level, small and scattered" economic scale to the "high-level, large and open" economy. It is not conducive to Zhejiang to produce knock-off products and keep the aircraft carrier enterprises as well as go global.

Bibliography

Abba, E. *Jewish History* [M]. Trans. Yan, R. Beijing: China Social Sciences Press, 1992.

Adam, S. *An Inquiry into the Nature and Causes of the Wealth of Nations* [M]. Trans. Guo, D. & Wang, Y. Beijing: The Commercial Press, 1981.

Alitto, G. S. *Anti-Modernization Thought Trends in a World-Wide Perspective* [M]. Trans. Tang, C. Guiyang: Guizhou People's Press, 1991.

Anuqin, B. A. *The Theoretical Issues of Geography* [M]. Trans. Li, D. & Bao, S. Beijing: The Commercial Press, 1994

Baldwin, E. et al. *Introducing Cultural Studies* [M]. Rev. ed. Trans. Tao, D. et al. Beijing: Higher Education Press, 2004.

Bao, W. *Studies on Zhejiang Regional History* [M]. Hangzhou: Hangzhou Publishing Group, 2003.

Bell, D. *The Cultural Contradictions of Capitalism* [M]. Trans. Zhao, Y., Pu, L. & Ren, X. Beijing: SDX Joint Publishing Company, 1989.

Bendix, R. *Max Weber: An Intellectual Portrait* [M]. Trans B. Liu. et al. Shanghai: Shanghai People's Publishing House, 2002.

Berger, P. L. *The Sacred Canopy Elements of a Sociological Theory of Religion* [M]. Trans. Gao, S. Beijing: People's Publishing House, 1991.

Blau, P. *Exchange and Power in Social Life* [M]. Trans. Sun, F. & Zhang, L. Beijing: Huaxia Publishing House, 1987.

Boissonnade, P. *Medieval European Life and Work (5th to 15th Century)* [M]. Trans. Pan, Y. Beijing: The Commercial Press, 1985.

Boudieu, P. & Haacke, H. *Free Exchange* [M]. Trans. Gui, Y. Beijing: SDX Joint Publishing Company, 1996.

Braudel, F. *Civilization and Capitalism, 15th to 18th Century* [M]. Trans. Gu, L., Shi, K. Beijing: SDX Joint Publishing Company, 1993.

Brook, T. *The Confusions of Pleasure: Commerce and Culture in Ming China* [M]. Trans. Fang, J., Wang, X. & Lou, T. Beijing: SDX Joint Publishing Company, 2004.

Bu, C. Theoretical explanation and modern connotation of "differential pattern" [J]. *Sociological Studies*, 2003(1).

Buchanan, J. M. *Liberty, Market and State* [M]. Trans. Ping, X. & Mo, F. Shanghai: SDX Joint Publishing Company, 1989.

Cai, H. *Urban Sociology: Theory and Vision* [M]. Guangzhou: Sun Yat-sen University Press, 2003.

Cao, J., Zhang, L. & Chen, Z. *Social and Cultural Changes of the Villages in Contemporary Northern Zhejiang* [M]. Shanghai: Shanghai Far East Publishers, 2001.

Cao, J., Zhang, L. & Cheng, Z. *Social and Cultural Changes of the Villages in Contemporary Northern Zhejiang* [M]. Shanghai: Shanghai Far East Publishers, 2001.

Cao, R. *Getting Out of Prisoners' Dilemma—An Analysis of Social Capital and System* [M]. Shanghai: SDX Joint Publishing Company, 2003.

Chayanov, A. *The Economic Organization of Peasants* [M]. Trans. Xiao, Z. Beijing: Central Compilation & Translation Press, 1996.

Chen, J. *Economic Development of China in Its Rapid Growth Areas—A Study on the Jiangsu and Zhejiang Patterns* [M]. Shanghai: SDX Joint Publishing Company, 2000.

Chen, L. *Market Rules and Culture* [M]. Hangzhou: Zhejiang People's Publishing House, 1999.

Chen, L. Regional industry and commerce cultural tradition and development of the modern economy—A comparative analysis of Huizhou, Shanxi and Zhejiang merchants [J]. *Zhejiang Social Sciences*, 2005(3).

Chen, L. *Urban Culture and Urban Spirit* [M]. Nanjing: Southeast University Press, 2002.

Cheng, X., Wang, Z. & Li, T. *Analysis of the Growth Model of Cluster Private Enterprises* [M]. Beijing: China Economic Publishing House, 2004.

Chu, X. & Li, H. Trust and the Growth of Family Business [J]. *Management World*, 2003(6).

Cipolla, C. M. *Economic History of Europe*: vol. 1 [M]. Trans. Xu, X. Beijing: The Commercial Press, 1988.

CPC Zhejiang Provincial Party History Lab & Contemporary Zhejiang Institute. *Brief History of Contemporary Zhejiang 1949—1998* [M]. Beijing: Contemporary China Publishing House, 2000.

CPPCC Taizhou City Cultural Information and Learning Committee & Zhejiang Taizhou Folk Literature and Art Association. *Grand View of Taizhou Folklore* [M]. Ningbo: Ningbo Publishing House, 1998.

Duan, B. & Shan, Q. *Modern Jiangnan Countryside* [M]. Nanjing: Jiangsu People's Publishing House, 1994.

Durkheim, E. *Methodology of Sociology* [M]. Trans. Hu, W. Beijing: Huaxia Publishing House, 1988.

Eggertsson, T. *New Institutional Economics* [M]. Trans. Wu, J. et al. Beijing: The Commercial Press, 1996.

Fang, W. How to form group symbol boundary? Take the Protestant Christian group in Beijing for example [J]. *Sociological Studies*, 2005(1).

Fei, X. *Earthbound China* [M]. Beijing: SDX Joint Publishing Company,1985.

Fei, X. *The Life and Change of Peasant in Jiangcun Village* [M]. Lanzhou: Dunhuang Literature & Art Publishing House, 1997.

Fukuyama, F. *Trust—The Social Virtues and the Creation of Prosperity* [M]. Trans. Li, W. Hohhot: Yuanfang Publishing House, 1998.

Gao, B. *Folk Culture and Folk Life* [M]. Beijing: China Social Sciences Press, 1994.

Gao, F. & Ni, K. "Grass-roots Culture" and Social and Economic Development in Taizhou [Z] // Conference Proceedings of the East Zhejiang School and Zhejiang Spirit Seminar, March 16-17, 2005.

Habermas, J. *Theory of Communicative Action* [M]. Trans. Cao, W. Beijing: SDX Joint Publishing Company, 2004.

Harding, T. et al. *Evolution and Culture* [M]. Trans. Han, J. & Shang, G. Hangzhou: Zhejiang People's Publishing House, 1987.

Hayek, F. V. *The Constitution of Liberty* [M]. Trans. Deng, Z. Beijing: Joint Publishing Company, 1997.

He, B. *Tracing to the Source of the Eastern Zhejiang School* [M]. Guilin: Guangxi Normal University Press, 2004.

He, F. *Overview of Zhejiang* [M]. Hangzhou: Zhejiang People's Publishing House, 2003.

Hegel. C. *The Philosophy of History* [M]. Trans. Wang, Z. Shanghai: Shanghai Bookstore Publishing House, 1999.

Herrmann-Pillath, C. *Internet Culture and Chinese Social and Economic Behaviors* [M]. Trans. Zhu, Q. Taiyuan: Shanxi Economic Publishing House, 1996.

Hodgson, G. M. *Economics and Institutions: A Manifesto for a Modern Institutional Economics* [M]. Trans. Xiang, Y. et al. Beijing: Peking University Press, 1993.

Hoyt, T. *Utilitarian Confucianism—Ch'en Liang's Challenge to Chu Hsi* [M]. Trans. Jiang, C. Nanjing: Jiangsu People's Publishing House, 1997.

Hsu, F. L. K. *American and Chinese—Passages to Differences* [M]. Beijing: Huaxia Publishing House, 1988.

Hsu, F. L. K. *Clan, Caste and Club* [M]. Trans. Xue, G. Beijing: Huaxia Publishing House, 1990.

Huang, G. Face and favor: The chinese power game [M] // Huang, G *The Chinese Power Game*. Taipei: Chuliu Publisher, 1988.

Huang, S. *Introduction to Property Economics* [M]. Jinan: Shandong People's Publishing House, 1995.

Huang, Z. *Small Peasant Families and Rural Development in the Yangtze Delta, 1350—1988* [M]. Beijing: Zhonghua Book Company, 2000: 263.

Huntington, S. P. & Harrison, L.E. *Culture Matters: How Values Shape Human Progress* [M]. Trans. Cheng, K. Beijing: Xinhua Publishing House, 2002.

Inkeles A. et al. *Becoming Modern—Individual Change in Six Developing Countries* [M]. Trans. Gu, X. Beijing: China Renmin University Press, 1992.

Jochim, C. *China's Religious Ethos* [M]. Trans. Wang, P. Beijing: The Chinese Overseas Publishing House, 1999.

King, Y. Confucian Ethics and Economic Development: A Review of Weber's Doctrine [A] // Zhang, W. & Gao, Z. Taiwan Scholars on of Chinese Culture. Harbin: Heilongjiang Education Press, 1989.

King, Y. *From Traditional to Modernised* [M], Beijing: China Renmin University Press, 1999.

Lewis, W. A. *The Theory of Economic Growth* [M]. Trans. Liang, X. Shanghai: SDX Joint Publishing Company, 1994

Li, H. & Yang, X. *Social Capital and Social Development* [M]. Beijing: Social Sciences Academic Press, 2000.

Li, L. & Li, H. *Resources, Power and Exchange in the Chinese Work Unit Organization* [M]. Hangzhou: Zhejiang People's Publishing House, 2000.

Li, P. *Transformation of China's Social Structure—A Sociological Analysis of the*

Economic System Reform [M]. Harbin: Heilongjiang People's Publishing House, 1995.

Li, P. Urban industry in China's countryside [J]. *Sociological Studies*, 1995(1).

Li, W. & Liang, Y. Special trust and universal trust: Structure and features of Chinese trust [M] // *Trust in Chinese Society*. Beijing: China City Press, 2003

Li, X. & Zhang, S. *Family Business: Organization, Behavior and the Chinese Economy* [M]. Shanghai: SDX Joint Publishing Company, Shanghai People's Publishing House, 2005.

Li, X. China's family business and business organizations [J]. *Chinese Social Sciences Quarterly (Hongkong)*, 1998(3).

Li, X. Trust, loyalty and the predicament that clannishness is in [J]. *Management World*, 2002(6).

Liang, L. *Religious Psychology of Chinese People—Theoretical Analysis and Empirical Study of Religious Identity* [M]. Beijing: Social Sciences Academic Press, 2004.

Liang, S. *The Essence of Chinese Culture* [M]. Shanghai: Xuelin Press, 1987.

Lin, Y. *Second Discussion on System, Technology and Agricultural Development in China* [M]. Beijing: Peking University Press, 2000.

Lin, Y. *System, Technology and Agricultural Development in China* [M]. Shanghai: SDX Joint Publishing Company, 1994.

Little John, S. W. *Human Communication Theory* [M]. Trans. Shi, A. Beijing: Tsinghua University Press, 2004.

Liu, J. Transferring non-agricultural occupations: a study of farmers' life history [J]. Research on Sociology, 2001(6).

Liu, S. *Introduction to the Analysis of Economic System Efficiency* [M]. Shanghai: SDX Joint Publishing Company, 1996.

Liu, S. *Research on Jiangnan Towns in the Ming and Qing dynasties* [M]. Beijing: China Social Sciences Press, 1987.

Lu, F. Unit: A special form of social organization [J]. *China Social Sciences*, 1989(1).

Lu, L., Bai, X. & Wang, Z. The Yiwu Fair—From Chicken Feather for Sugar to International Business and Trade [M]. Hangzhou: Zhejiang People's Publishing House, 2003.

Lu, X. *The New Institutional Economics* [M]. Rev. ed. Beijing: China Development Press, 2003.

Luo, G. & Liu, X. *Cultural Studies: An Essential Reader* [M]. Beijing: China Social

Sciences Press, 2000: 126.

McLuhan, E. & Zingrone, F. *Essential McLuhan* [M]. Trans. He, D. Nanjing: Nanjing University Press, 2000.

Mendras, H. *The Finality of Peasants* [M]. Trans. Li, P. Beijing: China Social Sciences Press, 1992.

Migdal, J. S. *Peasant, Politics and Revolution: Pressures toward Political and Social Change in the Third World* [M]. Trans. Li, Y. & Yuan, N. Beijing: Central Compilation & Translation Press, 1996.

Miyazaki, I. *Collection of Miyazaki Ichisada's papers* [M]. Trans. Institute of History, Chinese Academy of Sciences. Beijing: The Commercial Press, 1965.

Montesquieu. *The Spirit of the Laws* : vol. 1 [M]. Trans. Zhang, Y. Beijing: The Commercial Press, 1961.

Mu, W. *Research on the Historical Materials of Shanxi Merchants* [M]. Taiyuan: Shanxi People's Publishing House, 2001.

Nelson, R. R. & Winter, S. G. *Evolutionary Theory of Economic Change* [M]. Trans. Hu, S. Beijing: The Commercial Press, 1997.

North, D. C. & Thomas, R. *The Rise of the Western World* [M]. Trans. Li, Y. & Cai, L. Beijing: Huaxia Publishing House, 1999.

North, D. C. *Institutions, Institutional Change and Economic Performance* [M]. Trans. Liu, S. Shanghai: SDX Joint Publishing Company, 1994.

North, D. C. *Structure and Change in Economic History* [M]. Trans. Chen, Y. et al. Shanghai: SDX Joint Publishing Company, 1999.

Ostrom, E. et al. *Rethinking Institutional Analysis and Development* [M]. Trans. Wang, C. et al. Beijing: The Commercial Press, 1992.

Parsons, T. *Smale, Economy and Society* [M]. Trans. Li, J. et al. Beijing: Huaxia Publishing House, 1989.

Popenoe, D. *Sociology* [M]. Trans. Liu, Y. & Wang, G. Shenyang: Liaoning People's Publishing House, 1987.

Qian, H. & Cheng, Z. *Jiangnan Social Life in the 17th Century* [M]. Hangzhou: Zhejiang People's Publishing House, 1996.

Qian, H. & Xie, W. Clan problem: A perspective of contemporary rural studies [J]. *Social Sciences*, 1990(5).

Qian, H. Several Issues Concerning Religious Studies on Contemporary Rural China [J]. *Academic Monthly*, 1993(3).

Qian, H. The reconstruction and reconstruction environment of the contemporary patriarchal clan in China [J]. *Chinese Social Sciences Quarterly (Hongkong)*,

1994(1).

Qian, M. Eastern and Western Zhejiang Advancing Side by Side and The Connotation of "Zhejiang School" [Z] // Conference Proceedings of the Eastern Zhejiang School and Zhejiang Spirit Seminar (Unpublished).

Qin, H. & Su, W. *Pastorals and Rhapsodies* [M]. Beijing: Central Compilation & Translation Press, 1996.

Qin, P. *Social and Economic History Draft of the Ming and Qing dynasties* [M]. Beijing: China Ancient Books Publishing House, 1984.

Research Group of the Status Quo and Countermeasures of Ideological and Moral Education of Zhejiang's Operators and Administrators. The status quo and countermeasures of ideological and moral education of market managers and managers in Zhejiang province (I, II) [J], *Journal of Zhejiang Party School of C.P.C.*, 1998(6), 1999(1).

Rogers E. M. *Diffusion of Innovations* [M]. Trans. Xin, X. Beijing: Central Compilation & Translation Press, 2002.

Rosenberg, N. & Birdzell, L. E. Jr. *How the West Grew Rich* [M]. Trans. Liu, S. Hongkong: SDX Joint Publishing (Hongkong) Company Limited.

Rozman, G. *The Modernization of China* [M]. Trans. National Social Science Fund "Comparative Modernization" Research Group. Nanjing: Jiangsu People's Publishing House, 1995.

Samuelson, P. A. & Nordhaus, W. D. *Economics* [M]. Trans. Gao, H. et al. Beijing: China Development Press, 1992.

Schmidt A. *Under the Influence* [M]. Trans. Wang, X. & Zhao, W. Beijing: Peking University Press, 2004.

Schumpeter, J. *The Theory of Economic Development* [M]. Trans. Niu, Z. Beijing: China Social Sciences Press, 1999.

Scott, J. C. *The Moral Economy of the Peasant: Rebellion and Subsistence in Southeast Asia* [M]. Trans. Cheng, L., Liu, J. et al. Nanjing: Yilin Press, 2001.

Sha, L. et al. *Chinese Social and Cultural Psychology* [M]. Beijing: China Social Sciences Press, 1998.

Sheng, H. *Division of Labor and Transaction—A General Theory and Its Application Analysis on China's Nonprofessional Issues* [M]. Shanghai: SDX Joint Publishing Company, Shanghai People's Publishing House, 1995.

Sheng, S. & Zheng, Y. *"Zhejiang Phenomenon"—Industrial Cluster and Regional Economic Development* [M]. Beijing: Tsinghua University Press, 2004.

Sheng, S., Xu, M. et al. *Study on the Problems of Economic and Social Development in Zhejiang Province* [M]. Hangzhou: Zhejiang People's Publishing House, 1999.

Shi, J. & Luo, W. *Research on Zhejiang's Way of Modernization* [M]. Hangzhou: Zhejiang People's Publishing House, 2000.

Shi, J. et al. *Institutional Change and Economic Development: A Study of Wenzhou Pattern* [M]. Hangzhou: Zhejiang University Press, 2002.

Shiba, Y. *Study on the Economic History of Regions South of the Yangtze River in the Song Dynasty* [M]. Trans. Fang, J. & He, Z. Nanjing: Jiangsu People's Publishing House, 2001.

Shigeta, A. *Research on the Social and Economic History of the Qing Dynasty* [M]. Tokyo: Iwanami Shoten, 1975.

Shils, E. *Tradition* [M]. Trans. Fu, K. & Li, L. Shanghai: Shanghai People's Publishing House, 1991.

Simmel, G. *Modern People and Religion* [M]. Trans. Cao, W. et al. Beijing: China Renmin University Press, 2003.

Simmel, G. *The Philosophy of Fashion* [M]. Trans. Fei, Y. et al. Beijing: Culture & Art Publishing House, 2001.

Simon, H. A. *The Cornerstone of Modern Decision Theory* [M]. Trans. Yang, L. & Xu, L. Beijing: Beijing Institute of Economics and Management Press, 1989.

Tang, J. *Comparative Study of Chinese and Western Philosophy* [M]. Taipei: Taiwan Student Book Office, 1988.

Tang, L. *Social and Economic Research of Huizhou Since the Ming and Qing dynasties* [M]. Hefei: Anhui University Press, 1999.

Tominaga, K. *Principles of Sociology* [M]. Trans. Yan, L. et al. Beijing: Social Sciences Academic Press, 1992.

Tomlinson, J. *Cultural Imperialism* [M]. Trans. Feng, J. Shanghai: Shanghai People's Publishing House, 1999.

Tönnies, F. *Community and Civil Society* [M]. Trans. Lin, R. Beijing: The Commercial Press, 1999.

Toynbee, A. J. *A Study of History* [M]. Trans. Cao, M. et al. Shanghai: Shanghai People's Publishing House, 1966.

van Loon, H. W. *The Story of Mankind* [M]. Trans. Qin, Y. & Feng, S. Guilin: Guangxi Normal University Press, 2003.

Venblen, T. B. *The Theory of The Leisure Class* [M]. Trans. Cai, S. Beijing: The Commercial Press, 1964.

Wan, B. & Ge, L. *2005 Blue Book of Zhejiang* [M]. Hangzhou: Hangzhou

Publishing Group, 2005.

Wang, C. Social networks in motion: Wenzhou people's behavior patterns in Paris and Beijing [J]. *Sociological Studies*, 2000(3).

Wang, C. *Wenzhou People in Paris—The Social Construction of an Immigrant Group* [M]. Nanchang: Jiangxi People's Publishing House, 2000.

Wang, L. & Yang, X. *Globalization and World* [M]. Beijing: Central Compilation & Translation Press, 1998.

Wang, M. & Wang, S. *Order, Justice and Authority in Rural Society* [M]. Beijing: China University of Political Science & Law Press, 1997.

Wang, X. & Zhu, C. *Private Enterprises and Family Economy in Rural China* [M]. Taiyuan: Shanxi Economic Publishing House, 1996.

Wang, X. *Cultural Traditions and Economic Organizations* [M]. Dalian: Dongbei University of Finance & Economics Press, 1999.

Weber, M. *Economy and Society* [M]. Trans. Lin, R. Beijing: The Commercial Press, 1997.

Weber, M. *The Protestant Ethic and the Spirit of Capitalism* [M]. Trans. Yu, X., Chen, W. et al. Beijing: SDX Joint Publishing Company, 1987.

Weber, M. *Weber's Portfolio* [M]. Trans. Kang, L. & Wu N. Nanning: Guangxi People's Publishing House, 2004.

Weber. M. *Confucianism and Taoism* [M]. Trans. Hong, T. Nanjing: Jiangsu People's Publishing House, 1993: 273.

Wen, C. & Xiao, Y *The Chinese: Perceptions and Behaviors* [M]. Taipei: Taiwan Juliu Books, 1988.

Xiang, B. *Community Across Borders: Life History of "Zhejiang Village" in Beijing* [M]. Beijing: SDX Joint Publishing Company, 2000.

Xu, Z. *Introduction to Christian Theological Thoughts* [M]. Beijing: China Social Sciences Press, 2001.

Yang, C. *Economic Man and Analysis of Order* [M]. Shanghai: SDX Joint Publishing Company, Shanghai People's Publishing House, 1998.

Yang, N. *Modern Forms of Confucianism Regionalization: A Comparative Study of Three Knowledge Groups* [M]. Beijing: SDX Joint Publishing Company, 1997.

Yang, T. The Transmission and Inheritance Mechanism of the Academic Spirit of the Eastern Zhejiang School [Z] // Conference Proceedings of the Eastern Zhejiang School and Zhejiang Spirit Seminar, March 16-17, 2005.

Yang, Y. An Analysis of Interpersonal Relationships and Their Classification—A Deliberation with Mr. Huang Guangguo [J]. *Sociological Studies*, 1995(5).

Yang, Z. & Peng, S. Conceptualization of Interpersonal Trust in China: A Human Relationship Perspective [J]. *Sociological Studies*, 1999(2).

Ye, D. Traditional Borrowing Form and Modern Stock Ownership—The Relationship Between Economic Development and Folk Culture in Zhejiang [Z] // Conference Proceedings of the Eastern Zhejiang School and Zhejiang Spirit Seminar.

Ye, T. Study on economic thoughts of real learning in the East Zhejiang Practical Schools in the Song Dynasty—Centered on Ye Shi [J]. *Researches in Chinese Economic History*, 2000(4).

Yin, H. *Reappraisal of Culture Change in Modern China* [M]. Beijing: China Heping Publishing House, 1988.

Zhai, X. Social mobility and relationship trust—Relationship strength and job searching strategies of migrant workers [J]. *Sociological Studies*, 2003(1).

Zhang, H. & Zhang, H. *Ten Commercial Group in China* [M]. Hefei: Huangshan Publishing House, 1993.

Zhang, J. *Informal Institutions in the Process of Marketization* [M]. Beijing: Cultural Relics Press, 1999.

Zhang, J. *Transformation and Growth* [M]. Shanghai: Shanghai Far East Publishers, 2002.

Zhang, Q. *Social Capital Theory: Social Capital and Economic Growth* [M]. Beijing: China Social Sciences Press, 1997.

Zhang, W. Social capital: Theoretical argument and empirical study [J]. *Sociological Studies*, 2003(4).

Zhang, X. *The Irrational World in a Market Economy* [M]. Shanghai: Lixin Accounting Publishing House, 1995.

Zhang, Y. *Trust, Contracts and Its Rules* [M]. Beijing: Economy & Management Publishing House, 2004.

Zhang, Z. & Xue, H. *Selected Materials of Shanxi Merchants in the Ming and Qing dynasties* [M]. Taiyuan: Shanxi People's Publishing House, 1989.

Zhang, Z. *The Rise and Fall of Shanxi Merchants* [M]. Taiyuan: Shanxi Ancient Books Publishing House, 2001.

Zhao, L. *The Formation of the Merchant Class and Social Transformation in Western Europe* [M]. Beijing: China Social Sciences Press, 2004.

Zhejiang Administration for Industry and Commerce. *Zhejiang Individual and Private Economy Research Report* [R]. Beijing: China Workers Publishing House, 2000

Zhejiang Province Market Editorial Department. *Annals of the Markets in Zhejiang Province* [M]. Beijing: Local Records Publishing House, 2000.

Zhejiang Provincial Chronicle Compilation Committee. *Annals of Zhejiang* [M]. Shanghai: Zhonghua Book Company, 2001.

Zheng, Y. Endogenous civilian power promoting economic development: Zhejiang experience [J]. *Zhejiang Social Sciences*, 2001(2).

Zheng, Y. *Trust Theory* [M]. Beijing: China Radio and Television Publishing House, 2001.

Zheng, Y., Yuan, Y. & Lin, C. *Interpretation of the "Great Market Province"— Study on the Phenomenon of Zhejiang's Professional Market* [M]. Hangzhou: Zhejiang University Press, 2003.

Zhou, M. *Ye Shi and the Yongjia School* [M]. Hangzhou: Zhejiang Ancient Books Publishing House, 1992.

Zhou, X. *Peasants in the Process of Modernization* [M]. Nanjing: Nanjing University Press, 1998.

Zhou, X. *Tradition and Change: The Social Psychology of Peasants in Zhejiang and Jiangsu and Its Evolution since Modern Times* [M]. Beijing: SDX Joint Publishing Company, 1998.

Zhou, Z., Lin, S. & Chen, D. *Social Studies on Zhejiang's Clan Villages* [M]. Beijing: Local Records Publishing House, 2001.

Zhu, G. *Cultural Logic of Power* [M]. Shanghai: Shanghai People's Publishing House, 2004.

Zhu, G. *Economic Phenomena from a Sociological Perspective* [M]. Chengdu: Sichuan People's Publishing House, 1998.

Zhu, H. *Zhejiang Industrial Cluster—Industrial Network, Growth Trajectory and Development Motivation* [M]. Hangzhou: Zhejiang University Press, 2003.

Zhu, K. *The Change from the Bottom—A Case Study of Longgang's Urbanization* [M]. Hangzhou: Zhejiang People's Publishing House, 2003.

Zhuo, Y. Sweet potato, war and entrepreneurship—The causes and predicament of the Wenzhou pattern [J]. *Zhejiang Social Sciences*, 2004(3).